Romance languages

Ti Alkire and Carol Rosen trace the changes that led from colloquial Latin to five major Romance languages, those which ultimately became national or transnational languages: Spanish, French, Italian, Portuguese, and Romanian. Trends in spoken Latin altered or dismantled older categories in phonology and morphology, while the regional varieties of speech, evolving under diverse influences, formed new grammatical patterns, each creating its own internal regularities. Documentary sources for spoken Latin show the beginnings of this process, which comes to full fruition in the medieval emergence of written Romance languages. This book newly distills the facts into an appealing program of study, including exercises, and makes the difficult issues clear, taking well-motivated and sometimes innovative stands. It provides not only an essential guide for those new to the topic, but also a reliable compendium for the specialist.

TI ALKIRE is a senior lecturer in the Department of Romance Studies at Cornell University. Besides historical Romance linguistics, his research interests include stylistics, translation theory, and current variation in French and Italian.

CAROL ROSEN is a professor of Linguistics and Romance Studies at Cornell University. Her work in language typology, grammatical relations, and formal theory design lends a special character to her research in Romance linguistics, ranging over historical and contemporary topics.

Ti Alkire and Carol Rosen

Romance Languages
a historical introduction

CAMBRIDGE UNIVERSITY PRESS
Cambridge, New York, Melbourne, Madrid, Cape Town, Singapore,
São Paulo, Delhi, Mexico City

Cambridge University Press
The Edinburgh Building, Cambridge CB2 8RU, UK

Published in the United States of America by Cambridge University Press, New York

www.cambridge.org
Information on this title: www.cambridge.org/9780521889155

First published 2010
3rd printing 2012

Printed at MPG Books Group, UK

A catalogue record for this publication is available from the British Library

Library of Congress Cataloguing in Publication data
Alkire, Ti, 1961–
    Romance languages : a historical introduction / Ti Alkire, Carol Rosen.
        p.   cm.
    ISBN 978-0-521-88915-5 (hardback)
    1. Romance languages–History.   2. Romance languages–Grammar.
    I. Rosen, Carol G.   II. Title.
    PC45.A45 2010
    440.09–dc22   2010007559

ISBN 978-0-521-88915-5 Hardback
ISBN 978-0-521-71784-7 Paperback

Contents

Acknowledgements

Like general linguistics, Romance linguistics in the modern sense of the term traces its origins to the early decades of the nineteenth century. Given the weight of the accumulated scholarship, any work on the present topic will necessarily be derivative. In this book we do take some stands and venture some new analyses, but our debt to earlier researchers is immeasurable, beyond what our quotations and citations can convey.

We extend thanks to the colleagues who put their expertise at our disposal: Wayles Browne, Diego de Acosta, Anton Goţia, Wayne Harbert, Adam Ledgeway, Alan Nussbaum, Ştefan Oltean, Nigel Vincent, Michael Weiss, and especially Emily Scida, who contributed the chapter on Portuguese. In the production process the book benefited from the thoughtful and painstaking assistance of Chris Jackson and Kimberly Page Will. Heartfelt thanks go also to David Rosen for his concrete help and unflagging encouragement.

Introduction

Latin and the Romance languages occupy a vast space along at least three dimensions: geographical, temporal, and social. Once the language of a small town on the Tiber River in Latium, Latin was carried far afield with the expansion of Roman power. The Empire reached its greatest extent under the reign of the emperor Trajan (98–117 CE), at which point it included modern-day Britain, Portugal, Spain, France, Italy, Switzerland, Austria, and the Balkan peninsula, as well as immense territories in the Eastern Mediterranean and beyond, making it by far the largest single state the Western world had ever known. Even those distances are dwarfed by the extent of Western European colonial expansion in the 1500s and 1600s, which brought Spanish to most of Latin America and the Caribbean, Portuguese to Brazil, French to Canada, and all three to their many outposts around the world, where they engendered some robust creoles. On the time dimension, the colloquial speech that underlies the Romance languages was already a constant presence during the seven centuries that saw Rome grow from village to empire – and then their history still has twenty centuries to go. Their uses in society extend to every level and facet of activity from treasured world literature to instant messaging.

A truly panoramic account of Romance linguistic history would find few readers and probably no writers. The scope has to be limited somehow. Our decision, which may disappoint some readers, is to cover five languages: French, Italian, Portuguese, Romanian, and Spanish. Two criteria converge to justify the choice: these are the five that are national languages, and they have the greatest number of speakers, ranking as follows in terms of first-language speakers (Lewis 2009):

Language	Native speakers (millions)	Locations with most speakers (millions)	
Spanish	328.5	Latin America	249.5
		Spain	28.2

		United States	28.1
Portuguese	178.0	Brazil	163.0
		Portugal	10.0
French	67.8	France	53.2
		Canada	6.7
		Belgium	4.0
		Switzerland	1.5
Italian	61.7	Italy	55.0
		Argentina	1.5
Romanian	23.4	Romania	19.7
		Moldavia	2.7

In addition, Spanish is spoken as a second language by 60 million people (mostly in the United States and Brazil) and French by 50 million (mostly in Africa).

Venturing into the rest of the Romance languages and trying to count them, we encounter at once the word *dialect* used in contrast to *language*. Historically, our five languages are dialects of Latin, but we have no trouble calling them languages. The difference between *language* and *dialect*, however, is not always clear. The very word *dialect* is a trapdoor leading into a labyrinth of terminological confusion and clashing convictions (among linguists) as well as vested interests and aspirations to prestige (among the public at large). Consider this: one reputable source classifies Lombard, usually deemed a Gallo-Italian dialect, as both a language and a "group of dialects, some of which may be separate languages." Is there any reliable criterion that can distinguish *dialect* from *language*?

Even a seemingly simple extralinguistic criterion such as number of speakers can be problematic. Sicilian has over twice as many speakers as Sardinian, yet Sicilian is usually considered a dialect and Sardinian a language. And how does one count the speakers without having first established the boundaries of the variety to be evaluated? Should Occitan (as a cover term for Southern French) include speakers of Franco-Provençal and Gascon, which some consider separate languages?

A more nuanced criterion might rest on the idea that languages are the object of attention, elaboration, and social implementation, measured not only by number of speakers, but also by range of uses, size of lexicon, codification (dictionaries, grammars, academies), official status (e.g. in education), a continuous literary tradition, and use in mass media. But this constellation of measures does not yield a binary categorization into language versus dialect. Rather, it points to a continuum along which any variety – be it conventionally called language or dialect – is situated. Varieties conventionally called languages may rank at either end of the continuum, and so can varieties conventionally called dialects. Piedmontese, nominally a dialect, has many accoutrements of a language, while

Sardinian, said to be a language, has fewer. Ultimately, the terms *language* and *dialect* describe the same thing (a linguistic system), and the choice between the two is largely a matter of attitudes and ideology.

Let's rely on conventional wisdom, generated and endorsed by linguists, though in different versions. There are allegedly ten Romance languages, our top five plus these:

Language	Native speakers (millions)	Locations with most speakers (millions)	
Catalan	11.5	Spain	11.2
Occitan	2.0	France	1.9
Sardinian	1.0	Italy	1.0
Rheto-Romance	0.86	Italy, Switzerland	0.85
Dalmatian	0		

Other incipient Romance languages – the Latin of Britain and of North Africa – died in infancy, in the 400s and 700s respectively, and have no names.

Catalan is spoken in Catalonia, the northeastern coastal region of Spain, once a powerful kingdom whose influence peaked in the 1300s. Outside Spain, Catalan-speaking enclaves exist in the Eastern Pyrenees and in Sardinia. Ramon Llull, the most renowned and prolific figure in medieval Catalan literature, fostered its linguistic divergence from the Occitan of Southern France. Once associated with Aragon to the west, Catalonia remained on its own with the union of Aragon and Castile (1479). Over the centuries, Catalan declined in importance as Castilian rose. Championed by nineteenth-century authors and standardized for writing in the twentieth century, Catalan became an official language (1931–1939), lost that status during Franco's attempt to stifle it, regained it in 1978, and is today the language of a lively regional culture.

Occitan is one name for the language of southern France, but also denotes a particular variety. Others prefer Provençal, but this term also refers to a smaller variety. Here we use Occitan as a cover term that includes Gascon (in the southwest), North Occitan (Limousin, Auvergnat, Alpine Provençal) in the central south, Franco-Provençal (in the east), and Middle Occitan (Languedocian, Provençal) in the far south. Old Provençal was the language of a flourishing and enormously influential literature in the Middle Ages.

Sardinia was among the first territories the Romans wrested from their rival, Carthage (238 BCE). Isolated and weak in resources, the island lived under a long succession of ruling powers, the most influential being Catalonia and Spain. Sardinian is best known for retaining certain features of Latin elsewhere lost. Of the four varieties on the island, Logodurese and Campidanese are genuinely Sardinian, while Sassarese and Gallurese are considered to be closer to Tuscan Italian. Sardinian documents appear from 1080 on, and a literary tradition emerges in the Middle Ages, but there is no standard today.

Rheto-Romance is a group of dialects or languages (opinions differ) spoken in the Swiss and Italian Alps (hence one alternative name, Alpine Romance) stretching west to east from the Swiss canton of Graubünden (Grisons) to the Friuli-Venezia Giulia region in the northeastern corner of Italy. One group, Rhetic, includes the varieties spoken in Switzerland, often called Romansh. In 1938 it acquired the status of a national language in Switzerland. The other two groups are spoken in Italy: Dolomitic (known as Ladin < LATINU) in several valleys of the Dolomites, and Friulian in Friuli-Venezia Giulia.

Dalmatia is the Roman name for the eastern coast of the Adriatic, from Trieste in the north to Dubrovnik (Ragusa) in the south, today part of Slovenia and Croatia. Dalmatian, now extinct, was a relic of what must have been a wider range of dialects from the Latin of the Roman provinces there. Dalmatian is attested from 1325, and was submerged first in the south by Croatian. The northern variety, Vegliote, lived on until 1898.

This book, with some regret, ignores these five languages of the second tier. We first survey the historical phonology and morphology of Italian, Spanish, and French (Chapters 1–8). Portuguese has its own chapter (Chapter 9), as does Romanian (Chapter 10). The closing chapters, on the lexicon (Chapter 11) and the medieval emergence of the Romance languages (Chapter 12), deal with all five.

1 The evolution of stressed vowels

The languages of the Romance family are descended from Latin, but what kind of Latin? Just as Modern English exists in many varieties and registers, so also Latin came to be a socially complex language, extending over a vast territory and serving the needs of diverse speech communities. Among the educated, a codified literary Latin existed, enshrined in the classics and in treatises on grammar. But Latin also lived on as an evolving spoken language among the far-flung populations of the Roman Empire. The basic vocabulary of the Romance languages bears the imprint of a casual, spoken style of Latin, always open to change. In conservative social contexts, in the domain of religion and high culture, the frozen classical language remained an influential presence in the minds of the literate few, and became in later centuries a source of new layers of vocabulary.

1.1 Syllables and word stress in Latin

In this overview of the sound changes leading from Latin to the major Romance languages, we begin with the stressed vowels. Since the first requisite is knowing how to identify the stressed vowel, this lesson explains vowel quantity, syllable weight, and the rule that assigns stress in Latin.

1.1.1 Why word stress matters

Stress position in a Latin word (**etymon**) has a crucial effect on its Romance outcomes (**reflexes**). For example, consider these Latin infinitives and their reflexes:

Latin		Italian	Spanish	French
DEBERE	'owe'	dovere	deber	devoir
HABERE	'have'	avere	haber	avoir
VENDERE	'sell'	vendere	vender	vendre
PRENDERE	'take'	prendere	prender	prendre
PERDERE	'lose'	perdere	perder	perdre

5

The normal Latin spelling shows no difference in stress, but in fact these infinitives reflect two different classes: **arhizotonic** (stressed off the root, e.g. DEBERE and HABERE) and **rhizotonic** (stressed on the root, e.g. VENDERE, PRENDERE, PERDERE).

Italian preserves the original contrast in stress pattern. Spanish has neutralized the contrast in favor of arhizotonic infinitives. French, however, shows the drastic consequences of the difference in stress. The stressed vowel in the arhizotonic infinitives gives <oi> /wa/, but what happens to that same vowel in the rhizotonic infinitives?

DEBERE	HABERE	VENDERE	PRENDERE	PERDERE
devoir	avoir	vend re	prend re	perd re

Having seen the import of stress, how do we determine where it fell in a Latin word? Good news: Latin has an easy, exceptionless stress rule known as the **Penultimate Rule**. To understand it (an absolute prerequisite for all of our subsequent work) you need to consider three concepts: vowel quantity, syllable boundaries, and syllable weight.

1.1.2   Latin vowels

Latin has a typologically common vowel system: five vowels arranged in the usual triangle, with front-back contrast neutralized for the low vowel /a/.

$$\bar{\imath}\ \breve{\imath} \qquad\qquad \bar{u}\ \breve{u}$$
$$\bar{e}\ \breve{e} \qquad \bar{o}\ \breve{o}$$
$$\bar{a}\ \breve{a}$$

The only complication is quantity – each of these five vowels can be either long or short, a phonemic contrast seen in such **minimal pairs** as:

ĔST 'is'	VĔNIT 'comes'
ĒST 'eats'	VĒNIT 'came' [3rd sg.]

The vowel inventory also includes three diphthongs, written AE /aj/, OE /oj/, and AU /aw/. They count automatically as long vowels. The term **diphthong** means that the two elements (vowel + glide) belong to the same syllable. Caution! AE, OE, and AU are the only diphthongs in Latin.

1.1.3   Dividing syllables in Latin

More good news: English speakers understand most syllable boundaries intuitively. Stated in technical terms, the rule is: maximize the onset. This means: put as much material as possible into the later syllable, consistent with the requirement that its onset must be acceptable as the beginning of a word. Example: IM.PRI.MA.TUR, IN.FER.NU (because MPR, NF, and RN are not possible onsets, and MP. R is wrong because the onset is not maximized).

> **PRACTICE**
>
> Indicate syllable boundaries in these Latin words.
>
> | LACRIMA | PARTE | CANTU | PETRA | HERBA | OPTIMU |
> |---------|-------|-------|-------|-------|--------|
> | DECEMBER | ETERNU | MAXIMU (x stands for /ks/) | | | |

Sometimes you encounter two adjacent vowels (vowels in **hiatus**). Don't confuse these with diphthongs. Recall from § 1.1.2 that Latin has only three diphthongs: AE, OE, and AU. In other sequences written with two vowel graphemes <V V>, the two vowels belong to separate syllables. Example: SU.A.VE 'gentle', PA.LE.A 'straw'.

> **PRACTICE**
>
> Indicate where the syllable boundaries fall in these Latin words.
>
> FEBRUARIUS   HODIE   PIETATE   VITREU   FILIA

In addition to long vowels, Latin has long (**geminate**) consonants formed by adding an extra timing unit to the closure. Even though in pronunciation there are not really two consonant releases, you obtain the correct results by placing the syllable boundary between the two written consonants (GUT.TA, VIL.LA, etc.).

The one unexpected fact about Latin syllabification concerns /s/ + consonant occurring word-medially. The syllable boundary in this case runs between /s/ and the consonant, which seems contrary to the principle of maximizing the onset. But even though /s/ + consonant can begin a word, it cannot begin a medial syllable. For example: SPA.TA, but CRIS.PA not *CRI.SPA. This fact is inferred from clear linguistic evidence (§ 1.2.5). Interestingly, in some Romance languages /s/ + consonant proved to be an impossible onset even word-initially, as seen in Spanish *espada* 'sword' < SPATA and *escuela* 'school' < SCHOLA (§ 2.1.1).

1.1.4   The Penultimate Rule

This rule assigning word stress in Latin is stated in terms of syllable weight. Once you have identified the boundaries of a syllable, you have to determine whether it's heavy or light.

Definition: A syllable is **heavy** if it consists of two timing units. Otherwise stated, it contains a long vowel or ends in a consonant. Syllables meeting neither criterion are **light**.

> **PRACTICE**
>
> In these words you can't identify all the heavy syllables unless you know which vowels are long, but you can identify some on sight. Which ones?
>
> MULTU   NOCTE   UNDECIM   CAELU   AURORA   AUDIO

The Penultimate Rule stated below is so named because it looks at the next-to-last (**penultimate**) syllable. No other syllable is relevant. The rule says: if the penultimate syllable is heavy, stress it, otherwise stress the preceding syllable (the **antepenult**).

$$\sigma\, \underline{\sigma}\, \sigma\, \# \qquad \underline{\sigma}\, \sigma\, \sigma\, \#$$
$$H \qquad\qquad\ \ L$$

The Penultimate Rule establishes a regular relationship between syllable weight and stress position. Given Latin vowel quantity, we can deduce stress position. Vice versa, if we know the stress position (from Romance reflexes), we can deduce the weight of the penultimate syllable in Latin.

PRACTICE

(Latin → Romance) In the following words Latin vowel quantity is indicated when long. Syllabify and show which syllable is stressed.

DIFFICILE	MULIER	MULIĒRE
INIMĪCU	AQUILA*	EXEMPLU
FORMĪCA	DIRECTU	ROTUNDU

*QU counts as a consonant, /kʷ/.

PRACTICE

(Romance → Latin) Here vowel quantity is not shown. Try to infer the stress position from any Romance reflexes you may know, and from that, compute the weight of the penultimate syllable, and the vowel quantity when possible.

AMICA	'friend'	OPERA	'work'	NUMERU	'number'
LACTUCA	'lettuce'	CAMERA	'room'	CATENA	'chain'
INSULA	'island'	FARINA	'flour'	DOMINA	'lady'
ANIMA	'soul'	CONFLICTU	'conflict'		

In words containing only two syllables, the penultimate is stressed unconditionally, revealing nothing about vowel quantity.

1.2   Stressed vowels: the (almost) pan-Romance seven-vowel system

The most consequential of all the pre-Romance sound changes was the refashioning of the stressed vowel system. The Latin system has five vowels and a quantity contrast (ten phonemes in all). Out of the rearrangement came a seven-vowel system without quantity.

1.2.1   How the stressed vowel system changed

Almost certainly the contrast in quantity began to be replaced by a contrast in quality, the long vowel being tense and the short vowel lax.

The low vowel /a/ simply lost its quantity contrast. Therefore our starting-point is actually a nine-vowel system, as shown above.

> Question: Since quantity in the vowel /a/ is neutralized, would it follow that no Romance word can ever reflect the old difference between long and short /a/?
>
> Answer: Not quite. The Penultimate Rule decides stress at a time when /a/ still had the quantity contrast. For words like ANIMALE, SEPTIMANA, FONTANA, the Romance outcomes, if you know them, reveal by their stress that the penultimate was heavy, so the /a/ in that syllable must have been long. Of course, stress position reveals nothing in words like MARE 'sea', LANA 'wool'.

The data below show typical Romance outcomes of these nine stressed vowels. In these results, we can discern a further collapse of the system from nine to seven vowels.

The array of Latin words with their glosses is arranged according to the vowel triangle. For example, in AMĪCA and its group the stressed vowel is long, while in PILU and its group the stressed vowel is short. In DĒBET and its group the stressed vowel is long, while in PEDE and its group the stressed vowel is short. The reflexes in Italian, Spanish, and French appear below the array – the triangle has simply been flattened. Of course, when we say, for example, that PILU 'hair' becomes French *poil*, we are ignoring the intermediate stages. Our strategy here is to down-trace in one step all the way from Latin to the modern Romance languages.

As we examine the data, remember that we are focusing on *stressed* vowels only.

Latin stressed vowels and their outcomes in Italian, Spanish, and French

AMĪCA	'friend'
DĪCIT	'says'
NĪDU	'nest'
SPĪNA	'thorn'
FORMĪCA	'ant'
SCRĪPTA	'written'

PILU	'hair'
VIDET	'sees'
BIBIT	'drinks'
CRISPA	'curly'
LITTERA	'letter'
VIRIDE	'green'
DĒBET	'owes'
PARIĒTE	'wall'
HABĒRE	'have'
*MĒSE	'month'
VĒLA	'sail'
TĒRNU	'triad'

PEDE	'foot'
*MELE	'honey'
TENET	'holds'
HERBA	'grass'
TERRA	'earth'
PERDIT	'loses'

SALE	'salt'
MARE	'sea'
CAPUT	'head'
CAMPU	'field'
FLAMMA	'flame'
ARBORE	'tree'

NOVU	'new'
FOCU	'fire'
OVU	'egg'
HOSPITE	'host'
MORTE	'death'
PORCU	'pig'

GULA	'throat'
IUVENE	'young'
AUGUSTU	'August'
CURRIT	'runs'
BUCCA	'mouth'
FURCA	'fork'
SAPŌRE	'taste'
MELIŌRE	'better'
FLŌRE	'flower'
HŌRA	'hour'
SŌLU	'alone'
CŌRTE	'court'

CRŪDU	'raw'
IŪRAT	'swears'
SCŪTU	'shield'
ACŪTU	'sharp'
MATŪRU	'ripe'
SECŪRA	'safe'

Italian

amica	pelo	deve	piede	sale	nuovo	sapore	gola	crudo
dice	vede	parete	miele	mare	fuoco	migliore	giovane	giura
nido	beve	avere	tiene	capo	uovo	fiore	agosto	scudo
spina	crespo	mese	erba	campo	ospite	ora	corre	acuto
formica	lettera	vela	terra	fiamma	morte	solo	bocca	maturo
scritta	verde	terno	perde	albero	porco	corte	forca	sicura

Spanish

amiga	pelo	debe	pie	sal	nuevo	sabor	gola	crudo
dice	ve	pared	miel	mar	fuego	mejor	joven	jura
nido	bebe	haber	tiene	cabo	huevo	flor	agosto	escudo
espina	crespa	mes	hierba	campo	huésped	hora	corre	agudo
hormiga	letra	vela	tierra	llama	muerte	solo	boca	maduro
escrita	verde	terno	pierde	árbol	puerco	corte	horca	segura

French

amie	poil	doit	pied	sel	neuf	saveur	gueule	cru
dit	voit	paroi	miel	mer	feu	meilleur	jeune	jure
nid	boit	avoir	tient	chef	oeuf	fleur	août	écu
épine	crêpe	mois	herbe	champ	hôte	heure	court	aigu
fourmi	lettre	voile	terre	flamme	mort	seul	bouche	mûr
écrite	vert	terme	perd	arbre	porc	cour	fourche	sûre

1.2.2   Extremes of the vowel triangle: ī, ū, a

The group beginning with AMĪCA shows what happens to Latin /ī/: it gives /i/ in all three languages. Further examples confirming this generalization are:

Latin		Italian	Spanish	French
VĪTA	'life'	vita	vida	vie
VICĪNA	'neighbor'	vicina	vecina	voisine
FARĪNA	'flour'	farina	harina	farine
APRĪLE	'April'	aprile	abril	avril
MĪLLE	'thousand'	mille	mil	mille

The group beginning with CRŪDU shows what happens to Latin /ū/. In Italian and Spanish, Latin /ū/ gives /u/. In French the spelling might wrongly suggest /u/, but actually the pronunciation is /y/, a high rounded front vowel.

Many more examples confirm this regularity, including:

Latin		Italian	Spanish	French	
LŪNA	'moon'	luna	luna	lune	[lyn]
DŪRA	'hard'	dura	dura	dure	[dyʀ]
MŪRU	'wall'	muro	muro	mur	[myʀ]
SALŪTAT	'salutes'	saluta	saluda	salue	[saly]
PLŪMA	'feather'	piuma	pluma	plume	[plym]

The group beginning with SALE shows what happens to Latin /a/. In Italian and Spanish again there is no change: Latin /a/ gives /a/. In French, however, there are two outcomes. In certain words, Latin /a/ gives a front mid vowel usually written <e>, while in others Latin /a/ remains /a/.

Question: What determines the difference between the two outcomes?

Answer: The answer lies in Latin syllable structure. If the syllable ends in a consonant (**blocked syllable**), Latin /a/ remains /a/. If the syllable ends in a vowel (**free syllable**), Latin /a/ undergoes fronting and raising to /e/.

Further examples confirm the contrast between free and blocked syllables:

CLA.VE	'key'	clef	[kle]
NA.SU	'nose'	nez	[ne]
CA.SA	'house'	chez	[ʃe]
CA.RU	'dear'	cher	[ʃeʀ]
CAR.RU	'cart'	char	[ʃaʀ]
GRAN.DE	'big'	grand	[gʀɑ̃]
PAR.TE	'part'	part	[paʀ]

What matters for this rule is the syllable structure in Latin. For example, French *sel* 'salt' is a blocked syllable, but what matters is the Latin etymon SALE, where the stressed syllable is free, hence SALE becomes *sel*.

Closer phonetic detail: if you know French, you probably know that syllable structure in the *modern* language affects the pronunciation of this vowel. It has two allophones: the higher [e] in modern free syllables, and the lower [ɛ] in modern blocked syllables. Examples:

nez	'nose'	[ne]	nef	'nave'	[nɛf]
mes	'my'	[me]	mère	'mother'	[mɛʀ]
épée	'sword'	[epe]	épelle	'spells'	[epɛl]

1.2.3   The Great Merger

Next we turn to the momentous change that reduced the system from nine to seven stressed vowels. Not only Italian, Spanish, and French, but almost all of the Romance languages show evidence of having undergone the Great Merger.

Returning to the database (pp. 10–11), examine the outcomes of /ĭ/ and /ŭ/. They do not behave like their long counterparts. Instead, as we will see, they behave like /ē/ and /ō/, the next vowels down in the triangle. This is evidence for the Great Merger: in the spoken Latin of late antiquity, /ĭ/ merged with /ē/ to become one and the same vowel. Likewise, /ŭ/ and /ō/ merged. The Great Merger resulted in a seven-vowel system that looks like this:

This system has two kinds of mid vowel: high mids /e/ and /o/ result from the merger, and low mids /ɛ/ and /ɔ/ come from original /ĕ/ and /ŏ/. By the time the system reaches this stage, vowel quantity has long since been lost, but the contrasts in quantity are preserved indirectly. Original /ī/ as in NĪDU remains a high vowel, while original /ĭ/ as in BIBIT merges downward to become a high mid. Similarly, original /ē/ as in VĒLA merges upward to become a high mid, whereas original /ĕ/ as in PEDE becomes a low mid. Parallel developments occurred among the back vowels.

The next two sections examine in more detail how the mid vowels develop.

1.2.4   The high mid vowels

Italian and Spanish show no changes in the high mids. Examples from the database (pp. 10–11) include, for the front high mids:

	Latin		*Italian*	*Spanish*
BIBIT	'drinks'	beve	bebe
LITTERA	'letter'	lettera	letra
DĒBET	'owes'	deve	debe
TĒRNU	'triad'	terno	terno

and for the back high mids:

	Latin		*Italian*	*Spanish*
GULA	'throat'	gola	gola
CURRIT	'runs'	corre	corre
HŌRA	'hour'	ora	hora
CŌRTE	'court'	corte	corte

French high mids occupy the rest of this section. Their outcome depends (just as for /a/) on whether their syllable is free or blocked in Latin. Blocked syllables tend to block changes. The front high mid /e/ remains unchanged in blocked syllables.

LITTERA	'letter'	lettre
TĒRNU	'triad'	terne
CAVĒRNA	'cavern'	caverne

The back high mid /o/ also has a conservative development in blocked syllables: it simply drifts up to /u/, filling the space left in the vowel triangle when Latin /ū/ fronts to /y/. The sound /u/ is written <ou> since the letter <u> stands for [y].

CURRIT	'runs'	court	[kuʀ]
CŌRTE	'court'	cour	[kuʀ]

In free syllables, French high mids undergo drastic changes. Both begin by forming diphthongs: /e/ > /ej/ and /o/ > /ow/. They continue to change as follows:

/e/ > /ej/ > /oj/ > /oɛ/ > /wɛ/ > /wa/   and   /o/ > /ow/ > /ew/ > /ø/

For the front high mid /e/ in Latin free syllables, examples from the database include:

PILU	'hair'	poil	[pwal]
VIDET	'sees'	voit	[vwa]
BIBIT	'drinks'	boit	[bwa]
DĒBET	'owes'	doit	[dwa]
PARIĒTE	'wall'	paroi	[paʀwa]
HABĒRE	'have'	avoir	[avwaʀ]

and for the back high mid /o/ in Latin free syllables:

VŌTU	'vow'	voeu	[vø]
NEPŌTE	'nephew'	neveu	[nəvø]
PLŪVIT	'rains'	pleut	[plø]
SAPŌRE	'flavor'	saveur	[savœʀ]
MELIŌRE	'better'	meilleur	[mejœʀ]
HŌRA	'hour'	heure	[œʀ]
GULA	'throat'	gueule	[gœl]
IUVENE	'young'	jeune	[ʒœn]

Note that the French outcome has two pronunciations – higher [ø] in modern free syllables (*neveu*) and lower [œ] in most modern blocked syllables (*heure*).

The spellings are historically significant: <oi> for [wa] dates from a time when the pronunciation was [oj], and <eu> for [ø,œ] likewise reflects the earlier stage [ew]. Occasional <oeu> instead of <eu>, as in *voeu* 'vow', *soeur* 'sister', is purely ornamental, alluding to the Latin spelling.

PRACTICE

Check these cognate sets. Are there any words in which the stressed high mid vowel fails to conform to the rules we have just seen?

Latin		Italian	Spanish	French	
BŬRSA	'sack'	borsa	bolsa	bourse	[buʀs]
VAPŌRE	'steam'	vapore	vapor	vapeur	[vapœʀ]
SPĒRAT	'hopes'	spera	espera	espère	[ɛspɛʀ]
VĬCE	'stead'	vece	vez	fois	[fwa]
SĬCCA	'dry'	secca	seca	sèche	[sɛʃ]
IŬGU	'yoke'	giogo	yugo	joug	[ʒug]
MŬSCA	'fly'	mosca	mosca	mouche	[muʃ]
CRĒDIT	'believes'	crede	cree	croit	[kʀwa]

1.2.5   The low mid vowels

We have seen how the difference between Latin free and blocked syllables conditions some changes, so far only in French. For the low mids, however, the blocked versus free contrast is crucial in Italian as well as French. Let's start with blocked syllables, which are more conservative. Pick out from the sets starting with PEDE and NOVU (pp. 10–11) the stressed low mids in blocked syllables.

What happens to stressed low mid /ɛ/ in blocked syllables? In Italian and French /ɛ/ remains unchanged, while in Spanish it becomes a diphthong, /je/. Further examples:

Latin		Italian	Spanish	French
HIBERNU	'wintry'	inverno	invierno	hiver
APERTA	'open'	aperta	abierta	ouverte
SEPTE	'seven'	sette	siete	sept
CERVU	'deer'	cervo	ciervo	cerf
FERRU	'iron'	ferro	hierro	fer

Still in blocked syllables, stressed back low mid /ɔ/ remains intact in Italian and French, while in Spanish it becomes a diphthong, /we/. Examples confirming this regularity include:

Latin		Italian	Spanish	French
FORTE	'strong'	forte	fuerte	fort
PORTA	'door'	porta	puerta	porte
MORDIT	'bites'	morde	muerde	mord
OSSU	'bone'	osso	hueso	os
NOSTRU	'ours'	nostro	nuestro	notre
SORTE	'fate'	sorte	suerte	sort

Last on our agenda, and most changeable, are the stressed low mids in free syllables. This is the environment most conducive to diphthongization. In the database (pp. 10–11), select from the lists beginning with PEDE and NOVU the stressed low mids in free syllables.

The stressed front low mid /ɛ/ in a free syllable yields a diphthong [jɛ]/[je] in all three languages. Further examples:

Latin		Italian	Spanish	French
PETRA	'stone'	pietra	piedra	pierre
*FELE	'bile'	fiele	hiel	fiel
VENIT	'comes'	viene	viene	vient
HERI	'yesterday'	ieri	ayer	hier

What happens to stressed back low mid /ɔ/ in a free syllable? All three languages show a change. In Italian it becomes /wɔ/, and in Spanish /we/. In French the modern outcome is the same round front /ø/ mentioned earlier, typically spelled <eu> or <oeu> and pronounced [ø,œ]. Additional examples:

Latin		Italian	Spanish	French	
*MORIT	'dies'	muore	muere	meurt	[mœʀ]
MOVET	'moves'	muove	mueve	meut	[mø]
POTET	'can'	può	puede	peut	[pø]

The French development leading from words like FOCU to *feu* is reconstructed as follows:

$$/ɔ/ > /wɔ/ > /wɛ/ > /ø/$$

The first stage is the same diphthong as in Italian. The second seems to be a dissimilation (back glide versus front vowel), while in the third stage the round feature of the glide is superimposed on the vowel, yielding /ø/.

This is the same vowel /ø/ that also resulted from the back high mid /o/ in a free syllable. Both /o/ and /ɔ/ in free syllables end up converging to the same vowel /ø/, although they arrive via different paths. This /ø/, as we noted (§ 1.2.4), is realized phonetically as higher [ø] in modern free syllables, and as lower [œ] in most modern blocked syllables. Further examples:

veut	'wants'	[vø]	veulent	'want'	[vœl]
oeufs	'eggs'	[ø]	oeuf	'egg'	[œf]
gueux	'beggar'	[gø]	gueule	'face'	[gœl]

PRACTICE

Check these cognate sets. Are there any words in which the stressed low mid vowel fails to conform to the rules we have just seen?

Latin		*Italian*	*Spanish*	*French*	
CĔRTU	'certain'	certo	cierto	certes	[sɛʀt]
TŎRQUIT	'twists'	torce	tuerce	tord	[tɔʀ]
FĔRA	'wild'	fiera	hiera	fière	[fjɛʀ]
NŎVE	'nine'	nove	nueve	neuf	[nœf]
COPĔRTA	'covered'	coperta	cubierta	couverte	[kuvɛʀt]
BĔNE	'well'	bene	bien	bien	[bjɛ̃]

1.2.6   Review: primary diphthongs

We have seen that in Italian, Spanish, and French, mid vowels under stress break into diphthongs, but only under specific conditions that vary across the three languages. These Romance diphthongs are called **primary** or spontaneous, in contrast to **secondary** diphthongs that can arise in various other ways (§§ 2.3.3, 3.3.1, 4.3.8, 5.2.2, 5.3.1).

Summing up §§ 1.2.4–5, this diagram shows the contrasting conditions for primary diphthongization in Italian, Spanish, and French.

CONDITIONS FOR PRIMARY DIPHTHONGS

High mid free syllable	
Low mid free syllable	Low mid blocked syllable
Italian	Spanish French

As the chart shows, diphthongization affects free syllables more readily than blocked syllables, and low mids more than high mids. Italian requires both these conditions. Spanish diphthongs come only from low mids, but occur in blocked as well as free syllables. This accounts for such contrasts as:

Latin			*Italian*	*Spanish*
TEMPU	'time'		tempo	tiempo
TERRA	'earth'		terra	tierra
SEMPER	'always'		sempre	siempre
PONTE	'bridge'		ponte	puente
MORDIT	'bites'		morde	muerde

Only in French do the high mids produce diphthongs. At the first step in their evolution, a glide is generated after the vowel: /e/ > /ej/, /o/ > /ow/. Subsequent steps are reconstructed as we saw earlier (§ 1.2.4).

1.2.7   Stressed vowels in another perspective

The Great Merger, common to almost all Romance languages, produced a seven-vowel system which then evolved in different ways. As we saw, many of these subsequent changes depend upon whether the stressed syllable is blocked or free. This suggests another format for organizing the facts. Let's first consider all the changes occurring in blocked syllables, the more conservative environment. The seven-vowel system resulting from the Great Merger evolves as shown below:

CHANGES RESTRICTED TO BLOCKED SYLLABLES
Italian:	None
Spanish:	None
French:	o > [u], written <ou>

Some changes, oblivious to syllable structure, occur in both free and blocked syllables:

CHANGES IN ANY SYLLABLE, FREE OR BLOCKED
Italian:	None
Spanish:	Low mids diphthongize to [je] and [we]
French:	u > [y]

The changes restricted to free syllables are more numerous, especially in French.

CHANGES RESTRICTED TO FREE SYLLABLES
Italian:	Low mids diphthongize to [jɛ] and [wɔ]
Spanish:	None
French:	a > [e,ɛ]
	e > ej > … > [wa], typically written <oi>

o > ow > ... > [ø,œ], written <eu> or <oeu>
ε > [je]
ɔ > we > ... > [ø,œ], written <eu> or <oeu>

1.3   Special developments in stressed vowels

There are certain phonetic environments where the development of stressed vowels deviates from the patterns we studied in § 1.2.

1.3.1   Italian: failure of primary diphthongization

In Italian, even where the conditions for a primary diphthong are met (stressed low mid in free syllable), the diphthongization usually fails in **proparoxytones**, i.e. words stressed on the third syllable from the end. Examples:

LĔPORE	'hare'	lepre
TĔNERU	'tender'	tenero
GĔNERU	'son-in-law'	genero
PŎPULU	'people'	popolo
ŎPERA	'work' pl.	opera
ĔDERA	'ivy'	edera

There are some exceptions, such as TĔPIDU 'warm' *tiepido* and *LĔVITU 'yeast' *lievito*.

For other special developments in Italian, mainly vowel raising, see § 5.1.

1.3.2   Spanish: raising effects

You will encounter some Spanish words where the stressed vowel is higher than you would expect, based on the patterns presented so far. For example, MULTU, AUSCULTAT, and LUCTAT have /ŭ/ in Latin, which in the Great Merger should have become high mid /o/, but actually they have /u/. Likewise, LACTE, FACTU, BASIU, and CASEU yield reflexes with /e/ instead of /a/.

MULTU	'much'	mucho
AUSCULTAT	'listens'	escucha
LUCTAT	'struggles'	lucha
*LACTE	'milk'	leche
FACTU	'done'	hecho
BASIU	'kiss'	beso
CASEU	'cheese'	queso

This effect usually reflects the influence of a yod or similar palatal articulation later in the word.[1] These raising effects, prominent in Spanish, are covered in § 5.2.

1.3.3   French: stressed vowel before nasal consonant

Compare these three outcomes of Latin /a/ in French:

SALE	'salt'	sel
CARA	'dear'	chère
CASA	'house'	chez
SANU	'healthy'	sain
*DE-MANE	'tomorrow'	demain
AMAT	'loves'	aime
GRANDE	'large'	grand
CAMPU	'field'	champ
SANGUEN	'blood'	sang

Question: What happens to /a/ before a nasal consonant?

Answer: Judging from the spelling, /a/ before a nasal consonant apparently went through a stage where it diphthongized to [aj], but only in a free syllable.

The first group above shows the regular development of stressed /a/ in a free syllable (§ 1.2.2). The second group shows stressed /a/ in a free syllable before a nasal, and suggests that [a] went through a stage [aj]. In the third group /a/ remains unchanged before a nasal because the syllable is blocked. Further examples of this regularity include:

SCALA	'stair'	échelle
LANA	'wool'	laine
MANU	'hand'	main
FAMEN	'hunger'	faim
PANE	'bread'	pain
FLAMMA	'flame'	flamme

High mid /e/ behaves just like /a/. Compare these three groups:

DĒBET	'owes'	doit
VĒLA	'sail'	voile
MĒ	'me'	moi
PLĒNU	'full'	plein
SINU	'breast'	sein
VĒNA	'vein'	veine
VĒNDIT	'sells'	vend
INDE	'from there'	en

Question: What happens to the high mid /e/ before a nasal consonant?

Answer: As spelling again suggests, /e/ before a nasal consonant went through a stage where it diphthongized to /ej/, but only in free syllables.

Words of the first group above show the regular development of stressed /e/ in a free syllable (§ 1.2.4). The second group shows /e/ > <ei> in a free syllable before a nasal. In the third group /e/ remains <e> before a nasal consonant because the syllable is blocked. Further examples are:

PARIĒTE	'wall'	paroi
SĒRU	'evening'	soir
FRĒNU	'brake'	frein
*PĒNA	'punishment'	peine
FINDERE	'split'	fendre

These pre-nasal diphthongs offer an insight into how /a/ and /e/ developed historically. The nasal may be simply freezing the vowels at the first stage of their development. Pope (1934:107) suggests that stressed /a/ in *any* free syllable diphthongizes at first to /aj/, which later goes on to become /e/. The effect of a nasal consonant would be to freeze the /aj/ stage temporarily, long enough to motivate the <ai> spelling.

SALE	'salt'	*sajl	> sel
MARE	'sea'	*majr	> mer
PANE	'bread'	pain	
AMAT	'loves'	aime	

Even though these pre-nasal vowels have undergone further development in the modern language, their spelling would reflect this /aj/ stage. Now turn to stressed high mid /e/ in a free syllable. We have already hypothesized that its first change was to a diphthong, /ej/, which subsequently went on to become modern /wa/. In pre-nasal position it freezes at the first stage, /ej/, during a period when the spelling was established.

SĒRU	'evening'	> [sejr] > [sojr] > [soɛr] > [swɛr] > [swaʀ] *soir*
FRĒNU	'brake'	> [frejn] > … > *frein*

Thus the modern spelling reflects a stage where the nasal has blocked the usual further development of [ej] to [wa] as in *soir*.

Caution: the few insights we have drawn from these spellings – <ai> and <ei> before nasals – pertain only to the earliest stages of stressed vowel development in French. At a later stage, all pre-nasal vowels undergo nasalization (§ 5.4). Here we are scarcely touching upon the drastic and fairly complex effects that nasal consonants exert, over the centuries, upon all French vowels. Moreover,

/a/ and /e/ aside, for the other vowels shown below in pre-nasal position, modern spellings afford no special clues about the influence of nasals. In terms of spelling, nasal consonants have no effect on the development of low mid /ɛ/. These examples show pre-nasal /ɛ/ in free and blocked syllables:

BENE	'well'	bien
VENIT	'comes'	vient
VENTU	'wind'	vent
SENTIT	'feels'	sent

In the back of the vowel triangle the situation is the same:

HŌRA	'hour'	heure
DŌNU	'gift'	don
LŌNGE	'long'	long
SUNT	'are'	sont

We see the same outcomes from back low mid /ɔ/:

POTET 'can' > */pwɔte/ > /pwɛt/ > *peut* [pø]
BONU 'good' > */bwɔn/ > … > *bon* [bɔ̃]

HOMO	'man'	on
BONU	'good'	bon
SONU	'sound'	son
TONU	'tone'	ton
PONTE	'bridge'	pont

There is some early evidence that low mid /ɔ/ before nasals behaved almost like the front low mid /ɛ/, that is, stressed /ɔ/ in free syllables at first diphthongized to /wɔ/, as in Italian. The ninth-century *Cantilène de Sainte Eulalie* begins: *Buona pulcella fut Eulalia* …. Before nasals, both /ɛ/ and /ɔ/ at first had normal primary diphthongization to /jɛ/ and /wɔ/ in free syllables, but modern spelling reflects this only for /ɛ/.

The high vowels /i/ and /u/ show no spelling changes before nasal consonants:

VĪNU	'wine'	vin
LŪNA	'moon'	lune

PRACTICE

In these French words, do the stressed vowels before nasal consonants conform to the pattern outlined above?

Latin		Italian	Spanish	French	
CLAMAT	'calls'	chiama	llama	claimet (OFr)	[klajməθ]
SEPTIMANA	'week'	settimana	semana	semaine	[səmɛn]

GRANU	'grain'	grano	grano	grain	[gʀɛ̃]
VĔNTRE	'belly'	ventre	vientre	ventre	[vɑ̃tʀ]
CĒNA	'dinner'	cena	cena	Cène	[sɛn]
FŎNTE	'spring'	fonte	fuente	font	[fɔ̃]
CARBŌNE	'charcoal'	carbone	carbón	charbon	[ʃaʀbɔ̃]
ŬNDA	'wave'	onda	onda	onde	[ɔ̃d]

1.4   The three Latin diphthongs

To complete our survey of stressed vowels, we turn to the three original diphthongs of Latin and ask how they fit into the seven-vowel system.

1.4.1   Diphthongs from Indo-European simplify

Indo-European had many diphthongs. In Ancient Greek, the diphthongs were well preserved, but on the way to Latin, at a prehistoric stage, they began to be reduced to **monophthongs** (single vowels).

oj > ū   ŪNUS 'one'   ew, ow > ū   LŪNA 'moon'   ej > ī   DĪCIT 'says'

In the evolution to Latin, the simplification of the diphthongs didn't happen all at once: it was a long-term trend. At the time when Latin became standardized and codified, there were still three inherited diphthongs surviving: /aw/ (written AU), /aj/ (written AE), and a few instances of /oj/ (written OE). Romance handbooks and courses such as ours take standard Latin as their conventional point of departure. This is why we talk about these three diphthongs only, not those that had already been obliterated in the prehistory of Latin and in pre-Classical times. Obviously and instructively, the millennial trend toward simplification of the original Indo-European diphthongs, a trend already at work in the prehistory of Latin, continued in early Romance.

1.4.2   The fate of the three Latin diphthongs

The three diphthongs that survived this process in Latin not surprisingly went on to simplify to monophthongs, but at different rates. Our question here is how they fit into the seven-vowel system of Romance speech.

Many instances of /oj/ had already become /ū/ by the time of Classical Latin standardization; the few remaining instances gave high mid /e/.

Latin		*Italian*	*Spanish*	*French*
POENA	'punishment'	pena	pena	peine
FOEDU	'ugly'	....	feo	....

The diphthong /aw/ resolved to low mid /ɔ/, but not until after /ɔ/ had produced a primary diphthong. Low mids from /aw/ do not go on to produce diphthongs. Nonetheless, we do have evidence that /aw/ became a low mid: these words are

pronounced with the low mid in Italian, which retains to this day a distinction
between low mids and high mids among stressed vowels.

Latin		Italian	Spanish	French
AURU	'gold'	oro	oro	or
THESAURU	'treasure'	tesoro	tesoro	trésor
PAUPERU	'poor'	povero	pobre	pauvre
*AUSAT	'dares'	osa	osa	ose
LAUDAT	'praises'	loda	loa	loue
AUDIT	'hears'	ode	oye	oit (OFr)
PAUCU	'little'	poco	poco	peu

Exceptions in this array are instructive. The vowel /u/ in French *loue* results
from analogical leveling, common in verb paradigms (§ 6.7).

Question: What is special about the French outcome PAUCU > *peu* /pø/?

Answer: Unlike other instances of AU > /ɔ/, this one does go on to participate in primary diphthongization, ultimately giving the same result as other
Romance low mid /ɔ/.

This exception simply reminds us that changes hit different regions, and even
different words, at different times. Apparently, in Gaul PAUCU became PŎCU so
early that it developed like an original low mid /ɔ/. The French language retains
no memory that Popular Latin *PŎCU ever had a diphthong.

The diphthong /aj/ generally yields low mid /ɛ/, but sometimes high mid /e/.

Latin		Italian	Spanish	French
CAELU	'sky'	cielo	cielo	ciel
CAECU	'blind'	cieco	ciego	....
QUAERIT	'asks'	chiede	quiere	quiert (OFr)
SAETA	'silk'	seta	seda	soie
PRAEDA	'prey'	preda	....	proie

In SAETA and PRAEDA, apparently /aj/ gave high mid /e/, judging from the lack
of diphthongization in Italian and Spanish, and from the /wa/ in French.

Exercises

1. Check these cognate sets: there are a few which for some reason *fail* to conform
to our repertory of rules on the development of stressed vowels. Identify at least
six anomalous forms, and state how they differ from the expected outcome, without speculating on why the irregularity occurred. Latin vowel quantity is given (if
needed).

Latin		Italian	Spanish	French	
PLŪMA	'feather'	piuma	pluma	plume	[plym]

CAPRA	'goat'	capra	cabra	chèvre	[ʃɛvʀ]
LŬPU	'wolf'	lupo	lobo	loup	[lu]
CLAVE	'key'	chiave	llave	clef	[kle]
MŎVIT	'moves'	muove	mueve	meut	[mø]
CŎRPUS	'body'	corpo	cuerpo	corps	[kɔʀ]
BĔNE	'well'	bene	bien	bien	[bjɛ̃]
ĬNTRAT	'enters'	entra	entra	entre	[ɑ̃tʀ]
PLŬMBU	'lead'	piombo	plomo	plomb	[plɔ̃]
TĒ	'you'	te	te	toi	[twa]
*MĔNTIT	'tells lies'	mente	miente	ment	[mɑ̃]
TĔNET	'holds'	tiene	tiene	tient	[tjɛ̃]
AMŌRE	'love'	amore	amor	amour	[amuʀ]
CATTU	'cat'	gatto	gato	chat	[ʃa]
*FŎRTIA	'strength'	forza	fuerza	force	[fɔʀs]
NŌDU	'knot'	nodo	nudo	noeud	[nø]
MĪLLE	'thousand'	mille	mil	mille	[mil]
SŬRDA	'deaf'	sorda	sorda	sourde	[suʀd]
RŎTA	'wheel'	ruota	rueda	roue	[ʀu]
SAPŌNE	'soap'	sapone	jabón	savon	[savɔ̃]

2.   This is like the preceding exercise, except that Latin vowel quantities are not given. You make the best hypothesis about the quantity of the stressed vowel and see if there is some form which cannot be reconciled with that hypothesis.

Latin		*Italian*	*Spanish*	*French*	
NOSTRA	'our'	nostra	nuestra	notre	[nɔtʀ]
PIRA	'pear'	pera	pera	poire	[pwaʀ]
DENTE	'tooth'	dente	diente	dent	[dɑ̃]
*COCIT	'cooks'	cuoce	cuece	cuit	[kɥi]
COLORE	'color'	colore	color	couleur	[kulœʀ]
ROTUNDA	'round'	tonda	redonda	ronde	[ʀɔ̃d]
MINUS	'less'	meno	menos	moins	[mwɛ̃]
BATTUIT	'beats'	batte	bate	bat	[ba]
LACU	'lake'	lago	lago	lac	[lak]
PURA	'pure'	pura	pura	pure	[pyʀ]
APERTA	'open'	aperta	abierta	ouverte	[uvɛʀt]
*SITE	'thirst'	sete	sed	soif	[swaf]
DULCE	'sweet'	dolce	dulce	douce	[dus]
VENDIT	'sells'	vende	vende	vend	[vɑ̃]
DICIT	'says'	dice	dice	dit	[di]
SAPERE	'know'	sapere	saber	savoir	[savwaʀ]
SCALA	'stair'	scala	escala	échelle	[eʃɛl]
FEBRE	'fever'	febbre	fiebre	fièvre	[fjɛvʀ]
CORDA	'rope'	corda	cuerda	corde	[kɔʀd]
CLARA	'light'	chiara	clara	claire	[klɛʀ]

2   Early changes in syllable structure and consonants

2.1   Prosthetic vowels

One development that demonstrably dates back to Popular Latin speech is the word-initial support vowel (**prosthetic** vowel) added before /s/ + consonant.

2.1.1   Treatment of /s/ + consonant

Clusters of /s/ + consonant have special properties in the Western languages. We saw (§ 1.1.3) that in Latin they cannot begin a syllable word-medially: FESTA is syllabified FES.TA. This same prohibition began to apply to word-initial onsets. Apparently, in words like SPATA /s/ could no longer syllabify in the onset.

Latin		Old Italian	Spanish	Old French
SPONSA	'betrothed'	isposa	esposa	espose
SPATA	'sword'	ispada	espada	espede
STUDIU	'study'	istudio	estudio	estude
SPONGIA	'sponge'	ispugna	esponja	esponge
SCUTU	'shield'	iscudo	escudo	escut
*SCUTELLA	'dish'	iscodella	escudilla	escüelle
STRINGIT	'squeezes'	istringe	estriñe	estreint
STRICTU	'tight'	istretto	estrecho	estreit
SCRIPTU	'written'	iscritto	escrito	escrit

With the addition of the prosthetic vowel, the /s/ can syllabify as a coda of the first syllable, and thus conform to the ban on /s/ plus consonant in onsets.

On the way to Modern French, preconsonantal /s/ deletes, anywhere in the word:

Latin		Old French	Modern French
SPONSA	'betrothed'	espose	épouse
SPATA	'sword'	espede	épée
STUDIU	'study'	estude	étude

SPONGIA	'sponge'	esponge	éponge
SCUTU	'shield'	escut	écu
*SCUTELLA	'dish'	escüelle	écuelle
STRINGIT	'squeezes'	estreint	étreint
STRICTU	'tight'	estreit	étroit
SCRIPTU	'written'	escrit	écrit
BESTIA	'beast'	beste	bête
CRISPA	'curly'	crespe	crêpe
FESTA	'feast'	feste	fête
VESPA	'wasp'	guespe	guêpe
TESTA	'jug'	teste	tête
ASINU	'donkey'	asne	âne
ESSERE (Pop)	'be'	estre	être
INSULA	'island'	isle	île

Question: How does French orthography signal the deletion of preconsonantal /s/?

Answer: The vowel before the deletion site is marked with a diacritic: *accent aigu* for the /e/ of prosthetic origin (*épouse*), and circumflex elsewhere (*crêpe*, *île*).

2.1.2   Living versus dead rules

The constraint against word-initial /s/ + consonant persists even today in Spanish. The Spanish lexicon contains no such words. A non-native word such as *Schenectady*, pronounced in Spanish, gets a prosthetic vowel: /eskenektadi/. Not so in French, which in its formative period had the constraint but later lost it. When in force, the rule reshaped the lexicon in the ways we have just seen (*état*, *école*, etc.), but since its loss, new words beginning with /s/ + consonant have been freely introduced without vowel prosthesis (e.g. *sculpture*, *spécifique*). This is what accounts for such Spanish/French contrasts as:

Spanish	*French*
escorpión	scorpion
especial	spécial
esportiva	sportive

In Italian too, vowel prosthesis is a dead rule. Not only does Italian admit new words beginning with /s/ + consonant (e.g. *scultura*, *specifico*), but it also at some point removed prosthetic vowels. This must have happened at a time when variants with and without prosthesis (*isposa/sposa*) still coexisted.

Latin		Old Italian	Modern Italian
SPONSA	'betrothed'	isposa	sposa
SPATA	'sword'	ispada	spada
STUDIU	'study'	istudio	studio
SPONGIA	'sponge'	ispugna	spugna
SCUTU	'shield'	iscudo	scudo
*SCUTELLA	'dish'	iscodella	scodella
SCARLATTA	'rich cloth'	iscarlatta	scarlatta
STRINGIT	'squeezes'	istringe	stringe
STRICTU	'tight'	istretto	stretto
SCRIPTU	'written'	iscritto	scritto

A few frozen phrases contain relics of the prosthetic vowel: *per iscritto* 'in writing', *in Isvizzera* 'in Switzerland'.

A curiosity: Latin AUSCULTAT 'listens', probably *ASCULTAT in Popular Latin, gives Italian *ascolta*, which is regular. However, in Spanish *escucha* and French *écoute*, the initial vowel exhibits an irregular change. The likely explanation is that it was reinterpreted as a prosthetic vowel.

2.2   Syncope and new consonant clusters

Syncope, the deletion of an unstressed vowel in word-medial position, affected the shape of many words in early Romance. We observe the same tendency today in the pronunciation of English.

> Question: How many syllables do you count in these words: *several, every, groceries, history, evening, celery, dangerous*?
>
> Answer: Some might say these words have three syllables, but in casual speech most pronounce them with two.

Syncope in English is variable. You may or may not syncopate such words as: *funeral, nursery, numerous, camera*. Syncope is rare or impossible in such words as: *surgery, Mexico, feminine, imaginary, caliber, difficult, courteous, salivate*.

Caution: The term *syncope* is not used for all deletions. It customarily refers only to word-medial deletions that reduce the syllable count.

2.2.1   General patterns of syncope

Syncope is among the earliest changes affecting Popular Latin. Examples occur in Latin inscriptions and in the few surviving sources that reflect Popular Latin speech.

Standard Latin		Popular Latin	
OCULU	'eye'	OCLU	(CIL)[1]

| AURICULA | 'ear' | ORICLA | (Appendix Probi)[2] |
| CALIDU | 'hot' | CALDU | (Appendix Probi) |

Just as in today's English, it operates variably, hitting different words at different times and some not at all. But the typical patterns for our three languages are those shown here:

Latin		*Italian*	*Spanish*	*French*
LEPORE	'hare'	lepre	liebre	lièvre
CAPPARIS	'caper'	cappero	alcaparra	câpre
INSULA	'island'	isola	isla	île
ALTERA	'other'	altra	otra	autre
CALIDA	'hot'	calda	calda (OSp)	chaude
VIRIDE	'green'	verde	verde	verte
(DE-)POSITU	'place'	posto	puesto	dépôt

These examples, and more to come, show that the pressure to syncopate is greater in French and Spanish than in Italian. For example, no syncope occurs in Italian *cappero* and *isola*.[3]

Syncope may delete not only a single vowel, but even a whole syllable or more. Some words have been drastically shortened in French:

BLASPHEMARE	'blaspheme'	blâmer	'reproach'
TESTIMONIU	'testimony'	témoin	'witness'
MINISTERIU	'service'	métier	'job'
DESIDERAT	'desires'	désire	'desires'
SUBITANEU	'sudden'	soudain	'sudden'
MALE-HABITU	'in a bad way'	malade	'sick'
CONSUETUDINE	'habit'	coustume (OFr)	'habit'

> **PRACTICE**
>
> In the foregoing words, identify the material deleted by syncope.

2.2.2   New clusters from syncope: nasal + liquid

Syncope typically creates consonant clusters. When it creates a cluster of nasal + liquid, some special results ensue. In Italian, syncope is typically blocked in these cases. In Spanish and French, it does occur, and the resulting cluster is modified in a characteristic way.

Latin		*Italian*	*Spanish*	*French*
IN SEMEL	'once'	insieme	....	ensemble
HUMILE	'lowly'	umile	....[4]	humble
CINERE	'ash'	cenere	....	cendre

TENERU	'tender'	tenero	tierno	tendre
GENERU	'son-in-law'	genero	yerno	gendre
CAMERA	'room'	camera	....	chambre

> Question: How does Spanish treat nasal + liquid clusters arising from syncope?
>
> Answer: The unacceptable /nr/ cluster is resolved by **metathesis**: it becomes /rn/.

> Question: How does French treat nasal + liquid clusters arising from syncope?
>
> Answer: The nasal + liquid cluster is resolved by **epenthesis**: a consonant is inserted to resolve the cluster.

> Question: What consonant is inserted?
>
> Answer: From /ml/, /mr/, and /nr/ we get /mbl/, /mbr/, and /ndr/. The epenthetic stop is **homorganic** (having the same place of articulation) with the nasal.

There are some variant outcomes:

Latin		Italian	Spanish	French	
TREMULAT	'trembles'	tremola	tiembla	tremble	
PŌNĔRE	'put'	porre	poner	pondre	'lay eggs'

Spanish *tiembla* shows epenthesis, an effect more typical of French. Latin PŌNĔRE, a proparoxytone, does syncopate in Italian and /nr/ becomes /rr/, a case of **assimilation**: one segment changes to resemble another. This is how Italian resolves unacceptable consonant clusters: the first segment changes to match the second (**regressive** or **anticipatory** assimilation). French changes the second to match the first, as in NĪTĬDA 'shiny' > French *nette* 'clean', where /td/ > /t:/, later /t/ (**progressive** assimilation).

2.2.3   New clusters from syncope: nasal + nasal

Syncope can also create clusters of the form nasal + nasal.

Latin		Italian	Spanish	French
FEMINA	'female'	femmina	hembra	femme /fam/
HOMINES	'men'	uomini	hombres	hommes
SEMINAT	'sows'	semina	siembra	sème
DOMINA	'lady'	donna	dueña	dame

As we have seen, Italian is less given to syncope than the other languages. Spanish /mn/ merges with /mr/. Observe HUMERU 'shoulder' *hombro* with epenthesis, the same result seen above in *hembra, hombre, sembra*. In French /mn/ > /m:/ > /m/, written either <mm> or <m>.

DOMINA stands out, and the reason lies in its chronology. The frequency of this word probably fostered its early syncope everywhere, even in Italian. In the Popular Latin of Italy and Spain, this /mn/ cluster gives /n:/ (**regressive assimilation**) which then in Spanish acts like original Latin /n:/ (compare ANNU > *año* 'year' and cf. § 4.3.7 end). In the Popular Latin of Gaul, there was clearly no /n:/ stage, since the French outcomes all show **progressive assimilation**, /mn/ > /m:/ > /m/.

Here are some further examples involving Latin nouns that happen to have two stems, a shorter stem for nominative (subject) case, and a longer one for all other uses (§ 8.2). In these examples the long stem, after syncope, contains a cluster /mn/ which then develops normally.

Latin		Italian	Spanish	French
FAMEN	'hunger'	fame	....	faim
FAMINE	'hunger'	....	hambre	....
HOMO	'man'	uomo	....	on
HOMINE	'man'	....	hombre	homme
NOMEN	'name'	nome	....	nom
NOMINE	'name'	....	nombre	....

A more complex example is CULMEN 'summit', which in pre-French apparently metathesized to *kumle, and then with epenthesis, /ml/ > /mbl/.

Latin		Italian	Spanish	French
CULMEN, *CULMU	'summit'	colmo	....	comble
CULMINE	'summit'	....	cumbre	....

When a Latin noun has two stems, it may happen that both survive in different languages, or even in the same language, as seen here (more in § 8.7).

2.3   Merger of /b/ and /w/

In the early formative period of Romance, /b/ and /w/ were merging into one unit. Spelling confusion between them is rife in the sources that reflect Popular Latin speech. Evidence for the early date: all Romance languages show the merger. *Widespread* and *early* go together in the history of the Romance languages: an innovation, if early enough, affected the spoken Latin that was carried all over the expanding Roman territories.

In Italian and French, /b/ and /w/ remain distinct in certain protected positions, as we explain below. In Spanish the merger was complete. We survey the results after a brief word of caution.

2.3.1   Background on spelling convention

Romans regarded U and V as variant shapes of the same letter. It was V in the magnificent formal capitals, somewhat curvier in "rustic" capitals, and fully rounded U in Late Latin uncials. Depending on the hand, /wiwu/ 'alive' could be UIUU or VIVV.[5] However, since modern alphabets take <u> and <v> to be distinct items, we have a better convention for writing Latin nowadays: we use <u> when the value was vocalic (vowel /u/) and <v> when it was consonantal (glide /w/).

This modern convention is used in presenting Latin words throughout this book. Thus <v> in our Latin spelling always means /w/, for example NOVU /nowu/ 'new'. The fricative /v/ as in English *vote* did not exist in Latin. It developed as an innovation in most of the Romance languages. The purpose of this background is to emphasize that in this book, wherever you see <v> in Latin words, its value in Classical times was /w/.

2.3.2   Merger of /b/ and /w/

The **protected positions**, those where Romance consonants tend to resist change, are word-initial and postconsonantal.[6] Word-initially, /b/ and /w/ remain distinct in Italian and French:

Latin		*Italian*	*Spanish*		*French*
BARBA	'beard'	barba	barba	[barβa]	barbe
BUCCA	'mouth'	bocca	boca	[boka]	bouche
VACCA	'cow'	vacca	vaca	[baka]	vache
VINU	'wine'	vino	vino	[bino]	vin

Again, in the other protected position, postconsonantal, Italian and French keep /b/ and /w/ distinct, whereas in Spanish they merge. In Spanish the ultimate result of the merger is one phoneme with two allophones, [b] at the beginning of a breath group or post-nasally, and [β] everywhere else. To show this, we give phonetic, not phonemic, transcriptions here for Spanish:

Latin		*Italian*	*Spanish*		*French*
HERBA	'grass'	erba	hierba	[jerβa]	herbe
ALBA	'dawn'	alba	alba	[alβa]	aube
CARBONE	'coal'	carbone	carbón	[karβon]	charbon
MALVA	'mallow'	malva	malva	[malβa]	mauve
FERVENTE	'boiling'	fervente	hirviente	[irβjente]	fervent
SALVAT	'saves'	salva	salva	[salβa]	sauve
BUCCA	'mouth'	bocca	boca	[boka]	bouche
VACCA	'cow'	vacca	vaca	[baka]	vache
HIBERNU	'wintry'	inverno[7]	invierno	[imbjerno]	hiver

In the unprotected intervocalic position, all three languages merge /b/ with /w/. That is, within each language /b/ and /w/ give identical results. Italian and French have /v/.

Latin			Italian	Spanish		French
CABALLU	'horse'		cavallo	caballo	[kaβajo]	cheval
BIBAT	'drinks'		beva	beba	[beβa]	boive
DEBERE	'have to'		dovere	deber	[deβer]	devoir
CAVERNA	'cavern'		caverna	caverna	[kaβerna]	caverne
LAVARE	'wash'		lavare	lavar	[laβar]	laver
VIVUNT	'live'		vivono	viven	[biβen]	vivent

Spanish tends to favor spellings reminiscent of the Latin etymon, but in reality letters <b> and <v> are pronounced alike. Both represent a single phoneme, with its allophones [b] and [β] distributed as shown above.

2.3.3   /w/ in secondary diphthongs

The sound resulting from the /b/ and /w/ merger, probably [w] at first, was not always in a position to go on to the consonantal outcomes we have seen so far. In certain derivations it ended up in a syllable coda, and thus combined with the preceding vowel to form a secondary diphthong (§ 1.2.6).

PARABŎLA	'speech'	> *parawola	> *parawla	> parɔla	It *parola*, Fr *parole*
*AVĬCA	'goose'	> *awika	> *awka	> ɔka	It *oca*, Sp *oca*, Fr *oie*
FABRĬCA	'smithy'	> *fawrika	> *fawrdʒa	> fɔʀʒ	Fr *forge*
AVIS STRUTHĬU	'ostrich'	> *awistrytʃ	> *awstrytʃ	> otʀyʃ	Fr *autruche*
DEBĬTA	'debt'	> *dewida	> *dewda	> dewða	Sp *deuda*

2.4   Early consonant losses

Four changes, early and widespread, involve the loss of certain consonants.

2.4.1   Loss of /h/

Catullus (circa 84–54 BCE), in the four lines cited here, mocks a certain Arrius for his clumsy affectation of socially prestigious speech. The two basic ideas are that Arrius says 1) *chommoda* for the correct *commoda*, and 2) *hinsidias* for the correct *insidias*.

> *Chommoda* dicebat, si quando *commoda*
> vellet dicere, et *insidias* Arrius *hinsidias*,
> et tum mirifice sperabat se esse locutum,
> cum quantum poterat dixerat *hinsidias*.

> Arrius, whenever he meant *commoda*, would say *chommoda*,
> and *hinsidias* for *insidias*,
> and then he was sure he had spoken splendidly
> when he said at the top of his lungs, *hinsidias*.

Question: What makes Arrius think he should say *hinsidias*?

Answer: Uneducated people were no longer pronouncing /h/ in Popular Latin.

Evidently, Arrius is aware of a number of words existing in two socially marked variants, the higher one with word-initial /h/, and the lower without.

Standard Latin	Popular Latin	
HODIE	ODIE	'today'
HOMINE	OMINE	'man'
HORTU	ORTU	'garden'
HERBA	ERBA	'grass'
	INSIDIAS	'snares'

Hmm. It must be *hinsidias*

Arrius unconsciously uses a formula for the relation between lower and higher speech. He thinks words he normally pronounces with a word-initial vowel will sound "better" with a word-initial /h/. His mistake is to generalize this formula even to words that never had any /h/. This kind of overgeneralization is known as **hypercorrection**. We can see hypercorrection in today's English, for instance when speakers get the notion that *whom* is simply "better" than *who*, and say things like *Whom shall I say is calling?* Thus, what the poem tells us, reliably and vividly, is that when Catullus lived, the loss of /h/ was underway, and variants with and without /h/ actually coexisted, socially differentiated.

As for *chommoda*, Latin uses the <CH> spelling to render the voiceless velar fricative /x/ in borrowings from Greek. When a foreign word is borrowed, knowing its original pronunciation may be a sign of education or culture. But foreign borrowings inevitably adapt to the local phonological system, which in Latin meant changing /x/ to /k/. Thus, Greek borrowings formed another kind of doublet: higher /xorus/ versus lower /korus/ 'chorus'. What Catullus found amusing is that *chommoda* was actually a native Latin word, not Greek, so it had never had /x/. Here too the hapless Arrius was hypercorrecting.[8]

No Romance language retains any audible trace of original Latin /h/. In later centuries, as spelling was standardized, it became common practice to add an ornamental <h> as a reminiscence of Latin spelling, as in French *herbe* /ɛʀb/.

There have been three episodes where an actual audible [h] was introduced into individual Romance languages. First, certain Frankish borrowings into French brought their initial [h] with them. Though lost in Modern French, its earlier presence is still detectable because it blocks both **elision** and **liaison** as in: *le haricot, les haricots* /leaʀiko/ versus *l'hôtel, les hôtels* /lezotɛl/. This is the so-called **h aspiré** 'aspirated h', now a misnomer because it is entirely silent. Second, Medieval Spanish changed initial /f/ to /h/, but this /h/ too was later deleted: FARINA 'flour' > Old Spanish /harina/ > Modern Spanish /arina/

harina (§ 3.3.2). Third, Romanian acquired by contact an /h/ which it still has today: *hotar* [h] 'border'.

2.4.2   Loss of /n/ before /s/

In Popular Latin speech /ns/ reduced to /s/ at an early date. For instance, Latin MENSE becomes *MESE so early that the Romance languages retain no memory of the /n/. The stressed vowel develops as if in an original free syllable.

Classical Latin	Popular Latin		Italian	Spanish	French
MENSE	*MĒSE	'month'	mese	mes	mois
-ENSE	*-ĒSE	adj. suffix	-ese	-és	-ois
PENSU	*PĒSU	'weight'	peso	peso	poids

This feature of Popular Latin is vividly attested in the *Appendix Probi* (§ 2.5.3).

ANSA	non	ASA
MENSA	non	MESA
FORMOSUS	non	FORMONSUS
OCCASIO	non	OCCANSIO

Question: Why does the variation seem to go both ways, /ns/ > /s/ and /s/ > /ns/?

Answer: ASA, MESA reflect the regular change. FORMONSUS, OCCANSIO reflect hypercorrection: speakers know the variants /mensa/, /mesa/, know that /mensa/ is "better," and therefore tend to create /ns/ clusters where they do not belong.

The verb PENSARE preserved both variants with a split in meaning. Comparing them, we see evidence (where?) that this loss of /n/ induces lengthening of the preceding vowel.

Standard Latin	Popular Latin		Italian	Spanish	French
PENSAT	PENSAT	'thinks'	pensa	piensa	pense
PENSAT	PESAT	'weighs'	pesa	pesa	pèse

Loss of /n/ before /s/ is a dead rule today in Spanish and French. In Italian it persists, but in a less generalized form: /ns/ > /s/ only if a consonant follows (*istituto* 'institute', *trasporto* 'transportation', *ispettore* 'inspector', but *insegnare* 'teach', *insulto* 'insult').

2.4.3   Loss of intervocalic /g/

Also early and widespread is the loss of intervocalic /g/:

Latin		Italian	Spanish	French	
EGO	'I'	io	yo	je	
IAM MAGIS	'more'	giammai	jamás	jamais	'never'

MAGISTRU	'master'	maestro	maestro	maître
SAGITTA	'arrow'	saetta	saeta	saiete (OFr)
PAGENSE	'country'	paese	país	pays

In the very common word EGO, loss of /g/ leaves a vowel hiatus */eo/, which becomes monosyllabic /jo/ on the way to Spanish and French. In Italian *io*, however, the stress is still on the original initial syllable.

2.4.4   Loss of word-final /m/

From a remote pre-Classical period on, the weakening and loss of word-final /m/ is amply documented. Tagliavini (1964:202) cites an example in an inscription dating from 298 BCE. In fact, Latin poetic meter treated word-final /m/ as non-existent if the next word began with a vowel. Since /m/ was the main marker of the accusative singular, its loss profoundly disrupted the case system (§ 8.3). Today's linguists, displaying the sources of Romance nouns, customarily cite accusative forms without the prescribed final /m/.

2.5   In search of Popular Latin speech

The standardized Latin language enshrined in textbooks is like a photograph, a frozen moment in the long life of spoken Latin. Imagine a continuous natural evolution from Indo-European to today's Romance languages. Likewise over the same 5,000 years there has been a continuous evolution in, say, the Austronesian languages, or the languages of New Guinea, or those of the Amazon Basin. However, the history of Latin and Romance stands apart because of a momentous extra-linguistic event, the Roman Empire. It had social consequences: an ancient society with rich material culture, industry, bureaucracy, commerce, roads, aqueducts, theaters, apartment buildings and sewers in the metropolis, lawyers, rudimentary publishing, even how-to books, literary critics, and professional grammarians. Within this society, the Latin language became **standardized**. This means that paradigms were recorded in writing, prescriptive norms were fixed, gifted authors produced valued texts and created or adopted literary forms. Classical Latin poetic meters and rhetorical conventions were borrowed in large part from the pre-existing canon of Greek literature, which enjoyed enormous prestige among educated Romans. Drawing further upon the Greek tradition, Latin scholars wrote on both practical and philosophical matters, including the grammar and usage of their language.

Classical Latin literature is like a screen behind which the popular, colloquial, vernacular language continued its uninterrupted evolution. For example, the fate of the original diphthongs (§ 1.4) shows the working-out of a process over many centuries, both before and after the Classical period. The popular language was oblivious to the creation of a Classical Latin, a phenomenon that belonged to the world of the privileged and educated few.

2.5.1   Traces of Popular Latin

Obviously, we have records only of written Latin. Yet a few documentary sources do offer glimpses of the spoken language. At the beginnings of Latin literature, the plays of Plautus (254–184 BCE) and Terence (195–159 BCE) already display some of the same features of popular speech that emerge again in our post-Classical sources (§§ 8.3.1, 11.3.1). The dramatists necessarily use a colloquial style, because their language is meant to be heard on the stage rather than read. Classical constraints on grammar and diction, moreover, had not yet stabilized in their time. The language of the dramatists should cure us of the misapprehension that Popular Latin "begins" in post-Classical times. The loss of [h] in colloquial speech is vividly attested by Catullus, as we saw in § 2.4.1. Another famous source is the *Satyricon* of Petronius (fl. 60 CE), a fragmentary work relating a series of picaresque adventures in and around Rome. In the most complete surviving episode, *Trimalchio's Dinner*, the protagonists turn up as guests at the lavish party of a freedman depicted by Petronius as a comically vulgar *nouveau riche*. As the wine flows, the guests become more and more relaxed in their diction (§§ 8.5.1, 11.1).

Much more voluminous are the treatises on practical topics, texts having no pretensions to stylistic elegance. These include books on farm management by Cato (d. 149 BCE), Varro (d. 27 BCE), Columella (fl. 50 CE), and Palladius (fl. 350 CE?). Also surviving are such professional manuals as *De architectura* by Vitruvius (fl. 10 BCE) and *De re coquinaria*, a cookbook formerly ascribed to Apicius (fl. 25 CE). Veterinary medicine, important for farming and horse-racing, is the topic of handbooks by Martial (d. 102 CE), Palladius (fl. 350 CE?), and Vegetius (fl. 420 CE), among others.

Some writers even focus directly on matters of language. The unique and famous *Appendix Probi* tops the list (§ 2.5.3), but the writings of Latin grammarians form a substantial corpus teeming with scattered comments about style, pronunciation, and lexical choice. Useful information comes also from medieval glossaries, forerunners of the modern dictionary (§ 12.1.3).

There is also massive **epigraphic** evidence. Thousands of Latin inscriptions, both public and private, survive from antiquity, comprising all levels of formality: gravestones, commemorative inscriptions on buildings and sculptures, public notices, and so on down to lowly graffiti. Virtually all known (ancient) Latin inscriptions have been catalogued in a monumental work which we discuss next.

2.5.2   The Corpus Inscriptionum Latinarum

Published in seventeen volumes starting in 1863, the *Corpus Inscriptionum Latinarum* (CIL) assembled all the then known Latin inscriptions from all regions. Texts that come to us in the form of inscriptions have a unique status. Rare exceptions aside, stone and ceramic are the only writing materials that survive from antiquity. All other writings that reach us had to be valued enough to be copied and recopied over the years, a process that inevitably corrupts the text to some degree. An inscription, on the other hand, is an artifact that may be physically damaged, but otherwise does not change over time.

The popular features we have seen so far are well attested in the humbler inscriptions, since their writers were not always adhering to the Classical standard. For instance: DEUS MAGNU OCLU ABET instead of the "correct" DEUS MAGNUM OCULUM HABET 'God has a large eye' (CIL VI 34635[a]) shows loss of final [m], syncope, and loss of [h]. Some revealing examples from the CIL are:

Classical Latin			CIL
DOMĬNUS	'master'		DOMNUS
MASCŬLUS	'male'		MASCLUS
SUSPENDĔRE	'suspend'		SUSPENDRE
HABĔO	'I have'		AVEO
VIXIT	's/he lived'		BIXIT
LEVIS	'light'		LEBES
HIC HABITAT	'here lives'		IC AVETAT
SPERAVIT	's/he hoped'		ISPERABI
SPONSAE	'wife'		ISPOSE
MENSE	'month'		MESE
INSŬLA	'island'		ISULA
VŬLNUS	'wound'		VOLNUS

PRACTICE

Point out these sound changes in the foregoing examples: syncope, loss of [h], the [b]/[w] merger, prosthetic vowels, loss of [n] before [s], reduction of AE to E, and the merger of Ŭ and Ō.

2.5.3   What the Romans said about Popular Latin

The sources seen so far reflect features of Popular Latin but do not reflect *upon* it. There is, however, a tradition of grammatical and rhetorical writings that comment explicitly on the Latin of their time. Their remarks about colloquial features, though scattershot and sometimes opaque, can be informative. The *Institutio Oratoria* of Quintilian (d. 95 CE) documents several of the aforementioned sound changes. Here he tells us that unsyncopated CALIDUS 'hot' must have sounded pedantic and stuffy even as early as the first century BCE:

Augustus again in his letters to Gaius Caesar corrects him for preferring CALIDUS to CALDUS, not on the ground that the former is not Latin, but because it is unpleasing and, as he himself puts it in Greek, περίεργον 'affected'.[9]

Here Quintilian comments about the confusion surrounding the vanishing /h/:

Older authors used [H] but rarely even before vowels, saying AEDUS and IRCUS, while its conjunction with consonants was for a long time avoided, as in words such as GRACCUS or TRIUMPUS. Then for a short time it broke out into excessive use, witness such spellings as CHORONA, CHENTURIA or PRAECHO, which may still be read in certain inscriptions.[10]

Elsewhere he notes the loss of /n/ before /s/[11] ("We also find...CONSUL spelled without an N")[12] and alludes to the loss of word-final /m/:

wherever this same letter *m* comes at the end of a word it is, although written, so faintly pronounced...that it may almost be regarded as producing the sound of a new letter.[13]

The most revealing source of all for Popular Latin is an anonymous text known today as the *Appendix Probi*, surviving only in a single manuscript. Compiled presumably by some long-suffering schoolmaster, it consists of 227 corrections of the form PERSICA NON PESSICA ('peach'), admonishing against various errors in grammar, pronunciation, and spelling. All his effort was in vain, of course. The censured forms mostly reflect the very trends that live on in Romance.

When an anonymous text comes to light, scholars are likely to speak with more certainty about the physical manuscript than about where its content ultimately came from. For our text, there is little controversy about the one surviving manuscript. Around 700 CE, at the monastery of Bobbio (Northern Italy), the monks erased some biblical texts from a parchment and used it to copy a grammatical treatise attributed to a certain Probus. At the end they added five short texts of unknown authorship, of which the third is our so-called *Appendix Probi* (Väänänen 1983:254, paraphrased).

All other facts about the text – who composed it, when, and where – are open to scholarly speculation. The consensus of opinion, however, puts its composition at Rome in the third or fourth century CE. A few significant examples:

TRIBULA NON TRIBLA	AUCTOR NON AUTOR
VETULUS NON VECLUS	MENSA NON MESA
CLATRI NON CRACLI	TENSA NON TESA
BRAVIUM NON BRABIUM	CALCOSTEGIS NON CALCOSTEIS
TOLERABILIS NON TOLERAVILIS	NUMQUAM NON NUMQUA
AVUS NON AUS	OLIM NON OLI
HOSTIAE NON OSTIAE	COLUMNA NON COLOMNA
CITHARA NON CITERA	TURMA NON TORMA

PRACTICE

Point out evidence for these early changes:

merger of ŭ and ō	[b]/[w] merger
[w] in secondary diphthongs	loss of word-final [m]
loss of [n] before [s]	loss of intervocalic [g]
loss of [h]	syncope
metathesis	assimilation

Properly speaking, the name *Appendix Probi* should encompass all five texts. Besides the third, the less famous fourth is also informative. It elucidates pairs of words that were perceived as near-homonyms, often reflecting ongoing sound change (Stok 1997, Quirk 2006, Loporcaro 2007).

2.5.4   Latin speech: real versus reconstructed

Since the early 1800s, linguists have developed a set of procedures known as the **comparative method**. By comparing systematically the words and structures of daughter languages descended from a common parent, linguists can attempt to reconstruct the parent language even if it is undocumented. First, one assembles a set of cognate words from the daughter languages, and then one posits a parent form in such a way that the changes leading to the forms in the daughter languages will be as simple and plausible as possible. Even if there were no records of the Latin language, linguists could still attempt a reconstruction based on the Romance languages. By convention, such a reconstructed language is called *Proto-Romance*.

Many of the world's language families have only a shallow historical record, and for these families our only access to the parent language is through reconstruction. For Romance, on the other hand, the parent language is massively attested, at least in its written form. This means that the Romance family is a unique laboratory for historical linguistics, because the results of reconstruction can be confronted with the documented reality of spoken (and written) Latin.

Such a confrontation brings to light the built-in limitations of the comparative method. There is a dramatic difference between real spoken Latin and Proto-Romance, the result of reconstruction. Real spoken Latin, like any real language, includes a mixture of the old and the new. For instance, the dinner conversation represented in the *Satyricon* includes such words as EMIT 'buys' and AIT 'says', which could not possibly figure in Proto-Romance, because no trace of them survives in the daughter languages. Reconstruction can never give us access to those facets of real spoken Latin which vanished on the way to Romance. A reconstructed Proto-Romance, then, is necessarily a pallid and impoverished picture of the rich tapestry of Latin as it was spoken in its own time.

Exercises

1. Additional early changes in French
In Old French, word-final <e> represented /ə/ which was still pronounced throughout Middle French. It persists in spelling, as these words show.

PLUMBU	'lead'	plomb
PLUMA	'feather'	plume
CARU	'dear'	cher

CARA	'dear'	chère
COLORE	'color'	couleur
HORA	'hour'	heure

Form a generalization about what happened to word-final vowels in French. Next, what further word-final loss is illustrated in the following set?

Latin		*Italian*	*Spanish*	*French*
INFERNU	'hell'	inferno	infierno	enfer
HIBERNU	'wintry'	inverno	invierno	hiver
FURNU	'oven'	forno	horno	four
*RE-TORNU	'return'	ritorno	....	retour
DIURNU	'day'	giorno	....	jour
CARNE	'flesh'	carne	carne	chair
CORNU	'horn'	corno	cuerno	cor
VERME	'worm'	verme	....	ver

Why does it not occur in the following?

*RE-TORNAT	'returns'	retourne
*CORNA	'horns'	corne

2. More about relative chronology.
    Review what happens in French to stressed vowel + nasal consonant (§ 1.3.3).

LANA	'wool'	laine
AMAT	'loves'	aime
FAME	'hunger'	faim
PLENU	'full'	plein

Review and state the reason it doesn't happen in words like these:

CAMPU	'field'	champ
MENTHA	'mint'	menthe
GRANDE	'big'	grand
VENDIT	'sells'	vend

In the following words the Latin etymon looks like those in the first group, but the reflexes look like those in the second group. What might explain this result?

LAMINA	'blade'	lame
ANIMA	'soul'	âme
CAMERA	'room'	chambre
GENERU	'son-in-law'	gendre
CINERE	'ash'	cendre

What is the non-etymological <e> doing at the end of *gendre* and *cendre*?

3. An early consonant change with a secondary effect

Latin		*Italian*	*Spanish*	*French*	
DIGITU	'finger'	dito	dedo	doigt	[dwa]

a. The Spanish and French reflexes suggest that the stressed vowel in Latin was _____, but the Italian outcome suggests that it was _____.

b. We know that Spanish and French represent the regular development, while the /i/ in Italian is unexpected. How might this Italian outcome be explained?

Hint: One development involves a whole syllable, the other just a consonant.

4. Days of the week

Nominative case, used for subject	Genitive case ['of'] plus 'day'	Italian	Spanish	French
LUNA	LUNAE DĪE	lunedì	lunes	lundi
MARS	MARTIS DĪE	martedì	martes	mardi
MERCŬRIU	MERCŬRII DĪE	mercoledì	miércoles	mercredi
IOVIS	IOVIS DĪE	giovedì	jueves	jeudi
VENUS	VENERIS DĪE	venerdì	viernes	vendredi

Note: In forms like It *lunedì* and Fr *lundi*, the main stress is on the part that comes from DĪE. Nonetheless the Latin words in the LŪNAE column do develop like separate words, and their stressed vowels do follow the rules for stressed vowels (as you can see).

a. Find one example of plain syncope with no epenthesis, one example of syncope with consonant epenthesis, and one example of metathesis.

b. Sometimes a **sporadic** (wild, non-rule-governed) change can affect a single word. The segments most susceptible to sporadic changes are the liquids /l, r/. One factor seems to be a general dislike for words with two identical liquids.

Find two words in the data that show such changes.

c. How did Sp *lunes* and *miércoles* get their <s>?

d. The stress assigned by the Latin Penultimate Rule normally remains very stable in Romance. But there is one word in the data whose stress pattern evidently changed. The Penultimate Rule predicts one pattern, but the Romance words show another. Identify the word and explain how you know its stress pattern changed.

e. In Chapter 1 we used Romance cognate sets to calculate where a given stressed vowel belongs in the (almost) Pan-Romance seven-vowel system, and when possible, to go one step farther back and calculate vowel quantity in the Latin system.

This can be done for LUNAE. Answer:

Also fairly easy for VENERIS. Answer:

But IOVIS presents a problem. This will not be resolved here, only observed.

If <o> is long, then we don't know why...

Vice versa, if <o> is short, then we don't know why...

5. Slaughter of innocent vowels in Italian

What do these Italian words have in common? Answer: their initial /s/ + consonant cluster was originally not initial. The material that originally preceded this cluster was deleted at some point.

| AESTIMARE | 'judge' | stimare | |
| EXTRANEU | 'foreign' | strano | 'strange' |

HISPANIA	'Spain'	Spagna	
HISTORIA	'history'	storia	
INSTRUMENTU	'instrument'	strumento	
*ISTA SERA	'this evening'	stasera	
EXCAVARE	'dig out'	scavare	
EXPEDIRE	'disencumber'	spedire	'send'

What was the motive for removing the material preceding the cluster? When the deletion occurred, what did it delete? That is, what did each word look like at that time? Your answer should refer to the about-face treatment of words like SPONSA, STATU in Italian (§ 2.1.2). Explain why no such deletion occurred in words like these:

HOSTILE	'hostile'	ostile	not	*stile
*OSTRICA	'oyster'	ostrica	not	*strica
OBSTINATU	'obstinate'	ostinato	not	*stinato

3 Consonant weakening and strengthening

3.1 Degemination

Geminates, or long consonants, are formed by holding the articulatory position steady for two timing units rather than one. Geminates are written with a double letter, but beware: double letters in French don't represent a geminate.

Italian	fato	'fate'	[fato]	Italian	stalla	'stable'	[stal:a]
Italian	fatto	'done'	[fat:o]	French	stalle	'stable'	[stal]

Latin had several long consonants: /p:/ /t:/ /k:/ /f:/ /s:/ /m:/ /n:/ /l:/. Everywhere except in Italian and Sardinian, long consonants degeminated, becoming plain consonants. But they stop at that stage and do not feed into the further processes that affect original plain consonants (§ 3.2 below).

Latin		Italian		Spanish		French	
OSSU	'bone'	osso	[ɔs:o]	hueso	[weso]	os	[ɔs]
SUMMA	'sum'	somma	[som:a]	suma	[suma]	somme	[sɔm]
APPELLAT	'calls'	appella	[ap:ɛl:a]	apela	[apela]	appelle	[apɛl]
LITTERA	'letter'	lettera	[let:era]	letra	[letra]	lettre	[lɛtʀ]
SICCU	'dry'	secco	[sek:o]	seco	[seko]	sec	[sɛk]

Italian shows a predilection for geminates unique among the Romance languages. Besides preserving original Latin geminates, Italian also creates new ones by assimilation:

OB-SERVARE	'observe'	osservare
AD-MITTERE	'admit'	ammettere
ABDOMEN	'abdomen'	addome

In fact, five consonants in Italian (ts dz ʎ ɲ ʃ) are automatically long when intervocalic, presumably because they derive from clusters occupying two timing units (§§ 4.3.7, 4.3.9).

44

3.2   Lenition

Besides degemination, there is a weakening known as **lenition**, from Latin LENIS 'gentle', as in *lenient*, which affects the original Latin plain stops in unprotected position. Later we specify what 'unprotected position' means (§ 3.2.4).

3.2.1   The consonant strength gradient

Consonants are ranked according to articulatory effort, which in turn depends on manner of articulation. Stops, which completely stop the air flow, are stronger than fricatives, which allow air to pass through. From strongest (left) to weakest (right), the gradient looks like this:

pp	p	b	β/v	zero
tt	t	d	ð	zero
kk	k	g	ɣ	zero

The geminates are strongest because this articulation not only interrupts the air flow, but prolongs the interruption. In plain voiceless stops between vowels, vocal chord vibration has to stop and then restart. In voiced stops, the voicing of the surrounding vowels continues without interruption. Fricatives don't even obstruct the air flow completely and thus differ even less from their vocalic surroundings. In early Romance, overall, the plain stops drift rightward on the gradient, sometimes even reaching the final stage, deletion.

3.2.2   Lenition of intervocalic consonants

Lenition is more pervasive in some Romance languages than in others. Below, see how lenition affects intervocalic consonants:

Latin		*Italian*	*Spanish*		*French*
SAPORE	'flavor'	sapore	sabor	[saβor]	saveur
CAPUT	'head'	capo	cabo	[kaβo]	chef
COPERTU	'covered'	coperto	cubierto	[kuβjerto]	couvert
PIPER	'pepper'	pepe	pebre	[peβre]	poivre
VITA	'life'	vita	vida	[biða]	vie
FATA	'fairy'	fata	hada	[aða]	fée
CATENA	'chain'	catena	cadena	[kaðena]	chaîne
ROTA	'wheel'	ruota	rueda	[rweða]	roue
AMICA	'friend'	amica	amiga	[amiɣa]	amie
SECURU	'safe'	sicuro	seguro	[seɣuro]	sûr
FOCU	'fire'	fuoco	fuego	[fweɣo]	feu
IOCAT	'plays'	gioca	juega	[xweɣa]	joue
CABALLU	'horse'	cavallo	caballo	[kaβajo]	cheval
DEBERE	'owe'	dovere	deber	[deβer]	devoir

HABERE	'have'	avere	haber	[aβer]	avoir
BIBAT	'drinks'	beva	beba	[beβa]	boive
CRUDU	'raw'	crudo	crudo	[kruðo]	cru
CREDIT	'believes'	crede	cree	[kree]	croit
PEDE	'foot'	piede	pie	[pje]	pied
CADERE	'fall'	cadere	caer	[kaer]	choir
AUGUSTU	'August'	agosto	agosto	[aɣosto]	août
LIGARE	'bind'	legare	ligar, liar	[liɣar], [ljar]	lier
PAGANU	'pagan'	pagano	pagano	[paɣano]	païen
PLAGA	'wound'	piaga	llaga	[jaɣa]	plaie

Question: What happens to original voiceless stops /p t k/?

Answer: They remain intact in Italian, in these examples (but see below). In Spanish, they produce fricatives [β ð ɣ]. In French, which exhibits the most drastic lenition, /p/ survives as /v/ while /t/, /k/ lenite all the way to zero.

Question: What happens to original voiced stops /b d g/?

Answer: Italian keeps them intact except that the labial is /v/ (§ 2.3.2). Spanish generally has the same [β ð ɣ] as came from voiceless stops, except that original /d/ lenites all the way to zero in some words. In French, /b d g/ behave like /p t k/, namely: /b/ survives as /v/ while /d/, /g/ lenite all the way to zero.

In Spanish, the fricative series [β ð ɣ] enters into an allophonic relationship with [b d g]. The stop allophones occur in breath-group-initial and post-nasal positions. In addition, /ld/ clusters are [ld] not [lð]. Spanish is the only major Romance language that has no /v/. Letter <v> is only a variant spelling for the labial phoneme /b/ = [b, β]. This is why, when spelling a word aloud, some Spanish speakers say b [be] de burro or v [be] de vaca.

In Spanish and French, the series /p t k/ ultimately merged with the series /b d g/. Apparently, original /p t k/ continued along the path of lenition as far as the fricative stage, the same endpoint that /b d g/ had already reached – though some instances of original Latin /d/ had reached the zero stage. Some varieties of Spanish continue the process of lenition: the participle ending <-ado> is [aw] not [aðo] in Puerto Rican Spanish.

The fate of original /p t k/ in Italian is variable and debated. While our chart suggests that intervocalic /p t k/ always remain intact, they actually appear as /v d g/ in a fair number of words, for example:

RIPA	'shore'	riva
EPISCOPU	'bishop'	vescovo

PAUPERU	'poor'	povero
RECIPERE	'receive'	ricevere
SPATHA	'sword'	spada
STRATA	'paved'	strada
METIPSIMU	'same'	medesimo
QUIRĪTAT	'shouts'	grida[1]
LACU	'lake'	lago
LOCU	'place'	luogo
LACTUCA	'lettuce'	lattuga
PRECARE	'pray'	pregare

Results like these would be regular for Northern Italian dialects, which belong to the Gallo-Romance area. Diffusion of words from these dialects has been posited as the reason for the mixed results in Standard Italian, but the question remains unresolved (see Maiden 1995:59–63).

3.2.3   The fricative stage in Old French

In the evolution of French, lenition proceeds incrementally from one degree to the next:

$$/p, b/ \quad > \quad /v/$$
$$/t, d/ \quad > \quad /ð/ \quad > \quad zero$$
$$/k, g/ \quad > \quad */ɣ/ \quad > \quad zero$$

The labials show the most resistance, in that they reach only the fricative stage, not zero. The other stops have reached the zero stage, but demonstrably the dentals went through a prior fricative stage. For instance, in the earliest Old French (§12.2.1), we find two revealing spellings: *cadhuna* < CAT-UNA 'each', *aiudha* < *AD-IUTA 'help'. The <dh> surely reflects an attempt to spell [ð]. As for the velars, there is no parallel evidence for a [ɣ] stage, apparently because they had reached the zero stage even faster.

Further evidence comes from early Old French borrowings into English: FIDE > [fede] > [fɛjðə] > [fɛjθ] 'faith'. The devoicing of [ð] > [θ] exemplifies a general process in Old French: devoicing of word-final consonants. Conclusion: the [θ] of English *faith* reflects an earlier [ð] in Old French. Further examples of this word-final devoicing:

BOVE	'ox'	boeuf
CLAVE	'key'	clef
VIVU	'alive'	vif
NATIVU	'native'	naïf

in contrast to:

| VIVA | 'alive' | vive |
| NATIVA | 'native' | naïve |

3.2.4   The environment for lenition

Consonants undergo lenition if they occur in unprotected position, but what does this mean? So far, we have seen that word-initial position is protected, and intervocalic position is unprotected. Now observe what happens to consonants in word-medial clusters.

Latin		Italian	Spanish	French
*LEPRE	'hare'	lepre [pr]	liebre [βr]	lièvre [vr]
CAPRA	'goat'	capra [pr]	cabra [βr]	chèvre [vr]
PETRA	'stone'	pietra [tr]	piedra [ðr]	pierre [ʀ]
PATRE	'father'	padre [dr]	padre [ðr]	père [ʀ]
HEMI-CRANIA	'migraine'	emicrania [kr]	migraña [ɣr]	migraine [gʀ]
PIGRITIA	'sloth'	pigrizia [gr]	pereza [r]	paresse [ʀ]
SERPENTE	'snake'	serpente [rp]	serpiente [rp]	serpent [ʀp]
ALPES	'Alps'	Alpi [lp]	alpes [lp]	Alpes [lp]
RUMPERE	'break'	rompere [mp]	romper [mp]	rompre [p]
ORTICA	'nettle'	ortica [rt]	ortiga [rt]	ortie [ʀt]
MENTA	'mint'	menta [nt]	menta [nt]	menthe [t]
CANDELA	'candle'	candela [nd]	candela [nd]	chandelle [d]
ARCU	'arch'	arco [rk]	arco [rk]	arc [ʀk]
FALCONE	'falcon'	falcone [lk]	halcón [lk]	faucon [k]

> Question: Which sets display lenition, and what condition characterizes it?
>
> Answer: The top six lines. The leniting consonants are postvocalic.

In the remaining sets, the stops are protected by a preceding consonant. For instance, the /p/ of CAPRA undergoes lenition, but the /p/ of ALPES is protected (the nasals seen in the French spellings were formerly pronounced as consonants and did protect their adjacent stops). Moreover, under this rule, word-initial stops won't undergo lenition, since they are not postvocalic.

3.3   Other consonant weakenings

There are other episodes of consonant weakening that do not belong, strictly speaking, to the realm of lenition.

3.3.1   The fate of velarized /l/

A conspicuous change occurring in Old French is shown in the first set below. Note that nothing happens to /l/ in the second set.

Latin		Old French	Modern French	
TALPA	'mole'	[tawpə]	[top]	taupe
ALTERU	'other'	[awtrə]	[otʀ]	autre
FALCONE	'falcon'	[fawkũn]	[fokɔ̃]	faucon
ALBA	'white/dawn'	[awbə]	[ob]	aube
CALDA	'hot'	[tʃawdə]	[ʃod]	chaude
FALSA	'false'	[fawsə]	[fos]	fausse
PULMONE	'lung'	[powmũn]	[pumɔ̃]	poumon
*VOLVITA	'vault'	[vowtə]	[vut]	voûte
SOLIDARE	'solder'	[sowdɛr]	[sude]	souder
PULSU	'wrist'	[pows]	[pu]	pouls
LONGU	'long'	[lũŋ]	[lɔ̃]	long
VALERE	'be worth'	[valejr]	[valwaʀ]	valoir
*MELE	'honey'	[mjɛl]	[mjɛl]	miel

> Question: What happens to original /l/ on the way to Old French?
>
> Answer: In preconsonantal position /l/ becomes /w/.

A middle stage between [l] and [w] is the velar (so-called "dark") [ɫ]. As the articulation of [l] becomes increasingly velar, it comes to resemble [w], as happens in some varieties of English: *pill* [pɪw].[2]

The glide /w/ thus forms with the preceding vowel a secondary diphthong which, on the way to Modern French, simplifies to a monophthong, as most diphthongs do. Secondary /aw/ simplifies to /o/ just as original Latin /aw/ does, as in PAUPERU *pauvre* [povʀ]. Secondary /ow/ simplifies to /u/, unlike primary /ow/ (§ 1.2.4). Secondary /ew/ simplifies to /ø/ = [ø, œ], these vowels being allophones (§ 1.2.5). Here is a summary (based on Morin 1991:32) of all the diphthongs arising from velarized /l/, and their resolution into monophthongs.

$$
\begin{array}{lll}
/yw/ & > & /y/ \\
/iw/ & > & /i/ \\
/ew/ & > & /ø/ \\
/ɛw/ & > & /jaw/ > /o/ \\
/aw/ & > & /o/ \\
/ɔw/ & > & /u/ \\
/ow/ & > & /u/
\end{array}
$$

What stands out is the low mid in the combination /ɛl/, which first became /ɛw/, then produced a triphthong /jaw/, ultimately simplifying to /o/. The typical spelling <eau> (sometimes <iau> in Old French) reflects that intermediate stage /jaw/. Examples:

Gmc *helmu*	'helmet'	heaume
BELENA	'town near Dijon'	Beaune
*BELLITATE	'beauty'	beauté
APPELLET	'calls' (subjunc.)	apiaut (OFr)

The stressed vowel in Germanic *helmu* became a Romance low mid as seen in Spanish *yelmo*. In French, it developed along these lines:

helmu > [ɛlmu] > [ɛwm] > [jawm] > [om] *heaume*

Latin BELENA, *BELLITATE, and APPELLET, after syncopating, develop likewise:

BELENA > [bɛlna] > [bɛwnə] > [bjawnə] > [bon] *Beaune*
*BELLITATE > [bɛlte] > [bɛwte] > [bjawte] > [bote] *beauté*
APPELLET > [apɛlt] > [apɛwt] > [apjawt] *apiaut* (OFr)

Modern French is rife with alternations with or without velarization of /l/. These alternations arise in two ways. First, depending on morphological context, /l/ may be sometimes preconsonantal and sometimes not.

| CABALLU | 'horse' | cheval |
| CABALLOS | 'horses' | chevaux |

Second, velarization of /l/ was a **sandhi** phenomenon, i.e. it worked across word boundaries. If the following word began with a vowel, /l/ remained intact, but before a word beginning with a consonant, /l/ > /w/.

| NOVELLU AMICU | 'new friend' | nouvel ami |
| NOVELLU CANE | 'new dog' | nouveau chien |

This type of conditioning has since been blurred in many cases by a process known as analogical leveling (§ 6.7).

3.3.2   Word-initial /f/ in Spanish

The Old Spanish development exemplified here is of uncertain origin (Penny 2002:90–94). In place of Latin initial /f/, these words have a written <h>, now silent.

Latin		Italian	Spanish		French
FILU	'thread'	filo	hilo	[ilo]	fil
FERIRE	'wound'	ferire	herir	[erir]	férir
FERRO	'iron'	ferro	hierro	[jerːo]	fer
FAMEN, FAMINE	'hunger'	fame	hambre	[ambre]	faim
FALCONE	'falcon'	falcone	halcón	[alkon]	faucon
FARINA	'flour'	farina	harina	[arina]	farine
FATA	'fairy'	fata	hada	[aða]	fée
FORMICA	'ant'	formica	hormiga	[ormiɣa]	fourmi

| FURCA | 'fork' | forca | **h**orca | [orka] | fourche |
| FURNU | 'oven' | forno | **h**orno | [orno] | four |

The orthographic <h>, though silent today, actually reflects an Old Spanish stage when these words had initial [h]. For a time [f] and [h] were allophones, since the change [f] > [h] did not occur in clusters [fw], [fl], [fr]:

FOCU	'fire'	fuego	[fweɣo]
FORA	'outside'	fuera	[fwera]
FONTE	'font'	fuente	[fwente]
FRIGIDU	'cold'	frío	[frio]
FRONTE	'forehead'	frente	[frente]
FRUCTA	'fruit'	fruta	[fruta]
FLORE	'flower'	flor	[flor]
FLACCU	'flabby'	flaco	[flako] 'feeble'

Old Spanish writing treated the [f] and [h] allophones alike, both conservatively spelled <f>. Sometimes scribes wrote <ff>, as in *ffablo* 'spoke' (of uncertain interpretation). Finally, sixteenth-century writers introduced <h> to represent [h] unambiguously.

3.3.3   Weakening of /s/

In American Spanish, except in Mexico, Perù, and Andean Ecuador, /s/ > [h] in syllable coda, and /s/ > zero in word-final position before a pause.

	Peninsular Spanish	American Spanish
Hay dos patos.	[ajðospatos]	[ajðohpato_]
'There are two ducks.'		

The evidence adduced by Penny (2002:106–108) suggests that the loss of /s/ is a process where aspiration to [h] is the first stage, and deletion a more advanced stage.

French likewise deleted /s/ in preconsonantal position, as we saw (§ 2.1.1). Unlike Spanish, French has completed its /s/ deletion. In no present-day variety of French can we see the change in progress. Yet there is compelling evidence that in French too, /s/ deletion was the endpoint of a process: /s/ > [x] > zero (Pope 1934:151), much as in Spanish. French loan words in Medieval German poetry include such forms as *foreht* 'forest' rhyming with German *sleht* 'bad', *reht* 'right', where <h> is [x]. The *Orthographia Gallica*[3] even states explicitly:

*Quant s est joynt [a la t] ele avera le soun de **h**, come **est**, **plest** seront sonez **eght**, **pleght**.*

When *s* is joined [to *t*] it will sound like *h*, thus *est, plest* will be pronounced *eght, pleght*. (Cited in Pope 1934:151.)

3.3.4   Ordering of changes: an example

Some Romance words reveal the relative chronology of the changes that brought them to their present form. Consider this set:

Latin	Italian	Spanish	French
COLLOCARE	coricare	colgar	coucher
'put in a place'	'put to bed'	'hang'	'place horizontally (thing), put to bed (person)'

Apparently, degemination occurred early, since the results do not reflect original /l:/ (see §§ 3.1, 4.3.7). Italian *coricare*, not very revealingly, shows only a sporadic change to /r/. Spanish and French are more revealing.

Spanish *colgar* apparently has this derivation:

*COLOCARE > [kologar] > [kolɣar] *colgar*

Lenition must have occurred when /k/ was still intervocalic. If syncope had been first (*kolkar) it would have placed /k/ in a protected position /lk/, blocking any subsequent lenition. French *coucher* reflects a different sequence:

*COLOCARE > [kolkare] > [kowtʃer] > [kuʃe] *coucher*

The intervocalic /k/, though it becomes an affricate (§ 4.4), doesn't undergo the voicing characteristic of first-stage lenition. Hence, we posit early syncope to /kolkare/. The resulting /lk/ cluster both protects the /k/ from lenition and provides the environment for velarization of /l/.

3.4   Fortition

Some linguists believe that there are universal preferences regarding syllable structure.[4] In particular, strong onsets are favored, especially word-initially. In Romance, we saw that word-initial consonants are exempt from lenition, that is, they do not weaken. Conversely, when the weakest consonants, namely glides, occur in word-initial position, they have at times undergone **fortition** (strengthening).[5]

3.4.1   Word-initial fortition of /w/

Romance had two sources for /w/: native Latin words, and later borrowings from Germanic languages. Examples of both kinds follow:

Latin		Italian		Spanish		French	
VINU	'wine'	vino	[vi]	vino	[bi]	vin	[vɛ̃]
VENA	'vein'	vena	[ve]	vena	[be]	veine	[vɛ]
VENIT	'comes'	viene	[vjɛ]	viene	[bje]	vient	[vjɛ̃]
VASU	'vase'	vaso	[va]	vaso	[ba]	vase	[va]
*VOSTRU	'your'	vostro	[vɔ]	vuestro	[bwe]	votre	[vɔ]

Wilhelm	'William'	**Gu**glielmo	[gu][6]	**Gui**llermo	[gi]	**Gui**llaume	[gi]
**wisa*	'manner'	**gui**sa	[gwi]	**gui**sa	[gi]	**gui**se	[gi]
**werra*	'war'	**gue**rra	[gwɛ]	**gue**rra	[ge]	**gue**rre	[gɛ]
**warten*	'watch'	**gua**rdare	[gwa]	**gua**rdar	[gwa]	**ga**rder 'keep'	[ga]
**want*	'glove'	**gua**nto	[gwa]	**gua**nte	[gwa]	**gant**	[gɑ̃]

> Question: What happens to word-initial /w/ in words from Latin?
>
> Answer: In Italian and French, /w/ > /v/. In Spanish, /w/ > [b,β], specifically [b].

Word-initial /w/ from Germanic at first became [gw], which strengthened the onset. Spanish then reduces [gw] > [g] before front vowels, and French reduces [gw] > [g] unconditionally.

Strikingly, the words for 'ford, shallow place in a river' have different sources:

			Italian		*Spanish*		*French*	
Latin	VADU	'ford'	....		vado	[baðo]	....	
Germanic	**wado*	'ford'	guado	[gwado]	....		gué	[ge]

Spanish *vado* is apparently from the Latin word, judging by the treatment of the initial /w/. By the same criterion, the Italian and French words seem to have arrived by way of Germanic speech.[7]

3.4.2   Word-initial fortition of /j/

The glide /j/, when word-initial in Latin, underwent fortition in all three languages:

Latin		*Italian*		*Spanish*		*French*	
IOCU	'game'	**gio**co	[dʒɔ]	**jue**go	[xwe]	**jeu**	[ʒø]
IOVIS (DIE)	'Thursday'	**gio**vedi	[dʒɔ]	**jue**ves	[xwe]	**jeu**di	[ʒø]
IUVENE	'young'	**gio**vane	[dʒo]	**jo**ven	[xo]	**jeu**ne	[ʒœ]
IURAT	'swears'	**giu**ra	[dʒu]	**ju**ra	[xu]	**ju**re	[ʒy]
IUDICE	'judge'	**giu**dice	[dʒu]	**jue**z	[xwe]	**ju**ge	[ʒy]

Word-initial /j/ becomes an affricate /dʒ/ in Italian, a fricative /ʒ/ in French, and a fricative /x/ in Spanish, though actually in Spanish the picture is more complex (§ 4.3.1).

Exercises

1. Relative chronology in French
    a. Review and state (§ 2.2.2) how French resolves new sonorant + liquid clusters arising from syncope, as in these examples:

CAMERA	'room'	chambre	[ʃãbʀ]
NUMERU	'number'	nombre	[nõbʀ]
*SIMILAT	'resembles'	semble	[sãbl]
MINOR	'lesser'	moindre	[mwẽdʀ]

b. Review and state (§ 3.3.1) the condition under which /l/ becomes /w/ in French, as exemplified here, keeping in mind that /l/ remains intact in words like CALORE 'heat' *chaleur*, VALERE 'be worth' *valoir*, SOLA 'alone' *seule*.

CALVA	'bald'	chauve	[ʃov]
SALVAT	'saves'	sauve	[sov]
*wafla	'honeycomb'	gaufre 'waffle'	[gofʀ]
SULFUR	'sulfur'	soufre	[sufʀ]

c. The above-cited processes interact in words like these:

MOLERE	'grind'	moudre	[mudʀ]
PULVERE	'dust'	poudre	[pudʀ]
RESOLVERE	'resolve'	résoudre	[rezudʀ]
FULGURE	'lightning'	foudre	[fudʀ]

Let's select FULGURE as a representative of this group. Give an account: first, posit the relevant Latin vowel quantities, then show the steps leading to the modern word, especially the ordering of the above-mentioned rules (some other rules don't interact, so we can't see their ordering, ergo several variant answers are acceptable).

2. A scintillating problem
   a. What processes discussed so far can you identify in the following derivation?

   SCINTILLA 'spark' > stinkella > estĩntselə > etẽsɛl *étincelle*

   b. Eng *stencil* and *tinsel* both come from Fr *étincelle*. What happened in both cases? Which word can be clearly identified as the earlier borrowing?

3. Relative chronology in Spanish
   a. Sp *espalda* 'shoulder' (< Latin SPATULA) shows lenition, metathesis, prosthesis, and syncope. Starting with prosthesis, show the order of the other three changes.
   b. From Lat RETINA 'rein', what would we have instead of Sp *rienda* 'rein' if syncope had been the first development?
   c. Lat PIGNORA 'tokens', in becoming Sp *prenda* 'item', had to undergo epenthesis, metathesis, and syncope. In what order did these changes occur?

4. When 'same' is different

Latin		Italian	Spanish	French
METIPSIMU	'same'	medesimo	mismo (OSp meísmo)	même

The Italian reflex has four syllables, the Spanish two, and the French just one. Account for this difference, positing plausible intermediate stages in the derivations.

5. *Cultismos* in Romance
   Certain Romance words appear to have been unaffected by the changes we have studied. For example, CAPITALE > Fr *capitale* alongside *cheptel*. Such words as *capitale* are visibly **cultismos** (learnèd words), which means either of two things: words

coined at a late date drawing on the Latin tradition, or words that were constantly in use but resisted some or all sound changes for special reasons (typically, words heard in church, or in scholarly contexts, where Latin was still in use). Examine this set:

Latin		Italian	Spanish	French	
SPATIU	'space'	spazio	espacio	espace	[ɛspas]
SPIRITU	'spirit'	spirito	espíritu	esprit	[ɛspʀi]

a. Find two peculiarities in each of the French words.[8]
b. Find three peculiarities of Sp *espíritu*.
c. In the set below, comment on the variant forms in French and in the English borrowings.

HOSPITALE > Fr *hôpital*
> Fr *hôtel* > Eng *hostel* and Eng *hotel*

4 New palatal consonants

The Romance languages all have larger consonant inventories than Latin had. Some of the new consonants were mentioned earlier: as we saw in § 3.2.2 on lenition, Spanish added the fricative series [β ð ɣ], ultimately allophones of [b d g], while the other languages added /v/, as we saw in § 2.3 on the /b/ /w/ merger. But what chiefly accounts for the expanded consonant inventories is a new order of palatals, both fricatives and affricates, including among others: [ʃ] [ʒ] [ʧ] [ʤ] [ɲ] [ʎ]. This chapter explains how the new palatal consonants emerged and evolved.

4.1 About palatal articulation

The palate (roof of the mouth) is located midway in the range of points of articulation where consonant closures can be made. The relevant points are, from front to back: labial, dental, palatal, velar, uvular. Being in the middle, the palate is the target of various instances of **compromise articulation**: when a gesture aiming at one point of articulation is adjacent to a gesture aiming at a different point of articulation, the two tend to become simultaneous. In English, for instance, dental stops (actually alveolars) when followed by /j/ are pulled back to become palatal affricates, as in *did you* [dɪʤə], *can't you* [kæʧə]. Another example: among the unstable consonant clusters in Romance is /kt/ (velar + dental) which leads in Spanish, for instance, to a palatal compromise [ʧ].

DICTU	'said'	dicho
STRICTU	'tight'	estrecho
PECTU	'chest'	pecho
TECTU	'roof'	techo
NOCTE	'night'	noche
OCTO	'eight'	ocho

4.2   Yods old and new

The yod (/j/ in IPA) is the palatal gesture *par excellence*. Besides being itself a palatal, it also exerts a powerful pull on neighboring segments. The new palatal consonants typically have a yod involved somewhere in their origin. But what is the origin of the yods? Some existed in Latin, others result from high vowels losing their syllabicity, and still others arise from compromise articulation in certain consonant clusters. Our immediate purpose is only to exemplify these sources of yod. A systematic account of its effects starts in § 4.3.

4.2.1   Original yods

Some yods existed already in Latin, both word-initial (§ 3.4.2) and word-medial.

Latin		*Italian*	*Spanish*	*French*
IUSTU	'just'	giusto	justo	juste
(DE-) IAM	'already'	già	ya	déjà
IACET	'lies'	giace	yace	gît
IUNCTU	'joined'	giunto	junto	joint
IANUARIU	'January'	gennaio	enero	janvier
MAIUS	'May'	maggio	mayo	mai
MAIORE	'bigger'	maggiore	mayor	maieur (OFr)
CUIUS	'whose'	....	cuyo	....
PEIUS	'worse'	peggio	....	....

4.2.2   New yods from loss of hiatus

Remember that in Latin, apart from the diphthongs <AE OE AU>, any sequence written with two vowel graphemes represents two syllables (§ 1.1.3). But these sequences of adjacent vowels (vowels in hiatus) are disfavored in Popular Latin speech. There are three ways of eliminating vowel hiatus. Sometimes vowel hiatus is resolved simply by deleting one of the vowels, as seen here:

Latin		*Popular Latin*	*Italian*	*Spanish*	*French*
QUIĒTU	'quiet'	[kwetu]	cheto	quedo	coi
BATTŬIT	'beats'	[battit]	batte	bate	bat
FŬTŬIT	'fucks'	[fut(t)it]	fotte	jode	fout
PARIĒTE	'wall'	[parete]	parete	pared	paroi

Second, vowel hiatus may be resolved by inserting an epenthetic glide:

Latin		*Popular Latin*	*Italian*[1]	*Spanish*	*French*
GENUA	'Genoa'	[genuwa]	Genova	Genova	Gennes
MANUALE	'manual'	[manuwale]	manovale 'laborer'	...	...

RUINA	'ruin'	[ruwina]	rovina	ruina	ruine
VIDUA	'widow'	[viduwa]	vedova	viuda[2]	veuve
IOHANNES	'John'	[jo(w)annes]	Giovanni	Juan	Jean

The third and by far the most typical pattern: if one of the vowels is /i/ or /e/ it loses its syllabicity, becoming a glide, /j/:[3]

				Latin	*Popular Latin*
	PRETIU	'price'		[pretiu]	[pretju]
Pop Lat	FACIA	'face'		....	[fakja]
	HODIE	'today'		[hodie]	[odje]
	FAGEU	'beech tree'		[fageu]	[fagju]
	PALEA	'straw'		[palea]	[palja]
	SENIOR	'older'		[senior]	[senjor]

These new yods have far-reaching consequences, affecting the preceding consonants in ways we will see shortly.

4.2.3   New yods from palatalizing clusters

With certain consonant clusters the popular pronunciations involved a palatal gesture which in many cases generated a new palatal consonant. The palatalizing clusters to be studied in this chapter include these among others:

	Latin			*Italian*	*Spanish*	*French*
/kt/	FACTU	'done'		fatto	hecho	fait
/kl/	OCLU	'eye'		occhio	ojo	oeil
/gn/	DIGNU	'worthy'		degno	...	digne
/n:/	ANNU	'year'		anno	año	an
/l:/	CABALLU	'horse'		cavallo	caballo	cheval
/pl/	DUPLU	'double'		doppio	doble	double

You may or may not see a vestige of a yod in the spelling. There is typically no attested stage where the palatal gesture shows up as a separate segment in writing.

4.3   Yods and the growth of new consonants

This section surveys all the major sources of new palatal consonants in Romance arising under the influence of original or secondary yods. First, we treat three sources of palatal consonants which lead to the same endpoint. After we outline the data, you can verify that the three sources underwent a merger on the way from Latin to Romance (§ 4.3.4).

4.3.1   Original yod

Let's reconsider the examples of original yod given in § 3.4.2 and § 4.2.1. First the word-initial yods:

Latin		Italian		Spanish		French	
IACET	'lies'	**gia**ce	[dʒa]	**ya**ce	[ja]	**gî**t	[ʒi]
(DE-) IAM	'already'	**già**	[dʒa]	**ya**	[ja]	dé**jà**	[ʒa]
IOVIS (-DIE)	'Thursday'	**gio**vedì	[dʒɔ]	**jue**ves	[xwe]	**jeu**di	[ʒø]
IOCU	'game'	**gio**co	[dʒɔ]	**jue**go	[xwe]	**jeu**	[ʒø]
IOSEPHU	'Joseph'	**Giu**seppe	[dʒu]	**Jo**sé	[xo]	**Jo**sèphe	[ʒo]
IUDICE	'judge'	**giu**dice	[dʒu]	**jue**z	[xwe]	**ju**ge	[ʒy]
IUNIU	'June'	**giu**gno	[dʒu]	**ju**nio	[xu]	**jui**n	[ʒɥɛ̃]
IUNCTU	'joined'	**giu**nto	[dʒu]	**ju**nto	[xu]	**joi**nt	[ʒwɛ̃]
IURAT	'swears'	**giu**ra	[dʒu]	**ju**ra	[xu]	**ju**re	[ʒy]
*IEN[I/E]PERU	'juniper'	**gi**nepro	[dʒi]	enebro	[0]	**ge**nièvre	[ʒə]
IANUARIU	'January'	**gen**naio	[dʒe]	enero	[0]	**jan**vier	[ʒɑ̃]
IUDAEU	'Jew'	….		**ju**dío	[xu]	**jui**f	[ʒɥi]

> Question: What happens to original word-initial yod in the three languages?
>
> Answer: In Italian, it becomes affricate /dʒ/, in French, fricative /ʒ/. Spanish shows a three-way split: /j/ remains /j/ before stressed non-back vowels, /j/ deletes before unstressed non-back vowels, and /j/ > /x/ before back segments regardless of stress.

Original yod in word-medial position is exemplified here:

Latin		Italian		Spanish		French	
MAIU	'May'	maggio	[madʒ:o]	mayo	[majo]	mai	[mɛ]
MAIORE	'bigger'	maggiore	[madʒ:ore]	mayor	[major]	maieur (OFr)	[majewʀ]
RAIA	'ray fish'	razza	[radz:a]	raya	[raja]	raie	[ʀɛ]

> Question: What happens to original yod in word-medial position?
>
> Answer: In Italian, /j/ gives affricate /dʒ/, which typically becomes geminate in this position. In Spanish /j/ remains /j/, and in French, the result is not yet clear from the data.

The exceptional *razza* shows a development typical of Northern Italian dialects. We continue now with another source of the same palatals.

4.3.2   /d/ + yod and /g/ + yod

The sequences /dj/ and /gj/ behave like original Latin yods.

Latin		Italian	Spanish	French
*DIURNATA	'day'	giornata	jornada	journée
GEORGEU	'George'	Giorgio	Jorge	Georges
HODIE	'today'	oggi	hoy	hui
*AD-PODIU	'support'	appoggio	apoyo	appui
HORDEU	'barley'	orzo	…	orge
RADIU	'ray'	raggio	rayo	rai (cf. rayon)
MEDIANU	'middle'	mezzano	…	moyen
EXAGIU	'essay'	saggio	ensayo	essai
FAGEU/-A	'beech'	faggio	haya	…

To arrive at this generalization we must recognize two things. First, Italian *orzo* and *mezzano*, like *razza* above (§ 4.3.1), reflect the usual sporadic influence of Northern dialects. Second, the discrepancies in the French data are only apparent. They all reflect a first stage that must have been /j/. If postconsonantal (as in */ɔrdju/ > orge), these early yods behave as if word-initial.[4] In words like *rayon* and *moyen* the yod remains /j/ and syllabifies rightward. In words like *hui*, *appui*, *rai*, and *essai* the yod, being word-final, can only syllabify leftward, forming a secondary diphthong.[5] Old French *maieur*, where <i> stands for [j], shows the expected development of MAIORE, while today's *majeur* [maʒœʀ] appears to be a *cultismo*.

Next we turn to the third source of the same palatals.

4.3.3   /g/ + front vowel

The outcomes from /g/ + front vowel resemble those we saw for /j/, /dj/, and /gj/. The examples show /gi/ and /ge/ in these environments: initial stressed, initial unstressed, medial stressed, medial unstressed.

Latin		Italian	Spanish	French
GYPSU	'plaster'	gesso	yeso	…
GEMERE	'moan'	gemere	gemir	gémir
GENIU	'genius'	genio	genio	génie
GELAT	'freezes'	gela	hiela	gèle
GEMMA	'gem'	gemma	yema 'yolk'	…
GENERU	'son-in-law'	genero	yerno	gendre
GENTE(S)	'people'	gente	yente (OSp)	gens
GINGIVA	'gum'	gingiva	encía	gencive
GERMANU	'related'	germano	hermano	germain
GELARE	'freeze'	gelare	helar	geler
GENTILE	'clansman'	gentile	gentil	gentil 'kind'

FUGIRE	'flee'	fuggire	huir	fuir
REGINA	'queen'	regina	reina	reine
ARGENTU	'silver'	argento	argento	argent
LEGE	'law'	legge	ley	loi
FUGIT	'flees'	fugge	huye	fuit

The identity of the reflexes indicates that these sources of palatals – /g/ before front vowel, /j/, /dj/, and /gj/ – must have converged to a single sound, probably a slightly affricated /j/.

Abundant evidence from inscriptions (though hard to interpret phonetically) shows that the change in these sounds was underway in Popular Latin. For example: ZANUARIU for IANUARIU (CIL X 2466), ZIACONUS for DIACONUS (CIL III 8652), OZE for HODIE (CIL VIII 8424). Isidore of Seville (seventh century CE) reports, "solent Itali dicere ozie pro hodie" ("the Italians customarily say *ozie* for *hodie*"). This use of <z>, a letter borrowed from Greek (§ 11.2.1), is probably meant to represent the newly affricating /j/.

Before leaving /ge/ and /gi/, we recall (§ 2.4.3) that, from as early as the first century BCE, Popular Latin was losing intervocalic /g/.

Latin		*Italian*	*Spanish*	*French*
DIGITU	'finger'	dito	dedo	doigt
IAM MAGIS	'more'	giammai	jamás	jamais 'never'
MAGISTRU	'master'	maestro	maestro	maître
SAGITTA	'arrow'	saetta	saeta	saiete (OFr)
PAGENSE	'country'	paese	país	pays

So the /g/ of words like these was lost too early to participate in the merger.

4.3.4   Summary: the merger of /g/ before front vowels, /j/, /dj/, and /gj/

The result in Italian is simple: these sources all yield /dʒ/ which geminates intervocalically. The only complications are: a) occasional lack of gemination as in *regina* 'queen', *pagina* 'page', and b) words like *mezzano* which reflect developments in Northern Italian dialects.

In Spanish, the sound resulting from the merger is /j/, which in most environments remains intact. Word-initially it assimilates to a following back vowel, giving /x/, as in *joven* 'young'. The /j/ deletes in certain cases: a) the sequence /je/, if unstressed, reduces to /e/ as seen in *enebro* 'juniper', b) the /j/ deletes before a stressed /i/ – compare *huir* 'flee' and *huye* 'flees'. Lastly, word-initial /j/ from the merger is now archaic. Words like *yeso* 'plaster', with word-initial /j/ from the merger, are today far outnumbered by *cultismos* – compare Old Spanish *yente* and Modern Spanish *gente* /x/ 'people'.

In French, the /j/ from the merger strengthens to the Old French affricate /dʒ/ in initial position, which later deaffricates to /ʒ/. In medial position, /j/ remains, and if stranded in word-final position, will syllabify leftward as in *essai* 'essay', *hui* 'today'.

4.3.5   /k/ + front vowel

There is compelling evidence that Latin <c> always stands for [k] as in CENTU 'hundred' /kentu/, CIVES 'citizen' /kiwes/. Over time, however, the combination "velar plus front vowel" proved to be unstable, because the velar gesture is distant from the tongue position for front vowels. Only in Logudorese Sardinian, the most conservative of the Romance languages, and in Dalmatian (now extinct) did the original velar pronunciation survive. Elsewhere, /k/ before front vowels is pulled forward to the palatal or alveolar position. While /g/ yields to the same kind of pull (compare § 4.3.3), we will find that /k/ and /g/ before front vowels do not develop in perfectly parallel fashion.

For Italian, the new palatal consonant arising from /k/ + front vowel is /ʧ/. To remember the conditioning, think of *concerto*, where original /k/ remains intact before a back vowel and becomes /ʧ/ before a front vowel.

CENTU	'hundred'	cento	[ʧento]
CERVU	'deer'	cervo	[ʧɛrvo]
CIVITATE	'citizenship'	città 'city'	[ʧit:a]
*CINQUE	'five'	cinque	[ʧiŋkwe]
DICIT	'says'	dice	[diʧe]
DECEM	'ten'	dieci	[djɛʧi]

In Spanish and French, the new consonants arising from /k/ + front vowel are these:

Latin		Spanish		French	
CIVITATE	'citizenship'	ciudad 'city'	[siuðað]	cité 'city'	[site]
*CINQUE	'five'	cinco	[sinko]	cinq	[sɛ̃k]
CERVU	'deer'	ciervo	[sjerβo]	cerf	[sɛʀʀ]
CENTU	'hundred'	ciento	[sjento]	cent	[sɑ̃]
VICINA	'neighbor'	vecina	[besina]	voisine	[vwazin]
IACERE	'lie'	yacer	[jaser]	gésir	[ʒeziʀ]

Question: In Spanish and French, what happens to /k/ before /i/ or /e/?

Answer: Word-initially, /k/ before a front vowel yields /s/. Intervocalically, /k/ gives the same result, but then in French, /s/ voices to /z/.

These developments in the three languages reflect several stages. In all likelihood /k/ before /i/ and /e/ had become /ʧ/ in late Popular Latin, the stage that remains in Italian. A further fronting led to Old Spanish [ts] and Old French [ts], and both of these voiced to [dz] between vowels. In French, both allophones deaffricate, ending up as /s/ and /z/. Spanish, however, loses the allophonic voicing distinction, so [ts] and [dz] neutralize to /ts/ which then deaffricates, ending up as /s/, a pronunciation known as *seseo* [seseo].

In certain regional varieties of Spanish this trajectory took a different turn. At the stage where [ts] and [dz] were allophones reducing to /ts/, this sound was further fronted to /θ/, a pronunciation known as *ceceo* [θeθeo].

			seseo varieties	*ceceo* varieties
CENTU	'hundred'	ciento	/sjento/	/θjento/
SEMPER	'always'	siempre	/sjempre/	/sjempre/

Thus, in *seseo* varieties Latin /k/ before front vowel ends up merging with Latin /s/, whereas in *ceceo* varieties the reflexes are distinct, respectively /θ/ and /s/.

4.3.6   /t/ + yod and /k/ + yod

The sequences /tj/ and /kj/ behave like /k/ plus front vowel, except there is again a double outcome in Italian, reflecting dialect mixture in the standard language (as in §§ 4.3.1, 4.3.2).

Latin		*Italian*	*Spanish*	*French*	
MARTIU	'March'	marzo	marzo	mars	[maʀs]
DISTANTIA	'distance'	distanza	distancia	distance	[distãs]
*FORTIA	'strength'	forza	fuerza	force	[fɔʀs]
PUTEU	'well'	pozzo	pozo	puits[6]	[pɥi]
PLATEA	'open space'	piazza	plaza	place	[plas]
*FACIA	'face'	faccia	haz	face	[fas]
BRACHIU	'arm'	braccio	brazo	bras	[bʀa]
MINACIA	'threat'	minaccia	amenaza	menace	[mənas]
ERICIU	'hedgehog'	riccio	erizo	hérisson	[eʀisɔ̃]
CALCEA	'footwear'	calza	calza	chausse	[ʃos]
*CALCEU	'kick'	calcio	coz[7]	....	

In Spanish, the development of /tj/ and /kj/ is somewhat controversial, but at some stage they merged to /ts/, later deaffricating to /s/, which in *ceceo* varieties fronts to /θ/, as we saw. In Old French too, /tj/ and /kj/ gave /ts/, which becomes /s/. Later developments have deleted the /s/ in some environments.

Recalling § 4.3.5, you can verify that the reflexes of /tj/ and /kj/ are like those of /k/ before front vowel, which indicates that a three-way merger occurred. This merger is partly parallel to the one discussed in § 4.3.4. The sounds involved are:

voiceless:	[tj]		[kj] and [kⁱ˒ᵉ]
voiced:	[dj]	[j]	[gj] and [gⁱ˒ᵉ]

Both sets give rise to compromise articulations: palatal or prepalatal consonants. But the reflexes are not entirely parallel. Old French has [ts] from the voiceless set, but [dʒ] (not [dz]) from the voiced set. Likewise, Old Spanish had [ʦ] from the voiceless set, but [j], slightly affricated, and its further reflexes from the voiced set. Italian, with its double outcomes, has a different asymmetry: [tj] gives mostly [ʦ], rarely [ʧ], whereas [kj] gives mostly [ʧ], rarely [ʦ].

4.3.7   Sources of palatal n (ɲ) and palatal l (ʎ)

Prominent among the new palatal consonants are /ɲ/ and /ʎ/, which derive from several sources. They arise, for instance, when /n/ or /l/ is followed by a front vowel that becomes a yod, as in:

Latin		Italian	Spanish	French
SENIORE	'elder'	signore	señor	seigneur
HISPANIA	'Spain'	Spagna	España	Espagne
CICONIA	'stork'	cicogna	cigüeña	cigogne
ARANEA (-TA)	'spider'	ragno	araña	araignée
VINEA	'vineyard'	vigna	viña	vigne
ALIU	'garlic'	aglio	ajo	ail
MELIORE	'better'	migliore	mejor	meilleur
MELIUS	'better'	meglio	....	mieux
FILIA	'daughter'	figlia	hija	fille
FOLIA	'leaf'	foglia	hoja	feuille
PALEA	'straw'	paglia	paja	paille

> Question: What happens to /nj/ and /lj/ in the three languages?
>
> Answer: Their reflexes are: in Italian [ɲ] and [ʎ], in Spanish [ɲ] and [x], and in French [ɲ] and [j].

In Old French /lj/ first becomes [ʎ], which goes on to become [j] in the modern language (but see § 5.3.2 for more about [ɲ] [ʎ] in Old French). Like original plain /l/, new palatal /ʎ/ also velarizes before a consonant (§ 3.3.1), yielding /w/. For example:

MELIUS 'better' > [mjɛʎs] > [mjɛws] > [mjø] *mieux*

In Italian, /ɲ/ and /ʎ/ are always geminate when intervocalic: *ragno* [raɲːo], *paglia* [paʎːa], in keeping with the fact that their sources all consist of two segments.

Another source: the clusters /gn/ and /gl/, consisting of velar and dental, yield /ɲ/ and /ʎ/ as a palatal compromise.

Latin		Italian	Spanish	French	
LIGNA	'wood'	legna	leña	....	
DIGNA	'worthy'	degna	....	digne	[diɲ]
SIGNAT	'signs'	segno	seña	signe	[siɲ]
SIGNU	'sign'	segno	seño	seing	[sɛ̃]

STAGNU	'pond'	stagno	estaño	étang	[etã]
PUGNU	'fist'	pugno	puño	poing	[pwɛ̃]
COAGULAT	'curdles'	caglia	cuaja	caille	
STRIGILE	'scraper'	striglia	estrígil	étrille	'currycomb'

In Spanish, the [ʎ] ends up as [x]. The nasalization of *seing, étang, poing* is part of a much broader pattern: at a certain stage in Old French when final vowels other than Latin <A> had fallen, these words had [ɲ] word-finally. Like other nasal consonants in coda position, this [ɲ] nasalized the preceding vowel and later vanished (§ 5.3.2).

Lastly, Latin geminates /n:/ and /l:/ produce /ɲ/ and /ʎ/ in Ibero-Romance. In Spanish, /ʎ/ > /j/ in a pronunciation known as *yeísmo*, widespread in southern peninsular Spanish and in much of American Spanish. In Italian, of course, the original geminates remain.[8]

Latin		Italian	Spanish	French
ANNU	'year'	anno	año	an
CANNA	'cane'	canna	caña	canne
SOMNU/-A	'sleep'	sonno	sueño	somme
ANELLU	'ring'	anello	anillo	anneau
BELLU	'beautiful'	bello	bello	bel/beau
COLLU	'neck'	collo	cuello	col/cou
CABALLU	'horse'	cavallo	caballo	cheval

4.3.8   Palatalizing clusters with /l/

The sequences /pl/, /bl/, /fl/, /kl/, and /gl/ proved to be unstable in some contexts. Here are their reflexes in word-initial position (or morpheme-initial in the case of DE-/IN-GLUTTIRE):

Latin		Italian	Spanish	French
PLICAT	'folds'	piega	llega	plie
PLENA	'full'	piena	llena	pleine
PLANA	'plane'	piana	llana	plaine
*PLOVIT	'rains'	piove	llueve	pleut
PLANTA	'sole'	pianta	llanta	plante
Gmc *blank-*	'white'	bianca	blanca	blanche
Gmc *blond-*	'blond'	bionda	....	blonde
FLĒBILE	'pitiful'	fievole[9]	feble	faible
FLAMMA	'flame'	fiamma	llama/flama	flamme
Gmc *flank-*	'flank'	fianco	flanco	flanc
FLORE	'flower'	fiore	flor	fleur

CLAMAT	'calls'	chiama	llama	claimet (OFr)
CLARA	'clear'	chiara	clara	claire
CLAVE	'key'	chiave	llave	clef
CLAUSA	'closed'	chiuso	llosa 'estate'	close
GLANDE/-A	'acorn'	ghianda	....	gland
GLAREA	'gravel'	ghiaia[10]	glera	glaire
*GLUTTONE	'glutton'	ghiottone	glotón	glouton
DE-/IN-GLUTTIRE	'swallow'	inghiottire	deglutir	engloutir

Question: What happens to initial clusters /pl/ /bl/ /fl/ /kl/ /gl/ in Italian?

Answer: The /l/ becomes /j/.

Question: What happens to initial clusters /pl/ /bl/ /fl/ /kl/ /gl/ in Spanish?

Answer: The clusters /pl/ and /kl/ regularly produce palatal /ʎ/. Exception: *clara*. For /bl/, /fl/, and /gl/ the cluster is usually preserved. Exception: *llama* 'flame'.

Understandably, the palatal /ʎ/ is written <ll>. Given the development of original <LL>, as in COLLU > *cuello* /kweʎo/ (§ 4.3.7), the spelling <ll> came to stand for /ʎ/. This /ʎ/ is /j/ in *yeísmo* varieties of Spanish.

   The next data set shows these clusters word-medially. You will see a contrast between intervocalic and protected (postconsonantal) position. Most instances of the clusters are secondary, arising from syncope in Popular Latin.

Latin		*Italian*	*Spanish*	*French*
DUPLU	'double'	doppio	doble	double
COPULA	'couple'	coppia	....	couple
(RE-)IMPLET	'fills'	riempie	hinche	remplit
EXEMPLU	'example'	esempio	ejemplo	exemple
AMPLU	'wide'	ampio	ancho	ample
NEBULA	'fog'	nebbia	niebla	....
SABULA	'sand'	sabbia	sable (OSp)	sable
FABULA	'speech'	favola	habla	fable
TABULA	'table'	tavola	tabla	table
*AD-FLAT	'sniffs'	....	halla	....
SUB-FLAT	'blows'	soffia	sopla	souffle
CON-FLAT	'swells'	gonfia	....	gonfle
IN-FLAT	'inflates'	enfia	hincha	enfle
SIFILAT	'hisses'	....	silba[11]	siffle

AURICULA	'ear'	orecchia	oreja	oreille	[ɔʀɛj]
APICULA	'bee'	pecchia	abeja	abeille	[abɛj]
PARICULA	'little pair'	parecchia	pareja	pareille	[paʀɛj]
VERMICULU	'vermillion'	vermiglio	bermejo	vermeil	[vɛʀmej]
OCULU	'eye'	occhio	ojo	oeil	[œj]
*FENICŬLU	'fennel'	finocchio	hinojo	fenouil	[fənuj]
GENUCULOS	'knees'	ginocchi	hinojos (OSp)	genoux	[ʒənu]
QUACULA	'quail'	quaglia	coalla (OSp)	caille	[kaj]
CIRCULU	'circle'	cerchio	....	cercle	[sɛʀkl]
AVUNCULU	'uncle'	....	....	oncle	[ɔ̃kl]
TEGULA	'tile'	tegghia/teglia	teja	tuile	[tɥil]
COAGULAT	'curdles'	caglia	coaja	caille	[kaj]
UNGULA	'nail, claw'	unghia	uña	ongle	[ɔ̃gl]
CINGULA/-U	'girdle'	cinghia	cincho/ceño	cingle	[sɛ̃gl]

Question: What happens to word-medial clusters /pl/ /bl/ /fl/ /kl/ /gl/ in Italian?

Answer: Nearly always, /l/ > /j/. In intervocalic position, the obstruent before this /j/ geminates. In protected (postconsonantal) position, the obstruent remains single.

As for the deviations from the main pattern: a) *favola*, *tavola* did not syncopate and never contained /bl/ clusters, b) *vermiglio*, *teglia*, *caglia*, *quaglia* reflect the more French-like treatment prevailing in the Gallo-Italian (Northern) dialects.

Question: What happens to word-medial clusters /pl/ /bl/ /fl/ /kl/ /gl/ in French?

Answer: The clusters /pl/, /bl/, and /fl/ remain intact (apart from lenition in DUPLU > *double*). Clusters /kl/ and /gl/ also remain intact if in protected position: *oncle*, *ongle*. Intervocalically, /kl/ and /gl/ first produced palatal /ʎ/ (see § 4.3.7 on /gl/), which later becomes /j/ in Modern French.

Question: What happened to the /ʎ/ in *genoux* 'knees'?

Answer: Once /kl/ has become /ʎ/, the plural is something like /dʒənuʎs/, and the preconsonantal /ʎ/ will velarize to /w/ just as in *mieux* (§ 4.3.7).

But why is the singular *genou* 'knee' rather than **genouil*? In Old French, on the model of *genoux* /dʒənows/, a new singular was created by simply dropping the /s/.

This kind of analogy, where a supposedly more basic form (singular) is created from a supposedly more complex form (plural), is called **back formation** (§ 11.4.3).

> Question: What happens to word-medial clusters /pl/ /bl/ /fl/ /kl/ /gl/ in Spanish?
>
> Answer: Intervocalic /pl/ and /bl/ do not palatalize, they only show lenition. For /fl/, /kl/, and /gl/ we can posit an intermediate stage /ʎ/, which then typically ends up as /x/, the same result as seen in § 4.3.7. Some words such as *halla* and *coalla* stopped at the intermediate stage. When postconsonantal, all these clusters typically give /tʃ/, but /ngl/ may also give palatal /ɲ/, as in *uña*.

Of course, you will often encounter *cultismos*, and this is the most likely explanation of *ejemplo*.

There are also cases of /skl/, which evolve as shown here:

Latin		Italian	Spanish	French
MISCULAT	'mixes'	mischia	mezcla	mêle
MASCULU	'male'	maschio	macho	mâle

Popular Latin converted /sl/ to /skl/ as seen in the Romance word for 'slave':

Latin		Italian	Spanish	French
SLAVU	'Slav'	schiavo	esclavo	esclave

The rare cluster /tl/, a product of syncope, was adjusted to /kl/:

Latin		Italian	Spanish	French
VETULA	'old'	vecchia	vieja	vieille
SITULA	'bucket'	secchia	....	seille (OFr)
FISTULAT	'whistles'	fischia	....	....
*TESTULU	'clay pot'	teschio 'skull'	....	....

4.3.9   Clusters /sk/ + front vowel, /skj/, and /stj/

In Italian, these clusters are the main sources of the new palatal /ʃ/, which is automatically long between vowels. The spellings in bold type stand for /ʃ/ in Italian and /s/ in Spanish and French.

Latin		Italian	Spanish	French
SCAENA	'stage'	**sc**ena	e**sc**ena	**sc**ène
SCEPTICU	'sceptical'	**sc**ettico	e**sc**éptico	**sc**eptique
SCINDIT	'splits'	**sc**inde	e**sc**inde	**sc**inde
PISCINA	'pool'	pi**sc**ina	pi**sc**ina	pi**sc**ine
PASCIT	'grazes'	pa**sc**e	pa**c**e	pa**î**t
*NASCIT	'is born'	na**sc**e	na**c**e	na**î**t
SCIENTIA	'knowledge'	**sc**ienza	**c**iencia	**sc**ience

FASCIA(-ELLU)	'strip, band'	fascia	haza	faisceau
ANGUSTIA	'anguish'	angoscia	angustia	angoisse
OSTIU	'door'	uscio	....	huis
POSTEA	'afterwards'	poscia (OIt)	....	puis

French *paît* and *naît* have lost the expected /s/, but Old French had *paist* and *naist*. Also, the now silent <s> of *huis* and *puis* was formerly pronounced. An obvious *cultismo* is Spanish *angustia*.

4.3.10   Clusters /kt/, /ks/, and /sk/

A given cluster may create a palatal in some languages and not others. The Romance languages in their formative period all deem clusters /kt/ and /ks/ unacceptable and adjust them in different ways, but not always to palatals. For instance, in the case of /nkt/ and /nks/ the favored solution is to remove /k/, as seen here.

Latin		*Italian*	*Spanish*	*French*
*(DE-)PINCTU	'painted'	dipinto	pinto	peint
PLANCTU/-A	'lament'	pianto	llanto	plainte
SANCTA	'holy'	santa	santa	sainte
IUNCTA	'joined'	giunta	junta	jointe
PUNCTU	'point'	punto	punto	point
ANXIA	'distress'	ansia	ansia	....
DICTU	'said'	detto	dicho	dit
STRICTA	'narrow'	stretta	estrecha	étroite
DIRECTU	'straight'	dritto	derecho	droit
TECTU	'roof'	tetto	techo	toit
OCTO	'eight'	otto	ocho	huit
DIXI	'said'	dissi	dije	dis
FIXAT	'makes fast'	fissa	fija	fixe
*VEXICA	'bladder'	vescica	vejiga	vessie
TEXITORE	'weaver'	tessitore	tejedor	tisseur
AXILLA	'armpit'	ascella	axila	aisselle
FRAXINU	'ash'	frassino	fresno	frêne
COXAE	'hips'	cosce 'thighs'	....	cuisses
*COXĪNU	'hip rest'	cuscino	cojín	coussin

Question: What happens to intervocalic /kt/ and /ks/ in Italian?

Answer: Italian uses its typical device for repairing unwelcome clusters: the first consonant assimilates to the second, creating a geminate as in *detto*, *dissi*.

In French and Spanish, /kt/ and /ks/ affect the preceding vowel. Such changes in vowels are the topic of Chapter 5 (§§ 5.2.2, 5.3.3).

What about the exceptions, where Italian has /ʃ/, as in *cosce*? An appealing explanation: maybe /ks/ sporadically metathesized to /sk/. The cluster /sk/ does prove susceptible to metathesis. For instance, English *ask* /æsk/ was once (and still is, in some varieties) /æks/. Examples in Latin include MISCERE 'mix' /miskere/ with past participle MIXTU /mikstu/, and a Medieval Latin doublet TAXA /taksa/ 'work imposed' and TASCA /taska/.

With metathesis to /sk/, the words *vescica*, *ascella*, and *mascella* would be regular reflexes, the same as in PISCE 'fish' > *pesce*. A sample derivation would be:

*EX-ELIGO 'I choose' /ekseligo/ > /ekselgo/ > /eskelgo/ > /eʃelgo/ > /ʃelgo/ *scelgo*

During this sound change, the coexistence of variant pairs, first /ks/ ~ /sk/ (/ekselgo/ ~ /eskelgo/) and later /ks/ ~ /ʃ/ (/ekselgo/ ~ /eʃelgo/), allows speakers to replace /ks/ with /ʃ/ not only before front vowels, but also before other vowels.[12]

*EX-COLLIGO	'I loosen'	**scio**lgo	[ʃo]
*EX-AQUO	'I rinse'	**scia**cquo	[ʃa]
EXAMEN	'swarm'	**scia**me	[ʃa]

In Latin, the prefix EX- was [egz] before a vowel. Like [ks], this voiced [gz] also assimilates in Italian, but can't form a geminate (Italian has no [z:]). Thus it remains [z].

EX-ONERAT	'exonerates'	esonera	[z]
EX-ACTU	'precise'	esatto	[z]
EX-EMPTU(-E)	'exempt'	esente	[z]
EX-ORBITANTE	'exorbitant'	esorbitante	[z]
EX-ITU	'a going out'	esito	[z]

Sometimes a word with [ks] has two reflexes in Italian, one with [ʃ] and one with [z]:

EXAMEN	'swarm'	**sci**ame	'swarm'	/ʃ/	esame	'test'	/z/
EXEMPLU	'example'	**sc**empio	'slaughter'	/ʃ/	esempio	'example'	/z/

The derivations for *sciame* and *esame* are:[13]

EXAMEN 'swarm' > [eskame] > [iʃame] > [ʃame] *sciame* 'swarm'
EXAMEN 'swarm' > [eksame] > [egzame] > [ezame] *esame* 'test'

French has a similar pair that points to variants with /ks/ and metathesized /sk/:

LAXAT 'loosens' > [laksat] > [lajsə] > [lɛs] *laisse* 'lets'
LAXAT 'loosens' > [laskat] > [laʧə] > [laʃ] *lâche* 'releases'

4.3.11 /r/ + yod

These words show the effect of /j/ on a preceding /r/.

Latin		Italian	Spanish	French
IANUARIU	'January'	gennaio	enero	janvier
FEBRUARIU	'February'	febbraio	febrero	février
CORIU	'leather'	cuoio	cuero	cuir
COCHLEARIU (-A)	'spoon'	cucchiaio	cuchara	cuillère
PARIU	'pair'	paio	....	pair
GLAREA	'gravel'	ghiaia	glera	glaire
AREA	'area'	aia	era	aire
GLORIA	'glory'	gloria	gloria	gloire
HISTORIA	'history'	storia	historia	histoire
MATERIA	'matter'	materia	madera	matière
FURIOSA	'furious'	furiosa	furiosa	furieuse

The Spanish and French words, since they involve an early articulation of the yod and consequent changes of the vowel, belong to the topic of Chapter 5 (§§ 5.2.1, 5.3.1).

In Tuscan Italian, which forms the basis of the standard language, /r/ deletes before /j/. Southern dialects typically delete the /j/ instead, as in *San Gennaro*, patron saint of Naples, and *lupo mannaro* 'werewolf' < *LUPU HOMINARIU.

Since -ARIU was a suffix and remained productive in Romance, words of this class are numerous. In Italian, they fall into two main lexical fields: place for X (*acquaio* 'sink', *granaio* 'granary') and person who works with X (*lattaio* 'milkman', *marinaio*, *marinaro* 'sailor'). Modern Italian words of the form *-ario* (e.g. *ordinario*, *calendario*) are all *cultismos*.[14]

4.3.12 Labial + yod in French

One of the more remarkable sound changes in Romance is shown below. These words contain the cluster voiced labial (merged /b/ and /w/, § 2.3.2) plus yod.

TIBIA	'stalk'	tige	[tiʒ]	
RABIA	'rage'	rage	[ʁaʒ]	
CAMBIAT	'changes'	change	[ʃãʒ]	
*PLUMBIAT	'dives'	plonge	[plõʒ]	
GULBIA	'type of chisel'	gouge	[guʒ]	'gouge'
RUBEU	'red'	rouge	[ʁuʒ]	
*AD-SUAVIAT	'soothes'	assuage	[asɥaʒ]	
SALVIA	'sage'	sauge	[soʒ]	
SERVIENTE	'assistant'	sergent	[sɛʁʒã]	'sergeant'
*LEVIOR	'lighter'	léger	[leʒe]	'light'
DILUVIU	'flood'	déluge	[delyʒ]	
CAVEA	'cage'	cage	[kaʒ]	

Medial /bj/ and /wj/ clusters become /ʒ/. This development differs strikingly from other clusters of the form C + /j/. In clusters like /lj/, /nj/, /tj/, /dj/, both segments involve the tongue, so the competition between the two targets invites a compromise articulation, as we have seen: /ʎ/, /ɲ/, /ʧ/, /ʤ/. But in clusters like /bj, wj/, since the lips and tongue are independent, the segments are not in competition. Why do they end up forming a palatal? It has been suggested that at some point the newly created onsets like /bj, wj/ were disallowed, and that the chosen remedy was to shift the syllable boundary from, for example, /ra.bja/ to /rab.ja/. If that happened, /j/ would become the onset and would develop like word-initial /j/. The trajectory would be:

RABIA > [rabja] > [rabʤa] > [raʤə] > [ʀaʒ] *rage*

The cluster /mj/ develops in the same way. Its nasal feature persists and assimilates to the new palatal articulation. Ultimately, the nasal consonant deletes after having nasalized the preceding vowel (§ 5.4.1).

SIMIA	'monkey'	singe	[sɛ̃ʒ]
VINDEMIA	'harvest'	vendange	[vãdãʒ]
*SOMNIAT	'dreams'	songe	[sõʒ]
*RUMNIAT	'chews up'	ronge	[ʀõʒ]

For /pj/ the process is the same, except that the voiceless feature is imposed on the /ʤ/, giving /ʧ/, which regularly deaffricates to [ʃ].

SEPIA	'cuttlefish'	seiche	[sɛʃ]
SAPEAT	'knows'	sache	[saʃ]
PROPIU	'near'	proche	[prɔʃ]

A typical derivation would be:

SAPEAT > [sapjat] > [sapʤa] > [saʧə] > [saʃ] *sache* 'knows (subjunctive)'

4.4   Charles and Charlotte

English owes the special character of its lexicon largely to one historical event, the invasion and occupation of England in 1066 by a French-speaking people, the Normans, who were of Scandinavian origin, but had been living in northern France for some five or six generations (hence the name Normandy). For centuries thereafter, Anglo-Norman French was one of the spoken languages of the British Isles, and the most prestigious among them. English has adopted thousands of words from French, including the ones below.

What the listed words have in common, besides the fact that they came from French, is that they all derive from words that began with /ka/ at a pre-French stage. What is the difference between these two groups? You can hear it.

CATENA	chain	CARMEN	charm
CAMERA	chamber	CANTU	chant

CADENTIA	chance	CARITATE	charity
CAPELLA	chapel	*CAPTIA-	chase
CAMINATA	chimney	CATHEDRA	chair
CARRICA	charge	CANALE	channel
CAMISIA	chemise	CADUTA	chute
CAMPANIA	champagne	*CABALLERIA	chivalry
CAPUT	chef	CASTELLU	chateau
CAPRONE	chevron	CANDELARIU	chandelier

The loan words in the top group start with /ʧ/, while those in the bottom group start with /ʃ/. How might you account for the difference? It reflects a change that occurred in Old French. Unlike Italian and Spanish, Old French palatalizes /k/ before /a/. The immediate result is /ʧ/ which remained until at least 1100 and then became /ʃ/. So the first group consists of earlier borrowings, and the second of later borrowings.

In parallel fashion, /g/ > /ʒ/:

*galga (Frankish)		jauge	'gauge'
GAMBA	'hook, leg'	jambe	
*GARDINU	'enclosure'	jardin	
GAUDIA	'joy'	joie	

The same results are seen with word-medial /ka/ and /ga/ in protected position:[15]

BLANCA	'white'	blanche	
FRISCA	'fresh'	fraîche	
SICCA	'dry'	sèche	
MOSCA	'fly'	mouche	
BUCCA	'mouth'	bouche	
*BUCCARIU	'goat-meat vendor'	boucher	'butcher'
MASTICAT	'chews'	mâche	
(MALA) PERSICA	'Persian apple'	pêche	'peach'
LARGA	'broad'	large	

Both velars go through an intermediate affricate stage before reducing to fricatives.

before /a/: /k/ > OFr /ʧ/ > Mod Fr /ʃ/
before /a/: /g/ > OFr /ʤ/ > Mod Fr /ʒ/

This final change is part of a larger picture: all the affricates of Old French deaffricated:

ʧ >	ʃ	champ
ʤ >	ʒ	jardin (see also § 4.3.3)
ts >	s	cent (§ 4.3.5)
dz >	z	voi[dz]ine > voi[z]ine (§ 4.3.5)

The /ka, ga/ palatalization has revealing interactions with other processes. What happened here to CAU...?

| CAUDA | 'tail' | queue | [kø] | |
| CAUSA | 'cause' | chose | [ʃoz] | 'thing' |

The contrast between the reflexes reveals the timing of the reduction /aw/ > /o/. Apparently, CAUDA became *[koda] so early that the Charles and Charlotte rule never encountered any [ka] in that word. In CAUSA, the diphthong persisted longer, so when palatalization occurred, CAUSA behaved like other words beginning with [ka].

The relative chronology of sound changes is again the key to the voicing contrast in these examples:

CABALLICAT	'straddles'	chevauche	[ʃəvoʃ]
IMPEDICAT	'impedes'	empêche	[ãpɛʃ]
COLLOCAT	'lies down'	couche	[kuʃ]
CARRICAT	'loads'	charge	[ʃaʁʒ]
VENDICAT	'avenges'	venge	[vãʒ]
IUDICAT	'judges'	juge	[ʒyʒ]
FABRICAT	'makes'	forge	[fɔʁʒ]

In words where syncope occurred early, the syncopated form protected the /k/ from lenition. The protected /k/ before /a/ ends up as /ʃ/. But if the /k/ before /a/ stayed intervocalic for long enough, it first became /g/ by lenition, and then syncopated, giving such results as *charge* with /ʒ/.

Exercises

1. Each of these cognate sets diverges in some way from the outcomes predicted by the sound changes discussed in Chapter 4. Find the irregularities and comment.

VIGILAT	'is awake'	veglia	vela	veille
REGULA	'plowshare'	regola 'rule'	reja	règle 'rule'
CLAUSTRU	'closed place'	chiostro	claustro	cloître
PLAGIA	'cleared land'	spiaggia	playa	Plage 'beach'
ARGILLA	'clay'	argilla	arcilla	argile
GLĪRE/-U	'dormouse'	ghiro	lirón	loire
IULIU	'July'	luglio	julio	juillet
GIGANTE	'giant'	gigante	gigante	géant
FLAGELLU	'flail'	flagello	flagelo	fléau [fleo]
CIRCULU	'circle'	cerchio	círculo	cercle
CYGNU	'swan'	cigno	cisne	cygne [siɲ]

2. The Romance languages show reflexes not only of CANCRU 'crab', but also of diminutives *CANCRULU and *CANCRICULU. Show how these Latin etymons gave rise to the

following Romance reflexes: It *granchio* 'crab', Sp *cangrejo* 'crab', Fr *chancre* 'canker sore'. Do you have to posit any irregular or sporadic changes?

3.   Observe these Latin words and their Italian reflexes:

FALCE	'scythe, sickle'	falce	
FAUCES	'mouth, maw (gaping jaws)'	foci	'mouth of river'
		fauci	'maw'

   a.   Look up Sp *hoz*. Why does it have two strikingly different meanings?
   b.   The French reflex *faux* 'scythe' (OFr [fawts]) displays what two changes?

Now consider these Latin words and their Italian reflexes:

Popular Latin	FACIA (f.)	'face'	faccia	[faʧ:a]
	FASCE/*-IU (m.)	'bundle'	fascio	[faʃ:o]

   a.   Look up Sp *haz*. Why does it have two strikingly different meanings corresponding to different genders?
   b.   Show how these Latin words give Fr *face* [fas] and *faix* [fɛ] 'burden'. Regarding the semantics of *faix*: apparently the idea of 'bundle' as a form of humble luggage, hence something carried, drifted to the meaning 'burden'.

4.   Work out a derivation from Gmc *galbena* 'yellow' to Fr *jaune* [ʒon] 'yellow'. Name the changes that apply, and show their order when relevant.

5.   Apparently, Lat CUCURBITA 'gourd' lost its first syllable (a process known as **apheresis**) on the way to becoming Fr *courge* [kuʀʒ] 'squash'. Starting from *CURBITA, name the rules that apply and show their relative chronology when relevant. French also has *gourde* 'gourd'. Could it also be from CUCURBITA? Explain your answer.

6.   Getting the axe
   The Romance words for 'axe' (It *ascia*, Sp *hacha*, Fr *hache*) do not form a perfect cognate set. They have different sources, including Lat ASCIA, as well as a reconstructed Pop Lat diminutive *ASCULA, and possibly a variant *ACSA. Some scholars claim there was a Frankish *hapja* 'axe'.

   Pair up the Romance forms with their sources and indicate what regular sound changes are involved. How do you explain that Old French also had *aisse* 'axe'?

7.   Fr *abréger* 'shorten' comes from Lat ABBREVIARE, a derivative of BREVE 'short'. Show what sound changes lead from ABBREVIARE to *abréger*. Explain the relationship between Eng *abbreviate* and *abridge*.

8.   These Italian words both have a metathesis in their history.

FABULA	'tale'	fiaba
POPULU	'poplar'	pioppo

They differ in that gemination occurred in *pioppo* but not in *fiaba*. Can you use relative chronology to explain the difference?

9.   Some Latin 'boat' words
   a.   Related to Lat NAVE 'boat' are two words for 'sailor': NAVITA and NAUTA. What is the relationship between these two variants?

b. The Romance words for 'swims' come from NATAT 'swims' and *NAVITAT and NAVIGAT 'goes by water'. Assign each of these Romance words to its source, and explain how it developed: It *nuota*, Sp *nada*, Fr *nage*. What is unusual about the diphthong in *nuota* (§ 1.4.2)?

10. Here's a challenge

Eng *calumny* 'slander' is a *cultismo* from Lat CALUMNIA 'trickery, false accusation'. Given the verb CALUMNIARE, compute its expected outcome in French. What English word derives from it? How can you tell that English borrowed this word from Old French at an early date?

5 More about vowels: raising, yod effects, and nasalization

Under certain conditions, stressed vowels depart from the patterns we studied in Chapter 1. Many, but not all, of these special developments involve the influence of a palatal articulation, often a yod. The main pattern we will observe is that the high tongue position tends to be anticipated during the articulation of the preceding vowel. The same principle of anticipation makes vowels nasalize before nasal consonants in French (§ 5.4) and Portuguese (§ 9.3).

5.1 Vowel raising in Italian

Italian exhibits three distinct patterns of raising. Only the first involves yods.

5.1.1 Yod effects on vowels

In these Italian words the stressed vowel should have been a high mid under the rules of Chapter 1. The following consonant, we note, is [ɲ] or [ʎ].

FERRĪNEU	'iron-like'	ferrigno	
DULCĪNEU	'sweetish'	dolcigno	
TĬNEA	'tapeworm'	tigna	
PŬGNU	'fist'	pugno	
MIRABĬLIA	'amazing things'	meraviglia	
FAMĬLIA	'family'	famiglia	
CĬLIA	'eyelashes'	ciglia	
CONSĬLIU	'counsel'	consiglio	
MĬLIU	'millet'	miglio	
EX-CONBŬLLIO	'stew'	scombuglio	'disorder'

Regularly, stressed high mids followed by [ɲ] or [ʎ] raise one degree to become high vowels: /i/ instead of /e/, and /u/ instead of /o/.

In the same vein, words that develop a secondary yod tend to show sporadic raising of the preceding stressed vowel. This tendency usually involves high mids /e/ and /o/ raising to /i/ and /u/.

BĬBLIA	'Bible'	Bibbia	
DŬBIU	'doubt'	dubbio	
RADĬCULU	'root'	radicchio	'red chicory'
MŬMIA	'mummy'	mummia	
VĬSCULU	'sticky substance'	vischio	'bird lime'
BĒSTĬA	'beast'	biscia	'grass snake'
MŬSCULU	'moss'	muschio	
ŌSTĬU	'door'	uscio	
*MŬCULU[1]	'heap'	mucchio	

However, raising of the high mids fails in many words:

TRĪBULA	'instrument of torture'	trebbia	'threshing machine'
APĬCULA	'bee'	pecchia	
AURĬCULAE	'ears'	orecchie	
SĬTULU	'bucket'	secchio	
VINDĒMIA	'harvest'	vendemmia	
SĒPIA	'cuttlefish'	seppia	
DŬPLU	'double'	doppio	

The situation of the low mids is more complex. The words below all have a stressed low mid at the Romance starting-point. Its syllable is free in all except SŎMNIU.

MĔLIUS	'better'	meglio	
CON-VĔNIO	'assembly'	convegno	
RE-TĔNEO	'restraint'	ritegno	
FŎLIA	'leaves'	foglia	'leaf'
VŎLEO (Pop Lat)	'I want'	voglio	
SŎMNIU	'dream'	sogno	

These original low mids in free syllables should have diphthongized to [jɛ] and [wɔ]. Why no diphthong? Did these low mids [ɛ] [ɔ], anticipating the following [ɲ] or [ʎ], raise to [e] [o]? Apparently not, because in Standard Italian these vowels are not all high mids:

MĔLIUS	meglio	[mɛʎ:o]
CON-VĔNIO	convegno	[konveɲ:o]
RE-TĔNEO	ritegno	[riteɲ:o]
FŎLIA	foglia	[fɔʎ:a]
VŎLEO	voglio	[vɔʎ:o]
SŎMNIU	sogno	[soɲ:o]

Question: Under what conditions does a stressed low mid raise to become a high mid?

Answer: Low mids raise before /ɲ/. Before /ʎ/ they do not raise, but they still fail to produce a diphthong.

So let's ask again: why no diphthong? The best answer is that the original condition for primary diphthongs (i.e. free syllables only) acquired the status of a phonotactic constraint: no blocked syllable can ever contain a diphthong, even from a secondary source. Italian [ɲ] and [ʎ] are always geminate, thus blocking the preceding syllable so there can be no diphthong. Compare VŎLEO *voglio* but VŎLET *vuole*.

Corroboration comes from other words where early Italian developments result in a blocked syllable:

SPĔCULU	'mirror'	specchio	[spɛk:jo]
ŎCULU	'eye'	occhio	[ɔk:jo]
ŎPIU	'opium'	oppio	[ɔp:jo]
VĔTULU	'old'	vecchio	[vɛk:jo]
RŎTULU	'little wheel'	rocchio	[rɔk:jo]

These words develop a secondary yod, triggering consonant gemination (§ 4.3.8), which blocks the preceding syllable. Thus, while these stressed low mids do not raise, they do consistently fail to produce diphthongs.[2]

5.1.2   Raising before original nasal + velar

This is another environment where Latin vowels that should have become high mids [e] [o] end up instead as high [i] [u] in Italian.[3]

PERVĪNCA	'periwinkle'	pervinca
TĬNCA	'tench' (fish)	tinca
IŬNCU	'rush'	giunco
AD-ŬNCU	'hooked'	adunco
LĪNGUA	'tongue'	lingua
FĬNGO	'I pretend'	fingo
TĬNGO	'I dye'	tingo
*RINGULAT	'growls'	ringhia
ŬNGULA	'nail'	unghia
FŬNGU	'mushroom'	fungo
IŬNGO	'I join'	giungo
PŬNGO	'I sting'	pungo

This same pattern of raising from high mids to high [i] [u] also occurs before /ntʃ/ and /ndʒ/ from any source, often from normal palatalization of /nk/ and /ng/ (§§ 4.3.3, 4.3.5).

VĬNCIT	'wins'	vince
*CUM-INĬTIAT	'begins'	comincia
AD-NŬNTIAT	'announces'	annuncia
FĬNGIT	'pretends'	finge
TĬNGIT	'dyes'	tinge
IŬNGIT	'joins'	giunge
PŬNGIT	'stings'	punge
ŬNGIT	'anoints'	unge

In -NCT- the original velar deletes, but the modern word still shows the same raising pattern.

*VĬNCTU	'won'	vinto
TĬNCTU	'dyed'	tinto
ŬNCTU	'anointed'	unto
PŬNCTU	'stung'	punto

5.1.3   Pretonic raising

In Tuscan Italian, which provides the basis for the standard language, mid vowels in **pretonic** position (i.e. immediately before the stressed syllable) normally raise.[4] Included below are examples of /aw/ > /o/ > /u/.

FENESTRA	'window'	finestra
*FENICŬLU	'fennel'	finocchio
DECEMBER	'December'	dicembre
GENUCŬLU	'knee'	ginocchio
PEDUCŬLU	'louse'	pidocchio
SECŪRU	'free of worry'	sicuro
MEDULLA	'marrow'	midollo
SENIŌRE	'elder'	signore
AUDIRE	'hear'	udire
*AVICELLU	'bird'	uccello
COCHLEARĬU	'spoon'	cucchiaio
COXĪNU	'cushion'	cuscino
OFFICĬU	'service'	ufficio
POLĪRE	'clean'	pulire
IOSĒPHU	'Joseph'	Giuseppe

5.2   Yod effects in Spanish

Certain major "irregularities" in Spanish stressed vowels are actually attributable to the effect of a yod or equivalent palatal gesture coming later in the same word. Speakers tend to anticipate (prepare) the higher tongue position. Be warned that these effects in Spanish are complicated, more so than the related patterns we saw in Italian (§§ 5.1.1, 5.1.2). We depart from previous accounts (Menéndez Pidal 1966, Lapesa 1980, Lloyd 1987, Penny 2002) in the hope of achieving some simplification.

Some of these yod effects show up prominently in the verb system:

SERVIRE *servir*	but	SERVIO *sirvo*
CAPERE *caber*	but	CAPIO *quepo*

In verbs, these yod effects have spread beyond their original phonological environments and solidified into purely morphological patterns (§§ 6.6.2, 7.3.2, 7.5.2).

The apparent raising of a stressed vowel by a following high segment (yod or palatal consonant) actually happens in two ways: the high segment may be at a distance, and remain intact there (as does the [j] in VĪTREU 'glassy' > *vidrio* 'glass'), or else the high segment may be or become adjacent to the vowel, as in CASEU 'cheese' > [kasjo] > [kajso] > [keso] *queso*. Within each category we will also distinguish among different stressed vowels and different palatal consonants.

5.2.1   Effect of distant yod on stressed vowel

What is common to these examples is that a front vowel that became a yod still survives as yod and remains in its original position.[5]

VĪTREU	'glassy'	vidrio	'glass'
SĒPIA	'cuttlefish'	jibia	
VINDĒMIA	'vintage'	vendimia	
RŌSCIDU	'dewy'	rucio	'hoary'
PLŬVIA	'rain'	lluvia	
*RŬBEU	'red'	rubio	'blond'
NĔRVIU	'vigor'	nervio	
SUPĔRBIA	'pride'	soberbia	
PRAEMIU	'prize'	premio	
ŎSTREA	'oyster'	ostria (OSp)	
LABIU	'lip'	labio	
*SAPIU	'wise'	sabio	
*RABIA	'anger'	rabia	

The VĪTREU and RŌSCIDU groups have Latin stressed vowels that give Romance high mids. In Spanish, however, instead of [e] [o] they yield [i] [u], raising to anticipate the yod.[6]

In the NĔRVIU group and ŎSTREA, the evidence for raising is different. In these words, Latin ĕ ŏ yield Romance low mids [ɛ] [ɔ], which should diphthongize to [je] [we] respectively. By failing to diphthongize, these vowels are acting like high mids [e] [o].[7]

As the LABIU group shows, stressed [a] remains unaffected by a following non-adjacent yod.

5.2.2   Effect of adjacent yod on stressed vowel

A yod can become adjacent to a vowel in three ways. Sometimes lenition, by deleting an intervening consonant, brings a stressed vowel into contact with [i], which then becomes [j]. Sometimes the sequence VC + [j] metathesized to V[j]C. Thirdly, yods arise in the evolution of certain consonant clusters: [kt] [kl] [ks] [lt]. Not surprisingly, yod-like effects are also sometimes found before palatals [ɲ] and [ʎ].

In the first process, vowels in hiatus resolve to secondary diphthongs. Of these, [ej] [ɛj] [aj] reduce to simple vowels [e] [e] [e]. But [ej] remains intact if word-final.

CORRĬ(G)IA	'rein'	correa	'strap'
VĬ(D)EAT	'sees'	vea	
SĔ(D)EAT	'sits'	sea	'is' (subjunc.)
GRÉ(G)E	'herd'	grey	
LĒ(G)E	'law'	ley	
RĒ(G)E	'king'	rey	
LAICU	'lay'	lego	
CANTA(V)I	'I sang'	canté	
PLANTA(G)INE	'plantain'	llantén	
SARTA(G)INE	'skillet'	sartén	
HŎ(D)IE	'today'	hoy	
MŎ(D)IU	'bushel'	moyo	
PŎ(D)IU	'knoll'	poyo	'bench, ledge'

In the second process, diphthongs arise from metathesis when a yod migrates into the nucleus of the stressed syllable. Examples with front vowels and [a] are:

CERVĬSIA	'beer'	cerveza	
MATĔRIA	'material'	madera	'wood'
CERĔSIA[8]	'cherry'	cereza	
AREA	'area'	era	'threshing floor'
GLAREA	'gravel'	glera	
*CASARIU	'homemade'	casero	
FEBRUARIU	'February'	febrero	
*CABALLARIU	'horseman'	caballero	
BASIU	'kiss'	beso	
CASEU	'cheese'	queso	

As before, the resulting diphthongs reduce to simple vowels, e.g. CERVĬSIA 'beer' > [ʦerβejsa] > [serβesa] *cerveza* and BASIU 'kiss' > [basjo] > [bajso] > [beso]

beso. When yod migration gives rise to secondary [ɔj] or [oj], they reverse their syllabicity to become [we], a diphthong already existing in Spanish.

CŎRIU	'leather'	cuero
DŎRIU	'a river in Spain'	Duero
SALE MŬRIA	'brine'	salmuera
AUGŬRIU	'omen'	agüero
SEGŬSIU	'hound'	sabueso

In the third process, the clusters [kt], [kl], [ks], or [lt], while palatalizing, generate a [j] in the preceding stressed syllable, creating a secondary diphthong. Note in the second group, where the stressed vowel comes from Romance [ɛ], that primary diphthongization of [ɛ] > [je] is blocked.[9]

STRĬCTU	'tight'	estrecho	
APĬCULA	'bee'	abeja	
DIRĒCTU	'straight'	derecho	
TĒCTU	'roof'	techo	
PĔCTU	'chest'	pecho	
LĔCTU	'bed'	lecho	
SPĔCULU	'mirror'	espejo	
LACTE	'milk'	leche	
FACTU	'done'	hecho	
TAXU	'yew'	tejo	
AXE	'axle'	eje	
FRAXINU	'ash tree'	fresno	
MATAXA	'raw silk'	madeja	'skein'

The simple vowels come from secondary diphthongs just as we saw above, with [ej] [ɛj] [aj] becoming [e] [e] [e]. Typical derivations are:

STRĬCTU 'tight' > [estrekto] > [estrejto] > [estretʃo] *estrecho*
PĔCTU 'chest' > [pɛkto] > [pɛjto] > [petʃo] *pecho*
LACTE 'milk' > [lakte] > [lajte] > [letʃe] *leche*

Back vowels, when combined with [j] of consonantal origin, give secondary diphthongs that reduce as shown here: [oj] > [u] and [ɔj] > [o]. Note again in the second group that primary diphthongization of [ɔ] > [we] is blocked.

LŬCTAT	'struggles'	lucha
TRŬCTA	'trout'	trucha
MŬLTU	'much'	mucho
AUSCŬLTAT	'listens'	escucha
ŎCTO	'eight'	ocho
NŎCTE	'night'	noche
ŎCULU	'eye'	ojo

Typical derivations are:

MŬLTU 'much' > [molto] > [mojto] > [mujto] > [muʧo] *mucho*
NŎCTE 'night' > [nɔkte] > [nɔjte] > [noʧe] *noche*

Evidently [oj] on its way to [u] went through an intermediate stage [uj]. The stage [mujto] leading to [muʧo] is evident in the **apocopated** (truncated) form *muy* 'very' (and cf. Portuguese *muito*, § 9.2.2). This [uj] stage is even more conspicuous in *buitre* 'vulture':

VŬLTŬRE 'vulture' > [βoltre] > [bojtre] > [bujtre] > [bwitre] *buitre*

Since [ltr] could not become *[ʧr], its development stopped at the preceding stage [jtr].

Lastly, yod-like effects are sometimes produced by palatals [ʎ] and [ɲ], which involve a tongue position like that of [j].

CĪLIA	'eyelash'	ceja	'eyebrow'
CONSĬLIU	'advice'	consejo	
LĬGNA	'wood'	leña	
SĬGNA	'signs'	seña	'sign'
CASTĚLLU	'castle'	castillo	
CULTĚLLU	'knife'	cuchillo	
SĔLLA	'saddle'	silla	'chair'
PALEA	'straw'	paja	
ALIU	'garlic'	ajo	
ARANEA	'spider'	araña	
EXTRANEU	'foreign'	extraño	'strange'
ANNU	'year'	año	

The first group (high mids) show no visible effect, though they may have gone through a stage [ej] > [e] as we saw in examples like STRĬCTU 'narrow' *estrecho*. In the second group (low mids) we know the normal diphthongization [ɛ] > [je] did occur: the earliest attestations are *castiello, cuchiello, siella*.[10] So a later yod would give rise to a triphthong:

SĔLLA 'saddle' > [sɛʎa] > [sjeʎa] > [sjejʎa] > [siʎa] *silla*

The triphthong [jej] would reduce to [i], as happens in French (§ 5.3.4).[11] The third group shows that [a] remains intact before [ʎ] and [ɲ].

The back vowels too show multiple outcomes. The low mid [ɔ] dipthongizes before [ɲ], but not before [ʎ].

FŎLIA	'leaves'	hoja	'leaf'
SŎMNIU	'dream'	sueño	
SŎMNU	'sleep'	sueño	
DŎMINU	'master'	dueño	

The high mid [o] develops regularly before [ʎ] and has three distinct outcomes before [ɲ]:

BŬLLA,*-U	'round object'	bollo	'bun, puff'
MEDŬLLA	'marrow'	meollo	
PŬLLU	'chicken'	pollo	
CALŬMNIA	'slander'	caloña (OSp)	
TERRŌNEU	'piece of ground'	terruño	
CŬNEU	'wedge'	cuño	
PŬGNU	'fist'	puño	
ŬNGULA	'nail'	uña	
CICŌNIA	'stork'	cigüeña	
*RISŌNEU	'laughing'	risueño	'smiling'

In *caloña* there is no visible yod effect. The other outcomes find parallels in our previous examples. The PŬGNU 'fist' *puño* type resembles the LŬCTAT 'struggles' *lucha* development where we posit [oj] > [u]. The CICŌNIA 'stork' *cigüeña* type resembles the AUGŬRIU 'omen' *agüero* development where [oj] > [we].

5.2.3   The term *metaphony*

Despite the complexities we saw in §§ 5.2.1 and 5.2.2, these raising effects on stressed vowels all have something in common. Their similarity has given rise in Romance linguistics to the inclusive term **metaphony**, defined by Penny (2002:47) as "assimilatory raising of vowels, in anticipation of a following, higher, phoneme, typically a high vowel or a glide." But the broad scope of the term metaphony should not obscure the difference between the two processes it covers.

In one process, the high segment that triggers the raising becomes adjacent to the stressed vowel, typically forming a secondary diphthong. When it simplifies, the resulting vowel will generally be higher than the original, as in CASEU 'cheese' > [kasjo] > [kajso] > [keso] *queso*.

In the other process, the high segment that triggers raising occurs in a later, unstressed syllable and remains intact there, as in VĪTREU 'glassy' *vidrio* 'glass'. It exerts its effect at a distance. This is an instance of what linguists call **vowel harmony**.[12]

5.2.4   Pretonic raising as a yod effect

Like Italian (§ 5.1.3), Spanish shows raising of pretonic vowels, but only in words which have or had a yod in a later syllable. All kinds of yods, whatever their origin, trigger this effect. The yods in these examples are from vowels in hiatus.

MULIĒRE	'woman'	mujer
IANUARIU	'January'	enero

Palatalizing clusters trigger pretonic raising in the following examples:

COGNATU	'kinsman'	cuñado	'brother-in-law'
*COCHLEARA	'spoon'	cuchara	
GENUCŬLU	'knee'	hinojo (OSp)	
*FENUCŬLU	'fennel'	hinojo	
PEDUCŬLU	'louse'	piojo	
AFFECTIŌNE	'affection'	afición	'fondness'

Even a yod from primary diphthongization [ɛ] > [je] can exert a raising effect:

CAEMĚNTU	'mortar'	cimiento	'foundation'
FENĚSTRA	'window'	finiestra (OSp)	
TENĚBRAS	'darkness'	tinieblas	
FERVĚNTE	'boiling'	hirviente	

5.3   Yod effects in French

The tendency to anticipate a high tongue position is evident in French too. The main effect is that a stressed vowel acquires an adjacent yod, creating a secondary diphthong.

5.3.1   Yod metathesis: simple cases

These examples with [rj] and [sj] show the same pattern of metathesis as we saw in Spanish (§ 5.2.2): the yod appears to migrate leftward into the stressed syllable, creating a secondary diphthong, still reflected in spelling.[13]

AREA	'threshing floor'	aire	[ɛʀ]
GLAREA	'gravel'	glaire	[glɛʀ]
FERIA	'festival'	foire	[fwaʀ]
GLORIA	'glory'	gloire	[glwaʀ]
HISTORIA	'history'	histoire	[istwaʀ]

These secondary diphthongs continue to evolve into the modern language. Like inherited Latin [aj] (§ 1.4.2), this secondary [aj] resolves to [e, ɛ]. The new secondary [ej] also joins the primary diphthongs, becoming [oj] and ultimately [wa] (recall § 1.2.4).

Examples like these involve at some stage a yod that migrates leftward:

BASIARE	'kiss'	baiser	[beze]	
MA(N)SIONE	'dwelling'	maison	[mɛzɔ̃]	'house'
TO(N)SIONE	'shearing'	toison	[twazɔ̃]	'fleece'
*CLAUSIONE	'enclosure'	cloison	[klwazɔ̃]	'partition'

The suffix -ARIU/-ARIA (see also § 4.3.11) typically yields -ier [je]/-ière [jɛʀ]:

CANDELARIU	'candelabra'	chandelier	[ʃãdəlje]	
GRANARIU	'granary'	grenier	[gʀənje]	'attic'
AQUARIU	'sink'	évier	[evje]	
*SALARIA	'salt shaker'	salière	[saljɛʀ]	
PANARIU	'bread basket'	panier	[panje]	'basket'
*CABALLARIU	'horseman'	chevalier	[ʃəvalje]	
CAPRARIU	'goatherd'	chevrier	[ʃəvʀije]	
LACTARIU	'milkman'	laitier	[letje]	
*HOSPITALARIU	'innkeeper'	hôtelier	[otəlje]	
*SCOLARIU	'pupil'	écolier	[ekɔlje]	
IANUARIU	'January'	janvier	[ʒãvje]	

In today's *cultismos*, mainly adjectives, -ARIU has given rise to a suffix -*aire* [ɛʀ] as in:

LINEARIU	'linear'	linéaire	[lineɛʀ]
CIRCULARIU	'circular'	circulaire	[sirkylɛʀ]
SOLARIU	'solar'	solaire	[sɔlɛʀ]
*SIMILARIU	'similar'	similaire	[similɛʀ]
ORDINARIU	'ordinary'	ordinaire	[ɔrdinɛʀ]

5.3.2   Yod anticipation with [ɲ] and [l]

These words all contain, at some stage, [nj] or [lj], which become [ɲ] and [ʎ]. After that, however, the outcome depends on whether they had a following vowel in Old French. Final [a] survives as [ə] in Old French (see Exercise 2.1), so final [nja] [lja] become [ɲə] [ʎə], later [ɲ] [ʎ], today [ɲ] [j].

CICŎNIA	'stork'	cigogne	[sigɔɲ]	
HISPANIA	'Spain'	Espagne	[ɛspaɲ]	
LĪNEA	'line'	ligne	[liɲ]	
VĪNEA	'vineyard'	vigne	[viɲ]	
PALEA	'straw'	paille	[paj]	
VALEAT	'is worth' (subjunc.)	vaille	[vaj]	
FŎLIA	'leaves'	feuille	[fœj]	'leaf'
VIGĬLIA	'wakefulness'	veille	[vɛj]	
FĪLIA	'daughter'	fille	[fij]	

Thanks to the final vowel in Old French, [ɲ] and [ʎ] were able to syllabify rightward. With the loss of word-final [ə] in Modern French, [ɲ] remains while [ʎ] becomes [j].

If there was no final vowel in Old French, [ɲ] and [ʎ] ended up in syllable coda. In this case an anticipatory [j] appears in the nucleus of the stressed syllable, and the spelling reflects that stage.

CŬNEU	'wedge'	coin	[kwɛ̃]
IŪNIU	'June'	juin	[ʒɥɛ̃]
Gmc. *sunniu*	'care'	soin	[swɛ̃]
ŎLEU	'oil'	oil[14] (OFr)	[ɔjɫ]
FŎLIU	'leaf'	foil (OFr)	[fɔjɫ]
CONSĬLIU	'counsel'	conseil	[kɔ̃sɛj]

There are subsequent changes: final [ʎ] depalatalizes to [l], and final [ɲ], like [n] and [m], nasalizes the preceding vowel before vanishing (§ 5.4). There are also reversals of syllabicity, with [oj] > [wɛ] and [yj] > [ɥi]:

CŬNEU 'wedge' > [konj] > [kojɲ] > [kwɛɲ] > [kwɛ̃] *coin* 'corner'
IŪNIU > [dʒynj] > [dʒyjɲ] > [ʒɥiɲ] > [ʒɥĩ] > [ʒɥɛ̃] *juin* 'June'[15]

Palatal [ɲ] from original -GN- gives similar results:

| PŬGNU | 'fist' | poing | [pwɛ̃] |
| SĬGNU | 'sign' | seing | [sɛ̃] |

The orthographic <g> in Modern French is merely a reminiscence of the Latin etymon.

5.3.3 Yod from other palatalizing consonants

We saw that the cluster [kt] proved to be unstable in all three languages, and that its velar and dental may reach a palatal compromise (§ 4.3.10). The French solution is: [kt] > [jt].

STRĬCTA	'tight'	étroite	[etʀwat]
TĒCTU	'roof'	toit	[twa]
DIRĔCTA	'straight'	droite	[dʀwat]
FACTA	'done'	faite	[fɛt]
LACTE	'milk'	lait	[lɛ]

Old French already had, from other sources, the diphthongs [aj] (§ 1.3.3) and [ej], later [oj] (§ 1.2.4). The newly created instances of [aj] and [ej] (later [oj]) joined up with them and shared their subsequent developments.

STRĬCTA > [strekta] > [estrejtə] > [estrojtə] > [estrwɛtə] > [etʀwat] *étroite*

From cluster -NCT- a yod arises in the syllable nucleus:

IN-CĬNCTA	'pregnant'	enceinte	[ɑ̃sɛ̃t]
PĬNCTU	'painted'	peint	[pɛ̃]
*PLANCTA	'lament'	plainte	[plɛ̃t]
SANCTA	'saint'	sainte	[sɛ̃t]
PŬNCTU	'point'	point	[pwɛ̃]
IŬNCTU	'joined'	joint	[ʒwɛ̃]

This yod is clearly not from a primary diphthongization (cf. § 1.3.3), since the stressed vowels are in blocked syllables. Rather, it develops from [kt], as in previous examples like TĒCTU 'roof' *toit*.

Velars, we know, palatalize before front vowels (§§ 4.3.3, 4.3.5). This too is a yod-generating context:

		Old French	Modern French	
PĬCE	'pitch'	[pejts]	[pwa]	poix
PACE	'peace'	[pajts]	[pɛ]	paix
VŌCE	'voice'	[vojts]	[vwa]	voix
CRŬCE	'cross'	[krojts]	[kʀwa]	croix
NŬCE	'nut'	[nojts]	[nwa]	noix

A yod arises in the syllable nucleus adjacent to the palatalizing velar. Like other secondary diphthongs, these share the subsequent developments of their pre-existing primary counterparts: [oj] ends up as [wa]. English *voice* attests to the earlier [oj] stage.

Likewise from [tj], the palatalizing [ts] sends a yod into the preceding syllable:

POTIONE	'potion'	poison	[pwazɔ̃]	'poison'
SATIONE	'sowing'	saison	[sɛzɔ̃]	'season'
VENATIONE	'game'	venaison (OFr)		

A typical derivation is:

SATIONE 'sowing' [satjone] > [satsjone] > [sajtson] > [sajson] > [sɛzɔ̃] *saison* 'season'

Modern French also has many *cultismos* where -TIONE gives [-sjɔ̃]: NATIONE *nation* [nasjɔ̃] (not *naison), NOTIONE *notion* [nosjɔ̃] (not *noison).

5.3.4   Triphthong reduction

Why is it that DĔCEM 'ten' gives Italian *dieci*, Spanish *diez*, but French *dix* with a surprising vowel? Given the many sources for secondary yods, it may happen that a new yod joins a syllable that already contains a primary diphthong. In this way, triphthongs arise. For example:

DĔCEM 'ten' > [djɛjts] > [dits] > [dis] *dix*

The triphthong [jɛj] in Old French regularly reduces to [i] in Modern French. In this example, [jɛj] consists of the primary diphthong (as in *dieci, diez*) plus a new yod from the palatalizing velar (as in the PĬCE > [pejts] group above). Further examples:

PRĔTIU 'price' > [prjɛjts] > [prits] > [pʀi] *prix*
PĒIOR 'worse' > [pjɛjr] > [piʀ] *pire*
CERĒSIA 'cherries' > [tserjɛsjə] > [tserjɛjsə] > [səʀiz] *cerise* 'cherry'

IMPĔRIU 'empire' > [empjɛjr] > [ãpiʀ] *empire*
LĔGIT 'gathers' > [ljɛjt] > [li] *lit* 'reads'

Recall that Romance high mid [e] starts its Old French career by diphthongizing to [ej] in a free syllable (§ 1.2.4). If a secondary yod precedes this [ej], it forms the same triphthong [jej] by another route:

CĒRA 'wax' > [tsjejrə] > [ʦirə] > [siʀ] *cire*

In this example a yod arises in the syllable nucleus adjacent to the palatalizing segment [k] > [ts], just as in VŌCE > [vojts], but in the opposite direction (§ 5.3.3).

5.3.5   Back vowel plus yod

How does ŎLĔU, which gives Old French *oïl* [ɔjɫ], end up in Modern French as *huile* [ɥil]? The Old French form, as we saw, already involves these stages: [lj] gives [ʎ] which then depalatizes to [j] plus [l] (hence English *oil*):

ŎLĔU 'oil' > [ɔlju] > [ɔʎ] > OFr [ɔjɫ] *oïl*

On the way to Modern French, back vowel plus [j] undergoes further changes: [ɔj] raises to [uj], reverses syllabicity to [wi], and the glide then fronts to match the vowel, giving [ɥi], as seen here:

OFr *oïl* [ɔjɫ] > [ujl] > [wil] > [ɥil] *huile*

Any instance of back vowel plus [j] can undergo this process regardless of the source of the [j]. For example, the [j] may arise from a [kt] or [ks] cluster, as in:

NŎCTE	'night'	nuit	[nɥi]
ŎCTO	'eight'	huit	[ɥi]
CŎCTU	'cooked'	cuit	[kɥi]
CŎXA	'thigh'	cuisse	[kɥis]

An intervocalic velar can also produce a [j] and then [ɔj] > [uj] > [wi] > [ɥi]:

NŎCET	'harms'	nuit	[nɥi]
CŎCET	'cooks'	cuit	[kɥi]

In the following group, [ɔj] arises from metathesis and again gives [ɥi]:

CŎRIU	'leather'	cuir	[kɥiʀ]
ŎSTIU	'door'	huis	[ɥi]
PŎSTEA	'afterwards'	puis	[pɥi]

Certain words acquired [ɔj] when an intervening consonant deleted by lenition. Again the result is [ɥi]:

HŎDIE	'today'	hui	[ɥi]
AD-PŎDIU	'support'	appui	[apɥi]
IN-ŎDIAT	'bores'	ennuie	[ãnɥi]

Leaving [ɔj], we turn now to [oj], which also raises under the influence of [j], reverses syllabicity, and fronts the glide:

FRŬCTU 'fruit' > [frojθ] > [fruj] > [frwi] > [fRɥi] *fruit*
TRŬCTA 'trout' > [trojtə] > [trujtə] > [trwitə] > [tRɥit] *truite*
LŬCET 'shines' > [lojθ] > [luj] > [lwi] > [lɥi] *luit*
PŬTEU 'well' > [pojʦ] > [pujs] > [pwis] > [pɥi] *puits*

This [oj], being early and short-lived, never entered the path that leads to [wa]. The raising [oj] > [uj] was complete before the year 1100. It was only later, in the 1100s, that the primary diphthong [ej] (§ 1.2.4) gave rise to the later wave of secondary [oj] diphthongs which become [wa].

The blocking effects of nasal consonants in French (§ 1.3.3) show up here too:

| CŬNEU | 'wedge' | coin | [kwɛ̃] | 'corner' |
| Gmc *sunniu* | 'care' | soin | [swɛ̃] | |

Here we see only raising and reversal of syllabicity. Had there also been fronting of the glide, we would expect *cuin* [kɥɛ̃] and *suin* [sɥɛ̃].[16]

5.4   Nasal vowels in French

Compared to Italian and Spanish, a larger inventory of vowel phonemes arose in French, including until recently four nasal vowels: /ɛ̃/, /œ̃/, /ã/, /ɔ̃/. In Old French there was a tendency to anticipate lowering of the velum for the articulation of nasal consonants. The effect was that vowels became nasal before nasal consonants. What follows is a capsule history of the nasal vowels.

5.4.1   Nasalization

The first step in the process was assimilation: all vowels became phonetically nasal before a nasal consonant. The change affected different vowels at different dates, from the late 900s to the early 1100s. At this stage the distribution of the nasal vowels is entirely predictable, so nasal vowels are merely allophones of the oral vowels, much as in English (*cat* [kæt] versus *can* [kæ̃n]). At the next stage, nasal consonants in syllable coda vanish, so the conditioning factor for nasalization is often imperceptible. At that point, Middle French *chant* /ʃã/ and *chat* /ʃa/ form a minimal pair, so the nasal vowel has acquired phonemic status.

Ultimately, instead of there being a nasal counterpart to every oral vowel, the new nasal vowels collapse into the system of only four.[17] Middle French *chant* [ʃã], for example, ends up as [ʃã] in Modern French.

5.4.2   Denasalization

Now let's return to the stage where nasal vowels were only allophones of their oral counterparts. If the nasal consonant was not in syllable coda, it syllabified rightward and survived. In the 1500s and 1600s the nasal vowels preceding these surviving nasal consonants lost their nasal quality.

SANU (m.) 'healthy' > [sãjn] > [sẽjn] > [sɛ̃] *sain*

SANA (f.) 'healthy' > [sãjnə] > [sẽjnə] > [sɛ̃nə] > [sɛnə] > [sɛn] *saine*

Denasalization left many alternations between masculine and feminine forms, e.g. *bon* [bɔ̃], *bonne* [bɔn]; *plein* [plɛ̃], *pleine* [plɛn]; *sultan* [syltɑ̃], *sultane* [syltan], etc. However, a pair like *profond* [pʀɔfɔ̃] and *profonde* [pʀɔfɔ̃d] have [ɔ̃] in both masculine and feminine because both forms had the nasal consonant in syllable coda, where it vanished.

Exercises

1.   Oyster chowder
     For this chowder we need oysters. Indicate the regular changes that lead from Lat ŏSTRĔA to MFr *huître* [ɥitʀ] (§ 5.3.5). At what stage does English get *oyster*?
         Lat CALIDU 'hot' produces several nouns, including CALIDU 'hot drink' > Sp *caldo* 'broth'. Show how Lat CALDARIA 'pot for boiling' becomes Fr *chaudière* 'boiler'. Along the way, Old French gave us what English word?

2.   Mix well
     Pop Lat MĪSCŬLARE 'mix' (derived from MISCĒRE 'mix') yields two verbs in Italian, *mischiare* and *mescolare*. Starting from MĪSCŬLAT 'mixes', show how the two verbs evolve differently depending on whether syncope occurs. Why do the stressed vowels differ?

3.   Sprinkle with chives
     Columella, a first-century CE writer on husbandry, starts a recipe with: CAEPAM QUAM VOCANT UNIONEM RUSTICI ELIGITE 'take an onion, which the country folk call *unionem*' (*De re rustica* 12.10.1). Starting from Pop Lat CĒPA 'onion', show the regular changes leading to MFr *cive* [siv] 'scallion'. Along the way, Old French gave us what English word? Bear in mind that English has since undergone the Great Vowel Shift which takes [i] to [aj], as in the name of the letter <i>. What other adjustment did English make in the borrowed word?

4.   Show how NŬCLĔU 'kernel' becomes It *nocchio* 'knot, knob'. If you know Italian cooking, what is the mini-dumpling whose name derives from this word by metathesis?

5.   Sometimes an English word borrowed from French can pinpoint its stage of development in French at the time of its borrowing. For the following French words, posit the derivation and indicate at what stage each entered English:

QUIĒTU	'still'	coi	'silent'
FĒRIA	'festival'	foire	'fair'
GAUDIA	'joy'	joie	

Conversely, sometimes we can determine at what stage an English word was borrowed into French based on Modern French pronunciation. Fr *moire* [mwaʀ] 'watered (effect)' comes from Eng *mohair* (angora goat hair was used in creating the watered effect on silk and paper). Considering what you know about the sources of [wa] in Modern French, at what stage was the word borrowed into French?

6.   Latin STANNU 'tin' is not a plausible source for these Romance words:

		Italian	*Spanish*	*French*
Latin		stagno	estaño	étain
STANNU	'tin'			

Which of the three could come from STANNU? Would STANNEU 'made of tin' be a more convincing etymon? Explain.

7.   For the following three words we show the sound changes, roughly in order, leading from the etymon to the Modern French reflex. For each stage, (i) describe the change and (ii) find in this book (or cite from your knowledge) another French word exemplifying the same change. An example is given.

a. SCUTARĬU 'shield-bearer', derivative of SCŪTU 'shield'

SCUTARĬU		
[eskutariu]	_____	_____
[eskutarju]	_____	_____
[eskytarju]	_____	_____
[eskyðarju]	_____	_____
[eskyðjer]	_____	_____
[eskyjer]	_____	
[eskɥijer]	*reversal of syllabicity*	*juillet 'July'*
[ekɥije]	_____	_____
écuyer 'squire'		

What two English words came from the above? At what stage were they borrowed?

b. NAUSĔA 'seasickness', derivative of NAUS/NAVIS 'ship'

NAUSĔA		
[nawsja]	_____	_____
[nosja]	_____	_____
[nosjə]	_____	_____
[nojsə]	_____	_____
[nojzə]	*intervocalic voicing*	*potione > poison*
[nwazə]	_____	_____
[nwaz]	_____	_____
noise 'quarrel'		

At what stage did English borrow this word from French?

c. Gmc *kausjan* 'choose'

kausj-		
[kawsj-ir]	_____	_____
[ʧawsj-ir]	_____	_____

[ʧosj-ir]   _____   _____
[ʧojs-ir]   _____   _____
[ʃojs-ir]   _____   _____
[ʃojz-ir]   _____   _____
[ʃwaz-iʀ]   _____   _____
choisir 'choose'

What English noun comes from this root?

6 Verb morphology: the present indicative

The Romance languages in their diversity reflect the fact that Latin spread, with the expansion of Roman power, to regions where people learned it as adults, untutored. It is not far wrong to say that Latin passed through such a stage in every region where it was ever spoken. These conditions tended to foster change in favor of whatever the learner found easier.

We saw that the Romance languages ended up with larger phonemic inventories than that of Latin. In the realm of morphology, however, the Latin system was partially dismantled, certain distinctions were effaced, and new systems emerged, varying kaleidoscopically across the new languages.

Did the Romance languages "simplify" the Latin system? You decide. In the present tense, given that stem allomorphy is rare in Latin and rife in Romance (§ 6.6), you might well conclude that Latin was simpler.

Two principles become evident in Romance morphological change, chiefly in verb stems. First, there is a perpetual tension between the phonological changes that create allomorphy in the paradigms, and the force of analogy that tends to regularize paradigms. Second, regularizing does not always mean that a paradigm ends up with a single invariant stem morpheme. Rather, paradigms may gravitate by analogy toward some favored pattern of allomorphy. This chapter and the next present a panoramic overview of the Latin verb system and how it evolved in Italian, Spanish, and French.

6.1 Infinitives

Verbs in Romance, as in Latin, are divided into conjugation classes, represented here by their infinitives.

6.1.1   The conjugation classes

Latin had four classes:

Latin conjugation			Italian	Spanish	French
I	LAVĀRE	'wash'	lavare	lavar	laver
	PENSĀRE	'think'	pensare	pensar	penser
II	HABĒRE	'have'	avere	haber	avoir
	DEBĒRE	'owe'	dovere	deber	devoir
III[1]	PERDĔRE	'lose'	perdere	perder	perdre
	VENDĔRE	'sell'	vendere	vender	vendre
IV	DORMĪRE	'sleep'	dormire	dormir	dormir
	PARTĪRE	'depart'	partire	partir	partir

Question: Based on the Penultimate Rule (§ 1.1.4), which Latin infinitives are rhizotonic (stressed on the root)?

Answer: Only class III.

Question: In which of these languages were the rhizotonic infinitives retained?

Answer: In Italian and French: *perdere*, *vendere* and *perdre*, *vendre* with syncope.

6.1.2   Changes in conjugation class

The membership of these classes underwent some reshuffling on the way from Latin to Romance. The changes are most conspicuous in Spanish, which abolished class III, reassigning these infinitives either to class II or to class IV.

BIBĔRE	'drink'	beber	
CAPĔRE	'grasp'	caber	'fit'
PERDĔRE	'lose'	perder	
VENDĔRE	'sell'	vender	
VINCĔRE	'conquer'	vencer	
DICĔRE	'say'	decir	
FERVĔRE	'boil'	hervir	
FUGĔRE	'flee'	huir	
RECIPĔRE	'receive'	recibir	
VIVĔRE	'live'	vivir	

Migration of verbs from class III to class IV is seen in Italian too, but much less often, since the rhizotonic infinitive usually survives. Examples include:

AGĔRE	'act'	agire	
AD-VERTĔRE	'warn'	avvertire	
CAPĔRE	'grasp'	capire	'understand'
*DE-MINUĔRE	'lessen'	diminuire	
FUGĔRE	'flee'	fuggire	
RESTITUĔRE	'give back'	restituire	
RAPĔRE	'snatch'	rapire	'kidnap'

French also reclassifies some class III infinitives, but assigns them to class I about twice as often as to class IV. Many are Renaissance *cultismos*, which French regularly puts in the open class I.

CEDĔRE	'yield'	céder
CONSUMĔRE	'consume'	consommer
CORRIGĔRE	'correct'	corriger
DISCERNĔRE	'discern'	discerner
*DE-MINUĔRE	'lessen'	diminuer
DISTINGUĔRE	'distinguish'	distinguer
EVADĔRE	'escape'	s'évader
GERĔRE	'manage'	gérer
REPETĔRE	'repeat'	répéter
RESTITUĔRE	'give back'	restituer
EXISTĔRE	'exist'	exister
AGĔRE	'act'	agir
CURRĔRE	'run'	courir
FUGĔRE	'flee'	fuir
GEMĔRE	'groan'	gémir
SURGĔRE	'arise'	surgir

Italian and French hardly ever remake class III infinitives as class II. Here are some rare examples (Italian *ricevere* remains in class III).

Latin		Italian	French
CADĔRE	'fall'	ca<u>d</u>ere	<u>choir</u>
RECIPĔRE	'receive'	ri<u>ce</u>vere	rece<u>voir</u>
SAPĔRE	'know'	sa<u>pe</u>re	sa<u>voir</u>

Occasionally, an infinitive changes from one arhizotonic class (-ĒRE) to another (-ĪRE), as seen here. The infinitives in parentheses have not changed class.

Latin		Italian	Spanish	French	
ABOLĒRE	'destroy'	abolire	abolir	abolir	'abolish'
ABSORBĒRE	'swallow'	assorbire	(absorber)	absorber[2]	'absorb'
EXHIBĒRE	'present'	esibire	exhibir	exhiber[3]	
FLORĒRE	'bloom'	fiorire	…	fleurir	

GAUDĒRE	'rejoice'	(godere)	(gozar)[4]	jouir
IACĒRE	'lie down'	(giacere)	(yacer)	gésir
*(RE-)IMPLĒRE	'fill'	riempire	henchir	remplir
TENĒRE	'hold'	(tenere)	(tener)	tenir

Trends in the infinitive are strikingly different from trends in the finite (conjugated) forms. Oddly, while class III itself was to vanish as a distinct category (§ 6.2), Italian and French often changed class II infinitives to the rhizotonic format of class III.[5]

	Latin		Italian	French
	ARDĒRE	'burn'	ardere	….
	(DE-)PENDĒRE	'depend'	dipendere	dépendre
	FULGĒRE	'flash'	fulgere	….
	LUCĒRE	'shine'	….	luire[6]
	MORDĒRE	'bite'	mordere	mordre
	MOVĒRE	'move'	muovere	(mouvoir)
	NOCĒRE	'harm'	nuocere	nuire
	(RE-)SPONDĒRE	'respond'	rispondere	répondre
	RIDĒRE	'laugh'	ridere	rire
	SPLENDĒRE	'shine'	splendere	….
	TONDĒRE	'shear'	tondere	tondre
	TORQUĒRE	'twist'	torcere	tordre

Ultimately, class III survives as a distinct category in French and Italian only in infinitives.

6.1.3   Deponent verbs in Latin

Distributed across all four conjugation classes, deponents form a closed set of verbs which are active in meaning but passive in form. Popular Latin eliminates this category entirely. Their infinitives, originally passive, were uniformly remade into active infinitives, some of which also changed conjugation class.

Classical Latin	Popular Latin		Italian	Spanish	French
ADMIRARĪ	ADMIRĀRE	'admire'	ammirare	admirar	admirer
DOMINARĪ	DOMINĀRE	'reign'	dominare	dominar	dominer
PISCARĪ	PISCĀRE	'fish'	pescare	pescar	pêcher
MORĪ	MORĪRE	'die'	morire	morir	mourir
NASCĪ	NASCĒRE	'be born'	nascere	nacer	naître
SEQUĪ	SEQUĒRE	'follow'	seguire	seguir	suivre
DEMOLIRĪ	DEMOLĪRE	'demolish'	demolire	demoler	démolir

Henceforth, we ignore deponents, since they are all remade as normal active verbs.

6.2   Present indicative in Popular versus Standard Latin

While Latin distinguishes four conjugation classes, there are certain class III verbs that conjugate like class IV verbs in the first singular and third plural. We call them class IIIb. The present indicative forms are:

I	II	IIIa	IIIb	IV
LAVĀRE	TĬMĒRE	VENDĔRE	RECĬPĔRE	PARTĪRE
'wash'	'fear'	'sell'	'receive'	'depart'
LAVŌ	TĬMĔŌ	VENDŌ	RECĬPĬŌ	PARTĬŌ
LAVĀS	TĬMĒS	VENDĬS	RECĬPĬS	PARTĪS
LAVĂT	TĬMĒT	VENDĬT	RECĬPĬT	PARTĬT
LAVĀMUS	TĬMĒMUS	VENDĬMUS	RECĬPĬMUS	PARTĪMUS
LAVĀTIS	TĬMĒTIS	VENDĬTIS	RECĬPĬTIS	PARTĪTIS
LAVĂNT	TĬMĚNT	VENDŪNT	RECĬPĬŬNT	PARTĬŬNT

You need to know three things about the conjugations. First: applying the Latin Penultimate Rule (§ 1.1.4), you can verify that in classes I, II, and IV, stress falls on the root in four forms and off the root in the first and second plural. There is no fact more consequential than this for Romance verb morphology. Sound changes conditioned by stress will hit the four stressed verb roots and not the two unstressed roots, hence the many alternations like Spanish *vuelvo, volvemos* 'return' (§ 6.6.1).

Second, this stress alternation does not occur in class III. Again using the Penultimate Rule, observe that class III verbs are rhizotonic throughout the paradigm. So the property unique to class III is just the root stress in finite forms like VENDĬMUS and VENDĬTIS.

Third, this property of class III, apparently not salient enough to withstand the rough-and-tumble of second-language learning in the Romance context, proves to be doomed in all the Western Romance languages. The finite forms of verbs belonging to class III are adjusted to match the alternating stress patterns found in the other classes.[7]

I	II	III	IV
LAVĀRE	TĬMĒRE	VENDĔRE	PARTĪRE
'wash'	'fear'	'sell'	'depart'
LAVŌ	TĬM(Ě)Ō	VENDŌ	PART(Ĭ)Ō
LAVĀS	TĬMĒS	VENDĬS	PARTĪS
LAVĂT	TĬMĒT	VENDĬT	PARTĬT
LAVĀMUS	TĬMĒMUS	*VENDĬMUS	PARTĪMUS
LAVĀTIS	TĬMĒTIS	*VENDĬTIS	PARTĪTIS
LAVĂNT	TĬMĚNT	VENDŪNT	PART(Ĭ)ŬNT

The three parenthesized vowels typically delete by analogy with the other conjugations, but sometimes have consequences, as we will see (§§ 6.3.1, 6.6.2).

6.3   Present indicative in Italian

This chart displays the present tense in Popular Latin with the corresponding forms in Italian. The shaded elements call for comment in ensuing sections.

I		II	
LAVĀRE 'wash'	lavare	TĬMĒRE 'fear'	temere
LAVŌ	lavo	TĬM(Ĕ)Ō	temo
LAVĀS	lavi	TĬMĒS	temi
LAVĂT	lava	TĬMĔT	teme
LAVĀMUS	laviamo	TĬMĒMUS	temiamo
LAVĀTIS	lavate	TĬMĒTIS	temete
LAVĂNT	lavano	TĬMĔNT	temono

III		IV	
VENDĔRE 'sell'	vendere	PARTĪRE 'depart'	partire
VENDŌ	vendo	PART(Ī)Ō	parto
VENDĬS	vendi	PARTĪS	parti
VENDĬT	vende	PARTĬT	parte
*VENDĬMUS	vendiamo	PARTĪMUS	partiamo
*VENDĬTIS	vendete	PARTĪTIS	partite
VENDŬNT	vendono	PART(Ī)ŬNT	partono

6.3.1   First singular in Italian

Verb forms like TĬMĔO and PARTĬO (and class IIIb RECĬPĬO) have an unstressed <Ĭ> or <Ĕ> that becomes a yod. This yod never survives intact. Either it affects the stem-final consonant (TACĔO 'I am silent' *taccio*, cf. § 5.1.1, PARĔO 'I appear' *paio*, cf. § 4.3.11), or it simply deletes (TĬMĔO 'I fear' *temo*, PARTĬO 'I depart' *parto*).

6.3.2   Second singular in Italian

Since Latin second singulars end in <s>, how did Italian get -*i* as its second singular marker? A clue lies in other words that formerly ended in <s>:

CRAS	'tomorrow'	crai (OIt)	[kraj]
PŎS(T)	'after'	poi	[pɔj]
NŌS	'we'	noi	[noj]
VŌS	'you'	voi	[voj]

Word-final <s> becomes [j]. The resulting diphthongs, if unstressed (compare
IOHANNES > *Giovanni*), would become:

LAVĀS	>	[lavaj]	>	lave
TĬMĒS	>	[temej]	>	temi
VENDĬS	>	[vendej]	>	vendi
PARTĪS	>	[partij]	>	parti

In classes II–IV this accounts for today's forms. For verbs of the -*are* class, Old
Italian did have a second singular in -*e*. By 1300 it was being replaced by -*i* to
match the other three classes – a change induced by **analogy**. As we continue to
explore the reorganization of morphology from Latin to Romance, we will see
at every turn how the force of analogy can override the dictates of phonological
change.[8]

6.3.3   Third singular in Italian

Word-final <T> deletes. The third singular endings reflect the regular outcomes
for word-final unstressed vowels.

6.3.4   First plural in Italian

The Latin forms end in <US>. At an early unattested stage, this would be [oj],
which simplifies to [o]. The expected forms would thus be: *lavamo, tememo, ven-
demo, partimo*, which they were in Old Italian. Later, these endings were all
replaced by -*iamo*, originally a present subjunctive ending deriving from the last
three of these four subjunctive forms:

	LAVĒMUS	I
	TIMEĀMUS	II
VENDĀMUS >	*VENDEĀMUS	III
	PARTIĀMUS	IV

The first plural subjunctive had an exhortative use ('let's'), which presumably
fostered its extension to the indicative mood.

6.3.5   Second plural in Italian

From the Popular Latin starting-point LAVĀTIS, TĬMĒTIS, *VENDĬTIS, PARTĪTIS, with
final <s> becoming [j], we expect *lavati, *temeti, *vendeti, *partiti. Evidently,
the attested forms derive not from the indicative, but from the Latin imperative: LAVĀTE, TĬMĒTE, *VENDĬTE, PARTĪTE.

6.3.6   Third plural in Italian

The yod developing from forms like PARTĬUNT (and IIIb RECĬPĬUNT) behaves like
the yod in first singulars (§ 6.3.1). A major feature of Italian is that <ŬNT> from
class III verbs like VENDŬNT spreads to class II. Instead of TĬMĔNT, the analogical
*TĬMŬNT gives Italian *temono*. The ending -*eno* is attested in older Italian (Rohlfs
1968: II, 255).

Lastly, let's ask why third plurals in Italian end in -*o*, not directly from Latin. The answer lies in the verb 'be', where these two forms converged:

SŬM	'I am'	>	son
SŬNT	'they are'	>	son

Then *son* 'I am' acquired a variant *sono* by analogy to all other first singulars. At that point, given the first singular variants *son/sono*, it was natural for the homonymous third plural also to allow variants *son/sono*. On the analogical model of the high-frequency verb 'be', third plural verbs such as LAVANT > *lavan* were then felt to be *apocopated* (cut short), and thus acquired a variant *lavano*.[9]

6.4   Present indicative in Spanish

This chart displays the present tense in Popular Latin with the corresponding forms in Spanish. The three parenthesized vowels will vanish in the verbs shown here, but in some verbs they trigger metaphony (§ 6.6.2)

I		II		IV	
LAVĀRE 'wash'	lavar	DĒBĒRE 'owe'	deber	PARTĪRE 'depart'	partir
LAVŌ	lavo	DĒB(Ĕ)Ō	debo	PART(Ī)Ō	parto
LAVĀS	lavas	DĒBĒS	debes	PARTĪS	partes
LAVĂT	lava	DĒBĔT	debe	PARTĬT	parte
LAVĀMUS	lavamos	DĒBĒMUS	debemos	PARTĪMUS	partimos
LAVĀTIS	laváis	DĒBĒTIS	debéis	PARTĪTIS	partís
LAVĂNT	lavan	DĒBENT	deben	PART(Ī)ŬNT	parten

Spanish has a true three-conjugation system, with class III verbs assimilating totally to class II or IV, even in their infinitives. So VENDĔRE in the Popular Latin of Spain becomes *VENDĒRE and conjugates with class II.

6.4.1   Singular verbs in Spanish

With the loss of final <T> in the third singular, the verbs shown here derive regularly from Latin.

6.4.2   Plural verbs in Spanish

The first plural forms are normal reflexes of the Latin forms. In the second plural <T> shows up as <d> in Old Spanish -*ades*, -*edes*, -*ides*. Further lenition and subsequent changes bring the endings to -*áis*, -*éis*, -*is*. Third plural forms lose their final <T>. Important: the -*en* of class II spreads to class IV, the reverse of what happens in Italian.

6.5   Present indicative in French

This chart displays the present tense in Popular Latin with the corresponding forms in French. Again, the elements shaded are not phonological reflexes of the Latin.

I			II		
PORTĀRE	porter	[pɔʀte]	VĪDĒRE	voir	[vwaʀ]
'carry'			'see'		
PORTŌ	porte	[pɔʀt]	VĪD(É)Ō	vois	[vwa]
PORTĀS	portes	[pɔʀt]	VĪDĒS	vois	[vwa]
PORTĂT	porte	[pɔʀt]	VĪDĔT	voit	[vwa]
PORTĀMUS	portons	[pɔʀtɔ̃]	VĪDĒMUS	voyons	[vwajɔ̃]
PORTĀTIS	portez	[pɔʀte]	VĪDĒTIS	voyez	[vwaje]
PORTĂNT	portent	[pɔʀt]	VĪDENT	voient	[vwa]

III			IV		
CONCLUDĔRE	conclure	[kɔ̃klyʀ]	SERVĪRE	servir	[sɛʀviʀ]
'conclude'			'serve'		
CONCLUDŌ	conclus	[kɔ̃kly]	SERV(Ī)Ō	sers	[sɛʀ]
CONCLUDĬS	conclus	[kɔ̃kly]	SERVĪS	sers	[sɛʀ]
CONCLUDĬT	conclut	[kɔ̃kly]	SERVĬT	sert	[sɛʀ]
*CONCLUDĬMUS	concluons	[kɔ̃klyɔ̃]	SERVĪMUS	servons	[sɛʀvɔ̃]
*CONCLUDĬTIS	concluez	[kɔ̃klye]	SERVĪTIS	servez	[sɛʀve]
CONCLUDUNT	concluent	[kɔ̃kly]	SERV(Ī)ŬNT	servent	[sɛʀv]

6.5.1   Singular verbs in French

Recall that in Old French the vowel of a word-final syllable becomes [ə] if it comes from <A> or supports a consonant cluster, but otherwise it deletes. So in Old French the first singular forms of Latin class I verbs sometimes ended in [ə], but not always.

	Old French			*Old French*	
PORTŌ	port	[pɔrt]	INTRŌ	entre	[ẽntrə]
PORTĀS	portes	[pɔrtəs]	INTRĀS	entres	[ẽntrəs]
PORTĂT	porte	[pɔrtə]	INTRĂT	entre	[ẽntrə]

The [ə] in the second and third singular is from Latin <A>. Cluster support accounts for the [ə] in a first person form like *entre* 'I enter'.[10] Also regular is the loss of word-final <O> in *port*. But by analogy with forms like *entre* and the rest of the singular paradigm, [ə] spreads to all class I first singulars: *port* was replaced by [pɔrtə], today pronounced [pɔʀt].

Classes II, III, and IV fall together in French. For all these classes, the vowel of the final syllable, since it is not <A>, deletes. Hence the expected endings are: zero, -s, -t.

	Old French		Old French		Old French
VĬD(É)Ō	voi	CONCLUDŌ	conclu	SERV(Ĭ)Ō	serf
VĬDĒS	vois	CONCLUDĬS	conclus	SERVĪS	sers
VĬDĔT	voit	CONCLUDĬT	conclut	SERVĬT	sert

Later, the -s ending spreads to the first singular.[11] The analogical model for a paradigm -s, -s, -t lies in the inchoative verbs, e.g. *finis, finis, finit* (§ 6.9).

6.5.2   Plural verbs in French

In the first plural a new ending -*ons*, extracted from the verb 'be' (SUMUS > *sons*), was extended to all conjugations. In the second plural, -ATIS, -ĒTIS, and -ĪTIS all yield -*ez* (pronounced [ets] in Old French and [e] today), which spreads to class IV also. In the third plural, the Latin endings all collapse to [ənt]. The spelling was standardized to <ent> and with subsequent sound changes (loss of final [t], nasalization, loss of final [n]) the whole ending -*ent* has become silent.

6.6   Stem allomorphy in the present indicative

When a conditioned sound change occurs in a verb paradigm, it may affect some forms and not others. The result is patterned allomorphy, predictable alternations in the stem (or root) morpheme. The following sections cover the three main types of verb allomorphy in Romance.

6.6.1   Allomorphy induced by stress position

The diphthongization rules we studied in Chapter 1 apply only to stressed vowels. In the present tense paradigms of Popular Latin, the stress position alternates, as we saw (§ 6.2), producing stem allomorphy. Some typical examples are, in Italian:

CŎQUĔRE	cuocere	AUDĪRE	udire
'cook'		'hear'	
CŎQUŌ	cuocio	AUD(Ĭ)Ō	odo
CŎQUĬS	cuoci	AUDĪS	odi
CŎQUĬT	cuoce	AUDĬT	ode
*CŎQUĬMŬS	cociamo	AUDĪMŬS	udiamo
*CŎQUĬTĬS	cocete	AUDĪTĬS	udite
CŎQUUNT	cuociono	AUD(Ĭ)ŬNT	odono

In the paradigm of *udire*, it is not the stressed stem, but the unstressed stem, that has an allomorph from sound change: the arhizotonic forms show pretonic raising (§ 5.1.3).

In Spanish, allomorphy from diphthongization involves more verbs, since Romance low mid [ɛ] [ɔ] diphthongize in any stressed syllable, free or blocked (§ 1.2.5).

NĔGĀRE	negar	SŎNĀRE	sonar
'deny'		'sound'	
NĔGŌ	niego	SŎNŌ	sueno
NĔGĀS	niegas	SŎNĀS	suenas
NĔGĂT	niega	SŎNĂT	suena
NĔGĀMŬS	negamos	SŎNĀMŬS	sonamos
NĔGĀTĬS	negáis	SŎNĀTĬS	sonáis
NĔGĂNT	niegan	SŎNĂNT	suenan
PĔRDĔRE	perder	VŎLVĔRE	volver
'lose'		'roll'	'return'
PĔRDŌ	pierdo	VŎLVŌ	vuelvo
PĔRDĬS	pierdes	VŎLVĬS	vuelves
PĔRDĬT	pierde	VŎLVĬT	vuelve
*PĔRD<u>Ĭ</u>MŬS	perdemos	*VŎL<u>V</u><u>Ĭ</u>MŬS	volvemos
*PĔRD<u>Ĭ</u>TĬS	perdéis	*VŎL<u>V</u><u>Ĭ</u>TĬS	volvéis
*PĔRDĔNT	pierden	*VŎLVĔNT	vuelven

The conditions for diphthongization in French are reflected in the examples below (French *mène* [mɛn] contrasts with *menons* [mənɔ̃]):

Latin	Modern French	Latin	Old French	Modern French	Latin	Modern French
*MŎRĪRE[12]	mourir	MĬNĀRE	mener	mener	*ACQUĔRĪRE	acquérir
'die'		'lead'			'acquire'	
*MŎR(Ī)Ō	meurs	MĬNŌ	meine	mène	*ACQUĔR(Ī)Ō	acquiers
*MŎRĪS	meurs	MĬNĀS	meines	mènes	*ACQUĔRĪS	acquiers
*MŎRĬT	meurt	MĬNĂT	meine	mène	*ACQUĔRĬT	acquiert
*MŎRĪMŬS	mourons	MĬNĀMŬS	menons	menons	*ACQUĔRĪMŬS	acquérons
*MŎRĪTĬS	mourez	MĬNĀTĬS	menez	menez	*ACQUĔRĪTĬS	acquérez
*MŎR(Ī)ŬNT	meurent	MĬNĂNT	meinent	mènent	*ACQUĔR(Ī)ŬNT	acquièrent

Stress-induced allomorphy survives to varying degrees in the three languages. Italian and French often adjust the paradigms to eliminate the alternations (§ 6.7).

6.6.2   Metaphonic allomorphy in Spanish

A remarkable innovation in Old Spanish is the creation of a new class of stem-changing verbs that has its origin in metaphony. Recall that in Spanish, yod exerts a raising effect on a preceding stressed vowel (§ 5.2.2). The yod in the first singular of Latin class IV verbs has a major consequence, creating the

Spanish type shown below. The pattern is confined to a subset of -*ir* verbs, some that belonged to Latin class IV originally and others that joined the class.[13]

*MĒTĪRE[14]
'measure'

*MĒTĬŌ	mido
*MĒTĪS	mides
*MĒTĬT	mide
*MĒTĪMŬS	medimos
*MĒTĪTĬS	medís
*MĒTĔNT	miden

First singular *mido* has a high vowel from metaphony, while *mides, mide, miden* are analogical. Why would a single form, *mido*, extend its influence to three other forms of the paradigm? The best answer is that this alternation extends to fill out the boot template seen in § 6.6.1.

While the type *medir mido* has its origins in metaphony, a number of verbs joined this group by analogy, migrating from class II or III to class IV. Verbs like ĬMPLĒRE ĬMPLĔŌ 'fill' (probably via Popular Latin *ĬMPLĪRE *ĬMPLĬŌ), give modern *henchir hincho* with metaphony in *hincho*, the same as in *medir mido* above. But it takes a pure analogy to convert PĚTĔRE PĚTĬŌ 'ask for' (via Popular Latin *PĚTĪRE PĚTĬŌ) into today's *pedir pido*, since metaphony could not raise the low mid of PĚTĬŌ two degrees to the [i] of *pido* (see also § 6.6.4).

ĬMPLĒRE >	*ĬMPLĪRE	henchir	PĚTĔRE >	*PĚTĪRE	pedir
'fill'			'ask for'		
	*ĬMPLĬŌ	hincho		PĚTĬŌ	pido
	*ĬMPLĪS	hinches		*PĚTĪS	pides
	*ĬMPLĬT	hinche		*PĚTĬT	pide
	*ĬMPLĪMŬS	henchimos		*PĚTĪMŬS	pedimos
	*ĬMPLĪTĬS	henchís		*PĚTĪTĬS	pedís
	*ĬMPLĔNT	hinchen		*PĚTĔNT	piden

In Romanian, metaphonic allomorphy is extremely prominent and induces alternations in many paradigms (§ 10.1.3).

6.6.3   Allomorphy induced by consonant changes

Any sound change affecting a consonant produces allomorphy when it selectively hits the stem-final consonant in a verb paradigm. For example, Latin [k] [g] [sk] palatalize to Italian [tʃ] [dʒ] [ʃ] before a front vowel (§§ 4.3.3, 4.3.5). This produces such alternations as:

VINCĔRE	vincere	[vintʃere]		LĔGĔRE	leggere	[lɛdʒːere]
'vanquish'				'read'		
VINCŌ	vinco	[viŋko]		LĔGŌ	leggo	[lɛgːo]
VINCĪS	vinci	[vintʃi]		LĔGĬS	leggi	[lɛdʒːi]
VINCĬT	vince	[vintʃe]		LĔGĬT	legge	[lɛdʒːe]
*VINCĬMŬS	vinciamo	[vintʃjamo]		*LĔGĬMŬS	leggiamo	[lɛdʒːjamo]
*VINCĬTĬS	vincete	[vintʃete]		*LĔGĬTĬS	leggete	[lɛdʒːete]
VINCŬNT	vincono	[viŋkono]		LĔGŬNT	leggono	[lɛgːono]

CRĒSCĔRE	crescere	[kreʃːere]	
'grow'			
CRĒSCŌ	cresco	[kresko]	
CRĒSCĬS	cresci	[kreʃːi]	
CRĒSCĬT	cresce	[kreʃːe]	
*CRĒSCĬMŬS	cresciamo	[kreʃːamo]	
*CRĒSCĬTĬS	crescete	[[kreʃːete]	
CRĒSCŬNT	crescono	[kreskono]	

Italian has developed an affinity between the first singular and the third plural in paradigms having stem-consonant alternations. The foregoing examples show the reason.

> Question: What do the first singular and third plural have in common?
>
> Answer: They both have a back vowel immediately after the stem, as in *cresco* [kresko], *crescono* [kreskono]. So these forms have [k], [g], or [sk] rather than [tʃ], [dʒ], or [ʃ].

This pattern, which arises in many other verbs with stem-consonant alternation, has also spread by analogy.[15] In the *-are* class, however, stem-final consonants never alternate. There is a chronological reason:

Latin	*Pre-Italian*	*Italian*	
PACĀRE	[pagare]	pagare	
'pacify'		'pay'	
PACŌ	[pago]	pago	[pago]
PACĀS	[pagaj]	paghi	[pagi]
PACĂT	[paga]	paga	[paga]
PACĀMŬS	[pagamo]	paghiamo	[pagjamo]
*PACĀTE	[pagate]	pagate	[pagate]
PACĂNT	[pagan]	pagano	[pagano]

Quite simply, in Pre-Italian as reconstructed here, [g] never had a front vowel after it. It was only after the palatalization of velars ran its course that [pagaj] was altered to Old Italian [page], later analogical [pagi] *paghi*. The change from [pagamo] to [pagjamo] *paghiamo* was also late, post-dating by far the palatalization rule. Bear in mind that once palatalization has ended, [g] and [dʒ], as well as [k] and [tʃ], are distinct phonemes, not positional variants. So [spago] *spago* 'string' plus the diminutive suffix [et:i] -*etti* becomes [spaget:i] *spaghetti*, not *[spadʒet:i]. Likewise *pag* plus an inflection -*i* becomes [pagi] *paghi*.

With analogous changes in Spanish, Latin [k] remains velar only in the first singular, because the verbs involved have migrated to class II, so their third plural ending -ĕNT has a front vowel:

*FACĔRE	hacer	*COGNŌSCĔRE	conocer
'do'		'know'	
*FACŌ	hago	COGNŌSCŌ	conozco
*FACĒS	haces	*COGNŌSCĒS	conoces
*FACĔT	hace	*COGNŌSCĔT	conoce
*FACĒMŬS	hacemos	*COGNŌSCĒMŬS	conocemos
*FACĒTĬS	hacéis	*COGNŌSCĒTĬS	conocéis
*FACĔNT	hacen	*COGNŌSCĔNT	conocen

Palatalizations in Romanian create allomorphy even more extensive than in Italian or Spanish (§ 10.5.2, end).

In French, stem-consonant allomorphy is widespread and complex. The most salient pattern is one where the stem-final consonant is lost in the singular and retained in the plural. The rule ultimately responsible for this contrast is a familiar one: the vowel of a final syllable remains as [ə] if it came from Latin <A> or supports a cluster, but otherwise it deletes. This deletion brings the stem-final consonant into contact with a consonant ending or a vowel ending, with differing results:

Latin	Old French	Modern French	Latin		Old French	Modern French
VIVĔRE		vivre	vivre	VALĒRE		valeir	valoir
'live'				'be worth'			
VIVŌ	*viv >	vif	vis	VAL(Ē)Ō	*val >	vau	vaux
VIVĬS	*vifs >	vis	vis	VALĒS	*vals >	vaus	vaux
VIVĬT	*vift >	vit	vit	VALĔT	*valt >	vaut	vaut
*VIVĬMŬS		vivons	vivons	VALĒMUS		valons	valons
*VIVĬTĬS		vivez	vivez	VALĒTIS		valez	valez
VIVŬNT		vivent	vivent	VALĔNT		valent	valent

The resulting clusters C[s] and C[t] in the singular undergo regular sound changes. In the plural, the verb endings start with a vowel, no clusters are created, and so the consonant remains intervocalic in Old French, though ultimately third plural -*ent* becomes silent.

For the reasons seen here, Old French first singulars were always a unique allomorph because their stem-final consonant became word-final (VĪVŌ *vif*) or disappeared (VĒDŌ *voi*). First singulars were already being regularized in Old French: *vif* > *vis, voi* > *vois*.

Predictably, the clusters that produce stem allomorphy never arise in class I verbs in the indicative because -ĀS and -ĀT become [əs] and [ət] rather than losing their vowel. Stem-consonant allomorphy could arise in the first singular (e.g. CĪRCŌ > Old French *serc* 'I search' and CĪRCAS > Old French *serches* 'you search'), but was eliminated by analogy.

6.6.4   Patterns of allomorphy

In alternating paradigms, the distribution of allomorphs is not random, nor always entirely conditioned by sound changes. Rather, each language has certain favored patterns of allomorphy to which verbs may analogize.

Spanish has three major templates. One is the boot shape for vowel alternations:

1st sg.	1st pl.
2nd sg.	2nd pl.
3rd sg.	3rd pl.

Two sets of verbs conform to this template: the type *vuelvo volvemos* 'return' (§ 6.6.1), and the type *mido medimos* 'measure' (§ 6.6.2). It is common for verbs to be adjusted to match the template. For example:

SĔNTĪRE 'feel'	Expected forms	Analogical forms	SĔRVĪRE 'serve'	Expected forms	Analogical forms
SĔNTĬŌ	*sento	siento	SĔRVĬŌ	*servo	sirvo
SĔNTĪS	sientes		SĔRVĪS	*sierves	sirves
SĔNTĬT	siente		SĔRVĬT	*sierve	sirve
SĔNTĪMŬS	sentimos		SĔRVĪMŬS	servimos	
SĔNTĪTĬS	sentís		SĔRVĪTĬS	servís	
*SĔNTĔNT	sienten		*SĔRVĔNT	*sierven	sirven

The first singular forms *sento* and *servo* reflect metaphonic raising of low mid [ɛ] to high mid [e]. The analogical changes bring the paradigm into line with one or the other of the two types of verb that exhibit the boot pattern.[16] Analogy is at work here, but does not eliminate allomorphy.

Another template in Spanish has an allomorph confined to the first singular:

1st sg.	1st pl.
2nd sg.	2nd pl.
3rd sg.	3rd pl.

It originates in verbs with a stem-final velar such as *hago haces* and *conozco conoces* (§ 6.6.3). Only in the first singular does a back vowel follow the velar.

There is a third template that combines the preceding two, resulting in three allomorphs:

1st sg.	1st pl.
2nd sg.	2nd pl.
3rd sg.	3rd pl.

The verbs *tener* and *venir* exemplify this pattern. An anomalous first singular (§ 6.8) makes their stem-vowel alternation diverge from the boot pattern.

TĔNĒRE	tener	VĔNĪRE	venir
'hold'		'come'	
TĔNĔŌ	tengo	VĔNĬŌ	vengo
TĔNĒS	tienes	VĔNĪS	vienes
TĔNĔT	tiene	VĔNĬT	viene
TĔNĒMUS	tenemos	VĔNĪMŬS	venimos
TĔNĒTIS	tenéis	VĔNĪTĬS	venís
TĔNĔNT	tienen	*VĔNĔNT	vienen

Italian has three main patterns of allomorphy. For verbs with two allomorphs, besides the boot template shared with Spanish, there is another reflecting the affinity between first singular and third plural forms (§ 6.6.3):

1st sg.	1st pl.		1st sg.	1st pl.
2nd sg.	2nd pl.		2nd sg.	2nd pl.
3rd sg.	3rd pl.		3rd sg.	3rd pl.

The first template is exemplified by verbs like *cuocio cociamo* 'cook' (§ 6.6.1), and the second by verbs like *leggo leggiamo* 'read' (§ 6.6.3). The complement of the *cuocio* type forms in the first template consists of the arhizotonic forms *cociamo cocete*, which thus form an affinity of their own between first and second plural. The two templates have a unique way of combining in verbs with three allomorphs:

1st sg.	1st pl.
2nd sg.	2nd pl.
3rd sg.	3rd pl.

The three-part template is exemplified (as in Spanish) by the verbs *tenere* and *venire*.

TĚNĒRE	tenere	VĚNĪRE	venire
'hold'		'come'	
TĚNĚŌ	tengo	VĚNĬŌ	vengo
TĚNĒS	tieni	VĚNĪS	vieni
TĚNĚT	tiene	VĚNĬT	viene
TĚNĒMUS	teniamo	VĚNĪMŬS	veniamo
TĚNĒTIS	tenete	VĚNĪTĬS	venite
*TĚNŬNT	tengono	VĚNĬŬNT	vengono

French too has three main patterns of allomorphy. Alternations conditioned by stress alone conform to the boot template shared with Italian and Spanish. Alternations involving the stem-final consonant conform to another pattern, unique to French: singular versus plural.

1st sg.	1st pl.
2nd sg.	2nd pl.
3rd sg.	3rd pl.

1st sg.	1st pl.
2nd sg.	2nd pl.
3rd sg.	3rd pl.

The first template is exemplified by *meurs mourons* 'die', *mène menons* 'lead', *acquiers acquérons* 'acquire' (§ 6.6.1). For the second template our examples were *vis vivons* 'live', *vaux valons* 'be worth' (§ 6.6.3). When one template is superimposed on the other the result is:

1st sg.	1st pl.
2nd sg.	2nd pl.
3rd sg.	3rd pl.

The verbs *devoir* and *venir* exemplify this pattern. They exhibit both stem-consonant allomorphy (consonant retention in the plural) and stress-induced vowel allomorphy (diphthongs in the rhizotonic forms).

DĒBĒRE	devoir	VĚNĪRE	venir
'owe'		'come'	
DĒBĚŌ	dois	VĚN(Ĭ)Ō	viens
DĒBĒS	dois	VĚNĪS	viens
DĒBĚT	doit	VĚNĬT	vient

DĒBĒMUS	devons	VĔNĪMŬS	venons
DĒBĒTIS	devez	VĔNĪTĬS	venez
DĒBĔNT	doivent	VĔN(Ī)ŬNT	viennent

Many verbs gravitate to this pattern on the way from Old French to Modern French. One is *pouvoir* 'be able'. The starting point is PŎTĒRE 'be able', a Popular Latin creation (replacing Classical PŎSSE) which loses its [t] by lenition in Old French, and then gets a hiatus-breaking [v], probably by analogy with *devoir* 'owe' (above) and *savoir* (§ 6.7).

Latin	Old French	Modern French
PŎTĒRE	poeir	pouvoir
'be able'		
PŎT(Ĕ)Ō	pui	peux
PŎTĒS	puez	peux
PŎTĔT	puet	peut
PŎTĒMUS	poöns	pouvons
PŎTĒTIS	poëz	pouvez
PŎTĔNT	pueënt	peuvent

In Modern French, an analogical first singular *peux* serves to level the singular forms.[17] The new analogical plurals all share a stem-final consonant. The stem vowel, however, being stress-conditioned, conforms to the boot pattern. The result is three allomorphs: [pø] [puv] [pœv] conforming to our third template. Again, we learn from this example that the force of analogy does not necessarily simplify the paradigm, and may just assimilate it to an established model (cf. Spanish *sentir, servir* above). But typically, the force of analogy decreases (or, more rarely, increases) the number of allomorphs in a paradigm, as we see next.

6.7   Paradigm leveling

Verb allomorphy in the Romance languages would be much more extensive were it not for **paradigm leveling**, that is, analogical remodeling that reduces the number of allomorphs (not always to just one).

Latin	Old Italian	Italian	Popular Latin	Expected	Italian
PRŎBĀRE	provare	provare	QUĔRĔRE	chiedere	chiedere[18]
'try'			'ask'		
PRŎBŌ	pruovo	provo	QUĔRŌ	chiedo	chiedo
PRŎBĀS	pruove	provi	QUĔRĬS	chiedi	chiedi
PRŎBĂT	pruova	prova	QUĔRĬT	chiede	chiede

PRŎBĀMŬS	provamo	proviamo	*QUĔRĬMŬS	*chedemo	chiediamo
*PRŎBĀTE	provate	provate	*QUĔRĬTE	*chedete	chiedete
PRŎBĂNT	pruovano	provano	QUĔRŬNT	chiedono	chiedono

Both verbs formerly had an alternating paradigm resulting from regular sound change, but today they have a single invariant stem.

Question: How do these two instances of paradigm leveling differ?

Answer: In *provare* the unstressed stem prevails, while in *chiedere* the stressed stem prevails.

There is no telling which allomorph will spread in cases of leveling. Further examples:

Popular Latin	Old Italian	Italian	Popular Latin	Old Italian	Italian
*NŎTĀRE	notare	nuotare	NĔGĀRE	negare	negare
'swim'			'deny'		
*NŎTŌ	nuoto	nuoto	NĔGŌ	niego	nego
*NŎTĀS	nuote	nuoti	NĔGĀS	nieghe	neghi
*NŎTĂT	nuota	nuota	NĔGĂT	niega	nega
*NŎTĀMŬS	notamo	nuotiamo	NĔGĀMŬS	negamo	neghiamo
*NŎTĀTE	notate	nuotate	*NĔGĀTE	negate	negate
*NŎTĂNT	nuotano	nuotano	NĔGĂNT	niegano	negano

Italian has leveled nearly all the paradigms where it formerly had stem-vowel alternations. Perhaps a less obvious case of leveling, since stem-vowel allomorphy is still tolerated, is this one:

Popular Latin			
*CŎCĔRE	cuocere		
'cook'			
*CŎCŌ	cuocio	[kwɔtʃo]
*CŎCĬS	cuoci	[kwɔtʃi]
*CŎCĬT	cuoce	[kwɔtʃe]
*CŎCĬMŬS	cociamo	[kɔtʃjamo]
*CŎCĬTE	cocete	[kɔtʃete]
*CŎCŬNT	cuociono	[kwɔtʃono]

Question: How do we know that the shaded segments are analogical?

Answer: Popular Latin *CŎCŌ, *CŎCŬNT should give Italian *cuoco, *cuocono.

Even supposing a source *CŎCĪŌ, the result should be *coccio with gemination blocking the stressed syllable and precluding the diphthong (like nuocere, below). Conclusion: [ʧ] must have spread by analogy to the first singular and third plural. Rather than three allomorphs, *[kwɔk], [kwɔʧ], [kɔʧ], there are now two – another example of paradigm leveling.

Some Italian verbs even reduce from four to three allomorphs. Each paradigm below contains a finite form analogically adjusted to conform to the favored three-part template:

Latin	Old Italian	Modern Italian	Latin	Modern Italian
*MŎRĪRE	morire	morire	NŎCĒRE	nuocere
'die'			'harm'	
*MŎRĬŌ	muoio	muoio	NŎCĒŌ	noccio
*MŎRĪS	muori	muori	NŎCĒS	nuoci
*MŎRĬT	muore	muore	NŎCĒT	nuoce
*MŎRĪMŬS	moiamo	moriamo	NŎCĒMUS	nociamo
*MŎRĪTĬS	morite	morite	NŎCĒTIS	nocete
*MŎRĬŬNT	muoiono	muoiono	*NŎCŬNT	nocciono

Morire has [wɔ] in its root-stressed forms. It also reflects the Italian change [rj] > [j] as in paio (note 15 above and § 4.3.11). Modern Italian moriamo has analogized to morite, illustrating the affinity between first and second plural. Although nuocere shifted to class III, noccio still reflects a class II form NŎCĒŌ. This regular geminate [ʧ:] blocks the syllable and impedes diphthongization (§ 5.1.1). The third plural, as usual, matches the first singular (*NŎCŬNT would have yielded *nuocono). The first and second plural match, as expected.

In Spanish the class of verbs with stem-vowel allomorphy has gained some members (§ 6.6.4, § 6.8) and lost others to leveling. Examples of leveling are:

Latin	Old Spanish	Modern Spanish	Latin	Old Spanish	Modern Spanish
CONFŎRTĀRE	confortar	confortar	VĔTĀRE	vedar	vedar
'comfort'			'forbid'		
CONFŎRTŌ	confuerto	conforto	VĔTŌ	viedo	vedo
CONFŎRTĀS	confuertas	confortas	VĔTĀS	viedas	vedas
CONFŎRTĂT	confuerta	conforta	VĔTĂT	vieda	veda
CONFŎRTĀMŬS	confortamos	confortamos	VĔTĀMŬS	vedamos	vedamos
CONFŎRTĀTIS	confortades	confortáis	VĔTĀTIS	vedades	vedáis
CONFŎRTĂNT	confuertan	confortan	VĔTĂNT	viedan	vedan

Stem-consonant allomorphy, however, has been mostly effaced between Old Spanish and today's Spanish. For example:

Popular Latin	Old Spanish	Modern Spanish	Popular Latin	Old Spanish	Modern Spanish
*CŎCĔRE 'cook'		cocer	*ERĪGĔRE 'straighten'		erguir
*CŎCŌ	cuego	cuezo	*ERĪGĔŌ	yergo	yergo[19]
*CŎCĒS	cueces	cueces	*ERĪGĒS	yerzes	yergues
*CŎCĔT	cuece	cuece	*ERĪGĔT	yerze	yergue
*CŎCĒMŬS	cocemos	cocemos	*ERĪGĒMŬS	erzemos	erguimos
*CŎCĒTĬS	cocedes	cocéis	*ERĪGĒTĬS	erzedes	erguís
*CŎCĔNT	cuecen	cuecen	*ERĪGĔNT	yerzen	yerguen

Question: How do these two examples of leveling differ?

Answer: In *cocer* the first singular changes to match the rest ([s/θ]), while in *erguir* the velar of the first singular prevailed throughout the paradigm ([g]), a much rarer pattern.

In French, given its history of drastic sound change, allomorphy in verbs ran rampant, but has since been tamed by paradigm leveling.

Latin	Old French	Modern French	Latin	Old French	Modern French
LAVĀRE 'wash'	laver	laver	AMĀRE 'love'	amer	aimer
LAVŌ	lef	lave	AMŌ	aim	aime
LAVĀS	leves	laves	AMĀS	aimes	aimes
LAVĂT	levet	lave	AMĂT	aimet	aime
LAVĀMUS	lavons	lavons	AMĀMUS	amons	aimons
LAVĀTIS	lavez	lavez	AMĀTIS	amez	aimez
LAVĂNT	levent	lavent	AMĂNT	aiment	aiment

Question: How do these two instances of paradigm leveling differ?

Answer: In *aimer* the stressed stem prevails, while in *laver* the unstressed stem prevails.

The verbs NĔCĀRE 'kill' and NĔGĀRE 'deny' should have become homonymous in French with two allomorphs each. Instead, both have been leveled, but in opposite directions:

Latin	Old French	Modern French	Latin	Old French	Modern French
NĔCĀRE 'kill'	neyer	noyer 'drown'	NĔGĀRE 'deny'	neyer	nier

NĔCŌ	nie	noie	NĔGŌ	nie	nie
NĔCĀS	nies	noies	NĔGĀS	nies	nies
NĔCĂT	niet	noie	NĔGĂT	niet	nie
NĔCĀMUS	neyons	noyons	NĔGĀMUS	neyons	nions
NĔCĀTIS	neyez	noyez	NĔGĀTIS	neyez	niez
NĔCĂNT	nient	noient	NĔGĂNT	nient	nient

Rhizotonic forms like NĔCĂT and NĔGĂT should have both become [njɛjəθ], then [niəθ] by triphthong reduction in Old French (§ 5.3.4). Arhizotonic forms like NĔCĀMUS and NĔGĀMUS should both give [nejõns], ultimately [nwajõ]. Instead, each verb chose one allomorph and spread it throughout the paradigm.

Not all instances of leveling in French result in an invariant stem. Leveling in *savoir* 'know' reduces the count of allomorphs from three to two.

Popular Latin	Old French	Modern French
*SAPĒRE	saveir	savoir
'know'		
*SAPĔŌ	sai	sais
*SAPĒS	sais	sais
*SAPĔT	sait	sait
*SAPĒMUS	savons	savons
*SAPĒTIS	savez	savez
*SAPĔNT	sevent	savent

Regular sound change takes SAPĔNT to *sevent*, which later levels to *savent*, bringing the paradigm into line with the typical French singular versus plural template.

6.8   Paradigm disleveling

Sometimes the force of analogy increases allomorphy, making a non-alternating paradigm into an alternating one. There are far fewer examples of paradigm disleveling than of leveling. Examples from Spanish are:

Popular Latin	Expected	Spanish	Classical Latin	Expected	Spanish
*FĬNDĒRE	hender	hender	RĬGĀRE	regar	regar
'split'			'water'		
*FĬNDŌ	*hendo	hiendo	RĬGŌ	*rego	riego
*FĬNDĒS	*hendes	hiendes	RĬGĀS	*regas	riegas
*FĬNDĔT	*hende	hiende	RĬGĂT	*rega	riega
*FĬNDĒMŬS	hendemos	hendemos	RĬGĀMŬS	regamos	regamos
*FĬNDĒTĬS	hendéis	hendéis	RĬGĀTĬS	regáis	regáis
*FĬNDĔNT	*henden	hienden	RĬGĂNT	*regan	riegan

The stem vowel of *hender* and *regar* came from high mid /e/ and should not diph-thongize. These verbs have analogized to the class of verbs where these alterna-tions arise by regular sound change (*perder* etc.).

Verbs like PŌNŌ 'I put' > Italian *pongo* tell another story of analogical cre-ation of allomorphs. The process originates in the Latin verbs that already had stem-final [ŋg]. Before a front vowel, Latin [ŋg] yields Old Italian [ɲ] (or [n̪dʒ] in other dialects, not relevant here). Thus, these verbs have *-ngo* and *-ngono* alternating with *-gni* [ɲi] etc. Then [ɲ] spreads by analogy to the whole paradigm. So, for example, *frango* [fraŋgo] 'I break' acquires a variant *fragno* [fraɲo]:

Latin	Old Italian		Adding variants
FRANGĔRE	fragnere	[ɲ]	
'break'			
FRANGŌ	frango	[ŋg]	fragno, frango
FRANGĬS	fragni	[ɲ]	
FRANGĬT	fragne	[ɲ]	
*FRANGĬMŬS	fragnemo	[ɲ]	
*FRANGĬTĬS	fragnete	[ɲ]	
FRANGŪNT	frangono	[ŋg]	fragnono, frangono

The coexistence of these variants (rightmost column above) sets the stage for a spread in the opposite direction. Verbs of the type TĔNĒŌ 'I hold' (class II) and VĔNĬŌ/VĔNĬŪNT 'I/they come' (class IV), thanks to the Popular Latin [j] in these forms, go on to develop in Old Italian a stem-final [nj] > [ɲ]. This brings them into the orbit of verbs like *fragno/frango*. The analogical equation is:

$$\text{OIt } [fraɲo] : [fraŋgo] = [veɲo] : [veŋgo]$$

On the model of variants *fragno/frango*, verbs like VĔNĬŌ > *vegno* add the second variant, an analogical *vengo*. Likewise alongside VĔNĬŪNT > *vegnono* an ana-logical *vengono* arises.

The pattern spreads in two ways. Class II TĔNĒRE has a third plural TĔNĔNT lacking a yod. But given the Italian affinity between first singulars and third plurals (§ 6.6.4), *tengo* becomes the model for an analogical *tengono*.

The pattern also spreads to verbs like PŌNĔRE 'put' that never had a yod to initiate the process anywhere in the present indicative paradigm:

PŌNŌ	pongo
PŌNĬS	poni
PŌNĬT	pone
*PŌNĬMŬS	poniamo
*PŌNĬTĬS	ponete
PŌNŪNT	pongono

Pongo is clearly analogical (and brought *pongono* with it). But the model is harder to identify. Perhaps *pongo* was simply attracted to *tengo, vengo*, etc. But more likely, the Italian first plural was a model:

OIt [veɲjamo] : [veŋgo] = [poɲjamo] : [poŋgo]

Spanish, via the same analogical process, created *tengo, vengo*, and *pongo*. But unlike Italian, Spanish does not pair up its third plural with its first singular, hence *tienen, vienen*, and *ponen* without [g].[20, 21]

The model of *tengo* etc. found reinforcement in a few common verbs where a first singular stem allomorph ending in [g] came straight from Popular Latin, such as DĪCŌ 'I say', DĪCES 'you say' *digo dices* and FAC(I)Ō 'I do', FACIS 'you do' *hago haces*. The first singular [g] stem made further analogical gains between Old Spanish and Modern Spanish (for discussion see Penny 2002:176–178):

Latin		Old Spanish	Modern Spanish
AUDIŌ	'I hear'	oyo	oigo
CADŌ	'I fall'	cayo	caigo
TRAHŌ	'I drag'	trayo	traigo

6.9   A stem extender: *-sc-*

Latin has an affix *-sc-* which extends the stems of verbs and conveys an **inchoative** meaning (entry into a state) as in: FLORĒRE 'bloom', FLORESCĔRE 'begin to bloom'. A number of Latin verbs had the affix inherently: CRESCĔRE 'grow', ADOLESCĔRE 'become adult', VESPERASCĔRE 'become evening', COGNOSCĔRE 'get to know'. In the Popular Latin of Italy and France this *-sc-* began to be added to a subset of class IV verbs, losing its inchoative meaning, a process known as *semantic bleaching.* From its association with class IV, the affix is now synchronically *-isc-*.

Italian	French
finire	finir
finisco	finis
finisci	finis
finisce	finit
finiamo	finissons
finite	finissez
finiscono	finissent

The Italian distribution (no *-isc-* in the first and second plural) shows that *-isc-* is synchronically an affix: it is used only where needed to make the forms arhizotonic, and conforms to the principal pattern of stress-induced allomorphy. In French it occurs throughout the paradigm.[22] At first glance you might not see the presence of -*isc*- in a form like French *finit* 'finishes'. But without the -*isc*- we would have FINĪT > *fint* [fɛ̃]. In Spanish there is no evidence that -*sc*- was ever segmented out as an affix in the verbs where it occurs. It simply figures as a part of the stem throughout the paradigm: *obedecer* 'obey', *agradecer* 'thank', *establecer* 'establish', *blanquecer* 'turn white', etc.[23]

Popular Latin	Spanish
*FLORESCĒRE	florecer
'bloom'	
*FLORESCŌ	florezco
*FLORESCĒS	floreces
*FLORESCĒT	florece
*FLORESCĒMŪS	florecemos
*FLORESCĒTĬS	florecéis
*FLORESCĒNT	florecen

Before front vowels (everywhere except first singular), [sk] gives [ts] > [s] or [θ] according to region. Thus, the verbs from original inchoatives conform to one of the favored templates for Spanish allomorphy, an allomorph confined to the first singular (§ 6.6.3).

The class has also attracted new members: verbs like Old Spanish *yazer* having stem-final velars in the first singular replace the stem ending in -*g* with one ending in -*zc* from the inchoative paradigm.

Latin	Old Spanish	Modern Spanish	Latin	Old Spanish	Modern Spanish
IACĒRE	yazer	yacer	PLACĒRE	plazer	placer
'lie down'			'please'		
IACEŌ	yago	yazco	PLACEŌ	plago	plazco
IACĒS	yazes	yaces	PLACĒS	plazes	places
IACĒT	yaze	yace	PLACĒT	plaze	place
IACĒMŪS	yazemos	yacemos	PLACĒMŪS	plazemos	placemos
IACĒTĬS	yazedes	yacéis	PLACĒTĬS	plazedes	placéis
IACĒNT	yazen	yacen	PLACĒNT	plazen	placen

In French, the class of verbs with the affix from -*isc*- has greatly expanded to comprise almost all verbs ending in -*ir*.

6.10   Some truly irregular verbs: be, have, go

We have seen that "irregularities" in the present indicative tend to fall into certain regular patterns. However, in a few high-frequency verbs, genuine anomalies have been inherited or created. Different sources of irregularity are exemplified here with three sample verbs.

6.10.1   Outcomes of ESSE 'be'

Latin ESSE 'be' was already truly irregular. Popular Latin regularized only the infinitive, creating a class III ESSĔRE which continues in Italian (*essere*) and French ([ɛsːere] > [ɛsrə] > [ɛstrə] > [ɛtʀ] *être*), whereas Spanish replaced it with SĔDĒRE > *ser*.[24]

Latin	Italian	Spanish	French	
ESSE	essere	ser	être	[ɛtr]
SŬM	sono	soy	suis	[sɥi]
ĔS	sei	eres	es	[ɛ]
ĔST	è	es	est	[ɛ]
SŬMŬS	siamo	somos	sommes	[sɔm]
ĔSTĬS	siete	sois	êtes	[ɛt]
SŬNT	sono	son	sont	[sɔ̃]

In Italian, SŬM and SŬNT converge to Old Italian *son*. The first singular adds analogical *-o*, which then spreads to the third plural (§ 6.3.6). In the Popular Latin of Italy, the initial <s> of SŬM SŬMŬS SŬNT spread to form second singular *SĔS and second plural *SĒTĬS. The rule final [s] > [j] gives *sei* directly. In *siete* the diphthong is regular in a free syllable, and the ending *-te* matches all other second plurals.[25] In place of SŬMŬS, Old Italian had *semo*, predictably replaced by Modern Italian *siamo* (§ 6.3.4).

In Spanish, the non-etymological forms are *soy*, *eres*, and *sois*. SŬM gives regular *so*, which remains until the 1500s. How and why *so* became *soy* (and *esto*, *do*, *vo* became *estoy*, *doy*, *voy*) is controversial. Lloyd (1987:355–358) surveys six competing hypotheses, but deems plausible only two of them. One posits false segmentation of a postposed subject (*so yo* [soj:o] > *soy yo*). The other takes *soy* to be parallel to *hay* 'there is', known to consist of *ha* plus the locative clitic *y* < IBI.[26] To forestall homonymy of ĔS > *es* and ĔST > *es*, Spanish replaced the second singular with ĔRIS, salvaged from the moribund future paradigm of ESSE (§ 7.8.2). In the Popular Latin of Spain, an analogical *SŬTĬS arose on the model SŬM, SŬMŬS, SŬNT. Regular sound changes gave Old Spanish *sodes*, which became modern *sois*.

Of the French forms the most problematic is *suis*. Pope (1934:360) says: "The form *sui* appears to have been influenced by *fui* ['was', preterite from FUIT] but is not yet fully explained." But once we posit a final yod, albeit mysterious (perhaps *[sujo] modeled on *[ajo] < HABĔŌ),[27] the development to [sɥi] is regular (§ 5.3.5). In either case, today's orthographic final <s> is analogical (§ 6.5.1). The only irregularity in Old French *somes* [somǝs] and *estes* [ɛstǝs] is the preservation of the unstressed vowel of the final syllable. Later developments effaced [ə], and both preconsonantal and final [s], yielding today's *sommes* [sɔm] and *êtes* [ɛt]. For details see Fouché (1967:417 419) and Pope (1934:360).

6.10.2   Outcomes of HABĒRE 'have'

HABĒRE, unlike ESSE, was entirely regular. But as it came to be used as an auxiliary, it was subject to unusual phonetic attrition. The infinitive in all three languages is regular. Throughout these paradigms, <h> is purely a graphic reminiscence of the Latin etymon.

Latin	Popular Latin	Italian	Spanish	French
HABĒRE	*[aβere]	avere	haber	avoir
HABĔŌ	*[ajo], *[aw]	ho	he	ai
HABĒS	*[as]	hai	has	as
HABĔT	*[at]	ha	ha	a
HABĒMUS	*[aβemos]	abbiamo	hemos	avons
HABĒTIS	*[aβetis]	avete	habéis	avez
HABĔNT	*[ant]	hanno	han	ont

From *[ajo] Old Italian has *aggio* 'I have'. But *avere* belongs to a small, closed club of high-frequency verbs united by mutual analogical influences. Alongside attested *sao* 'I know', *vao* 'I go', and *fao* 'I do', we can posit **ao* 'I have', **dao* 'I give', and **stao* 'I stand', all of which would reduce to attested forms *so, vo, fo, ho, do, sto*. Even if **ao* never existed, the other verbs of the club would foster the creation of *ho*. Likewise *hai hanno* belong to a pattern shared among the six verbs. The geminate [n:] in these third plurals is variously explained (Maiden 1995:131, Tekavčić 1972:458).

The Spanish forms are regular from Popular Latin, except for *he* and *hemos*. Lloyd (1987:298) posits *[ajo] > [ej] > [e] *he*. Old Spanish, alongside *avemos avedes*, also had *emos edes* by **apheresis** (word-initial truncation), of which *hemos* survives.

Directly from *[ajo], Old French has [aj], which regularly yields Modern French [e] *ai*. For *ont*, Fouché (1967:432) agrees with Pope (1934:360) that there was an intermediate **HABŬNT > [awnt] > [ɔ̃nt] > [ɔ̃] which Fouché attributes to influence from SŬNT, hence the modern parallel *sont* [sɔ̃], *ont* [ɔ̃].

6.10.3   The verb 'go'

Romance verbs for 'go' combine forms drawn from three sources, possibly four, listed below. The convergence of formerly unrelated forms into one paradigm is called **suppletion**.

Latin			Popular Latin	Italian	Spanish	French
ĪRE	AMBŬLĀRE	VADĔRE		andare	ir	aller
'go'	'walk'	'go'				
ĔŌ	AMBŬLŌ	VADŌ	*[vaw]	vado	voy	vais
ĪS	AMBŬLĀS	VADĬS	*[va(j)s]	vai	vas	vas
ĬT	AMBŬLĂT	VADĬT	*[va(j)t]	va	va	va
ĪMŬS	AMBŬLĀMUS	VADĬMŬS		andiamo	vamos	allons
ĪTĬS	AMBŬLĀTIS	VADĪTĬS		andate	vais	allez
ĔŬNT	AMBŬLĂNT	VADŬNT	*[va(w)nt]	vanno	van	vont

Italian *andare, andiamo, andate* probably derive from AMBŬLĀRE 'go, walk' with the extra phonetic attrition often seen in high-frequency verbs:

AMBŬLĀRE > [amlare] > [amnare] > [annare] > [andare][28]

Another possible source is *AMBITARE 'go around' (Anderson and Rochet 1979:267, Elcock 1960:127). Spanish *ir* 'go' continues Latin ĪRE.[29] French *aller*, whatever its source, already appears in a Latinized form ALARE as early as the 700s.[30] It may be a drastically reduced form of AMBŬLĀRE. Another idea, neglected but intriguing, invokes the highly irregular past participle LATUS from FERRE 'carry'. Its compound ADFERRE 'bring, convey' might well form phrases like SE *ALLATUS EST 'went (betook himself)' which in turn could suggest an infinitive *ALLARE (Parker 1934, following Bauer 1878).

VADĔRE supplies all the remaining forms in all three languages. Like the auxiliaries, it developed reduced forms in Popular Latin. Italian *[vaw] > *vo* is regular, while *vado* is a restored, more conservative form (cf. *[faw] > *fo* 'I do' alongside [fakjo] > *faccio* 'I do'). Italian *vai, va, vanno* are parallel to *hai, ha, hanno* and other verbs of their club.

Modern Spanish *voy* from Old Spanish *vo* is poorly understood, as mentioned above (§ 6.10.1). From ĪMŬS, ĪTĬS Old Spanish had *imos, ides*, replaced by the syncopated reflexes of VADĬMŬS and VADĪTĬS, *vamos, vais*.[31]

French *vais* looks deceptively simple. But from Popular Latin *[vaw] it should be *[vo]. Moreover, Old French *vois* would remain unexplained. Pope (1934:362) suggests an analogical source: on the model of TRANSĔŌ 'I go' > *[trasjo], Old French created *[vawsjo], which becomes [vojs] (§ 5.3.1). By regular developments [vojs] > [vwɛs] > [vwɛ] > [vɛ].[32] Although early lenition took VADĬT to Old French *vait* [vajθ], the winning form was analogical *va* on the model of *avoir*: i.e. *as : a = vas : va*. *Vont*, the regular outcome of *[vawnt], falls into line with the third plurals of *être* and *avoir* (*sont, ont*) and may even have fostered the above-mentioned *[awnt] > *ont* (§ 6.10.2).

Exercises

1. These English verbs are borrowed from French. Are they borrowed from the infinitive? Explain. List some other members of this class.

Old French	English
accomplir	accomplish
brunir	burnish
chérir	cherish
eskermir	skirmish
esvanir	vanish
finir	finish
polir	polish
punir	punish
replenir	replenish

2. Old Italian was remarkably tolerant of variants, as is Modern Italian, to a lesser extent. This chart shows some variants in the conjugation of It *sedere* 'be seated'. Only the last of each group is standard today. Explain the origin of each form.

    SĔDĒRE
    'sit'

SĔD(Ĕ)Ō	seggio, seggo, siedo
SĔDĒS	
SĔDĔT	
SĔDĒMUS	sedemo, seggiamo, sediamo
SĔDĒTIS	
SĔDĔNT	seggiono, seggono, siedono

    In the verb *vedere* 'see', what Old Italian variants would you expect to find?

VĪD(Ĕ)Ō	– – – – – – – – – – – – – –
VĪDĒS	
VĪDĔT	
VĪDĒMUS	– – – – – – – – – – – – – –
VĪDĒTIS	
VĪDENT	– – – – – – – – – – – – – –

3. A lexical love story
    Once upon a time in Italy there were two etymologically unrelated words: ŌSTĬU 'door, portal' and EXĪRE 'go/come out', a compound of ĪRE 'go'. There was no special link between them. But as time went on, they had more and more in common. Today they are practically inseparable:

Latin	Popular Latin	Italian		
ŌSTĬU	[ostju]	uscio	[uʃːo]	'exit' (noun)
EXĪRE	[eksire]	uscire	[uʃːire]	'exit' (verb)
EXĔŌ	[eksjo]	esco	[ɛsko]	
EXĪS	[eksis]	esci	[ɛʃːi]	

EXĬT	[eksit]	esce	[εʃːe]
EXĪMŬS	[eksimus]	usciamo	[uʃːamo]
EXĪTĬS	[eksitis]	uscite	[uʃːite]
EXĔŬNT	[eksjunt]	escono	[εskono]

Does regular sound change account for the noun *uscio*? For the verb *uscire*? For all the finite forms of *uscire*? If these words were attracted to each other because of shared meaning, why is there still allomorphy? Comment on its distribution.

4. How do you account for the analogical (shaded) forms in Spanish? Hint: consider verbs like *pedir* (§ 6.6.2).

Latin	Expected outcome	Spanish	Popular Latin of Spain	Expected outcome	Spanish
RĪDĒRE 'laugh'	*rier	reír	*DĪCĒRE 'say'	*dicer	decir
RĪD(Ē)Ō	río	río	*DĪC(Ē)Ō	digo	digo
RĪDĒS	ríes	ríes	*DĪCĒS	dices	dices
RĪDĔT	ríe	ríe	*DĪCĔT	dice	dice
RĪDĒMUS	*riemos	reímos	*DĪCĒMUS	*dicemos	decimos
RĪDĒTIS	*riéis	reís	*DĪCĒTIS	*dicéis	decís
RĪDENT	ríen	ríen	*DĪCENT	dicen	dicen

5. *Volere* and *potere*

Lat VELLE 'want' was replaced by Pop Lat VŎLĒRE. In Old Italian, the distribution of allomorphs in the paradigm suggests the existence of a fourth template. How would you represent this template? Why do the diphthongs not occur in the boot pattern typical of stress-induced allomorphy? Are any of the Old Italian forms analogical? Note: *vuoi* is the Modern Italian second singular by regular change.

Lat PŎSSE 'be able' is irregular because it is a compound of ESSE 'be'. Which of these Old Italian forms come from Lat PŎSSE? Which are from Pop Lat PŎTĒRE? Explain the distribution of the diphthongs and comment on the Modern Italian forms *puoi* and *può*. What motivated the replacement of OIt *potemo* by modern *possiamo*?

Popular Latin	Old Italian		Classical Latin	Popular Latin	Old Italian	Modern Italian
VŎLĒRE	volere	[volere]	PŎSSE	PŎTĒRE	potere	potere
VŎL(Ē)Ō	voglio	[vɔʎːo]	PŎSSŬM	PŎT(Ē)Ō	posso	posso
VŎLĔS	vuoli > vuoi	[vwɔli]	PŎTĒS	PŎTĒS	puoti	puoi
VŎLĔT	vuole	[vwɔle]	PŎTĔST	PŎTĔT	puote	può
VŎLĒMŬS	vogliamo	[vɔʎːamo]	PŎSSŬMŬS	PŎTĒMŬS	potemo	possiamo
VŎLĒTĬS	volete	[volete]	PŎTĒSTĬS	PŎTĒTĬS	potete	potete
VŎLĔNT	vogliono	[vɔʎːono]	PŎSSŬNT	PŎTĔNT	possono	possono

6. Describe the sound changes from Lat CONSUĔRE 'sew' to Fr *coudre*. Why are its plural forms *cousons, cousez, cousent*, not *coudons, *coudez, *coudent*?

CONSUĒRE [konsuere]

[kosuere] ....

[kosere] ....

[kozere] ....

[kozrə] ....

[kuzrə] ....

[kuzdrə] ....

[kudrə] ....

[kudʀə] ....

[kudʀ] *coudre* ....

7. On the way from Old French to Modern French, [we] (written <ue>) and [wew] (written <ueu>) both became [ø] (written <eu>) in stressed free syllables. By another regular sound change, unstressed [o] becomes [u]. What *non-phonological* mechanisms have applied to yield the modern paradigm of *moudre* 'grind'? How do you explain the <d> in the singular forms (i.e. -*ds*, -*ds*, -*d*, not -*s*, -*s*, -*t*)?

Latin	Old French	Modern French	Latin	Old French	Modern French
*MŎVĒRE 'move'	moveir	mouvoir	MŎLĒRE 'grind'	moudre	moudre
*MŎV(Ē)Ō	muef	meus	MŎLŌ	muel	mouds
*MŎVĒS	mues	meus	MŎLĬS	mueus	mouds
*MŎVĒT	muet	meut	MŎLĬT	mueut	moud
*MŎVĒMŬS	movons	mouvons	*MŎLĬMŬS	molons	moulons
*MŎVĒTĬS	movez	mouvez	*MŎLĪTĬS	molez	moulez
*MŎVĒNT	muevent	meuvent	MŎLŬNT	muelent	moulent

8. These words show a sporadic change of [i] or [e] to round vowels [y], [o], or [u]:

Latin		Italian	Spanish	French
GEMELLU	'twin'			j**u**meau
BIBEBAT	'drank'			b**u**vait
EPISCOPUS	'bishop'		**o**bispo	
DEBILE	'weak'	deb**o**le		
REVERSAT	'overturns'	r**o**vescia		
DE-MANE	'tomorrow'	d**o**mani		
(IN-)DIVINAT	'guesses'	ind**o**vina		
*SIMILIAT	'resembles'	s**o**miglia		
-IBILE	'-ible'	-ev**o**le		

Considering what all the environments have in common, what two conditions favor the sporadic change?

From Lat DEBĒRE 'owe' Italian has a paradigm with stem alternation:

DEBĒRE   **do**vere

DEB(Ē)Ō   devo

DEBĒS	devi
DEBĔT	deve
DEBĒMUS	dobbiamo
DEBĒTIS	dovete
DEBĔNT	devono

Why do some of the stems have an [e] and others an [o]?

7   Verb morphology: systemic reorganization

The categories that figure in Latin finite verb morphology are all displayed below, but this book is not meant to teach Latin. What we do mean to show is how the Romance languages reorganize the Latin system, retaining some categories with their original morphology, retaining others with new or recycled morphology, and creating new categories unprecedented in Latin.

7.1   Map of the Latin verb system

The Latin verb system, itself the product of drastic innovation on the way from Indo-European, took on a squarish architecture characterized by three binary contrasts: voice (active and passive), mood (indicative and subjunctive), and aspect (infectum and perfectum), in addition to the familiar category of tense (present, past, and future). Chart 7.1 shows the complete conjugation of CANTĀRE 'sing' in the active voice. Its passive conjugation would occupy another chart of the same size (§ 7.9.4). This verb represents one of four conjugation classes. All four share identical endings in the perfectum.

From this display, what can we say about infectum forms and perfectum forms?

> Question: What do all perfectum forms in the chart have in common?
>
> Answer: They all begin with CANTĀV- [kan<u>taw</u>].

Every verb in Latin has one stem throughout the infectum and another throughout the perfectum. For CANTĀRE 'sing', the perfectum stem is CANTĀV- [kan<u>taw</u>].

7.1.1   About perfectum stems

The infectum stem appears in the present infinitive. Given the infinitive, you may be able to predict the perfectum stem. The perfectum in Latin had several

Chart 7.1

Active voice				
	INDICATIVE		SUBJUNCTIVE	
	Infectum	Perfectum	Infectum	Perfectum
p r e s e n t	(Present) CANTŌ CANTĀS CANTAT CANTĀMUS CANTĀTIS CANTANT	(Perfect) CANTĀVĪ CANTĀV ISTĪ CANTĀV IT CANTĀV IMUS CANTĀV ISTIS CANTĀV ERUNT	(Present) CANTEM CANTĒS CANTET CANTĒMUS CANTĒTIS CANTENT	(Perfect) CANTĀV ERIM CANTĀV ERĪS CANTĀV ERIT CANTĀV ERĪMUS CANTĀV ERĪTIS CANTĀV ERINT
p a s t	(Imperfect) CANTĀBAM CANTĀBĀS CANTĀBAT CANTĀBĀMUS CANTĀBĀTIS CANTĀBANT	(Pluperfect) CANTĀV ERAM CANTĀV ERĀS CANTĀV ERAT CANTĀV ERĀMUS CANTĀV ERĀTIS CANTĀV ERANT	(Imperfect) CANTĀREM CANTĀRĒS CANTĀRET CANTĀRĒMUS CANTĀRĒTIS CANTĀRENT	(Pluperfect) CANTĀV ISSEM CANTĀV ISSES CANTĀV ISSET CANTĀV ISSĒMUS CANTĀV ISSĒTIS CANTĀV ISSENT
f u t u r e	(Future) CANTĀBŌ CANTĀBIS CANTĀBIT CANTĀBIMUS CANTĀBITIS CANTĀBUNT	(Future Perfect) CANTĀV ERŌ CANTĀV ERIS CANTĀV ERIT CANTĀV ERIMUS CANTĀV ERITIS CANTĀV ERINT		

historical sources, and these are reflected in the four ways of forming stems: **waw** stems ([w]), **sigmatic** stems ([s]), long-vowel stems (V:), and reduplicated stems ([C₁V] > [C₁VC₁V]).

The waw stems are by far the most numerous. Virtually all verbs of class I (-ĀRE) and class IV (-ĪRE) have waw perfects. Waw perfects are common in the other conjugations too.

I	CANTĀRE	CANTĀV-IT	'he sang'
II	HABĒRE	HABŬ-IT	'he had'
III	GEMĔRE	GEMŬ-IT	'he groaned'
IV	DORMĪRE	DORMĪV-IT	'he slept'

Recall (§ 2.3.1) that Latin [w] in modern usage is spelled <U> when adjacent to a consonant and <V> otherwise. So, all the above examples have [w] as their perfect marker.

Sigmatic perfects are exemplified by:

SCRIBĔRE	SCRIPS-IT [bs] > [ps]	'he wrote'
DICĔRE	DIX-IT [ks]	'he said'

IUNGĔRE	IUNX-IT [gs] > [ks]	'he joined'
REMANĒRE	REMANS-IT	'he stayed'

Long vowels mark the perfect stem in such verbs as:

VĬDĒRE	VĪD-IT	'he saw'
CAPĔRE	CĒP-IT	'he seized'
FACĔRE	FĒC-IT	'he made'
VĔNĪRE	VĒN-IT	'he came'

Reduplicated stems, a much smaller class, include:

TANGĔRE	TETĬG-IT	'he touched'
POSCĔRE	POPOSC-IT	'he demanded'
TUNDĔRE	TUTUD-IT	'he beat'
CURRĔRE	CUCURR-IT	'he ran'

PRACTICE

These are Latin perfects in the third person singular. Identify the type of perfect marking: waw, sigmatic, long-vowel, or reduplicating.

LABORĀRE – LABORĀVIT 'worked'   PLANGĔRE – PLANXIT 'wept'

CANĔRE – CĔCĬNIT 'sang'   FINĪRE – FINĪVIT 'finished'   PLACĒRE – PLACŬIT 'pleased'

RĪDĒRE – RĪSIT 'laughed'   MORDĒRE – MOMŎRDIT 'bit'   FRANGĔRE – FRĒGIT 'broke'

ARDĒRE – ARSIT 'burned'   TACĒRE – TACŬIT 'kept silent'

7.1.2   Presence or absence of thematic vowel

We have seen all along how important stress position can be for Romance developments. Another zone where stress position has dramatic consequences is in the Romance synthetic pasts deriving from Latin perfects. Consider where the Latin Penultimate Rule places stress in these third singular perfects:

CANTĀRE	DELĒRE	PARTĪRE
'sing'	'destroy'	'depart'
CANTĀVIT	DELĒVIT	PARTĪVIT

In all these forms the stress is arhizotonic, falling right before the perfect marker [w] on a long vowel, Ā, Ē, or Ī, the **thematic vowel**. These arhizotonic forms are also known as **weak perfects**.

But many perfects, confined almost entirely to classes II and III, have no thematic vowel. Where does the Penultimate Rule place the stress in these perfects?

HABĒRE	VĪDĒRE	SCRĪBĔRE	DĪCĔRE	FACĔRE
'have'	'see'	'write'	'say'	'make'

HABŬIT	VĪDIT	SCRĪPSIT	DĪXIT	FĒCIT
[habwit]	[wiːdit]	[skriːpsit]	[diːksit]	[feːkit]

In all these forms the stress is rhizotonic. These **athematic perfects** (lacking a thematic vowel), known as **strong perfects**, are the main source of the irregular past tense forms in Romance (§§ 7.5.4–7).

> **PRACTICE**
>
> Of these perfect forms, which are strong and which are weak?
>
> AMĀVIT 'loved' POSŬIT 'put' ABOLĪVIT 'abolished' BĪBŬIT 'drank' MĪSIT 'put'
> PRECĀVIT 'prayed' MENTĪVIT 'lied' DIREXIT 'directed' AUDĪVIT 'heard'

Keep your eye on thematic vowels. They gain prominence in spoken Latin and become a force in shaping Romance verb systems. Stressed thematic vowels come to be the norm not only in Romance pasts (Chart 7.7), but also in other categories that have their origin in the Latin perfectum system.

7.2   How Romance reorganizes the Latin system

All categories of the Latin finite verb system – considered purely as categories – survive into Romance. Some categories, such as the present indicative, derive directly from Latin through regular sound change, plus analogical adjustments (§§ 6.6–8). But there are also systemic changes of two kinds. First, certain categories, though still existing as categories in Romance, begin to be expressed with morphology that in Classical Latin either did not exist or belonged to some other category. Second, Romance added two entirely new categories: the conditional, and the future subjunctive.

The three charts starting here show how the Popular Latin verb system took shape. The shaded parts represent respectively inherited morphology continuing into Romance, new or redeployed morphology, and new categories. These charts do not express chronology. In any form of language change, there is a period, possibly long, when the old and the new coexist in competition.

7.2.1   Old categories retaining original morphology

The forms expressing these four categories survived everywhere in early Romance.[1] (See Chart 7.2.)

The present indicative in Romance derives directly from the corresponding forms in Latin with the myriad analogical changes we saw in Chapter 6. The present subjunctive category and the forms that express it also persist into

Chart 7.2 Popular Latin: old categories with original morphology

'Active Voice'							
	Indicative				Subjunctive		
	Infectum		Perfectum		Infectum		Perfectum
p r e s e n t	(Present) CANTŌ CANTĀS CANTAT CANTĀMUS CANTĀTIS CANTANT		(Perfect) CANTĀVĪ CANTĀVISTĪ CANTĀVIT CANTĀVIMUS CANTĀVISTIS CANTĀVERUNT		(Present) CANTEM CANTĒS CANTET CANTĒMUS CANTĒTIS CANTENT		(Perfect)
p a s t	(Imperfect) CANTĀBAM CANTĀBĀS CANTĀBAT CANTĀBĀMUS CANTĀBĀTIS CANTĀBANT		(Pluperfect)[1]		(Imperfect)		(Pluperfect)
f u t u r e	(Future)		(Future Perfect)				

Romance with some adjustments (§ 7.3). Likewise, Romance retains the imperfect indicative with the inherited forms (§ 7.4). Finally, the Latin perfect indicative forms evolve into the Romance **synthetic** (one-piece) past, Italian *passato remoto*, Spanish *pretérito*, and French *passé simple* (§ 7.5), which have since seen new limits placed on their usage under pressure from the Romance **periphrastic** (two-piece) past (§ 7.9).

7.2.2   Old categories with non-original morphology

Certain categories existing in Classical Latin survive into Romance as categories, but have forms that either belonged to another category or were newly created in Romance. (See Chart 7.3.)

Romance imperfect subjunctives have two kinds of morphology, both recycled from elsewhere in the Latin system. Forms like CANTĀVERAT, originally pluperfect indicatives [A], and CANTĀVISSET, originally pluperfect subjunctives [B], both took on the value of imperfect subjunctive (§ 7.6).[2]

The Latin synthetic future (see Chart 7.1) was doomed. It was too similar to the imperfect indicative (CANTĀBIT – CANTĀBAT), and as its intervocalic [b] merged with [w] in Romance (§ 2.3.2), it was converging with the weak perfect indicative (CANTĀBIT – CANTĀVIT). The Latin synthetic future forms vanished and were replaced by a new periphrastic future (§ 7.8).

Chart 7.3 Popular Latin: old categories with non-original morphology

	Active voice					
	Indicative		Subjunctive			
	Infectum	Perfectum	Infectum		Perfectum	
p r e s e n t	(Present)	(Perfect)	(Present)		(Perfect)	
	CANTŌ	CANTĀVĪ	CANTEM			
	CANTĀS	CANTĀVISTĪ	CANTĒS			
	CANTAT	CANTĀVIT	CANTET			
	CANTĀMUS	CANTĀVIMUS	CANTĒMUS			
	CANTĀTIS	CANTĀVISTIS	CANTĒTIS			
	CANTANT	CANTĀVERUNT	CANTENT			
p a s t	(Imperfect)	(Pluperfect)	(Imperfect)		(Pluperfect)	
	CANTĀBAM		CANTĀVERAM	CANTĀVISSEM		
	CANTĀBĀS		CANTĀVERĀS	CANTĀVISSES		
	CANTĀBAT	[A] ⇒	CANTĀVERAT	CANTĀVISSET	⇐ [B]	
	CANTĀBĀMUS		CANTĀVERĀMUS	CANTĀVISSĒMUS		
	CANTĀBĀTIS		CANTĀVERĀTIS	CANTĀVISSĒTIS		
	CANTĀBANT		CANTĀVERANT	CANTĀVISSENT		
f u t u r e	(Future)	(Future Perfect)				
	CANTĀRE HABEŌ					
	CANTĀRE HABĒS					
	CANTĀRE HABET					
	CANTĀRE HABĒMUS					
	CANTĀRE HABĒTIS					
	CANTĀRE HABENT					

7.2.3   New categories

The Romance system adds three new categories unknown to Classical Latin: conditional, future subjunctive (§ 7.7), and inflected infinitive (§ 9.16.1). The last two are not Pan-Romance. (See Chart 7.4.)

Once Popular Latin had created a periphrastic future – consisting of an infinitive plus an auxiliary in the present tense – it was natural to allow the auxiliary to shift to another tense. The resulting "past of the future" took root in Romance grammars as the conditional (§ 7.8).

The Latin future indicative had no subjunctive counterpart, hence the conspicuous gap in Chart 7.1. Spanish and Portuguese (§ 9.7.4) filled this gap, creating a future subjunctive with morphology recycled from the Latin future perfect indicative [C] fused with the perfect subjunctive [D]. With this change, all the original morphology of the Latin perfectum system except the perfect indicative (and the pluperfect in Portuguese and Romanian, §§ 9.14.4, 10.6.5) had shifted to other functions or fallen into disuse. Already in Popular Latin, these synthetic forms were losing ground to the new periphrastic forms typical of Romance (§ 7.9).

Chart 7.4 Popular Latin: new categories

Active voice						
Indicative				Subjunctive		
Infectum		Perfectum		Infectum		Perfectum
	(Present)		(Perfect)		(Present)	(Perfect)
p **r** **e** **s** **e** **n** **t**	CANTŌ CANTĀS CANTAT CANTĀMUS CANTĀTIS CANTANT		CANTĀVĪ CANTĀVISTĪ CANTĀVIT CANTĀVIMUS CANTĀVISTIS CANTĀVERUNT		CANTEM CANTĒS CANTET CANTĒMUS CANTĒTIS CANTENT	[D] ⬇
p **a** **s** **t**	(Imperfect) CANTĀBAM CANTĀBĀS CANTĀBAT CANTĀBĀMUS CANTĀBĀTIS CANTĀBANT		(Pluperfect)		(Imperfect) CANTĀVERAM / CANTĀVISSEM CANTĀVERĀS / CANTĀVISSĒS CANTĀVERAT / CANTĀVISSET CANTĀVERĀMUS / CANTĀVISSĒMUS CANTĀVERĀTIS / CANTĀVISSĒTIS CANTĀVERANT / CANTĀVISSENT	(Pluperfect) ⬇
f **u** **t** **u** **r** **e**	(Future) CANTĀRE HABEŌ CANTĀRE HABĒS CANTĀRE HABET CANTĀRE HABĒMUS CANTĀRE HABĒTIS CANTĀRE HABENT		(Future Perfect) [C] ⇨		(Future) CANTĀVERIM CANTĀVERĪS CANTĀVERIT CANTĀVERĪMUS CANTĀVERĬTIS CANTĀVERINT	↩
c **o** **n** **d** **i** **t**	(Conditional)					
	CANTĀRE HABĒBAM CANTĀRE HABĒBĀS CANTĀRE HABĒBAT CANTĀRE HABĒBĀMUS CANTĀRE HABĒBĀTIS CANTĀRE HABĒBANT	~ HABUĪ ~ HABUISTĪ ~ HABUIT ~ HABUIMUS ~ HABUISTIS ~ HABUĒRUNT				

7.3   Present indicative and present subjunctive

Present indicative and present subjunctive existed in Latin and survive in all the Romance languages. The history of the present indicative is characterized by irregularities arising under sound change and gravitating into regular patterns under analogical pressure (Chapter 6). Present subjunctives developed in such a way as to mirror present indicatives, with which they now typically stand in a derivational relationship. Chart 7.5 shows the regular present subjunctive endings.

7.3.1   Present subjunctive in Italian

The first and second plural endings -iamo -iate, taken from Latin forms in -ĒĀMUS -ĒĀTIS (class II) and -ĬĀMUS -ĬĀTIS (classes IIIb and IV), were extended at

Chart 7.5 The present subjunctive

	Latin		Italian	Spanish	French
I	CANTEM	'I sing'	canti	cante	chante
	CANTĒS		canti	cantes	chantes
	CANTET		canti	cante	chante
	CANTĒMUS		cantiamo	cantemos	chantions
	CANTĒTIS		cantiate	cantéis	chantiez
	CANTENT		cantino	canten	chantent
II	VĬDEAM	'I see'	veda	vea	voie
	VĬDEĀS		veda	veas	voies
	VĬDEAT		veda	vea	voie
	VĬDEĀMUS		vediamo	veamos	voyions
	VĬDEĀTIS		vediate	veáis	voyiez
	VĬDEANT		vedano	vean	voient
IIIa	VĒNDAM	'I sell'	venda	venda	vende
	VĒNDĀS		venda	vendas	vendes
	VĒNDAT		venda	venda	vende
	VĒNDĀMUS		vendiamo	vendamos	vendions
	VĒNDĀTIS		vendiate	vendáis	vendiez
	VĒNDANT		vendano	vendan	vendent
IIIb	RECĬPĬAM	'I receive'	riceva	reciba	reçoive
	RECĬPĬĀS		riceva	recibas	reçoives
	RECĬPĬAT		riceva	reciba	reçoive
	RECĬPĬĀMUS		riceviamo	recibamos	recevions
	RECĬPĬĀTIS		riceviate	recibáis	receviez
	RECĬPĬANT		ricevano	reciban	reçoivent
IV	PARTĬAM	'I leave'	parta	parta	parte
	PARTĬĀS		parta	partas	partes
	PARTĬAT		parta	parta	parte
	PARTĬĀMUS		partiamo	partamos	partions
	PARTĬĀTIS		partiate	partáis	partiez
	PARTĬANT		partano	partan	partent

an early date to all verbs without exception.[3] Verb forms remade analogically also show this extension: *siamo siate* 'be', *stiamo stiate* 'stand', *diamo diate* 'give' (not derived from Classical Latin SĪMUS SĪTIS, STĒMUS STĒTIS, DĒMUS DĒTIS). As we saw, *-iamo* enjoyed an even greater success, spreading to all verbs in the indicative as well (§ 6.3.4).

The modern singular endings of the present subjunctive have been leveled. This development makes sense when we compare the older outcomes with the corresponding indicatives:

Latin subjunctive	Old Italian	Latin indicative	Old Italian
CANTEM	cante	CANTŌ	canto
CANTĒS	canti	CANTĀS	cante
CANTET	cante	CANTAT	canta
PART(I)AM	parta	PART(I)Ō	parto
PART(I)ĀS	parte	PARTĪS	parti
PART(I)AT	parta	PARTIT	parte

Recall that final [s] becomes [j], and that the resulting diphthongs simplify: [ej] > [i], [aj] > [e], and [ij] > [i] when unstressed (§ 6.3.2). So these Old Italian forms are in fact the expected forms. *Parta* (first and third singular) was distinctively subjunctive. *Parte* (second singular subjunctive), being identical to the third singular indicative, was disfavored and replaced with *parta*. Likewise *canti*, being distinctively subjunctive, replaced *cante* to avoid homonymy with the older second singular indicative. By a pattern already firmly established in the present subjunctive (and in class I present indicatives), the third plural *canteno* became *cantino* by analogy.

We turn now from endings to stems. In today's Italian, subjunctive stems offer a striking picture of how a language can reconcile the opposing forces of sound change and analogy.

If regular sound change had always had the upper hand, there would be far more allomorphy than there is. In class I, for instance, shouldn't we expect a stem-final velar to palatalize before the front vowel of the subjunctive ending, be it Latin [e] or modern [i]? Yet the stem remains invariant, here [k] not [tʃ]:

Latin indicative	Italian		Latin subjunctive	Italian	
IOCŌ	gioco	[ko]	IOCEM	giochi	[ki]
IOCĀS	giochi	[ki]	IOCĒS	giochi	[ki]
IOCAT	gioca	[ka]	IOCET	giochi	[ki]
IOCĀMUS	giochiamo	[kj]	IOCĒMUS	giochiamo	[kj]
IOCĀTIS	giocate	[ka]	IOCĒTIS	giochiate	[kj]
IOCANT	giocano	[ka]	IOCENT	giochino	[ki]

Question: Why are class I *subjunctive* stems immune to the palatalizing effect of a following front vowel or front glide?

Answer: Because they follow the model of class I *indicative* stems, which always remain invariant.

In the indicative, this property of class I verbs is historically justified (§ 6.6.3). Subjunctive stems simply follow suit. Elsewhere in the system too, we notice a formal link between indicative and subjunctive, apparently hardening into a derivational rule. The first singular indicative is key: every verb having a yod from <ĔŌ> or <ĪŌ> in its first singular also had a yod from <ĔA> or <ĪA> throughout its subjunctive paradigm (examine Chart 7.5, classes II, IIIb, and IV). In the examples below, regular sound change operated in both, with parallel results.[4]

Indicative – first singular				Subjunctive – (third) singular			
PARĔŌ	'I seem'		paio	PARĔAT	'seems'		paia
SĔDĔŌ	'I sit'	OIt	seggio	SĔDĔAT	'sits'	OIt	seggia
VĪDĔŌ	'I see'	OIt	veggio	VĪDĔAT	'sees'	OIt	veggia
TACĔŌ	'I am silent'		taccio	TACĔAT	'is silent'		taccia

FACĬŌ	'I make'		faccio	FACĬAT	'makes'		faccia
FUGĬŌ	'I flee'	OIt	fuggio	FUGĬAT	'flees'	OIt	fuggia
VĔNĬŌ	'I come'	OIt	vegno	VĔNĬAT	'comes'	OIt	vegna
SALĬŌ	'I go out'	OIt	saglio	SALĬAT	'goes out'	OIt	saglia

Verbs that drop the yod do so in both forms.

TĬMĔŌ	'I fear'	temo	TĬMĔAT	'fears'	tema

The same is true of analogically adjusted forms: when *fuggo* is created on the model of *leggo leggi*, the subjunctive *fugga* arises automatically. In short, when the boot-shaped template affects the present indicative, it has a parallel effect on the subjunctive paradigm. Other examples include: *muoia moriamo, oda udiamo, salga saliamo, venga veniamo, taccia taciamo*.

There are minor exceptions to the identity of the first singular indicative with the rhizotonic subjunctive stem. In two verbs, *avere* 'have' and *sapere* 'know', the subjunctives are regular, and the discrepancy is due to a radically reduced indicative:

HABĔŌ	'I have'	ho	HABĔAT	'has'	abbia
SAPĬŌ	'I know'	so	SAPĬAT	'knows'	sappia

The remaining exceptions are the truly irregular present subjunctives of *essere* 'be', *dare* 'give', and *stare* 'stay':

SŬM	'I am'	sono		SĬT	'is'	sia	
DŌ	'I give'	do		DĔT	'gives'	dia	
STŌ	'I stand'	sto	'I stay'	STĔT	'stands'	stia	'stays'

Latin subjunctives, fitted out with a new subjunctive ending -*a*, yield the amply attested Old Italian *dea stea* which give modern *dia stia* by regular sound change (cf. MĔA 'my' *mia*, DĔUS 'god' *dio*). Tekavčić (1972) posits the same process for the present subjunctive of ESSE 'be': SĬM, SĪS, SĬT, SĪMUS, SĪTIS, SĬNT were adjusted analogically to *SĬAM, *SĬAS, *SĬAT, *SĬAMUS, *SĬATIS, *SĬANT.[5]

7.3.2 Present subjunctive in Spanish

The endings are all regular reflexes of the Latin forms (Chart 7.5 above), except for yod deletion in such forms as VĬDĔAT 'sees' *vea* and PARTĬAT 'departs' *parta*. As in Italian, the subjunctive in Spanish ultimately settles into a derivational relationship with the indicative.

First, in class I, stem-final consonants remain invariant, showing no palatalization before the [e] of the subjunctive endings: PACET 'pays' *pague* [paɣe], *TOCCET 'touches' *toque* [toke]. The allomorphic diphthong of verbs like *quiero queremos* 'want' and *puedo podemos* 'can' is faithfully reproduced in their subjunctives: *quiera queramos, pueda podamos*. Among these, the -*ir* verbs also have metaphonic vowels in the arhizotonic stems of the subjunctive:[6] *sienta sintamos* 'feel' (indicative *siento sentimos*), *duerma durmamos* 'sleep' (indicative *duermo dormimos*). The metaphonic vowel of verbs like *mido medimos* 'measure' occurs throughout the present subjunctive paradigm: *mida midamos*, a reflex of the yod appearing in all the Latin endings.[7]

Another major pattern: wherever Spanish inherited or created a first person singular stem-final velar in the present indicative (§§ 6.8, 6.9), the velar is also found throughout the present subjunctive paradigm: *hago* 'I make' *haga hagamos*, *oigo* 'I hear' *oiga oigamos*, *conozco* 'I know' *conozca conozcamos*. Likewise, the stem-final yod in verbs like FŪGĬŌ 'I flee' *huyo*, AUDĬŌ 'I hear' Old Spanish *oyo*, DESTRŬŌ 'I destroy' *destruyo*, recurs throughout the present subjunctive (*huya huyamos*, etc.). This hiatus-breaking yod accounts for modern *vaya* 'goes' from VADAT and was extended to *haya* 'has'. An alternate explanation derives *haya* directly from Popular Latin *[ajo] (§ 6.10.2).

As for subjunctive *sea* 'is', the same reconstructed *SĬAM *SĬAS *SĬAT that leads to the Italian and French subjunctive would also account for *sea*. However, the scholars who derive the infinitive *ser* from **syncretism** (formal merging) of *ESSĔRE 'be' with SĔDĔRE 'sit' also derive *sea* from SĔDĔAT. Their view finds support in such forms as *siegat*, *siegan* in the tenth-century *Glosas Silenses* (§ 12.2.3).

7.3.3   Present subjunctive in French

The [ə] appearing regularly in the singular endings of class II, III, and IV verbs was extended by analogy to class I verbs in the early twelfth century. Of course, some class I verbs already had final [ə] for cluster support in their singular subjunctive endings: INTRET 'enters' > *entre* (§ 6.5.1). The first plural subjunctive endings in Old French, by sound change alone, would have been:

Class I		Classes II, IIIb, IV		Class IIIa	
-ĒMUS	> [ejns]	-ĔAMUS/-ĪAMUS	> [jens]	-AMUS	> [ens]
					> [jens][8]

In the west all these endings were replaced by the indicative *-ons* (and its variants) in the 1100s, whereas elsewhere *-iens* was favored. From a cross between *-iens* and *-ons* came today's *-ions* [jɔ̃]. Likewise, in the second plural the expected endings are:

Class I		Classes II, IIIb, IV		Class IIIa	
-ĒTIS	> [ojts]	-ĔATIS/-ĪATIS	> [jets]	-ATIS	> [ets]
					> [jets]

All are attested in Old French, but the ultimate success of *-ions* in all four classes assured that of *-iez* [jets], modern [je]. The third plural subjunctive, like the corresponding present indicative, had [ə] by regular sound change in all classes (§ 6.5.2).

The life story of the present subjunctive stems in French, in its general outlines, reflects again the tension between sound change and analogy. Thanks to
the [ə] from the subjunctive endings of class II, III, and IV verbs, the stem-final
consonant typical of plural forms of the indicative was retained also in the singular because it was not word-final. The property soon spread to include class
I verbs:

Latin indicative	French indicative		Latin subjunctive	Expected forms		French subjunctive	
CANTAT	chante	[ʃɑ̃t]	CANTET	chant	[ʃɑ̃]	chante	[ʃɑ̃t]
MŎVET	meut	[mø]	MŎV(Ĕ)AT	meuve	[mœv]	meuve	[mœv]
VENDIT	vend	[vɑ̃]	VENDAT	vende	[vɑ̃d]	vende	[vɑ̃d]
VĪVIT	vit	[vi]	VĪV(Ĭ)AT	vive	[viv]	vive	[viv]

The next factor in this mechanism is the template for stem-consonant allomorphy in the present indicative (§ 6.6.4). The formula that solidifies on the
way from Old to Modern French is one that extends the stem-final consonant
from the plural into the singular. Stem-vowel allomorphy in the subjunctive
has the same distribution as in the indicative. Therefore, the singular stem
of the present subjunctive will match the third plural form of the present
indicative:

Latin indicative	French indicative		Latin subjunctive	French subjunctive	
BĬBŌ	bois	[bwa]	BĬBAM	boive	[bwav]
BĬBĬS	bois	[bwa]	BĬBĀS	boives	[bwav]
BĬBĬT	boit	[bwa]	BĬBAT	boive	[bwav]
*BĬBĪMUS	buvons	[byvɔ̃]	BĬBĀMUS	buvions	[byvjɔ̃]
*BĬBĪTIS	buvez	[byve]	BĬBĀTIS	buviez	[byvje]
BĬBŬNT	boivent	[bwav]	BĬBANT	boivent	[bwav]

Given the many yods in the Latin present subjunctive endings (Chart 7.5) and
the drastic effects yods can have on preceding consonants (Chapter 4) and vowels (Chapter 5), shouldn't subjunctive stems often differ from indicative stems?
Some do. In verbs like *SAPĔRE 'know' and FACĔRE 'make', sound change has
prevailed, with the result that the subjunctive stem bears no synchronic relationship to the indicative.

Latin subjunctive	French subjunctive		French indicative	
*SAPĔAM	sache	[saʃ]	sais	[sɛ]
*SAPĔĀS	saches	[saʃ]	sais	[sɛ]
*SAPĔAT	sache	[saʃ]	sait	[sɛ]
*SAPĔĀMUS	sachions	[saʃjɔ̃]	savons	[savɔ̃]
*SAPĔĀTIS	sachiez	[saʃje]	savez	[save]
*SAPĔANT	sachent	[saʃ]	savent	[sav]

FACĬAM	fasse	[fas]	fais	[fɛ]
FACĬĀS	fasses	[fas]	fais	[fɛ]
FACĬAT	fasse	[fas]	fait	[fɛ]
FACĬĀMUS	fassions	[fasjɔ̃]	faisons	[fəzɔ̃]
FACĬĀTIS	fassiez	[fasje]	faites	[fɛt]
FACĬANT	fassent	[fas]	font	[fɔ̃]

But the yod of the subjunctive was not allowed to create permanent allomorphic chaos. In verbs like VALĒRE 'be worth' and *VŎLĒRE 'want', sound change has been reversed in the arhizotonic stems, leaving the palatalized stem to occupy the boot template.

Latin subjunctive	*French subjunctive*		*French indicative*	
VALĔAM	vaille	[vaj]	vaux	[vo]
VALĔĀS	vailles	[vaj]	vaux	[vo]
VALĔAT	vaille	[vaj]	vaut	[vo]
VALĔĀMUS	valions	[valjɔ̃]	valons	[valɔ̃]
VALĔĀTIS	valiez	[valje]	valez	[vale]
VALĔANT	vaillent	[vaj]	valent	[val]

Latin subjunctive	*French subjunctive*		*French indicative*	
VŎLĔAM	veuille	[vœj]	veux	[vø]
VŎLĔĀS	veuilles	[vœj]	veux	[vø]
VŎLĔAT	veuille	[vœj]	veut	[vø]
VŎLĔĀMUS	voulions	[vuljɔ̃]	voulons	[vulɔ̃]
VŎLĔĀTIS	vouliez	[vulje]	voulez	[vule]
VŎLĔANT	veuillent	[vœj]	veulent	[vœl]

Lastly, in some verbs, for example VĒNĪRE 'come', subjunctive stems were leveled to match those of the indicative.

Latin subjunctive	*Old French subjunctive*	*Modern French subjunctive*		*Modern French indicative*	
VĔNĬAM	viegne	vienne	[vjɛn]	viens	[vjɛ̃]
VĔNĬĀS	viegnes	viennes	[vjɛn]	viens	[vjɛ̃]
VĔNĬAT	viegne	vienne	[vjɛn]	vient	[vjɛ̃]
VĔNĬĀMUS	vegnons	venions	[vənjɔ̃]	venons	[vənɔ̃]
VĔNĬĀTIS	vegnez	veniez	[vənje]	venez	[vəne]
VĔNĬANT	viegnent	viennent	[vjɛn]	viennent	[vjɛn]

Verbs like *venir* confirm that on the way to Modern French a derivational relationship between present subjunctive and present indicative had emerged.

The verbs *avoir* 'have' and *être* 'be' have a puzzling present subjunctive.

Popular Latin	Old French I		Old French II		Modern French	
*SĬAM	seie	[sejə]	soie	[sɔjə]	sois	[swa]
*SĬAS	seies	[sejəs]	soies	[sɔjəs]	sois	[swa]
*SĬAT	sei(e)t	[sej(ə)θ]	soi(e)t	[sɔj(ə)]	soit	[swa]
*SĬĀMUS	seiiens	[sejẽns]	soiions	[sɔjũns]	soyons	[swajɔ̃]
*SĬĀTIS	seiiez	[sejets]	soiiez	[sɔjets]	soyez	[swaje]
*SĬANT	seient	[sejənt]	soient	[sɔjənt]	soient	[swa]

Recall that Popular Latin reduced HABĒŌ to *[ajo] because of its frequent use as an auxiliary (§ 6.10.2). Likewise subjunctive HABĔAM reduces to *[aja].

Latin	Popular Latin	Old French		Modern French	
HABEAM	*[aja]	aie	[ejə]	aie	[ɛ]
HABEĀS	*[ajas]	aies	[ejəs]	aies	[ɛ]
HABEAT	*[ajat]	aiet	[ejəθ]	ait	[ɛ]
HABEĀMUS	*[ajamus]	aiiens	[ejẽns]	ayons	[ejɔ̃]
HABEĀTIS	*[ajatis]	aiiez	[ejets]	ayez	[eje]
HABEANT	*[ajant]	aient	[ejənt]	aient	[ɛ]

Question: Which of these singular forms differ from all other singular present subjunctives in French? In what three ways?

Answer: (1) All other singular subjunctives have [ə] after the stem (unlike *sois, sois, soit*, and *ait*), (2) *soit* and *ait* are the only third singular subjunctives that end in -*t*, and (3) *sois* is the only first singular subjunctive that ends in -*s*.

Today these anomalies are only orthographic: the relevant [ə] and -*s* or -*t* are silent. Yet they point to a problematic history for which the standard manuals have no solid explanation (Nyrop II, Brunot 1899, Pope 1934, Fouché 1967).

7.4   Imperfect indicative

The history of the imperfect indicative is straightforward, consisting mostly of regular sound change with a few adjustments. Already in Popular Latin, class IV -IĒBAM was replaced by either -ĪBAM (in Italy and Spain) or -ĒBAM (in France). Class III abandoned -IĒBAM in favor of the -ĒBAM of class II. (See Chart 7.6.)

As a preliminary, apply the Latin Penultimate Rule to the paradigm. Where does the stress fall in CANTABĀMUS, CANTABĀTIS?

7.4.1   Imperfect indicative in Italian

The Italian forms retain the Latin stress pattern. That is, stress falls on the penultimate syllable throughout: *cantavamo, cantavate*. There are some departures from regular sound change: the endings -*i*, -*te*, -*no* spread from the present

Chart 7.6 The imperfect indicative

	Latin		Italian	Spanish	French
I	CANTĀBAM	'I was singing'	cantavo	cantaba	chantais
	CANTĀBĀS		cantavi	cantabas	chantais
	CANTĀBAT		cantava	cantaba	chantait
	CANTĀBĀMUS		cantavamo	cantábamos	chantions
	CANTĀBĀTIS		cantavate	cantábais	chantiez
	CANTĀBANT		cantavano	cantaban	chantaient
II	VĬDĒBAM	'I was seeing'	vedevo	veía	voyais
	VĬDĒBĀS		vedevi	veías	voyais
	VĬDĒBAT		vedeva	veía	voyait
	VĬDĒBĀMUS		vedevamo	veíamos	voyions
	VĬDĒBĀTIS		vedevate	veíais	voyiez
	VĬDĒBANT		vedevano	veían	voyaient
IV	PARTIĒBAM	'I was leaving'	partivo	partía	partais
	PARTIĒBĀS		partivi	partías	partais
	PARTIĒBAT		partiva	partía	partait
	PARTIĒBĀMUS		partivamo	partíamos	partions
	PARTIĒBĀTIS		partivate	partíais	partiez
	PARTIĒBANT		partivano	partían	partaient

indicative (§§ 6.3.2, 6.3.5, 6.3.6). So did first singular -o for expected -a, a change which gained favor only from the mid-1800s. In Old Italian, verbs outside the -are class had variants without [v] in the first and third singular and third plural (vedea 'I/he saw', venian 'they came'). These v-less variants are still alive in the poetic register.

The stems of the imperfect reflect older infinitives even where the modern infinitives have been abbreviated:

Latin infinitive		Old Italian infinitive	Modern infinitive	Imperfect
BĪBĔRE	'drink'	bevere	bere	beveva
DĪCĔRE	'say'	dicere	dire	diceva
DŪCĔRE	'lead'	-ducere	-durre	-duceva
FACĔRE	'make'	facere	fare	faceva
PŌNĔRE	'put'	ponere	porre	poneva
TRAHĔRE	'pull'	traere	trarre	traeva

The Latin imperfect of ESSE 'be' is reflected in a corresponding Italian paradigm. Notice the extra pretonic -av- in the first and second plural.[9]

ĒRAM	ero
ĒRĀS	eri
ĒRAT	era
ĒRĀMUS	eravamo
ĒRĀTIS	eravate
ĒRANT	erano

Tekavčić (1972:II, 486) notes that in Tuscan Italian, after [-jamo] had replaced [-amo] in the present indicative, the system had no first plural [-amo] endings except in the imperfect, where they were always preceded by [v]. Meanwhile, with a low-register deletion of post-tonic intervocalic [v] in Tuscan dialect, stigmatized forms like *cantamo* for *cantavamo* might have triggered hypercorrection: original *eramo* could sound like a "wrong" variant of *eravamo*.

7.4.2   Imperfect indicative in Spanish

Unlike Italian, Spanish regularizes stress in the imperfect to fall uniformly on the thematic vowel: CANTAB<u>Ā</u>MUS, CANTAB<u>Ā</u>TIS but *cant<u>á</u>bamos, cant<u>á</u>bais*. The intervocalic [β] of the imperfect endings remains intact in -*ar* verbs, but deletes in other verbs. Loss of intervocalic [β] is sporadic (cf. SCRĪBO 'I write' *escribo*, RĪVU 'stream' *río*), but its loss in the imperfect may have been triggered by its regular loss in the adjective-forming suffix -ĪVU/A (e.g. VACĪVU 'empty' *vacío*, AESTĪVU 'summery' *estío*, LIXĪVA 'of lye' *lejía*). By analogy -ĒBAM -ĒBAS etc. also lost their [β], becoming -*ea* -*eas* etc., and the two conjugations converge to -*ía*- by regular sound change (cf. MĔA 'my' *mía*).

A peculiar episode in the history of the Spanish imperfect is the emergence of forms in -*ié*- which competed successfully with older -*ía*- (in all but the first singular) in the 1200s and 1300s, but then receded in the 1400s. Their origin is a matter of debate.[10]

7.4.3   Imperfect indicative in French

Modern French has the same endings in all conjugation classes (Chart 7.6). However, Old French in some regions did show vestiges of distinct endings for classes I and IV (Pope 1934:345–346). These endings are shown below with the analogical forms shaded:

	Popular Latin	Old French (Western)	Old French (Central)	Old French (Eastern)
I	-ĀBAM	-oue	-eie	-eve
II, IIIa, IIIb	-ĒBAM	-eie	-eie	-eie
IV	-ĪBAM	-eie	-eie	-ive

The winning variety was the central one, where the -ĒBAM type endings had spread to all verb classes. But what steps lead from -ĒBAM, -ĒBAS, -ĒBAT to -*ais, -ais, -ait*? First, intervocalic [β] is lost for uncertain reasons.[11] As expected, stressed [e] gives [ej] (later [oj]), and [a] of the final syllable gives [ə]:

$$\text{-ĒBAM} > [eβa] > [ea] > [eja] > [ejə]$$

Thus, the earliest Old French endings are these, with raising of [e] to [i] when unstressed in the first and second plurals:

$$\text{-eie} > \text{-oie}$$
$$\text{-eies} > \text{-oies}$$

$$
\begin{aligned}
\text{-ei(e)t} &> \text{-oi(e)t} \\
\text{-iiens} &> \text{-iiens} \\
\text{-iiez} &> \text{-iiez} \\
\text{-eient} &> \text{-oient}
\end{aligned}
$$

For most of the Old French period, however, third singulars *-eit*, *-oit* were more common than *-eiet*, *-oiet*. Some link this change to a parallel one in the present subjunctive of *estre* 'be': *seiet*, *soiet* > *seit*, *soit*. The paradigms could easily have influenced each other:

Imperfect endings	*Present subjunctive of 'estre'*
-eie	seie
-eies	seies
-ei(e)t	sei(e)t
-iiens	seiiens
-iiez	seiiez
-eient	seient

Why *seiet* shrank to *seit* remains unclear. Once it did, the first and second singulars followed suit. Then the second singular *-s* spread to the first singular, as in the present indicative (§ 6.5.1). The change from *-iens* to *-ions*, reflecting the spread of a regional variant, is again strikingly similar to what happened in the present subjunctive. The second plurals were already identical in the two paradigms, so making the first plurals identical brings the first and second plural forms into line with the boot template.

How do we get from the older imperfect endings (above) to the modern ones? Recall (§ 1.2.4) that stressed [e] in a free syllable undergoes a long series of changes leading to modern [wa]:

$$
\text{MĒ 'me'} > \text{[me]} > \text{[mej]} > \text{[moj]} > \text{[moɛ]} > \text{[mwɛ]} > \text{[mwa]}
$$

Why then does the original [e] of the imperfect endings not become [wa]? Once [oɛ] became [wɛ] in the 1200s, there arose social variants [wa] and [ɛ]. At first limited to popular usage, these variants were later adopted by the court, perhaps under the Italian influence that prevailed in the 1500s. In time, the two variants were prescriptively assigned to different words, and the imperfect (and conditional) endings were to be pronounced [ɛ], though still spelled <oi>.[12]

The stems of the imperfect indicative today automatically match the arhizotonic plural stem of the present indicative, a derivational relationship that crystallized between Middle and Modern French.

Latin			*French*	
infinitive		*Infinitive*	*First plural*	*Imperfect stem*
BĬBĔRE	'drink'	boire	buvons	buv-
DĪCĔRE	'say'	dire	disons	dis-
FĪNĪRE	'finish'	finir	finissons	finiss-

IŬNGĔRE	'join'	joindre	joignons	joign-
MOLĔRE	'grind'	moudre	moulons	moul-
PREHENDĔRE	'grasp'	prendre	prenons	pren-
VENDĔRE	'sell'	vendre	vendons	vend-

The imperfect of ESSE 'be', retained in Italian and Spanish, survived in Old French into the 1300s: ĔRAM ĔRĀS ĔRAT > iere/ere, ieres/eres, iere/ere/ert. A regularized imperfect esteie, esteies, estei(e)t arose, based perhaps on Old French estre 'be', but quite possibly on Old French ester 'stand, stay' (from STARE).[13]

7.5   Perfect indicative: Romance synthetic past

Recall the contrast between weak (arhizotonic) perfects, having a long thematic vowel before their [w] marker, and strong perfects, having no such vowel (§§ 7.1.1–2):

- strong
- stress on root in most forms
- no thematic vowel

HABĒRE – HABŬĪ

- weak
- stress off root
- thematic vowel

CANTĀRE – CANTĀVĪ

Weak perfects, roughly speaking, became the "regular" synthetic pasts of Italian and Spanish. Verbs of classes I and IV almost invariably had weak perfects (Chart 7.7). Seemingly, there should also be weak perfects of classes II and III in -ĒVĪ, but these were few in number and did not survive in Romance (e.g. DELĒRE – DELĒVĪ 'I destroyed', CONSUĔRE – CONSUĒVĪ 'I got accustomed to'). The category was revived in Italian (§ 7.5.1) and for a time in Old Spanish (§ 7.5.2).

The weak perfect had long and short forms coexisting in Latin. The short forms, newer and not fully standardized, were gaining ground from pre-Classical times on. It is merely a matter of convention that today's Latin textbooks teach the long forms. (See Chart 7.7.)

The ancient testimony presents a picture of ongoing change. Second singulars in -ASTI/-ISTI are numerous in Plautus (254–184 BCE) and Terence (195–159 BCE). As early as the first century BCE, a short third plural form appears in the *Rhetorica ad Herennium* in a passage deliberately exemplifying informal style:

"Heus," inquit, "adolescens, pueri tui modo me *pulsarunt* [for *pulsaverunt*]..."[14]

In the same century, Lucretius writes INRITAT for INRITĀVIT 'spurred' (*De rerum natura* I, 70). Short third singular forms also occur in inscriptions: CURAUT 'cared for' (CIL IV 12700), DONAUT 'gave' (CIL VI 24481), EDUCAUT 'brought up' (CIL XI 1074), PETIUT 'asked' (CIL VI 36377), PUGNAT 'fought' (CIL X 7297), among many others.[15] The *Instituta artium*, an influential textbook in the post-Classical period, cites PROBASTI as standard, accepts PROBASTIS, PROBARUNT, and condemns PROBAI, PROBAISTI, PROBAIT,

Chart 7.7 The Latin weak perfect and Romance synthetic pasts

Long forms	Short forms		Italian	Spanish	French
CANTĀVĪ	CANTAI	'I sang'	cantai	canté	chantai
CANTĀVISTĪ	CANTA(I)STI		cantasti	cantaste	chantas
CANTĀVIT	CANTA(U)T/CANTAIT[17]		cantò	cantó	chanta
CANTĀVIMUS	CANTA(I)MUS		cantammo	cantamos	chantâmes
CANTĀVISTIS	CANTASTIS		cantaste	cantasteis	chantâtes
CANTĀVĒRUNT[16]	CANTARUNT		cantarono	cantaron	chantèrent
PARTĪVĪ	PARTII	'I left'	partii	partí	partis
PARTĪVISTĪ	PARTISTI		partisti	partiste	partis
PARTĪVIT	PARTI(U)T/PARTIIT		partì	partió	partit
PARTĪVIMUS	PARTIIMUS		partimmo	partimos	partîmes
PARTĪVISTIS	PARTISTIS		partiste	partisteis	partîtes
PARTĪVĒRUNT	PARTI(E)RUNT		partirono	partieron	partirent

and PROBAIMUS, thus attesting to their currency as well. In class IV, the author cites only the short forms, which evidently were then standard.

The change to short perfects apparently had two points of departure. According to Palmer (1961:274), loss of [w] in the perfect began between similar vowels, -īvī > -ī(ī) in class IV. This accords well with the treatment of class IV verbs in the *Instituta artium*. Second, the earliest short forms to take root in class I were those that brought the stress onto the thematic vowel: first -ASTI, soon followed by -ASTIS, -ARUNT, as the *Instituta artium* again seems to indicate.

7.5.1   Italian *passato remoto*: weak forms

From the short forms of the weak perfect in Latin, the changes yielding the *passato remoto* are minor. *Cantai/partii* and *cantasti/partisti* are straight from Latin. CANTAUT, with [aw] > [ɔ] and regular loss of final [t], gives *cantò*, while PARTIIT yields *partì*.

In the plural, the puzzling geminate of *cantammo/partimmo* has been variously attributed to: assimilation of a cluster [wm] (Tekavčić 1972:335, 373), avoidance of homonymy with the oldest present indicative *cantamo* (Rohlfs 1968:313), and analogy with *demmo* < DĒDĬMUS 'we gave', *stemmo* < STĔTĬMUS 'we stood', *fummo* < FŬĪMUS 'we were' (Rohlfs 1968:313, Tekavčić 1972:373). But given that CANTAIMUS is attested and *CANTAUMUS is not, the geminate is best attributed to a regular sound change: [jm] > [mm]. The high-frequency forms like *demmo* and *stemmo*, with their geminate resulting from syncope, may well have reinforced the change. The remaining plural forms have simple adjustments modeled on the present indicative (§§ 6.3.5–6):

> *cantati* > *cantate* motivates *cantasti* > *cantaste*
> *cantan* > *cantano* motivates *cantaro* > *cantarono*

In Chart 7.7 above, weak perfects with thematic vowel <ē> are conspicuously absent. But under several analogical pressures (§ 7.5.5), this type of weak perfect was recreated in Western Romance and has a few reflexes in Italian:

potere	'be able'
potei	'I was able'
potesti	
potè	
potemmo	
poteste	
poterono	

All verbs having weak *passato remoto* forms of the *-ei* type also have variants in *-etti* (§ 7.5.5). Nearly all have weak past participles, at least optionally (§ 7.11).

7.5.2   Spanish *pretérito*: weak forms

In Spanish too, the weak *pretérito* forms are mainly regular reflexes of the Latin short forms. The diphthongs in CANTAI, PARTII simplify to give *canté*, *partí*, while *cantaste*, *partiste*, and *partimos* reflect regular change in the unstressed final syllable. From the attested CANTAIMUS comes Old Spanish *cantemos* (with [aj] > [e] as in *canté*), analogically adjusted to modern *cantamos*. The expected second plurals *-astes* and *-istes* survived until the 1600s, but were adjusted to *-asteis* and *-isteis*, because all other second plurals ended in <*is*>.

The history of the third person *pretérito* has been controversial.[18] The most direct route to *partió* is via CANTAUT > *cantó*. This stressed *-ó* then motivates a stress shift in class IV, where PARTIUT gives not **partio* but *partió*. Similarly, a direct route to the third plural might be PARTĪVĒRUNT > PARTIERUNT and then *partieron* with a stress shift like that of *partió*. But another relevant fact is that Old Spanish had weak *pretéritos* of the *-er* class.[19] Malkiel (1976) proposes a derivation *-ĒVIT* > **-EUT* > [ew] > [jo] by regular sound change. As the *-er* and *-ir* classes merged their *pretérito*, *-ió* entered the resulting shared paradigm. Today's third plural *-ieron*, in Malkiel's view, is also a relic of the Old Spanish *-er* weak *pretérito*, which had plural endings *-iemos*, *-iestes*, *-ieron*.[20] The first two were lost, for unknown reasons, in the merging (**syncretism**) of the *-er* and *-ir* paradigms.

Simplest of all is to derive *partieron* from PARTIVĒRUNT, with loss of the [w] and no stress shift. Old Spanish had both *partieron* and *partiron*, which would derive from the full and short forms, respectively PARTIVĒRUNT and PARTIRUNT.

Spanish verb stems show metaphonic allomorphy in the *pretérito* just as they do in the present indicative (§ 6.6.2) and present subjunctive (§ 7.3.2). Metaphonic raising of the unstressed stem vowel is induced only by the [j] of *-ió* and *-ieron* and does not spread further, as it did in the present indicative. Curiously, only in *-ir* verbs do *-ió* and *-ieron* trigger metaphony: *temió temieron*, not **timió *timieron*.

| dormir 'sleep' | medir 'measure' | temer 'fear' |
| dormí | medí | temí |

dormiste	mediste	temiste
dormió	midió	temió
dormimos	medimos	temimos
dormisteis	medisteis	temisteis
durmieron	midieron	temieron

So, this metaphonic raising, at first phonologically motivated, now has morphological conditioning. Thus it conveys morphological information.

Does Spanish have three conjugations or two? Certainly the infinitives in *-er* and *-ir* have contrasting arhizotonic forms *-emos/-imos*, *-éis/-ís* in the present indicative, and the imperatives also differ, but otherwise these two classes are distinguished only by the presence or absence of metaphonic allomorphy in the weak *pretérito*.

7.5.3   French *passé simple*: weak forms

Two innovations are prominent in French. First, the verbs from Latin perfects settle into a three-class system not from Latin A E I (as in Italian and Old Spanish), but from Latin A U I. Second, the strong perfects all assimilate into the last two classes (§ 7.5.7).

The -ARE class, numerous and open, nearly always had weak perfects. The category survives in today's *passé simple* of *-er* verbs (Chart 7.7). Outside the -ARE class, the remaining Latin perfects have collapsed into two types of *passé simple* characterized by endings in [y] and [i]:

valus 'I was worth'	partis 'I left'
valus	partis
valut	partit
valûmes	partîmes
valûtes	partîtes
valurent	partirent

The newly created [y] *passé simple* has its origin in such waw strong perfects as VALŬĪ 'I was strong' and MŎLŬĪ 'I ground'. Popular Latin began to treat this [w] as a thematic vowel [u], creating short forms like those of the [a] and [i] classes (Chart 7.7), with [u] stressed throughout.

Latin	*New short forms*
VALUI	VALUI
VALUISTI	VALUSTI
VALUIT	VALUT
VALUIMUS	VALUMUS
VALUISTIS	VALUSTIS
VALUERUNT	VALURENT

The analogical forces motivating the new [u] class are double: not only does its stress pattern mimic that of the established short perfects in [a] and [i], but it also fills an empty space in the system. One of the forces that shape Romance verb morphology is a natural affinity between synthetic pasts and past participles.[21] Latin had three types of weak past participle: -ATU, -ITU, and -UTU, which was fairly rare in the standard language but gained ground in popular usage (§ 7.11). In pre-Old French the weak perfects developed a new tripartite system echoing the participles. In the newly formed [y] weak perfects, as in the other short forms, stress falls on the thematic vowel. Many originally strong waw perfects joined the new weak class. Further, a number of verbs forsook their original perfects to join the [u] class (CUCURRI 'I ran' becomes *CURRUI *courus*) and most of these verbs also have -UTU past participles (CURSU 'run' becomes *CURRUTU *couru*).

CANTATU	*CURRUTU	PARTITU
CANTAI	*CURRUI	PARTII
CANTA(I)STI	*CURRU(I)STI	PARTISTI
CANTA(U)T/CANTAIT	*CURRU(I)T	PARTI(U)T/PARTIIT
CANTAIMUS	*CURRUIMUS	PARTIIMUS
CANTASTIS	*CURRUSTIS	PARTISTIS
CANTARUNT	*CURRU(E)RUNT	PARTI(E)RUNT

Now for the endings. The endings for the *passé simple* of -er verbs are, mostly, regular reflexes of the Latin short forms in the -ARE class. The diphthong [aj] of CANTAI resoves to [e], though still written <ai>. From CANTASTI we would expect in Old French *chantast*. But as Pope notes (1934:372), the typical second singular marker is -s, not -st, and in the inverted order *chantast tu?* the [t] of the ending was inaudible. So Old French already has *chantas*. In the third singular -t weakens to [θ] and then disappears. From CANTAMUS CANTASTIS we would expect by regular sound change *chantens* (as in the present indicative before -ons took over, § 6.5.2) and *chantaz* (as in HOSTIS > Old French *oz* 'enemy'). The endings -ames -astes (and -imes -istes, -umes -ustes) have not been fully explained (Pope 1934:373). However, the first plural *chantames*, influenced by second plural *chantastes*, acquired in Middle French a spelling *chantasmes*, forerunner of today's *chantâmes*.[22] From CANTARUNT the regular *chantèrent* won out over a variant *chantarent* of dialectal origin.

In both the <i> and <u> *passé simple* the plural endings and second singular ending developed as explained above, but the first and third singular require comment. Nowhere in Latin was <s> a first singular ending. The French forms exemplified above (*valus, partis*) acquired their first singular -s analogically on the model of the present and imperfect indicative, with reinforcement from strong perfects like *mis* < MĪSĪ 'I put', *dis* < DĪXĪ 'I said', and *fis* < FĒCĪ 'I made', where the -s is etymological (§ 7.5.7). The third singular -t which had vanished in early Old French made a comeback in the 1200s in the <i> and <u> types of *passé simple*, fostered not only by the *-s -s -t* pattern of the present and imperfect indicative, but also by the preservation of third singular <t> in strong perfects (§ 7.5.7).

7.5.4   The strong perfect: pan-Romance trends

Popular Latin still had many verbs with a distinctive perfectum stem. Our example here is MITTĔRE 'send' with its sigmatic stem MĪS-.

Latin	*Popular Latin*
MĪSĪ	MISI
MĪSISTĪ	MISISTI
MĪSIT	MISIT
MĪSĬMUS	MISIMUS
MĪSISTIS	MISISTIS
MĪSĔRUNT/MĪSĒRUNT	MISERUNT/MISERUNT

Popular Latin preferred penultimate stress in the first plural, bringing the form into line with the present tense. For third plurals, we saw one reason to posit -ĒRUNT in Spanish to get *-ieron* (§ 7.5.2), while in Italian we will find evidence for the rhizotonic variant -ĔRUNT (§ 7.5.5).

Among the ways of forming perfectum stems (§ 7.1.1), Popular Latin obliterated the reduplicating type and nearly eliminated the long-vowel type. Vice versa, waw perfects and sigmatics became open classes that gained new members.

Latin		*Popular Latin*	*Romance*
CECĬDĪ[23]	'fell'	*CADUI	caddi (It)
MOMORDĪ	'bit'	*MORSI	morsi (It)
CĒPĪ	'seized'	*CAPUI	cupe (Sp)
LĒGĪ	'chose'	*LEXI	lessi (It)
PŌSUĪ	'placed'	POSI	posi (It), puse (Sp)

Strong perfects in waw, both old and new, undergo a further development in French (§ 7.5.3) and Romanian (§ 10.6.4), where the waw is reinterpreted as a thematic vowel, leading to a new class of weak perfects in <u>.

In Popular Latin the perfect of DARE generalized to its compounds and brought its stress with it, overriding the Penultimate Rule:

Infinitive		*Latin perfect*	*Popular Latin perfect*[24]
DARE	'give'	DĔDĪ	DĔDĪ
PERDĔRE	'lose'	PERDĬDĪ	PERDĔDĪ
VENDĔRE	'sell'	VENDĬDĪ	VENDĔDĪ
CRĒDĔRE	'believe'	CRĒDĬDĪ	CRĒDĔDĪ

These few, frequently used verbs ignite three developments that span Western Romance. They involve weak perfects: (1) the *-er* class in Ibero-Romance, (2) the

-*ei* and -*etti* endings in Italian, and (3) the [i] type for -*re* verbs in French. We will soon look at each of these stories in its context.

7.5.5   Italian *passato remoto*: strong forms

On the way from the Latin strong perfect paradigm to the Italian *passato remoto* two innovations took hold. One is the stress shift in the first plural (§ 7.5.4), modeled on a robust pattern: first plurals (and likewise their affiliated second plurals) are stressed on the penultimate syllable throughout the language. The other change, more dramatic, involves the stems:

MITTĔRE	mettere	SCRIBĔRE	scrivere
'send'	'put'	'write'	'write'
MĪSĪ	misi	SCRĪPSĪ	scrissi
MĪSISTĪ	mettesti	SCRĪPSISTĪ	scrivesti
MĪSIT	mise	SCRĪPSIT	scrisse
MĪSĬMUS	mettemmo	SCRĪPSĬMUS	scrivemmo
MĪSISTIS	metteste	SCRĪPSISTIS	scriveste
MĪSĔRUNT	misero	SCRĪPSĔRUNT	scrissero

> Question: Which forms retain the distinctively perfectum stem? What else do they have in common?
>
> Answer: Three of the forms, the first singular and third singular and plural, have the perfectum stem. They are also the only rhizotonic forms.

From today's perspective, *misi* and *scrissi* seem "irregular" – but the real irregularity resides in the shaded forms. We would expect the stem to remain constant, as it is in Latin, giving **misesti* 'you put', etc. Instead, the three shaded forms have converted to the infectum (infinitive) stem. This pattern recurs in all strong paradigms of the *passato remoto* except for *essere* 'be', *stare* 'stay', and *dare* 'give'.

All attempts to explain this innovation start by recognizing that it happens in the arhizotonic forms. Maiden (1995:141) downplays the factor of stress position a bit and draws more attention to the personal endings. His view is that Italian was at least toying with the idea of totally purging from the language all the strong stems like *misi* and *scrissi*, and that this process did reach fruition in the three shaded forms of the *passato remoto*, but could only go so far, because a major crisis of homonymy with the present indicative would have resulted if, for instance, *scrissi* and *scrisse* had been remade as **scrivi* 'I wrote' and **scrive* 'he wrote'. Maiden's view has the further merit of accounting for the infectum stem in the Italian imperfect subjunctive (§ 7.6.1).

Rohlfs (1966–69) and Tekavčić (1972) point instead to a stress-sensitive sound change affecting the waw perfects. Post-tonic waw survived in Popular Latin and caused, in Italian, doubling of the preceding stem consonant, while pretonic waw disappeared:

TENUĪ	tenni	[tɛn:i]		PLACUĪ	piacqui	[pjak:wi]
TENUISTĪ	tenesti	[tenesti]		PLACUISTĪ	piacesti	[pjatʃesti]

Consequently, arhizotonic forms, with their waw effaced, looked as if they had infectum stems. This pattern of allomorphy then generalized to all verbs with distinctive perfectum stems (i.e. Latin strong perfects), even those that were not of the waw type.

Latin	Expected	Italian
DĪXĪ	dissi	dissi
DĪXISTĪ	*dissesti	dicesti
DĪXIT	disse	disse
DĪXĬMUS	*dissemmo	dicemmo
DĪXISTIS	*dissesti	diceste
DĪXĔRUNT	dissero	dissero

The *passato remoto* paradigms of *stare* 'stay' and *dare* 'give' do not support the notion of a reversion to the infectum stem in arhizotonic forms, which would wrongly predict *stasti *stammo *staste etc. in the standard language. Rather, the *stare* forms support the idea of a gemination triggered by post-tonic waw, as mentioned above:

Popular Latin	Intermediate	Italian	Latin	Intermediate	Italian
*STETUI	stetti	stetti	DĔDĪ	diedi	diedi
*STETISTI	*stetesti	stesti	DĔDISTĪ	*dedesti	desti
*STETUIT	stette	stette	DĔDIT	diede	diede
*STET(I)MUS	*stet(e)mo	stemmo	DĔD(Ĭ)MUS	*ded(e)mo	demmo
*STETISTIS	*stetesti	steste	DĔDISTIS	*dedesti	deste
*STETUERUNT	stettero	stettero	DĔDĔRUNT	diedero	diedero

We posit for *STET(I)MUS and DĔD(Ĭ)MUS an early syncope, which precedes and precludes the usual shift to arhizotonic stress. The resulting *stemmo* and *demmo* may be the model for the reduced *stesti steste* and *desti deste*. Or these may reflect **haplology**, the loss of one of two adjacent identical syllables.

S*tare* and *dare* together have a far-reaching effect on the weak *passato remoto*. First, alongside *diedi diede diedero*, the variants *detti dette dettero* arose on the model of *stare*:

stetti	diedi	detti
stesti	desti	desti
stette	diede	dette
stemmo	demmo	demmo
steste	deste	deste
stettero	diedero	dettero

Next, the compounds of DARE get into the game, acquiring variants in *-etti*, etc.

Popular Latin	Expected	Old Italian/Modern Italian
DĔDĪ	diedi	diedi ~ detti
PERDĔDĪ	*perdiedi	perdetti
*VENDĔDĪ	*vendiedi	vendetti
*CREDĔDĪ	*crediedi	credetti

These form a new weak *passato remoto* in *-etti* that spreads to a few other *-ere* verbs.

These are exactly the same *-ere* verbs that also develop a weak *passato remoto* in <e>, on the model of the weak *passato remoto* of the *-are* and *-ire* verbs (§ 7.5.1):

Weak *-ere passato remoto* from compounds of DARE		Weak *-ere passato remoto* analogous to *-are* and *-ire* types
perdetti		perdei
perdesti	=	perdesti
perdette		perdè
perdemmo	=	perdemmo
perdeste	=	perdeste
perdettero		perderono

The weak *passato remoto* from the compounds of DARE may also have fostered the new paradigm by providing the endings *-esti -emmo -este*. On the other hand, the entire *perdei* type conjugation may be modeled on the *cantai* and *dormii* types. The fact remains that the two paradigms are typically in free variation. When this formula would generate awkward forms, grammars warn against them (*riflettei*, not *riflettetti* 'I reflected'), thus alluding to the formula.

The rhizotonic stems of the strong *passato remoto* result mainly from regular sound change. Assimilation is most conspicuous in the sigmatic class and gives rise to a series of stems with <ss> (or <s> if assimilation does not occur). Examples include: SCRIPSĪ 'I wrote' *scrissi*, DIXĪ 'I said' *dissi*, TRAXĪ 'I pulled' *trassi*, *MORSĪ 'I bit' *morsi*, *LEXĪ 'I read' *lessi*, *REDEMSĪ 'I redeemed' *redensi*. The waw, as we saw, causes doubling of the preceding stem consonant as in: TENUĪ 'I held' *tenni*, VOLUĪ 'I wanted' *volli*, HABUĪ 'I had' *ebbi*, SAPUĪ 'I knew' *seppi*,[25] *BIBUĪ 'I drank' *bevvi*, *RUPUĪ 'I broke' *ruppi*, *CADUĪ 'I fell' *caddi*.

One question about personal endings: why *dissero* 'they said', but *cantarono* 'they sang', *poterono* 'they were able', *dormirono* 'they slept'? Why does the strong *passato remoto* differ from the weak in its third plural ending? Since the regular outcome is *dissero*, the real question is: why did *dissero* not receive the analogical addition *-no*?

Long form	Short form	Old Italian	Modern Italian
CANTAVĔRUNT	CANTARUNT	cantaro	cantarono
PARTIVĔRUNT	PARTIRUNT	partiro	partirono
DIXĔRUNT	…	dissero	dissero
			*disserono

The best answer is that addition of *-no* would have engendered a family of verb forms stressed on the fourth syllable from the end, a format highly disfavored in Italian.

7.5.6   Spanish *pretérito*: strong forms

In Spanish, strong *pretéritos* do stand out as a class, but are far fewer today than in Italian or French.[26] The mass exodus of original strong perfects into the weak class started early and continued throughout Old Spanish:

Latin	Popular Latin		Old Spanish	Modern Spanish
	IACUĪ	'I lay'	yogue	yací
CRĒDĬDĪ	*CRĒDUĪ	'I believed'	crove	creí
	SCRIPSĪ	'I wrote'	escrise	escribí
TĒTĬGĪ	*TANXĪ	'I touched'	tanxe	tañí
	VĪDĪ	'I saw'	vide	vi

The strong perfects that do survive have only two rhizotonic forms, the first and third singular, and no stem alternation:

Popular Latin		Spanish
*PŎSĪ	'I placed'	puse
*PŎSISTĪ		pusiste
*PŎSĬT		puso
*PŎSĬMUS		pusimos
*PŎSISTIS		pusisteis
*PŎSĒRUNT		pusieron

Of the personal endings in the strong *pretérito*, only the first two are regular reflexes of the Latin forms. The third singular *-o* is imported from the weak perfects (*cantó* 'sang', *prendió* 'took', *partió* 'left', § 7.5.2), avoiding homonymy with the first singular. From class IV verbs comes the [i] in *-imos -isteis* (instead of *-emos -estes*). The third plural *-ieron* also originates in the weak conjugation.

All surviving Spanish strong *pretéritos* have a high stem vowel (e.g. *dije* 'I said', *pude* 'I was able') except *traer* 'bring' and its compounds (*traje* 'I brought', *atraje* 'I attracted').[27] How can this be explained? Three sources contribute to the pattern.

First, regular outcomes: Latin verbs with ī or ū in the stem yield a strong *pretérito* with [i] or [u] in the stem throughout the paradigm: (DĪXĪ *dije* 'I said', DĪXISTĪ *dijiste* 'you said', CONDŪXĪ *conduje* 'I led', CONDŪXISTĪ *condujiste* 'you led', etc.).

Second, glide anticipation regularly brings the waw perfect marker into the stem (compare § 5.2.2):

PŎSUĪ > *[pwɔswe] > *[pwɔwse] > *puse* 'I placed'
PŎTUĪ > *[pwɔdwe] > *[pwɔwðe] > *pude* 'I was able'

In rhizotonic forms like these (and the corresponding third singulars), meta-thesis of waw creates a triphthong that reduces to [u] (Penny 2002:225–226). This should have produced Old Spanish paradigms with high stem vowels in the two rhizotonic forms only.

Third, there are high stem vowels from metaphony. The earliest Old Spanish texts have *fize* 'I made' and *vine* 'I came', which leads several scholars to posit metaphony, induced (exceptionally) by the ī of FĒCĪ, VĒNĪ (Menéndez Pidal 1966:59, Lloyd 1987:308, Penny 2002:228).[28]

Thus, in Old Spanish, alongside the *pretéritos* with etymological high vowels [i] and [u] throughout, there must have existed at some point paradigms with [u] in just the rhizotonic forms, and paradigms with [i] in the first person only:

dixe	diximos		conduxe	conduximos
dixiste	dixisteis		conduxiste	conduxisteis
dixo	dixeron		conduxo	conduxeron

puse	posimos		fize	fezimos
posiste	posisteis		feziste	fezistes
puso	posieron		fezo	fezieron

The *puse puso* type soon attracted the *fize* type to produce a *fize fizo* type. A remarkably early recruit was *quise quiso* from *querer* 'want', which had no phonological motive for an [i] stem (regular *quese *queso are unattested).

fize	fezimos		quise	quesimos
feziste	fezistes		quesiste	quesistes
fizo	fezieron		quiso	quesieron

By the 1500s, the alternating paradigms had been leveled to match those with a high stem vowel throughout.

Meanwhile, other strong *pretéritos* that regularly had [e] or [o] in the stem were joining the trend toward high vowels:

Popular Latin	Intermediate		Old Spanish	Modern Spanish	
*PRĒSĪ	[prese]		prese ~ prise	prendí	'I took'
HABŬĪ	[awβe]	[oβe]	ove ~ uve	hube	'I had'
SAPŬĪ	[sawpe][29]	[sope]	sope ~ supe	supe	'I found out'
*CAPŬĪ	[kawpe]	[kope]	cope ~ cupe	cupe	'I fitted'

The high-frequency verb *hube* 'I had' engendered in turn an analogical stem consonant [β], as in *estuve* 'I stood', *tuve* 'I held', which are certainly not from *STETUĪ, TENUĪ.

7.5.7   French *passé simple*: the fate of the strong forms

Old and Middle French still had a class of strong perfects, but ultimately their distinctive properties were effaced. Today's French has three kinds of *passé simple*: an <a> type for -*er* verbs (*chanta* 'he sang'), an <i> type (*finit* 'he finished'), and a <u> type (*valut* 'he was worth'). Historically, a verb like Old French *mist* < MĪSĬT 'he put' was a strong perfect, but in today's *mit* the <i> might as well be part of the ending. This section explains how the original strong perfects were all made to fit into the <i> type or the <u> type.

The alternating stress in Popular Latin strong perfects caused allomorphy in the paradigms of Old French:

Popular Latin	Old French	
DĪXĪ	dis	'I said'
DĪXISTĪ	desis	
DĪXĬT	dist	
*DĪXĬMUS	desimes	
DĪXISTIS	desistes	
DĪXĚRUNT	distrent	

In Middle French the paradigms are leveled, some in favor of the rhizotonic forms and some the other way:

Old French		Modern French	Old French		Modern French	
dis	>	dis 'I said'	conduis		conduisis 'I drove'	
desis		dis	conduisis	>	conduisis	
dist	>	dit	conduist		conduisit	
desimes		dîmes	conduisimes	>	conduisîmes	
desistes		dîtes	conduisistes	>	conduisîtes	
distrent	>	dirent	conduistrent		conduisirent	

Paradigms leveled in favor of the arhizotonic stem are indistinguishable from the reflexes of original weak perfects. Paradigms leveled in favor of the rhizotonic stem are the only genuine survivors of the strong perfects, although synchronically they are unrecognizable.

The largest class of strong perfects to survive in Old French is the sigmatic type, which even gains new members in Popular Latin (e.g. PREHENDĪ > *PRĒSĪ 'I took'). A few survive into Modern French: MĪSĪ 'I put' *mis*, RĪSĪ 'I laughed' *ris*, DĪXĪ 'I said' *dis*, *PRĒSĪ 'I took' *pris*, for example. The rest either vanish (*FRANXĪ > Old French *frains* 'I broke') or are moved to the <i> class by leveling in favor of the arhizotonic stem, which sometimes even acquires an analogical consonant from the present tense:

Latin	Old French	Modern French
COXĪ	cuis	cuisis
COXISTĪ	cuisis	cuisis

TORSĪ	tors	tordis
TORSISTĪ	torsis	tordis
IUNXĪ	joins	joignis
IUNXISTĪ	joinsis	joignis
SCRIPSĪ	escris	écrivis
SCRIPSISTĪ	escrisis	écrivis

Strong perfects of the waw type ended up in today's <u> class by two paths. Gallo-Romance was already turning strong perfects into weak ones by converting their [w] to a thematic vowel [u], as in VALŬĪ > *VALŪĪ > *valu* 'I was worth' (§ 7.5.3). But even with their ranks depleted, strong waw perfects still survive as a small class in Old French, recognizable by their three rhizotonic forms. The Old French reflexes of SAPĔRE 'taste', later SAPĒRE 'know', exemplify a strong waw perfect on its way to the modern <u> class.

Popular Latin	Gallo-Romance	Old French	Modern French
SAPUĪ	*[sawwi]	soi	sus
SAPUSTĪ	*[sawus]	sous	sus
SAPUĬT	*[sawwit]	sout	sut
SAPUMUS	*[sawuməs]	soumes	sûmes
SAPUSTIS	*[sawustəs]	soustes	sûtes
SAPUERUNT	*[sawurənt]	sourent	surent

The three arhizotonic forms automatically joined the new weak <u> class. Later the rhizotonic forms followed suit.[30]

Of the Latin long-vowel perfects only three survive: FĒCĪ 'I made', VĒNĪ 'I came', and VĪDĪ 'I saw':

Popular Latin	Old French	Popular Latin	Old French	Popular Latin	Old French
FĒCĪ	fis	VĒNĪ	vin	VĪDĪ	vi
FĒCĬSTĪ	fesis	VĒNĬSTĪ	venis	VĪDĬSTĪ	veïs
FĒCĬT	fist	VĒNĬT	vint	VĪDĬT	vist
FĒCĬMUS	fesimes	VĒNĬMUS	venimes	VĪDĬMUS	veïmes
FĒCĬSTĬS	fesistes	VĒNĬSTĬS	venistes	VĪDĬSTĬS	veïstes
FĒCĔRŬNT	firent	VĒNĔRŬNT	vindrent	VĪDĔRŬNT	virent

The [i] of *fis* and *vin* supposedly resulted from metaphony[31] and spread from there to other rhizotonic forms. But there is no lack of analogical models for these alternating stems (e.g. *dis desis*, *mis mesis*, etc.). In Modern French these paradigms are leveled in favor of the rhizotonic stems, with an analogical <s> added in the first singular. The remaining long-vowel strong perfects were reassigned either to the more favored sigmatic and waw classes or else to the [i] class of weak perfects (VĪCĪ 'I won' but *vainquis*, RŪPĪ 'I broke' but *rompis*). Why to the [i] class?

Again, the answer lies in the Popular Latin remodeling of the compounds of DARE. Popular Latin disfavored perfects like PĚRDĬDĪ, VĚNDĬDĪ, *RENDĬDĪ and remade them – based on DĔDĪ 'I gave' – as PĚRDĔDĪ, *VĔNDĔDĪ, *RENDĔDĪ. When the intervocalic [d] vanishes by lenition, the result is a triphthong [jɛj] which regularly reduces to [i] (§ 5.3.4):

$$[perd\underline{\varepsilon}di] > [perdj\varepsilon ði] > [perdj\varepsilon j] > [perdi] > [pɛ\text{R}di]^{32}$$

These verbs sufficed to establish a pattern that attracted other -re verbs:

Infinitive	Past participle	Passé simple	
perdre	perdu	perdis	'I lost'
rendre	rendu	rendis	'I gave back'
vendre	vendu	vendis	'I sold'
rompre	rompu	rompis	'I broke'
vaincre	vaincu	vainquis	'I won'

The endings of the *passé simple* from strong perfects play a role in shaping the Modern French [y] and [i] paradigms (§ 7.5.3). The first singular -s is etymological only in reflexes of the sigmatic perfects: MĪSĪ > *mis* 'I put', DĪXĪ > *dis* 'I said', and in the reflex of FĒCĪ > *fis* 'I made'. From forms like these the -s spreads thoughout the [i] and [y] *passé simple*. As for the third singular, final T became [θ] in Old French and then deleted unless postconsonantal or following consonant + ĕ or ĭ: *PARTIIT > Old French *parti* 'he left', SŬNT > Old French *sont* 'they are', TĚNĚT > Old French *tient* 'he holds', ARSĬT > Old French *arst* 'he burned'. So, the third singular -t of the [i] and [y] *passé simple* is only etymological in the Old French reflexes of strong perfects such as MĪSĬT 'put' *mist*, DĪXĬT 'said' *dist*, FĒCĬT 'made' *fist*, etc. From here it spreads throughout the [i] and [y] *passé simple*:

Old French	Modern French	Old French	Modern French
parti	partis	valu	valus
partis	partis	valus	valus
parti	partit	valu	valut
partimes	partîmes	valumes	valûmes
partistes	partîtes	valustes	valûtes
partirent	partirent	valurent	valurent

Several third plural endings existed in Old French reflexes of the strong perfects. The sigmatics yielded both -istrent and -isdrent, while the waw class gave -urent. FĒCĔRŬNT 'they did' had two outcomes: *fistrent* (by palatalization of [k]) and *firent* (by syncope). Once preconsonantal [s] deletes (§§ 2.1.1, 3.3.3), the ending -itrent is found alongside a variant -isrent. Not surprisingly, confusion reigned for many centuries but by the late 1600s the (mostly) analogical -irent had prevailed.

7.6   Imperfect subjunctive

Romance languages retain the imperfect subjunctive as a category, but express it with morphology taken from two other Latin categories: the pluperfect subjunctive (in Italian, Spanish, and French) and the pluperfect indicative (in Spanish only).[33] These paradigms both belonged to the Latin perfectum system (see Chart 7.3) and were therefore built on perfectum stems, some of which end up as "irregular" forms in Romance.

But the overwhelming majority of perfectum stems are the weak type in [aw] and [iw], and these were soon replaced by short forms with no [w], as we saw (§ 7.5). With [w] gone, these verbs had no contrast between infectum and perfectum stems. This is why they are "regular" from the Romance perspective. Imperfect subjunctives of the weak type, like the weak synthetic pasts, have the same stem as the infinitive: see Chart 7.8.

Ancient sources confirm that short forms of the weak stem were in use throughout the whole perfectum system. For the subjunctives cited in Chart 7.8, the *Instituta artium* approves both forms in class I (PROBAVISSEM, PROBASSEM) and cites only the short forms in class IV (NUTRISSEM). Meanwhile, short forms like CANTASSEM and CANTASSET were being influenced by an archaic perfect subjunctive with forms like CANTASSIM and CANTASSIT. Some examples: LOCASSIM 'I set' (Plautus, *Aulularia* 2, 5, 51), NEGASSIM 'I denied' (Plautus, *Asinaria* 2, 4, 96), PECCASSIT 'he sinned' (Plautus, *Casina* 4, 4, 6), HABESSIT 'he had' (Cicero, *De legibus* 2, 8). These forms infiltrated the paradigm in Chart 7.8, with consequences for Italian (§ 7.6.1) and Romanian (§ 10.6.2).

As for the tense value, the *Instituta artium* still calls them pluperfect subjunctives, but we know that even much earlier they were beginning to function as imperfect subjunctives. An example from the first century BCE is:

seque paratos quaecumque *imperasset* [for *imperaret*], et libenti animo facturos pollicentur[34]

Chart 7.8 The Latin pluperfect subjunctive and Romance imperfect subjunctives

Long forms	Short forms	Italian	Spanish	French
CANTĀV ISSEM	CANTASSEM	cantassi	cantase	chantasse
CANTĀV ISSES	CANTASSES	cantassi	cantases	chantasses
CANTĀV ISSET	CANTASSET	cantasse	cantase	chantât
CANTĀV ISSĒMUS	CANTASSEMUS	cantassimo	cantásemos	chantassions
CANTĀV ISSĒTIS	CANTASSETIS[35]	cantaste	cantaseis	chantassiez
CANTĀV ISSENT	CANTASSENT	cantassero	cantasen	chantassent
PARTĪV ISSEM	PARTISSEM	partissi	partiese	partisse
PARTĪV ISSES	PARTISSES	partissi	partieses	partisses
PARTĪV ISSET	PARTISSET	partisse	partiese	partît
PARTĪV ISSĒMUS	PARTISSEMUS	partissimo	partiésemos	partissions
PARTĪV ISSĒTIS	PARTISSETIS	partiste	partieseis	partissiez
PARTĪV ISSENT	PARTISSENT	partissero	partiesen	partissent

While sliding into a meaning that belongs to the infectum system, will these forms retain a formal alignment with the perfectum system? We'll look at stems as well as endings.

7.6.1   The imperfect subjunctive in Italian

Take any verb with a distinctive perfectum stem, such as *mettere* 'put'. In a revision unique to Italian, one that we saw in the *passato remoto* (§ 7.5.3), the Latin perfectum stem in unstressed position is replaced by the infectum infinitive stem:

MITTERE 'send'	mettere 'put'	
Pluperfect subjunctive	*Imperfect subjunctive*	*Passato remoto*
MĪSĪSSEM	mettessi	misi
MĪSĪSSĒS	mettessi	mettesti
MĪSĪSSET	mettesse	mise
MĪSĪSSĒMUS	mettessimo	mettemmo
MĪSĪSSĒTIS	metteste	metteste
MĪSĪSSENT	mettessero	misero

In the *passato remoto* column, the three arhizotonic forms have switched to the unmarked infectum stem. In the imperfect subjunctive, all six forms are arhizotonic, and all have acquired the infectum stem. What happened here? There were two patterns exerting pressure: (a) the imperfect indicative, arhizotonic throughout its paradigm, has the infectum stem, and (b) weak perfectum stems, also arhizotonic, look like infectum stems once they are shortened. Under these pressures, Italian generalized the pattern: *all arhizotonic* verb forms must be built on the infectum stem.[36] The domain of the perfectum stem (as in *misi*, above) is severely reduced, confined to only three forms of the *passato remoto*, the rhizotonic ones.

Three verbs – *dare* 'give', *stare* 'stay', and *essere* 'be' – have exceptional imperfect subjunctives *desse*, *stesse*, and *fosse* deriving from short forms of the Latin pluperfect subjunctive.

Long forms	*Short forms*	
DEDISSET	DESSET	desse
STETISSET	STESSET	stesse
FŬISSET	FŬSSET	fosse

Question: What changes lead from DEDISSET to DESSET? How is this process like the change from CANTĀVISSET to CANTASSET? How is it different?

Answer: The <i> before <ss> deletes along with the preceding consonant, if any, as the stress shifts back to the preceding vowel.

Only in these three verbs does a strong perfect stem undergo this process of short-ening. These are consequently the only distinctively perfect stems in the Italian imperfect subjunctive.

Consider now the personal endings. Due to frequent confusion with the archaic perfect subjunctive paradigm having endings -SSIM, -SSIS, -SSIT, etc., the short forms above in Chart 7.8 had persistent variants. Old Italian had variants -*sse* and -*ssi* in both first and third singular. Today's Italian settled on -*ssi* for first person and -*sse* for third, probably on the model of the strong *passato remoto* (§ 7.5.5). Two endings of the imperfect subjunctive – the final /e/ of third singular -*asse* -*isse* and, with syncope, second plural -*aste* -*iste* – coincide with *passato remoto* endings. Based on that pattern, the endings -*assi* -*issi* (first singular) and -*assero* -*issero* (third plural) also copy the *passato remoto*, after much vacillation in Old and Renaissance Italian.[37] We might have predicted syncope in the first plural as well as the second, but there is an obstacle: the resulting [st] of the second plural is acceptable, while the potential [sm] of the first plural is disfavored, cf. -ISMU > -*esimo* '-ism' (Tekavčić 1972:II, 370).

7.6.2   Imperfect subjunctive in Spanish

Spanish has two imperfect subjunctive paradigms, both originating in the Latin perfectum system (Chart 7.3). One derives from the short forms of the Latin plu-perfect subjunctive (Chart 7.8) and the other from the short forms of the Latin pluperfect indicative, with the same leveling of stress that we saw in the Spanish imperfect (§ 7.4.2).

Remarks on the -*ir* class: the short forms of the Latin pluperfect indicative lose their waw. The resulting [i̯e], disallowed in Spanish, resolves to the diphthong [je], already prominent in the language. Again, stress in the first and second plural is leveled, shifting back to [je].

In the forms from the Latin pluperfect subjunctive (Chart 7.8), we would expect (*)*partise* instead of the attested *partiese*. The diphthong has spread from

Chart 7.9 The Latin pluperfect indicative and Spanish imperfect subjunctive[38]

Long forms	Short forms	Spanish
CANTĀV ERAM	CANTARAM	cantara
CANTĀV ERĀS	CANTARAS	cantaras
CANTĀV ERAT	CANTARAT	cantara
CANTĀV ERĀMUS	CANTARAMUS	cantáramos
CANTĀV ERĀTIS	CANTARATIS	cantarais
CANTĀV ERANT	CANTARANT	cantaran
PARTĪV ERAM	PARTIERAM	partiera
PARTĪV ERĀS	PARTIERAS	partieras
PARTĪV ERAT	PARTIERAT	partiera
PARTĪV ERĀMUS	PARTIERAMUS	partiéramos
PARTĪV ERĀTIS	PARTIERATIS	partierais
PARTĪV ERANT	PARTIERANT	partieran

the other imperfect subjunctive stem, with reinforcement from the *-ieron* ending of the third plural *pretérito* in the *-er* and *-ir* classes (§ 7.5.2).

In verbs that retain a distinctive perfectum stem from a Latin strong perfect, its reflex still shows up in both kinds of imperfect subjunctive (e.g. *ser* 'be', *fue* 'it was', *si fuese ~ si fuera* 'if it were').

Metaphony operates in both kinds of imperfect subjunctive stem. Again, as in the *pretérito*, its effects are limited to *-ir* verbs (§ 7.5.2). But the whole paradigm shows metaphony, since all forms have a yod (e.g. *sentir* 'feel', *sintiese ~ sintiera*, and *dormir* 'sleep', *durmiese ~ durmiera*).

7.6.3   Imperfect subjunctive in Old French

Though obsolete in speech and nearly so in writing,[39] the imperfect subjunctive has an interesting history displaying in several ways an allegiance to the *passé simple*. These two categories are naturally linked from Popular Latin on, since both are formed on Latin perfectum stems. Just as CANTAVISTI PARTIVISTI and CANTAVISSES PARTIVISSES had short forms CANTASTI PARTISTI and CANTASSES PARTISSES, so also the <u> forms that arose in the *passé simple* (e.g. VALUISTI > *VALUSTI) had corresponding short forms with stress retraction in the imperfect subjunctive (e.g. VALUISSES > *VALUSSES). The two categories continue to form matching pairs in modern French:

Infinitive		Passé simple	Imperfect subjunctive
chanter	'sing'	chantas	chantasses
valoir	'be worth'	valus	valusses
partir	'leave'	partis	partisses

Within the history of French, this affinity hardens into a derivational link: innovations in the *passé simple* are faithfully reflected in the imperfect subjunctive. As we saw (§ 7.5.7), the *passé simple* from Latin strong perfects leveled in favor of either the arhizotonic forms (e.g. *je peignis* 'I painted') or the rhizotonic forms (e.g. *je mis* 'I put') of Old French. Whenever the *passé simple* adopted the rhizotonic stem, the imperfect subjunctive followed suit, even though all its forms had originally been arhizotonic:

Latin	Old French		Modern French	
DĪCĔRE	dire			
'say'	'say'			
Pluperfect subjunctive	*Imperfect subjunctive*	*Passé simple*	*Passé simple*	*Imperfect subjunctive*
DIXISSEM	desisse	dis	dis	disse
DIXISSES	desisses	desis	dis	disses
DIXISSET	desist	dist	dit	dît
DIXISSEMUS	desissons	desimes	dîmes	dissions
DIXISSETIS	desisseiz	desistes	dîtes	dissiez
DIXISSENT	desissent	distrent	dirent	dissent

Ultimately, both the *passé simple* and the imperfect subjunctive fall into a tri-partite system, each class having its own "thematic vowel" ([a] [y] [i]). Yet Old French had forms that failed to conform. Whenever -ISS- has a stressed short vowel it should give -*ess*- [es], and in fact rare forms like *perdesse* (in the ninth-century *Cantilène de Sainte Eulalie*) attest to this outcome. But normally Old French has -*iss*-, as in DIXĪSSES 'you said' *desisses*, MISĪSSES 'you put' *mesisses*, FECĪSSES 'you made' *fesisses* from two analogical models: the class IV imperfect subjunctives like PARTISSES *partisses*, and the similarly positioned [i] of synthetic pasts like *perdis* 'I lost' and *dis* 'I said' (Pope 1934:383). Forms in -*iss*-, mysteri-ously, also occur in the first and second plural of -*er* verbs. Our chart shows *chantassions chantassiez*, but in Old French the usual forms were *chantissons chantissiez*. In fact, the *chantiss*- stem remained stable until the early 1500s.[40] Another possible model can be seen in the many -*ir* verbs having the root exten-sion -*iss*- (§ 6.9). Since already in Old French these verbs had -*iss(i)ons*, -*iss(i) ez* in their first and second plural present indicative and subjunctive as well as imperfect, they greatly increase the overall probability that in a sequence -*V.ssons* or -*V.ssez*, the vowel will be [i]. The [a] ~ [i] alternation was subject to leveling, occasionally in favor of [i] (e.g. Old French *chantisse*, etc.), but from 1600 on increasingly in favor of [a], leading to modern *chantassions chantassiez*.

For the personal endings, refer back to Chart 7.8. Regular sound change from CANTASSEM CANTASSES should have given *chantas *chantas, as in PASSUM 'step' > *pas*. The remodeled *chantasse chantasses* have been attributed to two factors: (a) influence of the present subjunctive (Nyrop:II, 153, Pope 1934:384) and (b) avoidance of homonymy between the first and second person (Fouché 1967:339) or of both with the second singular *passé simple* (Nyrop:II, 153). The second account correctly predicts that third singular *chantast*, being in no dan-ger of homonymic clash, would not need to be remodeled with an added [ə]. In the first and second plural, the modern endings -*ions* and -*iez* arise in the same way as in the present subjunctive (§ 7.3.3) and imperfect indicative (§ 7.4.3).

7.7   Future subjunctive

Two categories of the Latin perfectum system remain to be ousted from their original berths: the future perfect indicative and the perfect subjunctive. Besides differing in the first singular (CANTĀVERŌ CANTĀVERIM), the two paradigms would also have differed in stress position in the first and second plural due to the dis-crepancy between <ĭ> and <ī> in the endings (see Chart 7.1). But their short forms were sure to be confused, not only with each other but with the old imperfect sub-junctive.[41] This is because the short forms always retract stress to the thematic vowel (cf. Chart 7.7, second singular and plural).

	Latin short forms		Spanish
Future perfect indicative		*Perfect subjunctive*	*future subjunctive*
CANTĀRŌ		CANTĀRIM	cantare
CANTĀRIS		CANTĀRIS	cantares
CANTĀRIT		CANTĀRIT	cantare
CANTĀRIMUS		CANTĀRIMUS	cantáremos
CANTĀRITIS		CANTĀRITIS	cantareis
CANTĀRINT		CANTĀRINT	cantaren

These forms were lost in Italian, French, and Romanian. In Spanish and Portuguese (§ 9.16.2) they fuse into a single paradigm and end up as a future subjunctive. The Spanish future subjunctive has the same strong stems as do the other forms deriving from the Latin perfectum system: *tuvieron* 'they held' *tuvieren* 'they will hold', *quisieron* 'they wanted' *quisieren* 'they will want'. As expected, metaphonic raising occurs in *-ir* verbs: *durmieron* 'they slept' *durmieren* 'they will sleep', *sintieron* 'they felt' *sintieren* 'they will feel'. From the Golden Age on (about 1500–1680), the Spanish future subjunctive fades into disuse. By the 1700s it is purely literary and today survives only in legal usage and in some fixed expressions such as: *sea lo que fuere* 'whatever it may be', *venga lo que viniere* 'come what may'.

An amazing fact about the Latin paradigm we call the future perfect indicative (CANTĀVERŌ, short form CANTARO) is that Roman grammarians throughout antiquity were already calling it explicitly a future subjunctive.[42] With this label, it would belong in the empty *infectum* box of Chart 7.1, which is where it settles on the way to Romance ([C] in Chart 7.4).

But its forms contain the *perfectum* stem – a mismatch that irks Latin grammarians. The ancients are at pains to rationalize it, and the moderns finesse it by calling the paradigm a future perfect. But to ordinary pre-Romance speakers, especially Ibero-Romance, the mismatch would hardly be jarring, when they were importing other perfectum forms into the infectum category of imperfect subjunctive (see [B] and especially Ibero-Romance [A] in Chart 7.3). Moreover, this mismatch is mostly camouflaged, because Latin weak perfectum stems, when shortened, coincide with infectum stems. Only strong perfectum stems (and only a dwindling subset of these in Spanish) remain distinctly perfectum: *decir* 'say' but *dijo*, *dijese ~ dijera*, *dijere*. These few "irregularities" are absorbed and tolerated in Romance verb systems.

7.8   Future and conditional

Meet our candidate for the single most important concept in the historical study of verb systems: *periphrastic verb forms*. Examples in English are: *is stealing, has stolen, will steal*. These two-piece forms have a non-finite element conveying the lexical core, while the other element is an auxiliary, typically showing subject agreement. One appealing property of periphrastics is that the auxiliary itself can take on different tenses: given a progressive *is stealing*, a past progressive *was stealing* is available automatically. Whatever the reason for their success, periphrastics are a staple of the world's languages. In languages with long historical records, we often see new periphrastics gaining favor and replacing the old over the centuries (today, *will say* is losing ground to a newer future *is gonna say*, though they are by no means interchangeable).

7.8.1   The main Romance future

In Popular Latin, the old future (CANTĀBŌ etc. in Chart 7.1) had fallen into disuse by late antiquity and perhaps had never been favored in casual style.[43] The present tense was usually adequate to express future time. One ancient grammarian plainly documents this usage by deploring it:[44]

No other error is so commonly made, even by educated people. The present is while something is going on. Anything else, if it is not going on, is not present. I cannot say *lego* except while I am actually reading. So if you say to me, 'read me Virgil' and I reply *lego*, this is incorrect. Since I am not yet doing it, how can I use the present tense? Hence we must say *legam* 'I will read'.

Meanwhile, new periphrastics with a similar value were emerging, soon to take root as future tenses in Romance. While other formats occur (DEBEO 'must' plus infinitive, VOLO 'want' plus infinitive), the major Western languages adopted the format infinitive plus HABEO 'have' with the forms of HABEO shortened, as is typical of auxiliaries (§ 6.10.2):

Popular Latin	Italian	Spanish	French
CANTAR *[ajo]	canterò	cantaré	chanterai
CANTAR *[as]	canterai	cantarás	chanteras
CANTAR *[at]	canterà	cantará	chantera
CANTAR *[emos]	canteremo	cantaremos	chanterons
CANTAR *[etis]	canterete	cantareis	chanterez
CANTAR *[a(u)nt]	canteranno	cantarán	chanteront

Exploring the genesis of this Romance future, scholars have collected dozens of Latin examples like those below, showing how the early modal values ('have something to say' or 'have to say something') bleached to a plain future value.[45]

DE ... SOMNIIS QUID HABEMUS DICERE?
concerning ... dreams what have we to say (what can we say)?

(Cicero, *Academicae Quaestiones* 2, 136)

SIMON, HABEO TIBI ALIQUID DICERE
Simon, I have something to say to you

(Vulgate, Luke 7:40)

QUIDAM TEMPUS PRAESENS ESSE NEGANT, DICENTES RES AUT FACTAS ESSE AUT HABERE FIERI
some people deny the existence of a present tense, saying that things either were done or
will be done

(Sacerdos, *Ars Grammatica*. In Keil 1857:VI, 432)

TEMPESTAS ILLA TOLLERE HABET TOTAM PALEAM DE AREA
that tempest will lift all the chaff from the threshing floor

(Augustine, *In Evangelium Iohannis* 4, 1, 2)

COD ESTIS FUI ET QUOD SUM ESSERE ABETIS
what you are, I was, and what I am, you will be

(Diehl 1961 :3865)

Before the first Romance documents, the periphrastic future had already congealed into a single word, with the reduced forms of HABEO serving as inflections. In a famous early example, a seventh-century Latin chronicler juxtaposes the old and new futures: NON DABO 'I will not give' and DARAS 'you will give'.[46] Two centuries later, in the first Old French document, dated 842 (§ 12.2.1), there are fully fused Romance futures: *salvarai* 'I will save' < SALVARE[ajo] and *prindrai* 'I will take' < PRENDERE[ajo]. In Spanish, however, until well into the 1500s, there is still some awareness that the future consists of two pieces: they can be separated by clitic pronouns (nothing else). For example, alongside *le darás* 'you will give to him/her', there was also *dar le has* (Menéndez Pidal 1966:324). The same is true of Portuguese even today (§ 9.15.1).

Some future stems have a shortened form of the infinitive. A few infinitives, as we know, were shortened even in isolation (e.g. FACERE 'do' > Italian *fare* hence *farò* 'I will do'), but in a number of verbs the future acquires a syncopated stem of its own. This is because in the periphrastic, it is the auxiliary that carries the main stress of the whole phrase. So the penultimate vowel of the infinitive (even if stressed in the isolated word, as in POTERE below) is unstressed in the context of the future periphrastic. If it deletes by syncope, the result is a cluster of the form /Cr/:

Popular Latin		*Italian*	*Spanish*	*French*
*POTERE	'be able'	potere	poder	pouvoir
*POTER-AT	'will be able'	potrà	podrá	pourra

The /Cr/ clusters arising in syncopated infinitives may need adjustment to conform to the **phonotactics** of the language (constraints on permitted sequences of phonemes).

Latin	*Italian*		*Spanish*		*French*	
Infinitive	*Infinitive*	*Future*	*Infinitive*	*Future*	*Infinitive*	*Future*
TĒNĒRE 'hold'	tenere	terrà	tener	tendrá	tenir	tiendra
VALĒRE 'be worth'	valere	varrà	valer	valdrá	valoir	vaudra
PŌNĒRE 'put'	porre	porrà	poner	pondrá	pondre	pondra
VĔNĪRE 'come'	venire	verrà	venir	vendrá	venir	viendra

> Question: Recalling the examples of syncope in § 2.2.2, identify the mechanism of cluster resolution favored in each language. What is unusual about Old Spanish *porná* 'he will put', *verná* 'he will come'?
>
> Answer: Italian favors assimilation. Spanish and French favor epenthesis. The Old Spanish forms have metathesis, as seen in VENĔRIS 'Friday' *viernes* (§ 2.2.2).

Old Spanish had many syncopated future stems that have been replaced by regularized stems reflecting today's infinitive: e.g. *comer* 'eat' Old Spanish *combrá*, now *comerá*, and *doler* 'hurt' Old Spanish *doldrá*, now *dolerá*. Italian retains more syncopated future stems, including nearly all verbs of class II[47] and many in class III. Class IV has syncope only in *venire* 'come', and, in long-outmoded usage, *udire* 'hear', *morire* 'die'. Old Italian also had a few optionally syncopated future stems where today's language accepts only the regularized stem (e.g. *sciogliere* 'melt', Old Italian *scioglierà/sciorrà* 'will melt', now *scioglierà*).

In class I verbs, such syncopes never occur in Spanish, since [a] was immune to syncope. In Italian, the [a] of class I always weakens to [e], as in *CANTAR-ĄT cantèrà*, but does not delete (the sole exception is *andare* 'go', *andrà* 'will go'). In French, in this same context, class I verbs have [ə] by regular sound change, but in today's pronunciation it normally deletes: *CANTAR-AT > chantera* [ʃɑ̃təʀa] or [ʃɑ̃tʀa].[48]

The future stem of 'be' is a special case. Forms like Popular Latin *ESSER-AT, instead of syncopating, lose their initial syllable to give Italian *sarà* and French *sera*.[49] This apheresis, somewhat unusual in the history of Romance, was probably fostered by the present forms of 'be' that begin with [s]. The [a] in the Italian stem has been ascribed to analogy with *farà* 'will do', *darà* 'will give', and *starà* 'will stay', which in turn retain their [a] on the model of the monosyllabic present indicatives *fa*, *dà*, *sta* with stressed [a]. The three languages differ in the proximity of the future stem to the infinitive. They are identical in Spanish (*ser ~ ser-*), while in Italian and French the future stem has strayed away from the infinitives *essere* and *être*. *Être*, from Old French *estre*, results from the syncope of Popular Latin ESSERE followed by [t] epenthesis. It had its own future *estra* 'will be' competing in Old French with *sera* and with *iert/ert* (§ 7.8.2).

7.8.2   Relics of the original Latin future

The future of Latin ESSE 'be' was irregular and sufficiently distinct to be in no danger of homonymy with other paradigms. After surviving in Old French until the 1300s, it ceded its place to the periphrastic.

Latin	Old French	Modern French
ĔRŌ	ier ~ er	serai
ĔRIS	iers ~ ers	seras
ĔRIT	iert ~ ert[50]	sera
ĔRĬMUS	iermes ~ ermes	serons

| ĒRĬTIS | *iertz ~ *ertz | serez |
| ĒRUNT | ierent ~ erent | seront |

The forms with a diphthong are regular. But the verb *be* can also be unstressed, which accounts for the variants without the diphthong. The only modern relic of the Latin future paradigm is Spanish *eres* 'you are', which was redeployed as a present to avoid homonymy between the reflexes of ES EST (§ 6.10.1).

7.8.3   The new 'go' futures

Among the periphrastics that continue to arise over the centuries, one prominent formation is the future with a verb 'go' as auxiliary, the type Spanish *va a cantar*, French *il va chanter*, Brazilian Portuguese *vai cantar*, absent in Italian (in *va a cantare*, the verb 'go' can only be interpreted literally, i.e. he is going somewhere to sing). Evidence for the grammaticalization of 'go' as an auxiliary comes from such examples as *va a quedarse, il va rester* 'he's going to stay', and *va a llover, il va pleuvoir* 'it's going to rain', where a literal reading of the 'go' verb is unavailable. Like the English 'going to' type, these formations have encroached on an older future. This pattern is typical of the life cycle of periphrastics. New periphrastic (analytic) forms tend to replace older one-word (synthetic) forms, themselves originally periphrastic.

7.8.4   The invention of a new mood: conditional

Once a form like CANTARE HABET comes to mean 'will sing', a corresponding form CANTARE HABEBAT is potentially available to mean a future in the past.

In reported speech Latin used infinitives and participles to express the main verbs of the reported discourse. Here VENTURUM exemplifies the future participle:

| DICIT | MARCUM | VENTURUM | ESSE |
| he says | Marcus | going to come | be |

'he says Marcus will come'

| DIXIT | MARCUM | VENTURUM | ESSE |
| he said | Marcus | going to come | be |

'he said Marcus would come'

A major innovation in spoken Latin was the rise of complementizers (QUOD 'that' among others) introducing a clause with a finite verb:

| DICIT | QUOD | MARCUS | VENTURUS | EST |
| he says | that | Marcus | going to come | is |

'he says that Marcus will come'

| DIXIT | QUOD | MARCUS | VENTURUS | ERAT |
| he said | that | Marcus | going to come | was |

'he said that Marcus would come'

As the future participle receded and the new future periphrastic gained ground, it was natural for the contrast EST ~ ERAT to be reproduced in the new future auxiliary:

DICIT	QUOD	MARCUS	VENIRE	HABET
he says	that	Marcus	will come	

DIXIT	QUOD	MARCUS	VENIRE	HABEBAT
he said	that	Marcus	would come	

Such constructions are indeed attested, as in:

SANARE TE HABEBAT DEUS…SI FATERERIS
God would heal you…if you confessed

(Pseudo-Augustinus, *Sermones*, 253, 4)

Out of this combination grew a new paradigm that ultimately took over many uses of the Latin subjunctive, including conditional sentences. Latin had no single grammatical category corresponding to what was to become the Romance conditional mood.

Chart 7.10 The conditional

Latin	*Popular Latin*	*Italian*	*Spanish*	*French*
CANTARE HABĒBAM	CANTAR *[ea]	canterei	cantaría	chanterais
CANTARE HABĒBĀS	CANTAR *[eas]	canteresti	cantarías	chanterais
CANTARE HABĒBAT	CANTAR *[eat]	canterebbe	cantaría	chanterait
CANTARE HABĒBĀMUS	CANTAR *[eamus]	canteremmo	cantaríamos	chanterions
CANTARE HABĒBĀTIS	CANTAR *[eatis]	cantereste	cantaríais	chanteriez
CANTARE HABĒBANT	CANTAR *[eant]	canterebbero	cantarían	chanteraient

Question: What changes lead from the imperfect of HABĒRE to the reduced forms?

Answer: Apheresis and lenition.

Question: What happened to the stress position in the Spanish conditional?

Answer: In the first and second plural, stress retracts to the previous syllable just as in the imperfect indicative (§ 7.4.2).

Question: What is distinctive about the conditional in Italian?

Answer: The auxiliary portion derives from the perfect, not from the imperfect, of HABĒRE (§ 7.5.5).

7.9   A bombshell: the birth of periphrastic perfects

Another periphrastic that thrived in Romance is the type HABEO CANTATUM 'I have sung', consisting of an auxiliary and a past participle as in: Italian *ho cantato*, Spanish *he cantado*, French *j'ai chanté*, and their counterparts throughout the Romance family.[51] Besides examining its origin, a favorite topic of Romance linguists, we must also ask what functions it has acquired in the individual languages and understand how it was able to displace the entire Latin perfectum system.

7.9.1   Genesis of the periphrastic perfect

The Latin perfect has two values: CANTAVI means both 'I have sung' (true perfect) and 'I sang' (preterite), and there was no HABEO CANTATUM with either meaning. How did this major grammatical innovation get underway? In the first place, Latin HABERE 'have', like English *have*, is more than a verb of possession. To what extent do you think these English examples express possession?

a. Do you remember where I have the car parked?
b. They have us convinced now.
c. She has her lines memorized.

Clearly, these do not logically entail possession in the same way as, say, *I have my ticket.* In (a), (b), and (c) the subject is a person somehow involved in the achievement of a situation, and the rest of the sentence expresses that situation in a compact form. Furthermore, the subject is not necessarily the one who brings about the situation:

d. He has 200-year-old trees planted around his house.

This same *have* construction is attested throughout the history of Latin. For example:[52]

e. CAPUT CINCTUM HABEBANT FILO
    they had their heads girded with a cord

(Varro, *De lingua latina* 5, 15)

f. (MONACHUS) QUI HABET CURAM PEREGRINORUM DEPUTATAM
    (a monk) who has the care of visitors assigned (to him)

(Cassian, *Institutiones* 4, 7)

g. NAM CAPILLOS NOSTROS IPSE UTIQUE CREAVIT ET NUMERATOS HABET
    for He created our hairs and has them counted

(Augustine, *Sermones* 62, 10, 15)

Consider how the properties are similar to those of the English construction: HABERE does not express possession, and the subject is not necessarily the one who brings about the situation, as is clear in (f).

These constructions with HABERE are the source of the new periphrastic perfect, which, however, has different properties. In English, the main contrast we see is in word order and constituent structure:

h. She has [the key] [hidden].
i. She [has hidden] the key.

Have in (h) behaves like a main verb and in (i) like an auxiliary. This is evident because in English questions we use *do* with main verbs and inversion with auxiliaries:

j. Does she have the key hidden?
k. Has she hidden the key?

In the constructions exemplified in (a) through (h) a direct object is obligatory. But once HABERE becomes an auxiliary it can combine with intransitive verbs:

l. DE EA RE SUPRA SCRIPTUM HABEMUS
    we have written above on that matter

(Vitruvius, De architectura 9, 1, 4)

m. SICUT PARABOLATUM HABUISTIS
    as you had said

(Formulae Salicae Merkelianae 260.7)[53]

In (l) and (m), HABERE + past participle unambiguously reflects the new periphrastic perfect. Naturally, the periphrastic perfect could also be used with transitive verbs. In (n), HABERE is an auxiliary verb:

n. EPISCOPUM INVITATUM HABES
    you have invited the bishop

(Gregory of Tours, Vitae Patrum 3,1)

Meanwhile the older construction exemplified in (e), (f), and (g) still existed. Remarkable evidence that both constructions coexist comes from a third-century legal commentary:

"sive quid in id flumen ripamve eius immissum habes ... restituas ..." iubetur autem is qui factum vel immissum habet restituere quod habet ... haec verba "factum habes" vel "immissum habes" ostendunt non eum teneri qui fecit vel immisit, sed qui factum immissum habet

"*or if you have something extended into the river or the bank, you should restore it*" However, the one who has the thing built or extended is ordered to restore what he has ...The words "*you have something built*" or "*you have something extended into*" mean that the person held responsible is not the one who built or extended the thing, but the one who owns it now[54]

Ulpianus, the commentator, emphasizes that in this context HABET FACTUM means 'has something which is built' and not the perfect 'has built something'.

Why then do we take this to be evidence for the currency of the new periphrastic perfect? Because Ulpianus believed the phrase could be misconstrued as 'has built'.

7.9.2   The power of periphrastics: how they can rebuild the perfectum system

Look back to Chart 7.4, representing a stage where the Latin perfect indicative was the only element of the whole perfectum system still remaining vigorous in popular usage, while the other perfectum forms were either falling into disuse or shifting to other functions. The new periphrastic perfect begins life as an alternative perfect (HABEO CANTATUM competing with CANTAVI). By varying the tense and mood of its auxiliary, it has the potential to fill the empty boxes throughout the perfectum system. This is what happened in Popular Latin.

Chart 7.11 The new periphrastic perfects in Popular Latin

	INFECTUM				PERFECTUM	
	Old	New			Old	New
Present	CANTO	CANTO		Preterite	CANTAVI	CANTAVI
				True perfect	CANTAVI	HABEO CANTATU
Imperfect	CANTABAM	CANTABAM		Pluperfect	CANTAVERAM	HABEBAM CANTATU
Future	CANTABO	CANTAR[ajo]		Future perfect	CANTAVERO	HABER [ajo] CANTATU
Conditional	....	CANTAR[ea]		Past conditional	....	HABER [eam] CANTATU

Recognizable in Chart 7.11 is the architecture of the typical Romance verb system. The new periphrastic perfects are shaded. Even the new conditional mood was supplied with its own perfect.

The subjunctives in the perfectum follow suit. Perfect CANTAVERIM gives way to HABEAM CANTATU, and the pluperfect is supplied by HABUISSEM CANTATU.

7.9.3   Competition between synthetic and periphrastic forms

In Chart 7.11, CANTAVI and HABEO CANTATU share the same box. They are bound to be rivals. Recall (§ 7.9.1) that the Latin perfect has two values: CANTAVI means both 'I have sung' (true perfect) and 'I sang' (preterite). When HABEO CANTATU enters the system, it has true perfect meaning, 'I have sung', and can thus take over that half of the domain of CANTAVI:

	Latin	*Popular Latin*
True perfect	CANTAVI	HABEO CANTATU
	'I have sung'	'I have sung'
Preterite	CANTAVI	CANTAVI
	'I sang'	'I sang'

This is the scenario reflected in Standard European Spanish and in Standard Italian. In other Romance languages the periphrastic past continued to expand its domain. One possibility is for the periphrastic past to invade the domain of the Romance synthetic past (from CANTAVI), leaving it alive but in some way restricted:

	Popular Latin	Romance
True perfect	HABEO CANTATU	HABEO CANTATU
	'I have sung'	'I have sung'
Preterite	CANTAVI	HABEO CANTATU and CANTAVI
	'I sang'	'I sang'

This is the situation in French and in most Northern Italian varieties. Another possibility is for the periphrastic past to expand further and entirely supplant the synthetic past:

	Popular Latin	Romance
True perfect	HABEO CANTATU	HABEO CANTATU
	'I have sung'	'I have sung'
Preterite	CANTAVI	HABEO CANTATU
	'I sang'	'I sang'

This outcome, where reflexes of the Latin synthetic perfect have vanished from everyday usage, characterizes today's spoken French and spoken varieties of Northern Italian. In this system, a periphrastic form (HABEO CANTATUM) is doing the work of both preterite and true perfect, just as a synthetic form (CANTAVI) did in Latin.

In yet another scenario the periphrastic acquires a special aspectual value of its own and does not invade the domain of the CANTAVI type (Portuguese, Galician, Leonese, Sicilian, and southern Calabrian dialects).

In the subjunctive mood the periphrastic past has no rival: it expresses both true perfect and preterite meanings in all three languages with no competition from the old synthetic perfect subjunctive forms, which were forgotten or redeployed in another function (Chart 7.4 and § 7.7).

7.9.4   Morphosyntax of the periphrastic past

If you know Italian or French, you are aware that the periphrastic past, under some conditions, requires as its auxiliary not 'have' but 'be': Italian *è caduto*, French *il est tombé* 'he has fallen/he fell'. Descriptively speaking, the 'be' auxiliary is required with reflexive constructions and with a subset of the intransitive verbs. Two questions arise.

First, what determines which auxiliary is required in a given context? Since the 1970s, linguists have addressed this question with varying degrees of success.[55] Any attempt to do justice here to this chiefly synchronic issue would be a wrenching interruption in the agenda of this book.

The second question, more germane to our diachronic perspective, is how an alternation between 'have' and 'be' auxiliaries arose. On this matter scholarly opinion has

Chart 7.12

Passive voice						
INDICATIVE				SUBJUNCTIVE		
p r e s e n t	Infectum	Perfectum		Infectum	Perfectum	
	(Present)	(Perfect)		(Present)	(Perfect)	
	AMOR	AMĀTUS SUM		AMER	AMĀTUS SIM	
	AMĀRIS/AMĀRE	AMĀTUS ES		AMĒRIS/AMĒRE	AMĀTUS SĪS	
	AMĀTUR	AMĀTUS EST		AMĒTUR	AMĀTUS SIT	
	AMĀMUR	AMĀTĪ SUMUS		AMĒMUR	AMĀTĪ SĪMUS	
	AMĀMINĪ	AMĀTĪ ESTIS		AMĒMINĪ	AMĀTĪ SĪTIS	
	AMANTUR	AMĀTĪ SUNT		AMENTUR	AMĀTĪ SINT	
p a s t	(Imperfect)	(Pluperfect)		(Imperfect)	(Pluperfect)	
	AMĀBAR	AMĀTUS ERAM		AMĀRER	AMĀTUS ESSEM	
	AMĀBĀRIS/AMĀBĀRE	AMĀTUS ERĀS		AMĀRĒRIS/AMĀRĒRE	AMĀTUS ESSĒS	
	AMĀBĀTUR	AMĀTUS ERAT		AMĀRĒTUR	AMĀTUS ESSET	
	AMĀBĀMUR	AMĀTĪ ERĀMUS		AMĀRĒMUR	AMĀTĪ ESSĒMUS	
	AMĀBĀMINĪ	AMĀTĪ ERĀTIS		AMĀRĒMINĪ	AMĀTĪ ESSĒTIS	
	AMĀBANTUR	AMĀTĪ ERANT		AMĀRENTUR	AMĀTĪ ESSENT	
f u t u r e	(Future)	(Future Perfect)				
	AMĀBOR	AMĀTUS ERŌ				
	AMĀBERIS/AMĀBERE	AMĀTUS ERIS				
	AMĀBITUR	AMĀTUS ERIT				
	AMĀBIMUR	AMĀTĪ ERIMUS				
	AMĀBIMINĪ	AMĀTĪ ERITIS				
	AMĀBUNTUR	AMĀTĪ ERUNT				

long been fairly stable. Recall that Latin had a class of verbs known as deponents, active in meaning but passive in form (§ 6.1.3). Just as Chart 7.1 shows a sample conjugation in the active voice, Chart 7.12 shows a corresponding passive conjugation.

One key fact on display here is that Latin passives were periphrastic in form throughout the perfectum system. Caution: AMĀTUS EST means not 'he is loved' but rather 'he has been loved/was loved'.

Deponent verbs conjugate as in Chart 7.12, even though their meaning is active. Therefore, in a deponent verb such as MORĪ 'die', alongside MORĪTUR 'dies', the perfect is MORTUUS EST 'died/has died'. As the category of deponent verbs dissolves, their *infectum* system shifts to the ordinary active forms as in Chart 7.1, hence pre-Romance class IV MORĪRE and MŎRIT 'dies'. But, crucially, their *perfectum* system remains periphrastic. Thus, periphrastic perfects of the form EST MORTUUS were poised to enter into a paradigmatic relationship with those of the form HABET CANTATU. Both structures had the same tense and aspect values, and differed only in their auxiliary. Certain verbs that had never been deponent began to use the 'be' auxiliary:

SORORES	UNA	DIE	OBITAE	SUNT	(CIL VI 17633)
sisters	one	day	passed away	are	

'Sisters, they passed away on the same day'

Evidently a periphrastic past using both 'have' and 'be' auxiliaries arose in Popular Latin at some early stage and later receded in favor of 'have' in some regions. Vestiges of a two-auxiliary system appear in Old Spanish, Old Portuguese, and Old Catalan, and the two-auxiliary system still thrives in Italian, French, Occitan, and the Rheto-Romance varieties. Similar patterns exist in Balearic Catalan, Sardinian, and Dalmatian. The degree to which the alternation is systematic is not equally certain for all of these.[56]

Hand in hand with the retreat of auxiliary 'be' (for which agreement of the past participle with the subject was and has remained obligatory) goes an overall reduction in the syntactic environments for past participle agreement. We cannot cover the specifics of contemporary studies. Suffice it to say that at first the participle always showed adjective agreement with the direct object, a property inherited from the older 'have' construction (Pharies 2007:128):

UBI IPSI CASTRA POSITA HABEBANT
'where they had the camp located'

(Peregrinatio Aetheriae 9, 11)

A convincing example of agreement in the new periphrastic past is:

METUO ENIM NE VOS IBI HABEAM FATIGATOS
'for I fear that I may have tired you out'

(Augustine, *Sermones* 37, 27)

Here VOS imposes agreement on FATIGATOS (masculine plural accusative). But early evidence for the shrinkage of agreement environments is also found:

HAEC OMNIA PROBATUM HABEMUS
we have tried all these things

(Oribasius, *Synagogue medicae* 7, 48, pp. 189f.)

If the object OMNIA were imposing agreement like VOS in the preceding example, the past participle would be PROBATA (neuter plural accusative).

7.10   The passive voice

The Latin passive system exemplified in Chart 7.12 undergoes a drastic revision. The forms of the infectum, all synthetic, vanished entirely. They were replaced by what had been forms of the perfectum, all periphrastic. So AMĀTUR 'is loved' disappears, and instead AMĀTUS EST, formerly a perfect, takes on that present meaning. The same occurs in all the other tenses and moods. (See Chart 7.13.)

Chart 7.13 The passive shift in Popular Latin

Passive voice							
	INDICATIVE				SUBJUNCTIVE		
p r e s e n t	Infectum	Perfectum			Infectum	Perfectum	
	(Present) EST AMĀTU è amato es amado il est aimé	(Perfect) ⟵			(Present) SIT AMĀTU sia amato sea amado il soit aimé	(Perfect) ⟵	
p a s t	(Imperfect) ERAT AMĀTU era amato era amado il était aimé	(Pluperfect) ⟵			(Imperfect) FUERAT / FUISSET AMĀTU fosse amato fuera / fuese amado il fût aimé	(Pluperfect) ⟵	
f u t u r e	(Future) [ESSERE HABET] AMĀTU sarà amato será amado il sera aimé	(Future perfect) ⟵			(Future) FUERIT AMĀTU ... OSp fuere amado ...	not in Latin	
c o n d i t	(Conditional) [ESSERE HABĒBAT / HABUIT] AMĀTU sarebbe amato sería amado il serait aimé	not in Latin					

With this shift, the mismatch in Latin between the tense of the auxiliary and the tense of the passive verb as a whole (AMĀTUS EST originally meant 'has been/ was loved') is resolved so that the tense of the verb form equals the tense of the auxiliary (AMĀTUS EST comes to mean 'is loved'). As seen above, this shift also leaves the whole passive perfectum system in need of new morphology. The void is readily filled by putting the auxiliary into the newly available periphrastic forms:

è stata amata	ha sido amada	elle a été aimée	'she has been loved'
era stata amata	había sido amada	elle avait été aimée	'she had been loved'
sarà stata amata	será sido amada	elle aura été aimée	'she will have been loved'

For auxiliary ESSE 'be' to form a periphrastic perfect, it needs a past participle, which had not previously existed. Italian and French press into service the participle of STARE 'stand',[57] while Spanish creates *sido* 'been' based on *ser* 'be'.

7.11   Past participles old and new

Past participles in Latin were of two types: weak and strong. Like weak perfects (§ 7.1.2), weak past participles are arhizotonic: CANTĀTU 'sung', DELĒTU 'destroyed', BATTŪTU 'beaten', PARTĪTU 'departed'. The first and last types, typical of the large verb classes I and IV, were numerous and have reflexes in all Romance languages.

	Italian	Spanish	French
CANTĀTU	cantato	cantado	chanté
PARTĪTU	partito	partido	parti

Participles in -ĒTU, like perfects in -ĒV-, were rare, and none survive in Romance as participles. In Spanish, verbs of the -er class (from the merger of Latin classes II and III) regularly form weak participles in -ĪTU > -ido. The -ŪTU type, as we will shortly see, enjoys more widespread success.

7.11.1   Retention of strong participles

Strong participles, i.e. rhizotonic, were of the form -ĪTU (HABĬTU 'had'), -TU (SCRIPTU 'written'), or -SU (MISSU 'sent'), and belonged chiefly to classes II and III.[58] Italian retains many of these, French fewer, while Spanish tends to make past participles weak, leaving intact just a handful of strong participles.

Latin		Italian	Spanish	French
APĔRTU	'open'	aperto	abierto	ouvert
SCRIPTU	'written'	scritto	escrito	écrit
DICTU	'said'	detto	dicho	dit
FACTU	'done'	fatto	hecho	fait
MORTUU	'died'	morto	muerto	mort
POSĬTU	'put'	posto	puesto	...
FUSU	'melted'	fuso	...	...
CŬRSU	'run'	corso	...	...
COCTU	'cooked'	cotto	...	cuit
CLAUSU	'closed'	chiuso	...	clos
CONCLUSU	'concluded'	concluso	...	conclu

Syncope in forms like *PŌSTU < PŌSĬTU 'put' brings them into line with others like EXHAUSTU 'exhausted' and TOSTU 'roasted', probably fostering the spread of -STU in past participles.

Latin			Italian	Spanish
VIDĒRE	'see'	VISU	visto	visto
REMANĒRE	'remain'	REMANSU	rimasto	...
RESPONDĒRE	'respond'	RESPONSU	risposto	respuesto (OSp)

Modern French has reflexes of strong past participles that are unrecognizable as such because deletion of a final consonant makes them look like class IV weak participles:

Latin			Old French	Modern French
RIDĒRE	'laugh'	RĪSU	ris	ri
SUFFICĔRE	'suffice'	SUFFECTU	suffit	suffi

7.11.2   New weak participles

But overall the main trend is to replace strong past participles by weak ones. This can be accomplished in three ways. First and most conspicuously, in Italian and French the weak ending -ŪTU, at first confined to a few verbs, spreads dramatically, replacing nearly all of the -ĪTUS type past participles and further making inroads in classes II and III.

Latin			Innovations	Italian	French
HABĒRE	'have'	HABĬTU	*HABŪTU	avuto	eu
DEBĒRE	'owe'	DĒBĬTU	*DEBŪTU	dovuto	dû
VĒNDĔRE	'sell'	VENDĬTU	*VENDŪTU	venduto	vendu
PĔRDĔRE	'lose'	PERDĬTU	*PERDŪTU	perduto	perdu
CRĒDĔRE	'believe'	CREDĬTU	*CREDŪTU	creduto	cru
RECĬPĔRE	'receive'	RECEPTU	*RICEVŪTU	ricevuto	reçu
CADĔRE	'fall'	CASU	*CADŪTU	caduto	chu
CRESCĔRE	'grow'	CRĒTU	*CRESCŪTU	cresciuto	crû

POSSE 'can' and VELLE 'want' had no past participles, but when remade in Popular Latin as class II verbs, they are supplied with -UTU participles.

Latin			Popular Latin		Italian	French
POSSE	'can'	…	*PŎTĒRE	*POTUTU	potuto	pu
VELLE	'want'	…	*VŎLĒRE	*VOLUTU	voluto	voulu

Old Spanish also participates in the trend, but Modern Spanish has since eliminated all its -udo participles in favor of -ido ones.

Latin			Innovations	Old Spanish	Modern Spanish
COGNOSCĔRE	'know'	COGNĬTU	*COGNOSCUTU	cognozudo	conocido
MĬTTĔRE	'send'	MĬSSU	*METTUTU	metudo	metido
MŎVĒRE	'move'	MOVĬTU	*MOVUTU	movudo	movido
VĪNCĔRE	'win'	VĪCTU	*VINCUTU	vençudo	vencido

The spread of -UTU touched even a few class IV verbs, but Modern Italian retains only one and French two.

Latin			Innovations	Old Italian	Italian	French
FINĪRE	'finish'	FINĪTU	*FINUTU	finuto	finito	fini
SENTĪRE	'feel'	SENSU	*SENTUTU	sentuto	sentito	senti
VENĪRE	'come'	VENTU	*VENUTU	venuto	venuto	venu
VESTĪRE	'dress'	VESTĪTU	*VESTUTU	vestuto	vestito	vêtu

A second way of replacing strong participles with weak ones occurs in Spanish, where -*er* verbs can freely create participles in -*ido*.

Latin / Popular Latin				Spanish	
PRE(H) ENDĔRE	'hold'	PRE(H)ENSU		prender	prendido
VINCĔRE	'win'	VICTU		vencer	vencido
DEBĒRE	'owe'	DEBĬTU		deber	debido
MOVĒRE	'move'	MOVĬTU		mover	movido
*POTĒRE	'can'	*POTŪTU		poder	podido

Lastly, some verbs, chiefly in Spanish, moved wholesale into class IV (§ 6.1.2), thus automatically acquiring weak participles in -ĪTU (*recibido* etc.).

Latin			Italian	Spanish	French
RECĬPĔRE	'receive'	RECEPTU	…	recibir	…
VĪVĔRE	'live'	VĪCTU	…	vivir	…
SURGĔRE	'rise'	SURSU	…	surgir	surgir
AGĔRE	'do'	ACTU	agire	agir	agir

7.11.3   **Past participles and reflexes of the strong perfects: an analogical *pas de deux***

Nowhere in Latin is the force of analogy more busily intense than in pairing the strong perfects with strong participles. Always recessive, losing ground to productive weak forms, the surviving strong forms are "irregular" from today's perspective. As if to support each other, they gravitated into clusters conforming to some smaller regularity. There were analogical realignments in every possible direction, and sometimes in multiple directions, starting in Popular Latin and continuing for centuries.

For example, the way the sigmatic and waw classes of strong perfects gained new members (§ 7.5.4) was not random. Verbs with a participle in -SU often acquired sigmatic perfects, as in *MORSIT 'bit' replacing MOMORDIT on the model of MORSU 'bitten'. Certain frequent pairings of participle and perfect could attract new recruits: LĒGĬT 'he read' was replaced in this way.

Past participle	Perfect	
DICTU	DIXIT	'he said'
CONDUCTU	CONDUXIT	'he drove'
LECTU	*LEXIT	'he read'

In the same way, RŪPIT 'he broke' became RUPUIT, and BĬBĔRE 'drink', which had lacked a perfect, acquired one in Popular Latin:

Past participle	Perfect	
RAPTU	RAPUIT	'he seized'
RUPTU	*RUPUIT	'he broke'

HABĬTU	HABUIT	'he had'
BĬBĬTU	*BĬBUIT	'he drank'

Analogical interactions between past participles and reflexes of the strong perfects leave numerous traces in the Romance languages. Old Spanish has several strong *pretéritos* that are clearly reflexes of perfects remade to match their past participles:

	Latin		*Old Spanish*		
Perfect	*Past participle*		*Past participle*	*Pretérito*	
EXPĔNDĬT	EXPENSU		espeso	espiso	'he spent'
PRE(HE)NDĬT	PRĒ(HEN)SU		preso	priso	'he took'

Some Italian past participles were created analogically, copying established patterns. From the Latin EX-PANDĔRE 'spread out' EX-PANXIT EX-PANSU we expect Popular Latin *spandere spanse spanso*, but *spanso* was remade, joining this group:

Passato remoto	*Past participle*	
pianse	pianto	'wept'
punse	punto	'stung'
vinse	vinto	'won'
spanse	spanto	'spread out'

Similarly, from FĪGĔRE 'fix' FĪXĬT FĪXU the regular outcomes would be *figgere fisse fisso*, but the participle was changed to match another pattern:

Passato remoto	*Past participle*	
condusse	condotto	'driven'
lesse	letto	'read'
resse	retto	'supported'
fisse	fitto	'stuck, fixed'

Finally, Old Italian *vivuto* 'lived', formed from the infectum stem VIV-, was remade as *vissuto* based on the perfectum stem VIX-, so Old Italian *visse vivuto* becomes a modern matched pair *visse vissuto*.

In French, the perfects *dis* 'I said', *mis* 'I put', *pris* 'I took' provide the model for the past participles *dit, mis, pris* with analogical [i], not from DĪCTU, MĬSSU, PRĒSU. Sometimes the influence operated in both directions. The original past participle of VIVĔRE, VICTU, is remade as *VIXUTU to match the perfect VIXI and giving, with metathesis, Old French *vesqui vescu*. Later the past participle in turn launched a new <u> *passé simple*, hence Modern French *vécus vécu*. In another example of this type of double analogy, the original perfect of SĔDĒRE 'be located', SĒDĪ, is remade as *SĒSĪ on the model of the past participle SĒSSU giving *sis*, with metaphony (or by analogy to *dis, mis*, etc.). This *passé simple* in turn serves as the model for the past participle *sis*, which is not from SĒSSU.

Exercises

1. In these displays analogical forms are shaded.

Latin	Reconstructed Popular Latin of Spain	Expected outcome via regular sound change		Modern forms
CONCĬPĔRE 'conceive'	* CONCĬPĪRE	concebir	>	concebir
	CONCĬPĬŌ	concibo	>	concibo
	*CONCĬPĪS	concebes		concibes
	CONCĬPĬT	concebe		concibe
	*CONCĬPĪMUS	cocebimos	>	concebimos
	*CONCĬPĪTIS	concebís	>	concebís
	*CONCĬPĔNT	conceben		conciben

a. Comment on why three of the attested modern forms of *concebir* differ from what sound change alone would produce.

Latin	Reconstructed Popular Latin of Spain	Expected outcome via regular sound change		Modern forms
PĔTĔRE 'ask for'	*PĔTĪRE	pedir	>	pedir
	PĔTĬŌ	pedo		pido
	*PĔTĪS	piedes		pides
	PĔTĬT	piede		pide
	*PĔTĪMUS	pedimos	>	pedimos
	*PĔTĪTIS	pedís	>	pedís
	*PĔTĔNT	pieden		piden

b. What is the model for the analogical forms in today's paradigm of *pedir*? Could the paradigm have analogized to a different model? Comment on OSp *piedo*.

Latin	Reconstructed Popular Latin of Spain	Expected outcome via regular sound change		Modern forms
DĪCĔRE 'say'	*DĪCĪRE	dicir[59]		decir
	*DĪCĬŌ	digo	>	digo
	*DĪCĪS	dices	>	dices
	DĪCĬT	dice	>	dice
	*DĪCĪMUS	dicimos		decimos
	*DĪCĪTIS	dicís		decís
	*DĪCĔNT	dicen	>	dicen

Latin	Reconstructed Popular Latin of Spain	Expected outcome via regular sound change		Modern forms
RĪDĔRE 'laugh'	* RĪDĪRE	riír		reír
	*RĪDĬŌ	río	>	río

*RĪDĪS	ríes	>	ríes
*RĪDĬT	ríe	>	ríe
*RĪDĪMUS	riímos		reímos
*RĪDĪTIS	riís		reis
*RĪDĚNT	ríen	>	ríen

c. How do the analogical adjustments in today's paradigms of *decir* and *reír* differ from those seen in *concebir* and *pedir*?

Latin	Reconstructed Popular Latin of Spain	Expected outcome via regular sound change		Modern forms	Old Spanish
SCRĪBĚRE 'write'	*ESCRĪBĪRE	escribir	>	escribir	?
	*ESCRĪBĬŌ	escribo	>	escribo	
	*ESCRĪBĪS	escribes	>	escribes	
	*ESCRĪBĬT	escribe	>	escribe	
	*ESCRĪBĪMUS	escribimos	>	escribimos	?
	*ESCRĪBĪTIS	escribís	>	escribís	?
	*ESCRĪBĚNT	escriben	>	escriben	

d. All the modern forms of *escribir* come directly from Popular Latin. What analogical forms could you expect to find in Old Spanish?

Latin	Reconstructed Popular Latin of Spain	Expected outcome via regular sound change		Modern forms
RECĬPĔRE 'receive'	* RECĬPĪRE	recebir		recibir
	RECĬPĬŌ	recibo	>	recibo
	*RECĬPĪS	recebes		recibes
	RECĬPĬT	recebe		recibe
	*RECĬPĪMUS	recebimos		recibimos
	*RECĬPĪTIS	recebís		recibís
	*RECĬPĚNT	receben		reciben

In contrast to the foregoing data, describe how the remodeling of *recibir* stands out. Could the paradigm have been remodeled in a different way?

2. Old Italian imperfect subjunctive *cantasseno* became *cantassero* by analogy to the *passato remoto* (§ 7.6.1). Old Italian also had the variants *cantassino* and *cantassono*. What are their analogical models? Old Italian even has a **hypercharacterized** (doubly marked) variant *cantasserono*. What is its source? Why do we not also find **cantassenero*?

3. Italian *dare* and *stare* revisited
    a. *Dare* 'give' and *stare* 'stay' are anomalous in that they belong, on the face of it, to the *-are* class and yet they have strong preterites *diede* 'gave' and *stette* 'stayed'. Wouldn't *dare*, *stare* have been under pressure to replace these with an analogical *passato remoto*? Using Chart 7.7, create a hypothetical *passato remoto* for *dare*, *stare* on the model of other *-are* verbs. Why would such a paradigm be rejected?

b. In the imperfect subjunctive, on the other hand, colloquial Italian favors forms like *dasse, stasse* instead of prescriptively correct *desse, stesse* (§ 7.6.1). Show with a mini-diagram what analogical model gives rise to *dasse, stasse*.

4. Back to the future
   a. Explain what the inflection *-AT comes from and why it is stressed (§ 7.8.1).

Latin	Pre-Romance		Italian	Spanish	French	
HABĒRE	*HABER-AT	'will have'	avrà	habrá	aura	[ɔʀa]
SAPĒRE	*SAPER-AT	'will know'	saprà	sabrá	saura	[sɔʀa]
VALĒRE	*VALER-AT	'will be worth'	varrà	valdrá	vaudra	[vodʀa]
VOLĒRE	*VOLER-AT	'will want'	vorrà	....	voudra	[vudʀa]
VOLĀRE	*VOLAR-AT	'will fly'	volerà	volará	volera	[vɔl(ə)ʀa]

b. Show in order the sound changes leading to Sp *sabrá* [saβra].
c. Do the same for Fr *saura, vaudra*. Show why *vaudra* has a [d] and *saura* doesn't.
d. Why does It *volerà* not show syncope while *vorrà* does? At the pre-Romance stage, *VOLER-AT, *VOLAR-AT form a **minimal pair**: they have only one difference.

5. The [i] *passé simple*
   The French *passé simple* in *-is -is -it* etc. has four sources. Identify in §§ 7.5.3 and 7.5.7 an example of each category:
   a. Latin weak perfects of class IV (-ĪRE verbs)..
   b. Sigmatic strong perfects...
   c. Long-vowel strong perfects with <ī> in the stem..
   d. Compounds of DARE 'give' where -DĔDI > /djɛj/ > /di/.......................................

   Then sort the following into the proper categories:

   voir → je vis 'I saw'   *vendre → je vendis* 'I sold'
   couvrir → je couvris 'I covered'   *écrire → j'écrivis* 'I wrote'

6. The creeping <n>
   Certain Latin verb stems have a mobile /n/ in their coda, mobile in the sense that it occurs in the infectum stem but not in the perfectum stem: VINCĔRE 'win', VĪCĪ 'I won'. At least that was the original inherited distribution of this /n/. Based on the data below, what trend do you see in its distribution in Latin? Does this trend continue in Italian? Any exceptions?

	Latin			Italian		
infinitive	perfect	past participle	infinitive	passato remoto	past participle	
CINGERE	CINXI	CINCTU	cingere	cinsi	cinto	
EX-STINGUERE	EX-STINXI	EX-STINCTU	estinguere	estinsi	estinto	
DE-STINGUERE	DE-STINXI	DE-STINCTU	distinguere	distinsi	distinto	
FINGERE	FINXI	FICTU	fingere	finsi	finto	

FRANGERE	FREGI	FRACTU	frangere	fransi	franto
IUNGERE	IUNXI	IUNCTU	giungere	giunsi	giunto
DE-PINGERE	DE-PINXI	DE-PICTU	dipingere	dipinsi	dipinto
PUNGERE	PUNXI	PUNCTU	pungere	punsi	punto
STRINGERE	STRINXI	STRICTU	stringere	strinsi	stretto
TINGERE	TINXI	TINCTU	tingere	tinsi	tinto
VINCERE	VICI	VICTU	vincere	vinsi	vinto

7.   The *passé simple* of *vouloir* 'want'
      Pop Lat VŎLĒRE 'want' had a strong waw perfect, from which Old French developed
      these paradigms:

Latin	Old French	
VŎLŬĪ	voil	voli
VŎLŬISTĪ	volis	volis
VŎLŬIT	volt	voli
VŎLŬĬMUS	volimes	volimes
VŎLŬISTIS	volistes	volistes
VŎLŬĔRUNT	voldrent	volirent

      There existed a few other competing paradigms, however, one of which was:

Popular Latin	Old French	
*_____	vols	_____
*_____	volsis	_____
*_____	volst	_____
*_____	volsimes	_____
*_____	volsistes	_____
*_____	volstrent	_____

      What is the origin of this paradigm, and what other paradigm would you expect to
      arise analogically? Finally, to what source would you attribute the paradigm that
      finally won out, giving the MFr *passé simple*: *voulus, voulus, voulut, voulûmes*, etc.?

8.   VĒNĪ VĪDĪ VĪCĪ: the fate of three long-vowel perfects in Italian
      Displayed below are perfect paradigms for VENĪRE 'come', VIDĒRE 'see', and
      VINCĔRE 'conquer' with Italian outcomes, both hypothetical and actual, includ-
      ing certain changes that we have shown as "expected" – first plural stress shift (§
      7.5.4) and long /m:/ (§ 7.5.1), second plural /-e/ (§ 7.5.1).

Latin	Expected	Italian	Latin	Expected	Italian
VĒNĪ	veni	venni	VĪDĪ	vidi	vidi
VĒNISTĪ	venesti	venisti	VĪDESTĪ	videsti	vedesti
VĒNIT	vene	venne	VĪDIT	vide	vide
VĒNĬMUS	venemmo	venimmo	VĪDĬMUS	videmmo	vedemmo

| VĒNISTIS | veneste | veniste | VĪDISTIS | videste | vedeste |
| VĒNĔRUNT | venero | vennero | VĪDĔRUNT | videro | videro |

Latin	Expected	Italian
VĪCĪ	vici	vinsi
VĪCISTĪ	vicesti	vincesti
VĪCIT	vice	vinse
VĪCĬMUS	vicemmo	vincemmo
VĪCISTIS	viceste	vinceste
VĪCĔRUNT	vicero	vinsero

a. Which one of these long-vowel perfect stems has reflexes in Italian? In what forms do they occur? How can you explain the corresponding forms in the other two verbs?

b. Explain the analogical adjustment that all three paradigms undergo on the way to Italian. What analogical adjustment occurs in only one paradigm?

8   Noun and adjective morphology

Learning to inflect Latin nouns, adjectives, and pronouns is an onerous task that scarcely finds a parallel in the Romance languages. The history we trace in this chapter is one of simplification, the ongoing loss of categories and contrasts that had existed in Latin. We look first at the categories affected – declension class, case, gender – and then at how Popular Latin reshapes them, favoring economy and regularity.

8.1   The starting-point: Latin noun and adjective morphology

Latin nouns fall into five classes called **declensions**, differing in their morphology. Each noun varies in form according to its **case**, determined by its grammatical context. Broadly speaking, subjects are in the **nominative** case, direct objects in the **accusative**, indirect objects in the **dative**, while **genitive** expresses the 'of' relation often associated with possession, and the **ablative** case marks a variety of spatial and instrumental relations.[1] Chart 8.1 shows a noun from each class declined in these cases, singular and plural.

Chart 8.1 The five noun declension classes

		1	2	3	4	5
S	Nom	CAPRA	MŪRUS	PANIS	FRŪCTUS	DIĒS
I	Gen	CAPRAE	MŪRĪ	PANIS	FRŪCTŪS	DIEĪ
N	Dat	CAPRAE	MŪRŌ	PANĪ	FRŪCTUĪ ~ FRŪCTŪ	DIEĪ
G.	Acc	CAPRAM	MŪRUM	PANEM	FRŪCTUM	DIEM
	Abl	CAPRĀ	MŪRŌ	PANE	FRŪCTŪ	DIĒ
P	Nom	CAPRAE	MŪRĪ	PANĒS	FRŪCTŪS	DIĒS
L	Gen	CAPRĀRUM	MŪRŌRUM	PANIUM	FRŪCTUUM	DIĒRUM
U	Dat	CAPRĪS	MŪRĪS	PANIBUS	FRŪCTIBUS	DIĒBUS
R.	Acc	CAPRĀS	MŪRŌS	PANĒS	FRŪCTŪS	DIĒS
	Abl	CAPRĪS	MŪRĪS	PANIBUS	FRŪCTIBUS	DIĒBUS
		'goat'	'wall'	'bread'	'fruit'	'day'

Adjectives fall into two classes: some follow the first declension when feminine and the second when masculine or neuter, while others belong to the third declension, and their gender marking, if any, is effaced in Popular Latin.

Each noun, besides belonging to a declension class, also has a **grammatical gender**: masculine, feminine, or neuter. Adjectives agree in gender and number with the noun they modify. Gender is not systematically shown in the morphology of the noun itself. Gender does correlate with declension class, but not reliably. Typical correlations are shown here, with exceptions demonstrating that genders do cross-cut declensions.

Declension	Typical gender	Typical example	Exceptional example
1	Feminine	CAPRA BONA	NAUTA BONUS
2	Masculine/neuter	MURUS BONUS	HUMUS BONA
3	Any gender	....	....
4	Masculine	FRUCTUS BONUS	DOMUS BONA
5	Feminine	FIDES BONA	DIES BONUS /-A

Neuter nouns also occur in the third declension, and the fourth has a few, but the neuter gender is ultimately dismantled (§ 8.5).

8.2   From five to three declension classes

The fourth and fifth declensions begin to dissolve in Popular Latin as their nouns relocate to the more populated first and second declensions. In the process, the first declension bonds more firmly with the feminine gender and the second with masculine.

8.2.1   The fourth declension dissolves

Most nouns of the predominantly masculine fourth declension are reassigned to the second declension, which they already resemble in their most frequent forms (FRŪCTUS like MŪRUS). Their migration to the second makes them masculine. However, nouns like NŬRUS 'daughter-in-law' or SŎCRUS 'mother-in-law' can hardly be made masculine. The *Appendix Probi* (§ 2.5.3) cites:

NURUS NON NURA

SOCRUS NON SOCRA

Question: What happens to these fourth declension nouns in Popular Latin?

Answer: Since they need to remain feminine, they move to the predominantly feminine first declension.

MANUS 'hand', a feminine of the fourth declension, exceptionally retained both its form and gender, yielding "irregular" Italian and Spanish *la mano*.[2]

8.2.2   The fifth declension dissolves

Nouns of the fifth declension, nearly all feminine, move to the first declension based on their gender:

Latin		Popular Latin	Romance		
FACIES	'face'	FACIA	It	faccia	
GLACIES	'ice'	GLACIA	Fr	glace	
MATERIES	'material'	MATERIA	Sp	madera	'wood'
RABIES	'anger'	RABIA	Fr	rage	'rabies'

A few fifth declension nouns resist the exodus to the first, e.g. FIDĒS 'faith' > Italian *fede*, Spanish *fe*, French *foi*, and REM 'thing' > Fr *rien* 'nothing'. The modern languages also adopt some fifth declension nouns as *cultismos*, such as Italian *serie* 'series', *specie* 'species', *carie* 'caries'.[3]

8.3   From six to two cases

On the way from Indo-European to Latin the case system had already been reduced. Indo-European had eight cases, including an **instrumental** ('means by which') and a **locative** ('place where'). The instrumental merges with the ablative ('direction from'), while the locative merges with the genitive or dative. But signs of further decay of the case system appear from early Latin onward.

8.3.1   Loss of oblique cases

Prepositions could stand in for cases. Instead of the genitive case, DE + noun occurs as early as the second century BCE. Plautus writes DIMIDIUM ... DE PRAEDA 'half of the booty' (*Pseudolus* 1164). In the same period we find FAECEM ... DE VINO 'dregs of the wine' (Cato, *De agricultura* 96, 1) and GRANA DE FICO 'fig seeds' (Varro, *De re rustica* 1, 41). This construction persists, and in the 500s Benedict of Nursia writes DE EADEM LIBRA TERTIA PARS 'a third of the same weight', and Theodosius MONASTERIUM ... DE CASTAS 'a convent of nuns'.[4] Relics of the genitive case include Italian *terremoto* 'earthquake' < TERRAE MOTU 'movement of the earth', Italian *lunedì* 'Monday' < LUNAE DIES 'day of the moon', Spanish *jueves* 'Thursday' < IOVIS 'of Jupiter'.

Also by the second century BCE, the dative case begins to be replaced by AD + noun. Plautus writes PRAECIPE QUAE AD PATREM VIS NUNTIARI 'Tell me what you want said to your father' (*Captivi* 360), but forty lines later expresses the idea 'to your father' with the dative PATRI. In Later Latin the AD + noun construction begins to be common, as in this not atypical example from the *Mulomedicina Chironis* (454): AD EOS DES MANDUCARE 'give them something to eat' (Herman 2000:61).

Latin grammar prescribes which case(s) to use with each preposition, e.g. A, AB 'from, by', DE 'of', CUM 'with', PRO 'for' take ablative, CONTRA 'against', PER 'through' take accusative. But these rules are frills. After all, in CUM AMICIS 'with friends', PRO AMICIS 'for friends', it is the preposition, not the ablative case, that carries the meaning 'with' and 'for'.[5] Popular Latin blurs the case rules and favors the accusative, which gradually becomes an all-purpose non-subject case. These "wrong" accusatives become typical (Herman 2000:53):

CUM DISCENTES SUOS	'with his pupils'	CIL IV 698
CUM IUMENTUM	'with a draft animal'	CIL IV 8976
CUM FILIOS SUOS TRES	'with his three children'	CIL VIII 3933
POSITA A FRATRES	'placed by his brothers'	CIL VIII 20300
PRO SE ET SUOS	'for himself and his family'	CIL XII 1185

8.3.2   The Popular Latin two-case system

Alongside these morphological trends, early sound changes were also undermining the case contrasts: loss of final [m] (§ 2.4.4), reduction of AE [aj] to [e] (§ 1.4.2), and loss of quantity in unstressed vowels. By the 400s or before, Popular Latin was using only three declensions and two cases: see Chart 8.2.

Chart 8.2 Reconstructed Popular Latin two-case system

		1	2	3
sg.	Nom	CAPRA	MŪRUS	PANIS
	Non-Nom	CAPRA	MŪRU	PANE
pl.	Nom	CAPRE/CAPRAS	MŪRI	PANES
	Non-Nom	CAPRAS	MŪROS	PANES

In this reduced system the first declension singular is already caseless. Its plural soon tends to neutralize case, with -AS spreading to subjects.[6] Inscriptions from late antiquity show the beginnings of this change:

BENE QUIESCANT RELIQUIAS   (CIL V 5078)
'may these remains rest well'

HIC QUESCUNT DUAS MATRES, DUAS FILIAS   (CIL III 3551)
'here lie two mothers, two daughters'

AQUAS COQUENDAE SUNT   (Oribasius 5, 9)
'the waters are to be cooked'

SI DUAS PLAGAS FUERINT   (*Edictus Rothari* 46)
'if there be two wounds'

8.4   Romance noun and adjective morphology

Italian and Spanish, by the time of their earliest surviving documents in the 900s, no longer have any case contrast in nouns (§ 8.8). French, when first attested in the 800s, does have a two-case system, which remains in place for most of the Old French period and gradually crumbles in the 1200s.

8.4.1   Nouns and adjectives in Italian

The three main classes of Italian nouns, continuing the three declensions of Popular Latin, form their plurals with these vowels: *capra capre*, *muro muri*, *pane pani*. Comparing these with the reconstructed Western Romance system in Chart 8.2 above, one may be tempted to say that Italian discards the accusative form and retains the nominative. Not so fast.

Check that hypothesis against the Italian sound changes involving word-final [s] (§ 6.3.2). Starting from the Western Romance system in Chart 8.2, and applying these sound changes, we obtain the hypothetical pre-Italian paradigm in Chart 8.3.

Chart 8.3 Reconstructed pre-Italian noun morphology

sg.	Nom	capra	muro	pani (<ıs)
	Non-Nom	capra	muro	pane
pl.	Nom	capre (<ae/as)	muri	pani (<es)
	Non-Nom	capre (<as)	muro	pani (<es)
		'goat'	'wall'	'bread'

With the expected [as] > [aj] > [e], our *capre* plurals come from either case. So sound change alone neutralizes the case contrast in the whole first declension. In the second declension, [os] > [oj] (unstressed) > [o][7] results in case neutralization to *muro* in the singular, while the plural would still have a contrast. In the third declension, the rules [es] > [ej] (unstressed) > [i] and [is] > [ij] > [i] give the indicated results. At this point, with the case contrast dying, Italian selected from each pair the one unambiguous form. The boxed forms in Chart 8.3 are those that survive. Adjectives simply follow suit: *buono buoni*, *buona buone*, *grande grandi*.

Given that in reflexes of the first two classes Italian makes its noun and adjective plurals by changing low or back vowels to mid or high front vowels, what happens when the stem ends in a velar? Will it palatalize? The answer is complex and unresolved for masculines, but straightforward for feminines.

m. sg.		m. pl.		f. sg.	f. pl.	
cuoco	'cook'	cuochi	[ki]	cuoca	cuoche	[ke]
amico	'friend'	amici	[ʧi]	amica	amiche	[ke]
simpatico	'nice'	simpatici	[ʧi]	simpatica	simpatiche	[ke]
carico	'loaded'	carichi	[ki]	carica	cariche	[ke]

The plurals in [ki] versus [ʧi] are not entirely predictable and have shown variation over the centuries. The feminine forms, however, consistently keep their stem-final velar unpalatalized. There is a good reason, the same one that accounts for the non-palatalization of stem-final velars in *-are* verbs (§ 6.6.3). In the derivation AMICAS [amikas] > [amikaj] > [amike], the last change, giving a front vowel, occurs at a time when palatalization was no longer a living rule.

8.4.2   Nouns and adjectives in Spanish

From the Popular Latin two-case system in Chart 8.2, one step leads to the Spanish system: the case contrast collapses in favor of the accusative.

Chart 8.4 Early Spanish noun morphology

sg.	cabra	muro	pan(e)[8]
pl.	cabras	muros	panes

Although Spanish lost the case marking system of Latin, it did acquire one new case marker, the "personal *a*," which marks definite human direct objects, as in *Juanito quiere a Conchita* 'Johnny loves Connie'. This *a* served originally to forestall ambiguities and was grammaticalized in the 1600s (Penny 2002:115–116).

8.4.3   Nouns and adjectives in French

In this area of morphology, French is in one way more conservative than Italian or Spanish, and in another way more innovative. On the conservative side, Old French maintains a case contrast (*cas sujet* versus *cas régime*) not only in the earliest texts, but for several centuries thereafter. On the innovative side, the third declension melts away in the Old French period, as its forms are assimilated either to the first or to the second, according to gender.

Starting from Chart 8.2, one arrives at the two main noun paradigms by way of familiar sound changes, plus two analogical adjustments. Here our example from the Latin third declension is a masculine noun:

Chart 8.5 The main noun declensions in Old French

sg.	Nom	chevre	murs	pains
	Non-Nom	chevre	mur	pain
pl.	Nom	chevres	mur	pain
	Non-Nom	chevres	murs	pains

In plurals of the first declension, the spread of *-s* to the *cas sujet* was at least prefigured, if not completed, in late antiquity (§ 8.3.2). The second and third declension masculines, with their seemingly strange distribution of *-s*, come straight from regular sound change, except that nominative plural *pain* < PANES lost its *-s* in analogizing to *mur* < MŪRI.

Chart 8.5 depicts Old French noun morphology in the broadest strokes. However, Old French had another two declensions, each having a historically induced peculiarity in its nominative singular. Feminines of the third declension such as FINIS 'end' give rise to one special declension, and masculines like LIBER 'book' to the other:

Chart 8.6 The minor noun declensions in Old French

sg.	Nom	fins	livre
	Non-Nom	fin	livre
pl.	Nom	fins	livre
	Non-Nom	fins	livres
		'end'	'book'

The *fins* type develops like the other feminines (*chevre*), except that it retains the nominative singular *-s* of the Latin third declension (Chart 8.1). Vice versa, the *livre* type develops like the other masculines (*murs*, *pains*) except that the language remembers, amazingly, that in Latin, nouns like LIBER had no nominative singular *-s*.

Unlike the *cas sujet* with its complex (and synchronically unmotivated) distribution of *-s* versus no *-s*, the *cas régime* is entirely regular: its singular never has affixal *-s* and its plural always does. In the 1200s, the *cas régime* inflections increasingly displace those of the *cas sujet*, hence today's pattern of regular *-s* plurals. In short, French went the way of Spanish, but several centuries later.

Adjectives underwent a major overhaul in Middle French.[9] Adjectives that belonged to the Latin third declension are easily recognized in Italian and Spanish because they have no gender contrast: *forte forti* and *fuerte fuertes* can modify both masculine and feminine nouns. The same was true of Old French *fort forz*.

		Popular Latin		Italian	Spanish	Old French	Modern French
1st/2nd declension	m. sg.	SICCU	'dry'	secco	seco	sec	sec
	f. sg.	SICCA		secca	seca	seche	sèche
	m. pl.	SICCOS		(secchi)	secos	secs	secs
	f. pl.	SICCAS		secche	secas	seches	sèches
3rd declension	m. sg.	FORTE	'strong'	forte	fuerte	fort	fort
	f. sg.	FORTE		forte	fuerte	fort	forte
	m. pl.	FORTES		forti	fuertes	forz	forts
	f. pl.	FORTES		forti	fuertes	forz	fortes

Question: How does adjective inflection change between Old and Modern French?

Answer: Third declension adjectives assimilate to first/second declension adjectives.

The -A of the Latin first declension endings, surviving as [ə] in Old French, came to be perceived as a mark of the feminine in adjectives and spread to the feminine forms of third declension adjectives. Isolated examples occur from the early texts on, but the change is fully generalized only in Middle French. Even today, relics of Old French third declension adjectives survive in such fixed expressions as *grand-mère* 'grandmother', *grand-messe* 'High Mass', *pas grand-chose* 'nothing much', and *Rochefort* < ROCCA FORTE. The French language now treats *fort forte* just as if the adjective were derived from **FORTU **FORTA. With this change, the Latin third declension as a category no longer has any clear footprint in Modern French. Yes, there are still adjectives remaining invariable for gender, but some reflect spelling conventions (*facile* 'easy') and others result from Middle French levelings (LARGU LARGA 'wide' > *larc large*, later *large large*). The feminine nouns without final [ə] (e.g. *la fin* 'the end') are the only synchronically identifiable survivors of the third declension.

8.5   The neuter diaspora: from three to two genders

If we were unaware that a neuter gender existed in Latin, we might still be able to reconstruct it from its scattered relics in Romance. Neuter nouns in Latin occur mainly in the second and third declensions, and the fourth has a few. Neuters have two distinctive properties: (1) a special nominative and (2) an accusative always identical to the nominative:

		2	3	4
sg.	Nom	PRATUM	TĔMPUS	GĔLU
	Gen	PRATĪ	TĔMPORIS	GĔLŪS
	Dat	PRATŌ	TĔMPORĪ	GĔLŬĪ
	Acc	PRATUM	TĔMPUS	GĔLU
	Abl	PRATŌ	TĔMPORE	GĔLŪ
pl.	Nom	PRATA	TĔMPORA	GĔLŬA
	Gen	PRATŌRUM	TĔMPORUM	GĔLŬUM
	Dat	PRATĪS	TĔMPORĬBUS	GĔLĬBUS
	Acc	PRATA	TĔMPORA	GĔLŬA
	Abl	PRATĪS	TĔMPORĬBUS	GĔLĬBUS
		'meadow'	'time'	'frost'

In Popular Latin and Romance the neuter gender as a category was dismantled and its members were relocated in several ways.

8.5.1   From neuter to masculine

Neuters of the second and fourth declensions could easily become masculine:

Latin		Italian	Spanish	French	
PRATUM	'meadow'	prato	prado	pré	
ŎSSUM	'bone'	osso	hueso	os	
CŎLLUM	'neck'	collo	cuello	col	'collar'
VĪNUM	'wine'	vino	vino	vin	
GĔLU	'frost'	gelo	hielo	gel	

In the *Satyricon* (§ 2.5.1), slippage from neuter to masculine is one of the features Petronius uses to mark the speech of unrefined characters: FATUS for FATUM 'fate' (42, 71, 77), CAELUS for CAELUM 'sky' (45), and accusative LACTEM for LAC 'milk' (38, 77). A guest at Trimalchio's dinner, blathering about nothing much, regenders neuter nouns BALNEUM 'bath' and VINUM 'wine' (41):

Et mundum frigus habuimus. Vix me **balneus** calfecit. Tamen calda potio vestiarius est. Staminatas duxi, et plane matus sum. **Vinus** mihi in cerebrum abiit.

And we've had cold weather. The **bath** barely warmed me up. But a hot drink is as good as a coat. I knocked back a few pitchers, and I'm totally bombed. The **wine** has gone to my head.

Neuters of the third declension have two stems, one long and one short. Their nominative singular ending is zero. In the chart above (§ 8.5), TĔMPUS is the short stem and TĔMPOR- the long one.[10] But Romance speakers were bound to equate TĔMPUS to masculine nouns of the second declension like CAMPUS 'field', where the stem is CAMP- throughout. So, neuters like TĔMPUS also slid easily into the second declension, taking on masculine gender:

Latin		Italian	Spanish	Old French	Modern French
TĔMPUS	'time'	tempo	tiempo	tens	temps
CŎRPUS	'body'	corpo	cuerpo	cors	corps
PĔCTUS	'chest'	petto	pecho	piz	....
LATUS	'side'	lato	lado	lez	....

8.5.2   From neuter to feminine

The neuter plural ending -A was always open to reinterpretation as a feminine singular ending of the first declension. Popular Latin abounds with examples attesting to this trend. Accius (170–86 BCE) writes: CASTRA HAEC VESTRA EST 'this is your camp', where the first three words are ambiguous between feminine singular and neuter plural, but the singular verb disambiguates. In Columella we find alongside the original neuter RAPUM 'turnip' (plural RAPA) evidence of a new feminine RAPA RAPAE:

Ceterum Augusto … tertia satio est eaque optima radicis et **rapae**
Also in August, … comes the third sowing, and this is the best one for [= of] radish, and turnip   (*De re rustica* 11, 3, 18)

Neuter ŎPUS 'work' survives only marginally in Romance,[11] but its plural ŎPĔRA became a feminine singular which gained currency even in literary Latin:

Alterum est vitium, quod quidam nimis magnum studium multamque **operam** in res obscuras atque difficiles conferunt easdemque non necessarias.

Another fault is that some devote too much study and **work** to obscure and difficult things that are also unnecessary   (Cicero, *De officiis* 1, 19)

Reflexes of these new feminines include:

	Latin neuters		*Romance feminine singulars*		
sg.		pl.	*Italian*	*Spanish*	*French*
ŎPUS	'work'	ŎPĔRA	opera	obra	oeuvre
				huebra (OSp)	
MIRABILĬUM	'marvel'	MIRABILĬA	meraviglia	maravilla	merveille
RAPUM	'turnip'	RAPA	rapa	....	rave
PECUS	'sheep'	PECORA	pecora	....	....
MŌRUM	'mulberry'	MORA	mora	mora	mûre
					meure (OFr)

Sometimes both the singular and plural have survived as *singulars* in the same or different languages:

Latin		*Italian*	*Spanish*	*French* (Old French)
FOLĬU	'leaf'	foglio 'leaf' (paper)	....	....
FOLĬA	'leaves'	foglia 'leaf' (plant)	hoja	feuille
CŎRNU	'horn'	corno	cuerno	cor 'horn' (musical)
CŎRNŬA	'horns'	....	....	corne 'horn' (animal)
GAUDĬU	'joy'	....	gozo	....
GAUDĬA	'joys'	gioia (< OFr)	....	joie
LĬGNU	'wood'	legno 'wood'	leño 'wood, log'	....
LĬGNA	'woods'	legna 'firewood'	leña 'firewood'	(leigne 'firewood')

8.5.3   Ambigeneric nouns

Italian and Romanian (§ 10.7.2) have nouns known as *ambigenerics* which are masculine in the singular but feminine in the plural. Italian has about thirty of them. Only in these Italian nouns does the Latin neuter plural -A survive in Romance with a plural meaning.

Latin		*Italian*	*Latin*		*Italian*
ŎVUM	'egg'	uovo	ŎVA	'eggs'	uova
PARĬUM	'pair'	paio	PARĬA	'pairs'	paia

Evidently, awareness of the feminine feature elsewhere associated with -*a* intervened to make the plurals feminine: *uova buone* 'good eggs'. This pattern is attested in a ninth-century Roman inscription: NON DICERE ILLE SECRITA ABBOCE 'don't say the secret things aloud', where the demonstrative ILLE, used as an article, shows that SECRITA is feminine plural. An inscription from Dalmatia shows the same pattern: OSSA EXTERAE 'bones that don't belong here' (CIL III 9450 7).

Most Italian ambigenerics have in addition a masculine plural with a different shade of meaning:

BRACHĬUM	'arm'	braccio	BRACHĬA	braccia	'arms' (human)
				bracci	'arms' (chair)
MĔMBRUM	'member'	membro	MĔMBRA	membra	'members' (body)
				membri	'members' (group)
CŎRNU	'horn'	corno	CŎRNŬA	corna	'horns' (animal)
				corni	'horns' (instruments)

Strangely, a few originally masculine nouns joined the ambigenerics, acquiring a feminine plural in -*a*:

DĬGĬTUS	'finger'	dito	DĬGĬTI	diti	'fingers' (individually)
				dita	'fingers' (together)
MŪRUS	'wall'	muro	MŪRI	muri	'walls' (of building)
				mura	'walls' (of city)

8.6   Toward gender marking

Neuter nouns in the process of becoming masculine or feminine end up mostly in the second and first declensions, respectively. The third declension does keep some of its former neuters (FLUMEN 'river' > Italian *fiume* (m.), MARE 'sea' > Italian *mare*, Spanish *mar* (m.),[12] French *mer* (f.), RETE 'net' > Italian *rete* (f.), etc.), but it does not attract newcomers. What speakers liked about the second and first declensions, no doubt, was that the marking of their declension class was becoming equatable to gender marking. This makes for an easier grammar than one in which gender must be learned separately from form.

This predilection for clearer gender marking shows up as early as Plautus: PAUPERA HAEC RES EST 'this is a poor thing' (*Vidularia* 17d) instead of PAUPER, a third declension adjective which should remain unmarked for gender, as it does in Spanish *pobre*. The *Satyricon* too shows this trend: NON ES NOSTRAE FASCIAE, ET IDEO PAUPERORUM VERBA DERIDES 'you are not of our class, and that's why you mock the speech of the poor' (46). The usage figures in the *Appendix Probi*: PAUPER MULIER NON PAUPERA MULIER 'poor woman'. The stigmatized popular form PAUPERA and the genitive plural PAUPERORUM (instead of third declension PAUPERUM) prefigure Italian *povero povera*. Again,

SENIOR 'elder', a third declension adjective, was originally the same for both
genders. In its Romance use as an honorific, it urgently needed gender marking, hence Italian *signora*, Spanish *señora* from an innovative *SENIORA. Other
defections from the third declension include (for SOROR) *SORA > Italian *suora*
'nun', (for COMPANIO) *COMPANIA > French *compagne* 'female companion', (for
FASCIS) *FASCIUS > Italian *fascio* 'bundle', (for ACER, SUBER, PAPAVER) *ACERUS,
*SUBERUS, *PAPAVERUS > Italian *acero* 'maple tree', *sughero* 'cork tree', *papavero*
'poppy', and (for ARBOR) *ARBORUS > Italian *albero* 'tree'.

8.7   Imparisyllabic nouns and adjectives

Third declension nouns and adjectives fall into two classes according to the
form of their nominative singular. **Parisyllabics** are those whose stem has the
same number of syllables throughout the declension (PANIS PANEM 'bread',
PATER PATREM 'father'). **Imparisyllabics** have a nominative singular stem shorter
in syllable count than the stem of the remaining forms.[13] Popular Latin tends
to level the paradigm by creating a nominative singular based on the longer
stem.

			Latin		*Popular Latin*
Nom	[*bow-s]	>	BOS	'ox'	*BOVIS
Acc	[*bow-em]	>	BOVEM		BOVEM
Nom	[*dent-s]	>	DENS	'tooth'	*DENTIS
Acc	[*dent-em]	>	DENTEM		DENTEM
Nom	[*ped-s]	>	PES	'foot'	*PEDIS
Acc	[*ped-em]	>	PEDEM		PEDEM
Nom	[*reg-s]	>	REX	'king'	*REGIS
Acc	[*reg-em]	>	REGEM		REGEM

These analogical nominatives turn up from early Latin on: SORTIS 'fate' for
SORS (Plautus, *Casina*), STIRPIS 'lineage' for STIRPS (Livy, *Ab urbe condita*). The
imparisyllabic neuter LAC, LACT- 'milk', with accusative LAC, becomes a parisyllabic *LACTIS, LACTE in: LACTE GALLINACEUM SI QUAESIERIS, INVENIES 'if you want
chicken milk, you'll find it' (*Satyricon* 38). The *Appendix Probi* too attests to
this trend:

PECTEN NON PECTINIS	'comb'
GLIS NON [G]LIRIS	'dormouse'
GRUS NON GRUIS	'crane'

When an imparisyllabic noun is made parisyllabic, the case distinction in its
paradigm is further undermined.

Of course, the creation of these new nominative singulars has no long-term consequences, because the vast majority of Romance nouns and adjectives derive from the accusative. Exceptionally, however, distinctive nominatives do survive. Among the imparisyllabics that were not leveled, some have nominative singulars that continue into Romance. Below, the short stems and their surviving reflexes appear in boldface. Stress position (recall the Penultimate Rule, § 1.1.4) often reveals which stem is the etymon. For example, given CANTOR CANTŌRE 'singer', the source of French *chantre* 'cantor' can only be the short stem, and *chanteur* 'singer' can only derive from the long stem CANTŌRE.

Nom	Non-Nom		Italian	Spanish	French
CAPUT	CAPĬTE	'head'	**capo**	**cabo**	**chef**
MULĬER	MULIĒRE	'woman'	**moglie**	mujer	....
CURCULĬO	CURCULIONE	'weevil'	....	**gorgojo**	....
TRADĬTOR	TRADITŌRE	'traitor'	traditore	traidor	**traître**

Sometimes reflexes of both the long and short stems survive in the same language:[14]

	Latin		Italian	Spanish	French
Nom	**SERPENS**	'snake'	**serpe**	**sierpe**	....
Non-Nom	SERPENTE		serpente	serpiente	serpent
Nom	**TITĬO**	'ember'	**tizzo**	**tizo**	....
Non-Nom	TITIŌNE		tizzone	tizón	tison
Nom	**HOMO**	'man'	**uomo**[15]	....	**on**
Non-Nom	HOMĬNE		....	hombre	homme
Nom	**FALCO**	'falcon'	**falco**	....	....
Non-Nom	FALCŌNE		falcone	halcón	faucon
Nom	**PASTOR**	'herdsman'	....	....	**pâtre**
Non-Nom	PASTŌRE		pastore	pastor	pasteur

PRACTICE

Given these four imparisyllabic nouns, identify the Romance words that derive from the short (nominative singular) stem:

SARTOR, SARTŌRE 'tailor'	Italian *sarto*, Spanish *sastre*, Old French *sartre*
MĬNOR, MĬNŌRE 'lesser'	Italian *minore*, Spanish *menor*, French *mineur*, French *moindre*
LATRO, LATRŌNE 'thief'	Italian *ladro*, Italian *ladrone*, Spanish *ladrón*, Old French *larron*, Old French *lerre*
PI(N)CTOR, PI(N)CTŌRE 'painter'	Italian *pittore*, Spanish *pintor*, French *peintre*

Chart 8.7

		Latin	Italian	Tonic/Heavy Spanish	French	Atonic/Light Italian	Spanish	French
1st sg.	Subject	ĒGO	io	yo	moi	....	....	je [ʒə]
	Non-subject	MĒ	me	mí	moi	mi	me	me [mə]
2nd sg.	Subject	TŪ	tu	tú	toi	....	....	tu [ty]
	Non-subject	TĒ	te	tí	toi	ti	te	te [tə]
1st pl.	Subject	NŌS	noi	nosotros	nous	....	....	nous
	Non-subject	NŌS	noi	nosotros	nous	ci	nos	nous
2nd pl.	Subject	VŌS	voi	vosotros	vous	....	....	vous
	Non-subject	VŌS	voi	vosotros	vous	vi	os	vous

8.8   Romance personal pronouns

Two major innovations shaped the Romance personal pronoun system. In Latin, every personal pronoun was capable of standing alone, for example as a short answer: CUI? MIHI 'to whom? to me'. Romance, besides having pronouns of that kind, also created a new category of pronouns known as **clitics**, which cannot stand alone and which behave more like verb affixes than like full-fledged words. The pronouns that can stand alone are called *tonic* (stressed) or *heavy*, while the clitic type are called **atonic** (unstressed) or *light*. The other innovation, already apparent in Popular Latin, is the replacement of old third person pronouns IS EA ID (and their declensions) by demonstrative pronouns, especially ILLE ILLA ILLUD 'that one'. The Romance personal pronoun system also has a conservative trait: it preserves the Popular Latin two-case system and even a distinct dative in the third person (§ 8.8.2).

8.8.1   First and second person pronouns

Chart 8.7 shows the Latin first and second person pronouns and the corresponding Romance pronouns, both tonic and atonic.

For Italian, the tonic forms are entirely regular. Spanish *mí* and *tí* are attributed to datives MĬHĪ and TĬBĪ, which became arbitrarily limited to stressed contexts (Lloyd 1987:278). From NŌS VŌS come Old Spanish *nos vos*. Today's forms *nosotros vosotros* (from NŌS VŌS plus ALTĔRŌS 'others'), originally highlighting contrast with some other referent,[16] lost their contrastive meaning by the late Middle Ages. In French, the regular non-subject forms *moi toi* are now also employed as tonic subject pronouns, while *nous vous* are regular outcomes in both tonic and atonic contexts. Italian and Spanish use subject pronouns only for emphasis: *tu sei scemo, tú eres tonto* 'you are foolish' (with emphasis), *sei scemo, eres tonto* 'you are foolish' (without emphasis). Otherwise stated, their atonic subject pronouns are zero (note the blanks on the atonic side of Chart 8.7). A different story in French: ĒGO and TŪ yield the atonic pronouns *je* and *tu*. In French, subject clitics are mandatory and do not indicate emphasis. To provide

Chart 8.8 Singular forms of ĬLLĔ

	Latin		Popular Latin
(m.)	*'that (one)'*	*'who, which'*	
Nom	ĬLLĔ	QUĪ	ĬLLĔ / ĬLLĪ
Gen	ĬLLĪŬS	CŬĬŬS	ĬLLŬĬŬS
Dat	ĬLLĪ	CŬĬ	ĬLLŬĬ
Acc	ĬLLŬM	QUĔM	ĬLLŬ
Abl	ĬLLŌ	QUŌ	ĬLLŌ

emphatic subjects, there being no such forms from ĒGO and TŪ, the non-subject forms are pressed into service: *toi tu es niais* 'you are foolish' (with emphasis), *tu es niais* 'you are foolish' (without emphasis).

Among the atonic pronouns, Italian *ci* and *vi* are innovations. They both derive from locative expressions (EC)CE HIC 'here' *ci*, and IBI 'there' *vi*. Although Old Italian regularly had *no* < NŌS 'us/to us' and *vo* < VŌS 'you/to you', with reduction of [oj] to [o] in unstressed position (§§ 6.3.2, 8.4.1), somehow the pair *ci vi* managed first to rival and ultimately to supplant *no vo*.[17] Pretonic raising in Italian accounts for *mi ti*, as opposed to tonic *me te* (§ 5.1.3).

Spanish *os*, originally *vos*, lost its initial [β] in post-verbal position: **despertad vos > despertaos* 'wake up'. This form then generalized in the 1500s. With *nos* in post-verbal position, the preceding consonant deletes: **vamos nos > vámonos* 'let's go'.

In French, regular sound change accounts for today's atonic personal pronouns. The source of *je* is: ĒGO > [eo] > [jo] > [dʒə] > [ʒə]. The consonant is regular for yod-initial words (§§ 3.4.2, 4.3.1), and Old French *jo* is attested.[18] The first and second singular forms reflect the regular development of their unstressed vowels: [e] > [ə], [u] > [y]. The [o] of NŌS VŌS behaves the same in unstressed blocked syllables as in stressed ones (§ 1.2.4), so the [u] of *nous vous* is expected in the atonic forms.

8.8.2   Third person pronouns in pre-Romance

The old pronouns IS EA ID 'he she it' were apparently vanishing from popular speech by the first century CE, replaced by the demonstrative pronoun ĬLLĔ ĬLLA ĬLLŬD 'that (one)', the source of nearly all third person pronouns in Romance. This being such a common word, documentary sources show amply not only how its meaning was shifting, but also how its case forms were modified at the beginning of their journey into Romance. An early example of demonstratives used as plain third person pronouns occurs in the Pompeii graffiti:

SUCCESSUS TEXTOR AMAT COPONIAES ANCILLA ... QUAE QUIDEM **ILLUM** NON CURAT, SED **ILLE** ROGAT, **ILLA** COMISERETUR
Successus the weaver loves the innkeeper's maid, who doesn't care about him, but he begs her to take pity on him

(CIL IV 8259)[19]

Chart 8.9 Singular forms of ĬLLĂ

	Latin		Popular Latin
(f.)	'that (one)'	*1st decl.*	
Nom	ĬLLĂ	-Ă	ĬLLĂ
Gen	ĬLLĪŬS	-AE	ĬLL(A)E / ĬLL(A)EĬŬS
Dat	ĬLLĪ	-AE	ĬLL(A)E / ĬLL(A)EĪ
Acc	ĬLLĂM	-ĂM	ĬLLĂ
Abl	ĬLLĀ	-Ā	ĬLLĀ

Latin has a special pronominal declension, used for ĬLLĔ ĬLLA (Charts 8.8–10) and several other common words. Three endings depart from the normal second and first declensions – nominative ĬLLĔ (m. sg.), genitive ĬLLĪŬS (m./f. sg.), dative ĬLLĪ (m./f. sg.) – and these three anomalies encountered some resistance in Popular Latin.

Among the masculine singular forms, the analogical trend seems to aim at matching them with the paradigm of the relative and interrogative pronouns.[20] Formal similarity in the plural (Chart 8.10) brings about formal similarity in the singular: QUĪ = ĬLLĪ but QUĪ ≠ ĬLLĔ, so ĬLLĔ >> ĬLLĪ. This analogical replacement is attested in early medieval documents:[21]

QUODSI **ILLI** AUT ALIQUA PERSONA ... PRESUMPSERIT
if he or any person should presume

(Formulae Andecavenses 4)

ILLI VENIENS AD PRESENTIAM NOSTRAM SUGGESSIT
he came into our presence and suggested

(Formulae Malcufi 13)

A similar impulse must have hit the genitive: in the plural QUŌRŬM = ĬLLŌRŬM but singular CŪĬŬS ≠ ĬLLĪŬS, so ĬLLĪŬS >> ĬLLŬĬŬS (and likewise ISTĪŬS >> ĬSTŬĬŬS 'of this one', IPSĪŬS >> ĬPSŬĬŬS 'of this very one'). The newly minted genitive singular had a domino effect on the dative singular: CŪĬŬS = ĬLLŬĬŬS but CŪĬ ≠ ĬLLĪ, so ĬLLĪ >> ĬLLŬĬ. The new forms are attested in Latin inscriptions and medieval formularies:

ROFINA FILIA **IPSUIUS**...
Rofina his daughter [lit. daughter of him]

(CIL X 5939)

IADE CONTUBERNALI SUO DIGNISSIMO QUOI NON LICUIT IN SUIS MANIBUS ULTIMUM **ILLUI** SPIRITUM UT EXCIPERIT
Iade [set this stone] for his very worthy comrade to whom it was not granted to draw his last breath in his [Iade's] arms

(CIL X 2564)

AB IPSO PRINCIPE ILLO MEMORATO **LUI** FUISSE CONCESSA[22]
was ceded to him by the aforementioned prince

(Formulae Marculfi 54)

Chart 8.10 Plural forms of ĬLLĔ and ĬLLA

	(m.)	(f.)
Nom	ĬLLĪ	ĬLLAE / ĬLLĀS
Gen	ĬLLŌRŬM	ĬLLĀRŬM
Dat	ĬLLĪS	ĬLLĪS
Acc	ĬLLŌS	ĬLLĀS
Abl	ĬLLĪS	ĬLLĪS

In the feminine singular, analogical ĬLL(A)E is simply a reversion to the normal first declension endings. This variant appears as early as Cato (234–149 CE): ILLAE REI 'for that purpose', literally 'to that thing' (*De agricultura* 153, 154). Either on the model of the analogical masculine ĬLLŪĪ, or by blending the original dative ĬLLĪ with the new analogical ILLAE, Popular Latin produced another feminine dative ILLEI, attested in a second-century letter written by one of Trajan's soldiers:

DICO **ILLEI** ET EGO
I too say to her[23]

Also documented is a new genitive ILLEIUS, which likely arrived by a similar path:

NICAON AMATOR **ILLEIUS**
Nicaon her devoted friend

(CIL VI 14484)

Analogical forms of the relative/interrogative QUAE may also have played a role. Inscriptions show that, in Popular Latin, feminine CUIUS CUI was becoming QUEIUS QUEI:

INCOMPARABILISSIMAE FEMINAE **QUEIUS** DE VITA
a most incomparable woman, concerning whose life

(CIL X 3980)

BON[AE] MEMORIAE PRIMITIBA … **QUEI** BENE FICERUN FILI EIUS
Primitiva of fond memory … for whom her sons made this [stone]

(CIL X 8082)

Just as masculine ĬLLĪŬS ĬLLĪ assimilated to the relative/interrogative CUIUS CUI, so the feminine ĬLLĪŬS ĬLLĪ may have assimilated to QUEIUS QUEI.

The plural forms have the same endings as the second and first declensions. But recall that the feminine accusative plural was supplanting the nominative plural (§ 8.3.2). (See Chart 8.10.)

8.8.3   Third person pronouns in Romance

Starting from the weakening demonstrative pronouns of standard and colloquial Latin, the Romance third person pronouns took shape as outlined below.

From Popular Latin ĬLLĪ came Old Italian *elli* which became *egli*, first in pre-vocalic position, and later everywhere. Since ĬLLĪ was also plural, an additional marker -*no*, taken from third plural verbs, was supplied: *ellino*, *eglino* 'they'.

The ending then spreads to the feminine plural to give *elleno*. All the foregoing pronouns are limited to animate subjects.

A second series of tonic pronouns, more successful, arose from Popular Latin datives (ĬLLUĪ *lui*, ĬLLEĪ *lei*) and from the masculine genitive plural (ĬLLŌRŬ *loro*). All three had in Old Italian both genitive and dative meaning.[24] But as early as Dante they were becoming caseless, usable in all contexts regardless of case.

Italian third person pronouns

	Tonic				Atonic			
	Nom		*Non-Nom*		*Acc*			*Dat*
m. sg.	ĬLLĪ	egli	ĬLLUI	lui	ĬLLU	lo	ĬLLĪ	gli
	ĬPSU	esso	ĬPSU	esso				
f. sg.	ĬLLA	ella	ĬLLEI	lei	ĬLLA	la	ĬLL(A)E	le
			ĬPSA	essa				
m. pl.	ĬLLĪ	eglino	ĬLLŌRŬ	loro	ĬLLI	li	ĬLLŌRŬ	loro
			ĬPSI	essi				
f. pl.	ĬLL(A)E	elleno	ĬLLŌRŬ	loro	ĬLL(A)E	le	ĬLLŌRŬ	loro
			ĬPSE	esse				

Italian also has a set of tonic personal pronouns from another Latin demonstrative ĬPSE ĬPSA, which developed in Popular Latin a masculine singular ĬPSU. The resulting *esso essa essi esse* coexisted with the tonic pronouns from ĬLLE, but were limited to non-human referents until the 1800s, when *essi esse* began to replace *eglino elleno*. Later, *essa* takes over for *ella*, but *egli* and *esso* continue to coexist, *egli* specialized for animates, *esso* for inanimates. Gradually, and to the dismay of purists, both sets of tonic subject pronouns fall victim to the spread of *lui lei loro*, fairly complete within the 1800s. But these can only stand for animates. *Esso essa essi esse* still survive weakly as the only available direct and indirect object tonic pronouns for inanimates. In colloquial style they are replaced by demonstratives *questo* 'this', *quello* 'that'.

The history of atonic *lo la li le* echoes the evolution of first and second declension nouns and adjectives (§ 8.4.1). In prevocalic position *li* palatalized to *gli*, which then generalized to all positions. But by the early 1800s direct object *gli* was replaced by *li*, matching the other three. The atonic dative pronouns *gli le* develop regularly from ĬLLĪ ĬLLAE ĬLLĪS. The palatalized *gli* from ĬLLĪ ĬLLĪS occurs before vowels originally and then spreads to other contexts.

Spanish third person pronouns

	Tonic		Atonic			
	(Caseless)		*Acc*		*Dat*	
m. sg.	ĬLLE	él	ĬLLU	lo	ĬLLĪ	le
f. sg.	ĬLLA	ella	ĬLLA	la	ĬLLĪ	le

m. pl.	ĬLLOS	ellos	ĬLLOS	los	ĬLLĪS	les
f. pl.	ĬLLAS	ellas	ĬLLAS	las	ĬLLĪS	les

Hispano-Romance is the branch that most consistently adopts the Latin accusative for its noun and adjective forms (§ 8.4.2). The third person tonic pronouns mostly follow suit, although Old Spanish has *elle* from nominative ĬLLE. Admittedly, ĬLLA > *ella* is a form where nominative and accusative converged in late Roman times, but *ellos ellas* make it clear that Spanish selected the accusative. The same holds for atonic accusatives *lo la los las*. In its atonic dative pronouns, Spanish remains faithful to the old pronominal declension (ĬLLĪ > *le* for both genders) and does not welcome the popular creations ĬLLUI ĬLLEI that take hold in Italian and French.[25]

French third person pronouns

	Tonic		*Atonic*					
	(Caseless)			*Nom*		*Acc*		*Dat*
m. sg.	ĬLLUI	lui	ĬLLĪ	il	ĬLLU	le	ĬLLUI	lui
f. sg.	ĬLLA	elle	ĬLLA	elle	ĬLLA	la	ĬLLUI	lui
m. pl.	ĬLLOS	eux	ĬLLĪ	ils	ĬLLOS	les	ĬLLŌRŬ	leur
f. pl.	ĬLLAS	elles	ĬLLAS	elles	ĬLLAS	les	ĬLLŌRŬ	leur

The French tonic pronouns evolve regularly. ĬLLA ĬLLAS give Old French *ele eles*, which in the Renaissance reacquired <ll>, alluding to their Latin lineage. The derivation ĬLLOS > *els* > *eus* > *eux* [ø] is unproblematic,[26] as is ĬLLUI > *lui* [lɥi].[27] Among the modern subject clitics, *elle elles* develop like their tonic counterparts. Masculine singular *il* (instead of *el*) is attributed to metaphony induced by final long ī (cf. FĒCĪ > *fis*, § 7.5.7). The plural ĬLLĪ also gave *il*, which did not become *ils* until the 1300s, when *-s* was becoming the regular plural marker (§ 8.4.3). The accusative clitics went through a stage *lo la los las* in Old French and only later do their vowels diverge from the expected outcomes, due to stress variations and perhaps the influence of the definite article, giving today's *le la les* [lə la le].

Certainly the most successful personal pronoun in French is masculine singular ĬLLUI *lui*. It replaces not only the Old French *tonic* subject pronoun *il* < ĬLLĪ, but also, in Middle French, the *atonic* masculine and feminine dative singulars *li* < ĬLLĪ and *lillei/lie* < ĬLLE(I). The dative plural *leur* is supplied by originally genitive ĬLLŌRŬ, which also takes over for feminine ĬLLĀRŬ.

8.9   Birth of the definite article

Latin had no definite article, but pre-Romance speech was already creating one from the demonstrative ĬLLE ĬLLA. As we saw, ĬLLE ĬLLA standing alone as a pronoun gave rise to Romance personal pronouns ('that one' > 'he she it'). In the same way, ĬLLE ĬLLA as an adjective gradually lost its demonstrative meaning to become a definite article ('that ...' > 'the ...'). Possibly a stepping-stone is the construction where forms of ĬLLE ĬLLA mean 'the one/s' plus a modifier:

MENDICUS ATQUE ILLE OPULENTISSIMUS
the beggar and the very wealthy man

(Plautus, *Trinummus* 493)

MELA ... QUAE DULCIA SUNT, BONA SUNT ... NAM ILLA ACIDA NON SUNT CONGRUA
apples ... that are sweet, are good ... for the sour ones are not suitable

(Anthimus, *De observatione ciborum* 84)

But sometimes ĬLLE ĬLLA seem more like genuine definite articles modifying nouns:

FAVA ... COCTA ... MELIUS CONGRUA EST QUAM ILLA FAVA FRESA QUIA GRAVAT STOMACHUM
[the] cooked bean ... is better suited than the crushed bean, for it weighs on the stomach

(Anthimus, *De observatione ciborum* 65)

OPTIMUM EST NON MOVERE ILLUM IUMENTUM DE LOCO
it is best not to move the animal

(*Mulomedicina Chironis* 470)

A fourth-century travel narrative known as the *Peregrinatio Aetheriae* (Aetheria's Pilgrimage) shows vividly how the nascent definite article figured in pre-Romance informal usage. Like the earlier *Appendix Probi*, this famous text barely made it to our times, surviving only in a single eleventh-century copy that lacks unknown amounts at the beginning and end. Discovered in a monastic library in Arezzo, Italy, it was first published by Gamurrini (1887).[28] In it a Christian woman of ample means – nothing is known of her except what scholars deduce from the text – recounts her travels in the Holy Land and in Constantinople over a period of three years, 381–384 by some calculations. Escorted by local Roman authorities and hosted *humanissime* 'most cordially' by local clerics, her party visits Old Testament sites, even some as difficult of access as the summit of Mount Sinai. She addresses her readers as *dominae venerabiles* 'venerable ladies' and *sorores* 'sisters' – were she and they fellow nuns in a convent back home? No one knows. Nor is there any consensus about her homeland.[29]

The one trait of her chatty style most significant for us is the way she overuses – hugely, by the standards of Classical Latin – forms of IPSE and ILLE. With its old meaning 'he himself, the very one' now fading, Aetheria's IPSE seems to mean just 'the' or at most 'the aforementioned':

TUNC DIXIT NOBIS IPSE SANCTUS PRESBYTER
then the holy priest [just mentioned] said to us ...

(15, 3)

Chart 8.11 Romance definite articles

	Italian sg.	pl.	Spanish sg.	pl.	Old French[30] sg.	pl.	French sg.	pl.
m.	il	i	el	los	li	li	le (l')	les
	lo (l')	gli			los, le	los, les		
f.	la (l')	le	la (el)	las	la	les	la	les
					la	les		

Aetheria's ILLE is also bleached, both as a pronoun and as an adjective. As an adjective it is usually better translated as 'the' than as 'that', or else as a pronoun, as in the first example below:

REQUISIVI AB EO DICENS: «ROGO TE, DOMINE, UT DICAS MIHI, QUOD DESIDERO AUDIRE.» ET ILLE AIT: «DIC, FILIA, QUOD VIS, ET DICAM TIBI, SI SCIO.»
I asked him, saying: "I ask you, sir, that you tell me something which I wish to hear." And he said, "Say, daughter, what you wish, and I will tell you, if I know."

(20,9)

OSTENSUS EST NOBIS ET ILLE LOCUS, IN QUO CONFIXUM [A] MOYSE EST PRIMITUS TABERNACULUM
they also showed us the place where Moses set up the first tabernacle

(5,9)

ILLOS SANCTOS MONACHOS, QUI IBI MANEBANT
the holy monks who resided there

(11,2)

The trend continues over the centuries. This passage from an eighth-century monastic rule suggests that forms of ILLE have completed their transformation into definite articles:

ILLA MEDIA PARS CLERI QUI SENIORES FUERINT ANNIS SINGULIS ACCIPIANT CAPPAS NOVAS, ET VETERES QUAS PRAETERITO ANNO ACCEPERUNT SEMPER REDDANT, DUM ACCIPIANT NOVAS. ET ILLA ALIA MEDIETAS CLERI ILLAS VETERES CAPPAS QUAS ILLI SENIORES ANNIS SINGULIS REDDUNT ACCIPIANT, ET ILLI SENIORES ILLAS CAPPAS QUAS REDDERE DEBENT NON COMMUTENT.
The half of the clergy who are older are to receive new cloaks every year, and they are always to turn in the old ones which they received the previous year, when they get the new ones. And the other half of the clergy are to receive the old cloaks which the elders turn in each year, and the elders are not to sell the cloaks which they have to turn in.

(*Regula Chrodegangi* 1–6, cited in Muller and Taylor 1932:243)

By the time of the earliest Romance documents (§ 12.2) the definite article is a fully grammaticalized category: see Chart 8.11. The Oaths of Strasbourg (§ 12.2.1) and the Cassino Depositions (§ 12.2.2) – both probably translated from Latin – have no definite articles, but the *Cantilène de Sainte Eulalie* (882) has twelve unmistakable examples.

In Modern Italian, the masculine articles vary according to the beginning of the next word: *lo* before [s] + consonant,[31] *lo* reducing to *l'* before a vowel, and *il* elsewhere. The plural *gli*, derived from Old Italian *li* before vowels (§ 8.8.3), occurs under the same conditions as *lo*, while *i* occurs elsewhere. In the feminine singular *la* reduces to *l'* before a vowel, while plural *le* remains invariant. In Old Italian, *lo* was less restricted and a form *'l* is also frequent. Leon Battista Alberti (1404–1472), in the first ever grammar of Italian (Florentine, in his case), reports a system much like the modern one, except with *el e* instead of *il i* (a change due to pretonic raising) and with no elision of *lo la* before vowels.

Used as a definite article, ILLE was unstressed. In Spanish, under this condition its LL reduces to [l] rather than palatalizing to [ʎ] (§ 4.3.7). This yields in Old Spanish *ele ela elos elas*. The redundant first syllable was later lost in all but the masculine singular. Exception: *ela* elided to *el*, at first before any vowel, and later only before stressed /a/:

el águila	'the eagle'	la aguja	'the needle'
el agua	'the water'	la anguila	'the eel'

Old French nominative singular and plural *li* both derive from ILLI (Chart 8.8). The masculine forms of the *cas régime* derive from ILLU ILLOS and, in keeping with the larger trend in French nouns and adjectives, ultimately supplant the *cas sujet*. In the feminine singular and plural the case contrast is neutralized already in Old French.

Exercises

1. From these Latin neuters Italian has two plurals, masculine and feminine. Why? Explain the process.

		m. pl.		f. pl.	
CEREBELLUM	'little brain'	*cervelli*	'minds'	*cervella*	'brains'
FILUM	'thread'	*fili*	'threads'	*fila*	'strands'
FUNDAMENTUM	'foundation'	*fondamenti*	'fundaments'	*fondamenta*	'foundations'
LABRUM	'lip'	*labbri*	'edges'	*labbra*	'lips'
VESTIGIUM	'trace'	*vestigi*	'traces'	*vestigia*	'traces'

2. Why do so many French names have a final <s> (e.g. *Charles, Denis, Georges, Gilles, Jacques, Jules, Louis, Yves*)? Why only men's names?

    Louis derives from Germanic *Lodovicus*. Does *Louise* derive from a potential **Lodovica*? How do you know? What does the <s> in *Louise* tell you about the period of French when this name was formed? The same goes for *Denis, Denise*.

3. Given these Latin imparisyllabic nouns and adjectives, identify the Romance words that derive from the short (nominative singular) stem:

		Italian	Spanish	French (Old French)	Portuguese
MĒLĬOR, MĔLĬŌRE	'better'	migliore	mejor	meilleure (mieildre)	....
PĒĬOR, PĔĬŌRE	'worse'	peggiore	peor	pire	....
PŪLVUS, PŬLVĔRE	'dust'	polvere	polvo	(pous)	pó
DRACŌ, DRACŌNE	'dragon'	drago dragone	dragón	dragon	dragão
FŬLGOR, FŬLGŌRE	'brightness, lightning'	folgore	fulgor	foudre	....

4.   The link between neuter ŏPUS 'work' and its plural ŏPĔRA dissolves as ŏPĔRA becomes feminine singular in Romance (§ 8.5.2). But ŏPUS does leave relics in the medieval languages: OFr *ues* 'need, task'. The idiom EST ŏPUS 'it is needful' lives on in OIt *è d'uopo*, OSp *uebos (me) es* and in OFr *estovoir* 'be needful', *estuet* 'it is needful'.

a. Show how Old French created *estuet* and *estovoir*.
b. If OFr *ues* had survived, what would its pronunciation be today?

5.   What morphological innovation appears in this Spanish pair?

		Italian	Spanish
TEXTORE	'weaver' (m.)	tessitore	tejedor
TEXTRICE	'weaver' (f.)	tessitrice	tejedora

6.   Review § 8.4.3 on French nouns and adjectives, then read this passage from the Old French *Chanson de Roland* (early 1100s).

Li empereres se fait e balz e liez   The emperor becomes bold and cheerful,
Cordres ad prise e les murs peceiez,   He has taken Cordoba and smashed its walls,
Od ses cadables les turs en abatiéd   With his catapults has felled its towers
Mult grant eschec en unt si chevaler   His knights have great spoils from it
D'or e d'argent e de guarnemenz chers.   Gold, silver, and finery.

a. Indicate in which of the following words <s>/<z> is a plural marker. *empereres   balz   liez   murs   ses cadables   turs   chers*
b. Which plural noun in the text does not have <s>? Why?

7.   These four Latin words were imparisyllabics with two stress patterns, one for nominative singular, the other for everything else. Three of these words have the property that their nominative singular had no <s>, a property that Old French often retains (Chart 8.6):

ANTECESSOR	IMPERĀTOR	INFANS	PASTOR
ANTECESSŌRE	IMPERĀTŌRE	INFANTE	PASTŌRE
'ancestor'	'emperor'	'infant'	'shepherd'

a. Which of these nouns are in the *cas sujet*?
   empere(d)re   pasteur   enfant   ancestre   empereur   enfes   ancesseur   pastre
b. If you find forms like *empere(d)res, ancestres, pastres,* how can you explain the <s>?
c. What is unusual about ModFr *ancêtre*?

9 History and structure of Portuguese: an overview

Portuguese is spoken by about 10,000,000 people in Portugal, plus about 165,000,000 in Brazil. There are another 750,000 native speakers in France, and Portuguese remains the official language of many former colonies. In number of speakers, it is second only to Spanish among the Romance languages.

9.1 Stressed vowels: the seven-vowel system

Portuguese, like Standard Italian, has maintained the seven-vowel system resulting from the Great Merger (§ 1.2.3). In a few contexts, /e/ and /ɛ/ are distinguished in writing: high mid /e/ = <ê> and low mid /ɛ/ = <é>. See the table on p. 210.

9.1.1 Extremes of the vowel triangle: ī, ū, a

Latin /ī/, /ū/, and /a/ are well preserved. This mini-triangle gives further examples:[1]

VĪTA	'life'	vida				LŪNA	'moon'	lua
VICĪNA	'neighbor'	vizinha				DŪRU	'hard'	duro
FARĪNA	'flour'	farinha				MŪRU	'wall'	muro
APRĪLE	'April'	abril				PLŪMA	'feather'	pluma
NĪDU	'nest'	ninho				ACŪTU	'sharp'	agudo
SPĪNA	'thorn'	espinha				SECŪRA	'safe'	segura

			CLAVE	'key'	chave
			CASA	'house'	casa
			CARU	'dear'	caro
			CARRU	'cart'	carro
			FLAMMA	'flame'	chama
			GRANDE	'big'	grande

Latin stressed vowels and their outcomes in Portuguese

Latin	gloss	Portuguese
AMĪCA	'friend'	amiga
DĪCIT	'says'	diz
FORMĪCA	'ant'	formiga
SCRIPTU	'written'	escrito
PILU	'hair'	pêlo
CITO	'quickly'	cedo
CRISPU	'curly'	crespo
LITTERA	'letter'	letra
DĒBĒRE	'owe'	dever
PARIĒTE	'wall'	parede
*MĒSE	'month'	mês
CRĒSCIT	'grows'	cresce
PEDE	'foot'	pé
SEPTE	'seven'	sete
HERBA	'grass'	erva
PERDIT	'loses'	perde
SALE	'salt'	sal
MARE	'sea'	mar
CAMPU	'field'	campo
ARBORE	'tree'	árvore
NOVA	'new'	nova
HOSPITE	'host'	hóspede
MORTE	'death'	morte
PORTA	'door'	porta
SUPER	'over'	sobre
AUGUSTU	'August'	agosto
BUCCA	'mouth'	boca
DUPLU	'double'	dobro
SAPŌRE	'taste'	sabor
NERVŌSU	'nervous'	nervoso
FLŌRE	'flower'	flor
CŌRTE	'court'	corte
CRŪDU	'raw'	cru
IŪRAT	'swears'	jura
SCŪTU	'shield'	escudo
MATŪRU	'ripe'	maduro

9.1.2   The high mid vowels

After Latin stressed /ĭ/ /ē/ merge to pre-Romance /e/, it remains /e/ in Portuguese. Likewise, after Latin /ŭ/ /ō/ merge to /o/, it remains /o/.

LĬTTĔRA	'letter'	letra	BŬCCA	'mouth'	boca
VĬRĬDE	'green'	verde	AUGŬSTU	'August'	agosto
PARIĔTE	'wall'	parede	VŌTA	'vows'	boda
HABĒRE	'have'	haver	FLŌRE	'flower'	flor

Deviations from this pattern are common, mainly because the expected high mid vowels are often altered by metaphony (§ 9.4).

9.1.3   The low mid vowels

After Latin /ĕ/ /ŏ/ become pre-Romance low mids /ɛ/ /ɔ/, these remain /ɛ/ /ɔ/. The primary, stress-induced diphthongs of Italian, Spanish, and French (§§ 1.2.4–6) have no counterpart in Portuguese. Further examples:

DĔCE	'ten'	dez	/dɛz/	MŎRIT	'dies'	morre	/mɔxe/
PĔTRA	'stone'	pedra	/pɛdra/	PŎTET	'is able'	pode	/pɔde/
*MĔLE	'honey'	mel	/mɛw/	ŎVA	'roe'	ova	/ɔva/
CĔRVU	'deer'	cervo	/sɛrvo/	FŎRTE	'strong'	forte	/fɔrte/
FĔRRU	'iron'	ferro	/fɛxo/	NŎSTRA	'our'	nossa	/nɔsa/

Certain departures from this pattern are covered below (§§ 9.2, 9.4).

9.1.4   The Latin diphthongs

The three Latin diphthongs /aw/, /aj/, and /oj/ reduced to simple vowels (§ 1.4). The rare Latin /oj/ became high mid /e/ in Portuguese:

POENA	'punishment'	pena
FOEDU	'ugly'	feio

As in Italian, Spanish, and French, Latin /aj/ gave either low mid /ɛ/ or high mid /e/:

CAELU	'sky'	céu	/sɛw/
CAECU	'blind'	cego	/sɛgo/
QUAERIT	'asks'	quer	/kɛʀ/
SAETA	'silk'	seda	/seda/
FAECES	'dregs'	fezes	/fezes/

Latin /aw/ became /ow/ in Old Portuguese, and stayed /ow/ in northern dialects. By the 1500s, /ow/ had simplified to high mid /o/ in Standard Portuguese.

CAUSA	'thing'	cousa	[o]
AURU	'gold'	ouro	[o]
THESAURU	'treasure'	tesouro	[o]

PAUCU	'little'	pouco	[o]
AUDIT	'hears'	ouve	[o]

9.2 More on stressed vowels: secondary diphthongs

While Portuguese has no primary diphthongs like those of Italian, Spanish, and French (§§ 1.2.4–6), it does have secondary diphthongs from other sources, as we see next.

9.2.1 Diphthongs from glide metathesis

As in Spanish, /j/ and /w/ in contact with certain consonants are anticipated, moving into the preceding syllable to form a diphthong. Usually the vowel raises (assimilating to the glide), and the diphthong simplifies.

PRIMARĬU	'first'	primeiro
SAPĬAT	'knows'	saiba
*RABĬA	'anger'	raiva
BASĬU	'kiss'	beijo
CASĔU	'cheese'	queijo
IANUARĬU	'January'	janeiro
PASSIŌNE	'passion'	paixão
MATĔRĬA	'material'	madeira
CERĔSĬA	'cherry'	cereja
FERĬA	'festival'	feira
CŎRĬU	'leather'	coiro
*MŎRĬO	'I die'	(OPo) moiro
PLŬVĬA	'rain'	(OPo) chuiva > chuva
RŬBĔU	'red'	ruivo
SAPŬIT	'knew'	soube
PŎTŬIT	'was able'	(OPo) poude > pôde

The diphthong /aj/ from yod metathesis has two outcomes: /ej/ from early metathesis and in words from northern dialects, and /aj/ from later metathesis and in southern dialects (Williams 1962:§ 33.2). Diphthongs formed with mid vowels plus metathesized yod generally simplify, except before /r/. Metathesized /w/ gives /ow/, which then becomes /o/.

9.2.2 Diphthongs from palatalization and raising

The medial consonant clusters /kt/ /ks/ /kl/ /sk/ /lt/ generate an anticipated yod, often forming new diphthongs (compare §§ 4.3.8–10).

SAXU	'stone'	seixo		
LACTE	'milk'	leite		
FACTU	'done'	feito		
FASCE	'bundle'	feixe		
LĔCTU	'bed'	leito		
SPĔCŬLU	'mirror'	espelho		
VĔTŬLU	'old'	velho		[ɛ]
DIRĒCTU	'straight'	direito		
STRĬCTU	'narrow'	estreito		
APĬCŬLA	'bee'	abelha		
AURĬCŬLA	'ear'	orelha		
PĬSCE	'fish'	peixe		
NŎCTE	'night'	noite		
ŎCTU	'eight'	oito		
ŎCŬLU	'eye'	olho		[o]
RŎTŬLA	'little wheel'	rolha		[o]
CŎXA	'thigh'	coixa	> coxa	[o]
LŬCTAT	'struggles'	luita	> luta	
AUSCŬLTAT	'listens'	escuita	> escuta	
TRŬCTA	'trout'	truita	> truta	
VŬLTŬRE	'vulture'	abuitre	> abutre	
MŬLTU	'much'	muito		
FRŪCTU	'fruit'	fruito	> fruto	
LŪCTU	'mourning'	luito	> luto	

The yod from palatalizing clusters /kt/ /ks/ /sk/ /lt/ was generally maintained and induced raising, except with /u/ and high mid /e/. The sequence /uj/ tended to become /u/. Portuguese *muito* is frozen in an intermediate stage, perhaps through influence of the apocopated form *mui* (Williams 1962:§ 94.2). The yod from /kl/ deletes, but does trigger raising of stressed low mids (*velho* is an exception) and of stressed /o/.

As new palatal consonants arose, stressed vowels raised under certain conditions (§ 9.5). Stressed mid vowels raise in contact with the new palatals /ɲ/ and /ʎ/:

FĪLĬA	'daughter'	filha	
VĪNĔA	'vinyard'	vinha	
LĬGNA	'wood'	lenha	
CĬLĬA	'eyebrow'	celha	
VĔNĬO	'I come'	venho	[e]
TĔNĔO	'I hold'	tenho	

PALĔA	'straw'	palha	
ALĬU	'garlic'	alho	
ARANĔA	'spider'	aranha	
EXTRANĔU	'foreign'	estranho	
FŎLĬA	'leaves'	folha 'leaf'	[o]
SŎMNĬU	'dream'	sonho	[õ]
CICŌNĬA	'stork'	cegonha	
TESTIMŌNĬU	'witness'	testemunho	
PŬGNU	'fist'	punho	
CŬNĔU	'wedge'	cunho	

The stressed low mids /ɛ/ /ɔ/ raise to /e/ /o/ as in sets two and four above. Stressed /e/ shows no raising effect, while the stressed high mid /o/ in set five may or may not raise.

The palatalization of /d/ plus yod to /ʒ/ also raises stressed /ɛ/ /ɔ/ to /e/ /o/:

SĔDĔAT	'sits'	seja	'is'	[e]
HŎDĬE	'today'	hoje		[o]
PŎDĬU	'knoll'	pojo		[o]

Like Spanish and Italian (§§ 5.1.1, 5.2.4), Portuguese shows raising of pretonic vowels triggered by yod or a palatalizing cluster in a later syllable.

MŬLIĒRE	'woman'	mulher	
COGNATU	'kinsman'	cunhado	
DŎRMIAMUS	'we sleep'	durmamos	
CŬLTELLU	'knife'	cuitelo	> cutelo
SERVIAMUS	'we serve'	sirvamos	
VINDĒMIARE	'harvest'	vindimar	
LĔCTURA	'reading'	leitura	

Usually /aj/ raises to /ej/ which then remains:

BASIARE	'kiss'	beijar
LACTUCA	'lettuce'	leituga
LAXARE	'loosen'	leixar (OPo)

9.2.3   Diphthongs /ow/ and /oj/

We saw that stressed Latin /aw/ became /ow/, then /o/ in Standard Portuguese: PAUCA > *pouca*. Metathesis of yod and palatalization of /k/ created a new diphthong /oj/. Latin medial /kt/ gave Portuguese /jt/ or sometimes /wt/.

NŎCTE	'night'	noite
DOCTU	'learnèd'	douto

Perhaps for this reason, /ow/ and /oj/ became interchangeable for some time in many words, /ow/ being more literary and /oj/ more colloquial (Williams 1962:§ 92.7).

CAUSA	'cause'	cousa, coisa
AURU	'gold'	ouro, oiro
DORIU	'[river name]'	Douro, Doiro
NŎCTE	'night'	noute, noite

9.2.4   Diphthongs from vowel hiatus

Vowel hiatus, whether original or from loss of intervocalic consonants, often resulted in diphthongs, some of which underwent further changes:

MALU	'bad'	mau				
PĔDE	'foot'	pee	>	pé		
SŌLA	'alone'	soa	>	soo	>	só
SAGĬTTA	'arrow'	saeta	>	seeta	>	seta
PŎPŬLU	'people'	poboo	>	povo		
LĒGE	'law'	lei				
RĒGE	'king'	rei				
GREGE	'herd'	grei				
LAICU	'lay'	leigo				
CANTA(V)I	'I sang'	cantei				

When an intervocalic consonant deleted, the threat of vowel hiatus was often averted by inserting an anti-hiatic glide, either /j/ or /w/, to harmonize with the preceding vowel. The /w/ later strengthens to /v/, as in *ouve, louva*:

CRĒDO	'believe'	creo	>	creio
TĒLA	'cloth'	teia		
AUDIT	'hears'	ouve		
LAUDAT	'praises'	louva		

9.3   More on stressed vowels: nasalization

Stressed vowels followed by /n/ or syllable-final /m/ were nasalized. Intervocalic /n/ later deletes (§ 9.6.4):

PANE	'bread'	pã (OPo)
MANU	'hand'	mão
PONIS	'put'	pões

Sometimes word-initial /m/ nasalizes a following vowel:

MATRE	'mother'	mãe	
MIHI	'me'	mim	[mĩ]
MŬLTU	'much'	muito	[mũĩtu]

9.3.1   The spread of /-ão/

In the 1300s and 1400s, word-final stressed /ã/ and /õ/ merged with final /-ão/ from Latin -ANU. But earlier plural forms were maintained:

					Plural
CANE	'dog'	cã	>	cão	cães
RATIONE	'reason'	razon	>	razão	razões
LECTIONE	'lesson'	liçõ	>	lição	lições
LEONE	'lion'	leon	>	leão	leões
NON	'not'	non	>	não	
SUNT	'are'	son	>	são	

9.3.2   Coalescence and denasalization

In the 1400s, after the spread of final /-ão/, like vowels in hiatus coalesce:

BŎNU	'good'	bõo	>	bom	[bõ]
LANA	'wool'	lãa	>	lã	
GERMANA	'sister'	irmãa	>	irmã	

The stressed nasal diphthongs /ão/, /õe/, and /ãe/ remained nasal, but other nasal vowels in hiatus were generally denasalized after the 1500s.

BŎNA	'good'	bõa	>	boa		
PERSONA	'person'	pessõa	>	pessoa		
TĔNĒRE	'hold'	tẽer	>	teer	>	ter
VĒNA	'vein'	vẽa	>	vea	>	veia
VĔNĪRE	'come'	vẽir	>	viir	>	vir

9.3.3   Anti-hiatic /ɲ/

When stressed nasal /ĩ/ was followed by /o/ or /a/, the hiatus was broken by inserting a palatal /ɲ/. Sometimes this occurred after intervocalic /n/ deleted (§ 9.6.4): FARĪNA > farĩa > farinha.

MĔA	'my'	mĩa	>	minha
SPĪNA	'thorn'	espinha		
FARĪNA	'flour'	farinha		
MŎLĪNU	'mill'	moinho		

9.3.4   Diphthongization

When a stressed front mid vowel precedes a final nasal consonant, the vowel becomes nasal /ẽ/ and then /ẽj/.

QUEM	'whom'	quem	[kẽj]
BENE	'well'	bem	[bẽj]
VENIT	'comes'	vem	[vẽj]

9.4   Raising effects

Stressed mid vowels raise in contact with certain triggers. When nasalized, they become high mids:

SŎNU	'sound'	som			[õ]
BŎNA	'good'	bõa	>	boa	[o]
DĔNTE	'tooth'	dente			[ẽ]
LŎNGE	'long'	longe			[õ]

Stressed high mids before [ŋk] or [ŋg] can raise to /i/ or /u/, as in Italian (§ 5.1.2).

LĬNGUA	'tongue'	língua
NŬMQUAM	'never'	nunca
IŬNCU	'rush'	junco

A yod in the following syllable can also raise a stressed mid vowel:

SUPĔRBIA	'pride'	soberba	[e]
NĔRVIU	'vigor'	nervo	[e]
TĔRTIU	'third'	terço	[e]
SĒPIA	'cuttlefish'	siba	[i]
VINDĒMIA	'vintage'	vindima	[i]
FŎRTIA	'force'	força	[o]

Stressed high mids followed by a syllable with word-final /i/ became high vowels, a type of metaphony also posited in Spanish (§ 6.6.2).

FĒCĪ	'did'	fiz		
VĪGĬNTĪ	'twenty'	viinte	>	vinte
PŎTŬĪ	'I could'	*podi	>	pude
ŬBĪ	'where'	u (OPo)		

9.5   Early changes in consonants

Portuguese shares with other Western Romance languages the effects of early sound changes dating from Popular Latin (Chapter 2).

9.5.1   Prosthesis

Like other Western Romance languages (§ 2.1), Portuguese added a prosthetic vowel to words beginning with /s/ + consonant.

SPONSA	'betrothed'	esposa
SPATA	'sword'	espada
STUDIU	'study'	estudo
SPONGIA	'sponge'	esponja
STRICTU	'tight'	estreito
SCRIPTU	'written'	escrito

Prosthesis still applies to modern loan words: *espaguete* 'spaghetti', *esnobe* 'snob', *escorpião* 'scorpion'.

9.5.2   Early syncope

The loss of word-medial unstressed vowels created new consonant clusters, some tolerated and others modified. Nasal + liquid clusters are treated as shown here:

TENERU	'tender'	terno, tenro
GENERU	'son-in-law'	genro
HUMERU	'shoulder'	ombro
SIMILAT	'resembles'	sembra
MEMORAT	'remember'	lembra
CUCUMERE	'cucumber'	cogombro

These new nasal clusters are relatively few in Portuguese, because in many words intervocalic /n/ deleted early, before syncope.

DOMINA	'lady'	dona		
FEMINA	'female'	fêmea		
SEMINAT	'sows'	semea		
HOMINES	'men'	homães	>	homens [õmẽjs]

For denasalization of <ea>, see § 9.3.2. In *homens* the intervocalic /n/ nasalizes the preceding vowel, then deletes, then [ẽe] > [ẽj]. The <n> merely marks the nasality.

9.5.3   Merger of /b/ and /w/

Unlike Spanish (§ 2.3), Portuguese keeps /b/ and /w/ distinct word-initially and sometimes in internal protected position, but /b/ becomes /v/ twice as often as it remains /b/, and /v/ never becomes /b/, as it can in Romanian (§ 10.4.1).

BASSU	'low'	baixo
BUCCA	'mouth'	boca
VACCA	'cow'	vaca
VINU	'wine'	vinho
BARBA	'beard'	barba
SUPERBU	'haughty'	soberbo

BULBU	'bulb'	bulbo
CARBONE	'coal'	carvão
HERBA	'grass'	erva
TURBIDU	'clouded'	turvo
ARBORE	'tree'	árvore
ALBU	'white'	alvo
CERVU	'deer'	cervo
FERVENTE	'boiling'	fervente
SALVAT	'saves'	salva
CABALLU	'horse'	cavalo
HABERE	'have'	haver
CAVERNA	'cavern'	caverna
LAVAT	'washes'	lava
VIVIT	'lives'	vive

9.5.4   Early consonant losses

Portuguese shows the effects of consonant losses dating from Popular Latin (§ 2.4), loss of /h/, and the reduction /ns/ > /s/:

HOMINE	'man'	homem	[õmẽj]
MENSE	'month'	mês	
PENSU	'weight'	peso	
SPONSU	'spouse'	esposo	

Portuguese reflects the early loss of intervocalic /g/, mostly before /e/ or /i/.

EGO	'I'	eu
IAM MAGIS	'more'	jamais
MAGISTER	'master'	mestre
SAGITTA	'arrow'	seta
PAGENSE	'country'	país

9.6   Consonant weakening and strengthening

Portuguese shares certain Romance processes of consonant weakening and strengthening (Chapter 3) and has others of its own.

9.6.1   Degemination

Latin geminates reduce to plain consonants in Portuguese, as they do in Spanish and French (§ 3.1).

OSSU	'bone'	osso [oso]
SUMMA	'sum'	suma

CABALLU	'horse'	cavalo
LITTERA	'letter'	letra
SICCU	'dry'	seco
CUPPA	'cup'	copa
ANNU	'year'	ano

9.6.2   Lenition

In unprotected position (intervocalic in these examples), Latin voiceless stops /p t k/ become voiced /b d g/, but do not go on to [β ð ɣ], as they do in Spanish.

SAPORE	'flavor'	sabor	
CAPUT	'head'	cabo	
COPERTU	'covered'	coberto	
OPERA	'works'	obra	
VITA	'life'	vida	
FATA	'Fate'	fada	'fairy'
CATENA	'chain'	cadeia	
ROTA	'wheel'	roda	
AMICA	'friend'	amiga	
SECURU	'safe'	seguro	
FOCU	'fire'	fogo	
IOCAT	'plays'	joga	

Sometimes Latin /p/ becomes /v/: POPULU *povo* 'people', SCOPA *escova* 'broom'.

Unprotected /b/ survives as /v/, reflecting the /b/ /w/ merger, while /d/ lenites all the way to zero, and /g/ stays intact except before front vowels: SIGILLU 'seal' *selo* (§ 9.5.4).

CABALLU	'horse'	cavalo
DEBERE	'owe'	dever
HABERE	'have'	haver
CRUDU	'raw'	cru
CREDIT	'believes'	crê
PEDE	'foot'	pé
CADERE	'fall'	cair
AUGUSTU	'August'	agosto
LIGARE	'bind'	ligar
PAGANU	'pagan'	pagão
PLAGA	'wound'	chaga

In word-medial consonant clusters, postvocalic stops as in *LEPRE do undergo lenition, while postconsonantal stops as in SERPENTE do not (§ 3.2.4).

*LEPRE	'hare'	lebre	
CAPRA	'goat'	cabra	
PETRA	'stone'	pedra	
PATRE	'father'	padre	
FLAGRAT	'burns'	cheira	'smells'
SERPENTE	'snake'	serpente	
RUMPIT	'breaks'	rompe	
URTICA	'nettle'	urtiga	
MENTHA	'mint'	menta	
PERDIT	'loses'	perde	
ARCU	'arch'	arco	
FALCONE	'falcon'	falcão	

9.6.3   Vocalization of /l/

As in French (§ 3.3.1), Latin /l/ in syllable-final position becomes /w/ in some Portuguese words, via an intermediate velarization to [ł]: SALTU > [sałto] > [sawto] > [sowto] > [soto] *souto*.

ALTERU	'other'	outro
SALTU	'leap'	souto

In Modern Brazilian Portuguese, /l/ becomes /w/ word-finally too:

sol	[sow]	'sun'
final	[finaw]	'final'
alto	[awtu]	'tall'
Brasil	[braziw]	'Brazil'

9.6.4   Loss of /l/ and /n/

Intervocalic /l/ and /n/ delete, an early change peculiar to Portuguese:

SALIRE	'leap'	sair
DOLORE	'pain'	dor
NEBULA	'cloud'	névoa
CALENTE	'hot'	quente
PERICULU	'danger'	perigo
CAELU	'sky'	céu
MANU	'hand'	mão
GERMANU	'brother'	irmão
CANES	'dogs'	cães
LANA	'wool'	lã
PERSONA	'person'	pessoa
TENERE	'have'	ter

Before deleting, intervocalic /n/ nasalized the preceding vowel, but in some environments nasalization was later reversed (§ 9.3.2).

9.6.5   Fortition

Word-initial glides are replaced by stronger consonants (§ 3.4). Word-initially, Latin /w/ becomes /v/, while Germanic /w/ becomes /g/ before front vowels and /gw/ elsewhere (§ 3.4.1). Word-initial /j/ is strengthened to /ʒ/ (§ 9.7.1).

VINU	'wine'	vinho	
VENA	'vein'	veia	
VENIT	'comes'	vem	
VASU	'vase'	vaso	
VOSTRU	'your'	vosso	
*werra	'war'	guerra	[ge]
*wisa	'manner'	guisa	[gi]
*warten	'watch'	guardar	[gwa]
IOCU	'game'	jogo	
IUVENE	'young'	jovem	
IURAT	'swears'	jura	
IUDICE	'judge'	juiz	

9.7   New palatal consonants

The Romance languages developed a new order of palatal consonants which greatly expanded their phonemic inventories (Chapter 4). These palatals arose from contact with a yod or in response to unstable consonant clusters.

9.7.1   Original yods

Latin word-initial /j/ becomes Portuguese /ʒ/, as shown above. In word-medial position it normally becomes /ʒ/:

CUIU	'whose'	cujo
IEIUNARE	'fast'	jejuar
HABEAT[2]	'has'	haja

9.7.2   /d/ + yod and /g/ + yod

These sequences behave like original yods, as seen in Italian, Spanish, and French (§ 4.3.2).

HODIE	'today'	hoje
FUGIO	'I flee'	fujo
ADIUTAT	'helps'	ajuda
VIDEO	'I see'	vejo

PODIU	'knoll'	pôjo
RADIU	'ray'	raio

The regular outcome of Latin medial /j/, /dj/, or /gj/ is /ʒ/. Words like *raio* that maintain the yod appear to be loan words from Spanish or *semicultismos*.

9.7.3   /g/ + front vowel

Latin /g/ plus front vowel develops like /j/, /dj/, and /gj/:

GYPSU	'plaster'	gesso	
GEMIT	'moans'	geme	
GEMMA	'gem'	gema	
GENERU	'son-in-law'	genro	
GENTE	'people'	gente	
GINGIVA	'gum'	gengiva	
GELAT	'freezes'	gela	
GENTILE	'clansman'	gentil	'graceful'
REGE	'king'	rei	
LEGE	'law'	lei	
GREGE	'flock'	grei	

Latin /g/ plus front vowel becomes /ʒ/ in protected positions – word-initial or postconsonantal (§ 3.2.4). Elsewhere it deletes.

9.7.4   /k/ + front vowel

The velar /k/, pulled forward toward the palatal articulation of front vowels, becomes /s/, which voices to /z/ when intervocalic.

CIVITATE	'citizenship'	cidade
CERVU	'deer'	cervo
CENTU	'hundred'	cento
*CINQUE	'five'	cinco
DICIT	'says'	diz
DECEM	'ten'	dez
VICINA	'neighbor'	vizinha
IACET	'lies'	jaz
FACIT	'makes'	faz

In Portuguese, /k/ before front vowels went through stages partly similar to those in Italian, Spanish, and French. First, /k/ plus /i/ or /e/ yielded /tʃ/ in late Popular Latin and then, in Old Portuguese, fronted to /ts/, voicing to /dz/ when intervocalic. These deaffricated to /s/ and /z/ in Modern Portuguese.

9.7.5   /t/ + yod and /k/ + yod

The regular result of medial /kj/ was first /ts/, which deaffricated to /s/, but sometimes /z/ appears instead, as in *juizo*. Postconsonantal /tj/ gave /ts/ > /s/.

Intervocalic /tj/ gave /dz/ > /z/, but in some words /tj/ > /ts/ > /s/ without lenition.

*FACIA	'face'	face
BRACHIU	'arm'	braço
MINACIA	'threat'	ameaça
CALCEA	'footwear'	calça
IUDICIU	'trial'	juizo
MARTIU	'March'	março
*FORTIA	'strength'	força
TERTIARIU	'third'	terceiro
PUTEU	'well'	poço
PLATEA	'open space'	praça
PALATIU	'palace'	paço
RATIONE	'reason'	razão
PRETIAT	'prizes'	preza

Summing up: the reflexes from the sets below are parallel only in part (compare § 4.3.6). The voiceless set yields Old Portuguese [ts] or [dz], but the voiced set gives [dʒ] (not [dz]), which becomes [ʒ] in Modern Portuguese.

voiceless:	[tj]		[kj] and [k ^{i,e}]
voiced:	[dj]	[j]	[gj] and [g ^{i,e}]

In Old Portuguese, the affricates [ts] and [dz] from the voiceless set above contrasted with [s̺] and [z̺], which had an apicoalveolar articulation.

se̱nhor [s̺]	ce̱nto [ts] > [s]
ca̱sa [z̺]	faze̱r [dz] > [z]

As we saw, [ts] and [dz] deaffricated, yielding [s] and [z], but with a dorsoalveolar articulation. Old Portuguese retained a four-way distinction, [s] / [z] and [s̺] / [z̺]. In the 1500s the place contrast neutralized, creating the modern standard distinction [s] / [z].[3]

9.7.6   Palatals /ɲ/ and /ʎ/

The new Romance palatals /ɲ/ and /ʎ/ come from various sources, notably Popular Latin /nj/ and /lj/.

SENIORE	'elder'	senhor
HISPANIA	'Spain'	Espanha
CICONIA	'stork'	cegonha
ARANEA	'spider'	aranha
CUNEU	'wedge'	cunho
ALIU	'garlic'	alho
MELIORE	'better'	melhor

FOLIA	'leaf'	folha
PALEA	'straw'	palha
MULIERE	'woman'	mulher

Latin /gn/ /gl/ also palatalize to [ɲ] [ʎ]:

LIGNA	'wood'	lenha	
SIGNA	'signs'	senha	'sign'
STAGNU	'pond'	estanho	
PUGNU	'fist'	punho	
TEGULA	'tile'	telha	
COAGULAT	'curdles'	coalha	

But the Latin geminates /nː/ /lː/ do not become [ɲ] [ʎ], as they do in Spanish. They simply degeminate:

ANNU	'year'	ano
CANNA	'cane'	cana
SOMNU	'sleep'	sono
ANELLU	'ring'	anel
BELLU	'beautiful'	belo
COLLU	'neck'	colo
CABALLU	'horse'	cavalo

9.7.7   Palatalizing clusters with /l/

Latin clusters /pl/ /bl/ /fl/ /kl/ /gl/ develop as exemplified here. The popular outcome of /pl/ /fl/ /kl/ is the fricative /ʃ/, written <ch>. In less frequent words and in *cultismos*, the original clusters are maintained or become /pr/ /fr/ /kr/. Apparently /bl/ and /gl/ never palatalize.

PLICAT	'folds'	chega	'arrives'
PLENA	'full'	cheia	
*PLŬVIT	'rains'	chove	
PLORAT	'cries'	chora	
PLAGA	'wound'	chaga	
PLANA	'plane'	plana	
PLACERE	'pleasure'	prazer	
Gmc *blank*	'white'	branco	
BLITU	'blite'	bredo	
BLANDU	'flattering'	brando	'soft'
FLAMMA	'flame'	chama	
FLAGRAT	'burns'	cheira	'smells'

FLAMMŬLA	'flame'	chámoa
FLACCU	'weak'	fraco
FLORE	'flower'	flor
CLAMAT	'calls'	chama
CLAVE	'key'	chave
CLAUSA	'enclosed place'	chousa
CLARA	'clear'	clara
CLAVU	'nail'	cravo
GLANDE	'acorn'	lande
GLAREA	'gravel'	leira
*GLUTTONE	'glutton'	glutão

Protected in postconsonantal position, /pl/ /fl/ /kl/ become /ʃ/, as they do word-initially (see *enche, acha, incha, mancha*), except in *cultismos* like *exemplo*. In the unprotected intervocalic position, /pl/ > /br/ and /bl/ > /l/. Medial /tl/ /kl/ /gl/, formed by early syncope, become /ʎ/. Words like *tábua, névoa* lost their intervocalic /l/ before the cluster could materialize.

DUPLU	'double'	dobro
IMPLET	'fills'	enche
EXEMPLU	'example'	exemplo
FABULAT	'speaks'	fala
*TABULARIA	'records'	taleira
TABULA	'table'	tábua
NEBULA	'fog'	névoa
*AFFLAT	'sniffs out'	acha
INFLAT	'inflates'	incha
AURICULA	'ear'	orelha
APICULA	'bee'	abelha
SPECULU	'mirror'	espelho
PARICULA	'pair'	parelha
VERMICULU	'vermilion'	vermelho
OCULU	'eye'	olho
GENUCULU	'knee'	joelho
MA(N)CULA	'stain'	mancha
VETULU	'old'	velho
TEGULA	'tile'	telha
COAGULAT	'curdles'	coalha
UNGULA	'nail'	unha

9.7.8   Clusters /sk/ + front vowel, /skj/, and /s:j/

These clusters are another source of the new palatal consonant /ʃ/ in Portuguese.

SCINDO	'split'	escindo
SCAENA	'stage'	cena
SCIENTIA	'knowledge'	ciência
PISCE	'fish'	peixe
MISCERE	'mix'	mexer
FASCE	'bundle'	feixe
FASCIA	'band'	faixa
*NASCIT	'is born'	nasce
*RUSSEU	'red'	roxo
PASSIONE	'passion'	paixão
*BASSIARE	'lower'	baixar

The regular development of word-initial /sk/ plus front vowel is /s/ with prosthetic /e/, as in *escindo*. For medial /sk/ + front vowel or yod, the regular outcome is /ʃ/. Popular Latin /s:j/ palatalizes to /ʃ/.

9.7.9   Clusters /kt/ and /ks/

Latin medial clusters /kt/ and /ks/ are modified in most Romance languages, sometimes creating a yod.

*PINCTU	'painted'	pinto	
PLANCTU	'lament'	pranto	
SANCTU	'holy'	santo	
IUNCTU	'joined'	junto	
PUNCTU	'point'	ponto	
ANXIA	'distress'	ânsia	
DICTU	'said'	dito	
STRICTU	'tight'	estreito	'narrow'
DIRECTU	'straight'	direito	
NOCTE	'night'	noite	
OCTO	'eight'	oito	
FACTU	'made'	feito	
LECTU	'bed'	leito	
LACTE	'milk'	leite	
DIXIT	'said'	disse	
FIXAT	'makes fast'	fixa	
*VEXICA	'bladder'	bexiga	
FRAXINU	'ash tree'	freixo	
COXA	'hip'	coxa	'thigh'

Postconsonantal /kt/ /ks/ lose the /k/. Otherwise, /kt/ gives /jt/, and this yod can affect the preceding vowel (§ 9.2.2). Intervocalic /ks/ gives /ʃ/, or sometimes /s/, as in *disse*.

9.7.10   /s/ + yod

As described above (§ 9.7.8), the sequence /s:j/ gives Portuguese /ʃ/. Similarly, intervocalic /sj/ palatalizes to /ʒ/, and the yod may migrate leftward (§ 9.2.1).

CASEU	'cheese'	queijo
CERESIA	'cherry'	cereja
BASIU	'kiss'	beijo
ECCLESIA	'church'	igreja

9.8   Noun and adjective morphology

9.8.1   Noun declensions

The first and second declension classes of Latin, increasingly bonding with genders, left in Portuguese the same imprint as in Spanish and Italian, namely feminine nouns in /-a/ and masculine nouns in /-o/.

FILIA	'daughter'	filha
PORTA	'door'	porta
LUPU	'wolf'	lobo
AMICU	'friend'	amigo

From the mixed-gender third declension, Portuguese inherits nouns ending in consonant or (now or formerly) in /-e/.

SOLE	'sun'	sol
REGE	'king'	rei
SENIORE	'lord'	senhor
NOMEN	'name'	nome
RATIONE	'reason'	razão

9.8.2   Recategorizing nouns

As exemplified in § 8.2, § 8.5, and below, pre-Romance times saw the dissolution of the neuter gender and of the fourth and fifth declensions. Such nouns found refuge in the favored first and second declensions, or less commonly in the third.

Neuter nouns of the second and fourth declensions became masculine: CORNU 'horn' *corno*, VINU 'wine' *vinho*. Feminine nouns of the second and fourth declensions moved to the first (SOCRU 'mother-in-law' *sogra*, NURU 'daughter-in-law' *nora*, SAPPHIRU 'sapphire' *safira*) or became masculine, joining the second declension (FRAXINU 'ash tree' *freixo*). Exceptionally, MANU > *mão* 'hand' remained feminine.

Some neuter plurals in /-a/ became feminine singulars and acquired analogical plurals:

Singular	*Plural*	*Singular*		*Plural*	
VOTU	VOTA	boda	'wedding'	bodas	'wedding anniversary'
LIGNU	LIGNA	lenha	'lumber, beam'	lenhas	'beams'
FOLIU	FOLIA	folha	'leaf'	folhas	'leaves'

Neuter plurals in final /-a/ from the third declension adopted plural endings in /es/ from masculine and feminine forms: MARE, MARIA >> *mar, mares*.

In certain neuter singulars of the third declension, final /en/ was reanalysed as /em/ and the nasal fell: NOMEN 'name' *nome*, LUMEN 'light' *lume*, with new plurals *nomes, lumes*. Their long stems like NOMINE, LUMINE (Spanish *nombre, lumbre*) leave no trace in Portuguese.

Third declension neuters with stem-final /us/ were reanalysed as masculines of the second declension:

Singular	*Plural*	*Singular*		*Plural*
CORPUS	CORPORA	corpo	'body'	corpos
TEMPUS	TEMPORA	tempo	'time'	tempos
PECTUS	PECTORA	peito	'chest'	peitos

Nouns of the fifth declension were assimilated into the first or third:

RABIES	'rage'	raiva	
DIES	'day'	dia	
MATERIES	'material'	madeira	'wood'
FIDES	'faith'	fé	
FACIES	'face'	face	

Some nouns from the third and fifth declensions joined the first and second:

PASSERE	'sparrow'	pássaro
CUCUMERE	'cucumber'	cogombro
GRAMEN	'grass'	grama
SEPTEMBRE	'September'	setembro

Third declension nouns are invariant for gender, but some acquired a new feminine form in /-a/:

SENIORE	'lord'	senhor	senhora[4]
INFANTE	'infant'	infante	infanta
PARENTE	'relative'	parente	parenta
LEONE	'lion'	leão	leoa

9.8.3   Vestiges of other cases

Portuguese, like Spanish, loses all case contrasts in nouns, typically keeping the accusative. But scattered vestiges of other cases do survive. Names, certain pronouns, and a few other nouns derive from nominatives.

EGO	'I'	eu
TU	'you'	tu
ILLE	'he'	ele
DEUS	'God'	deus
SOROR	'sister'	sor
CAROLUS	'Charles'	Carlos
MARCUS	'Mark'	Marcos

Vestiges of the ablative case are fossilized in a few adverbs (HAC HORA 'now' *agora*, IN BONA ORA 'eventually' *embora*) and in the suffix -*mente* '-ly' < MENTE 'mind' (§ 11.2.9). The genitive case is preserved in words for the days of the week in other Romance languages (see Exercise 2.4), which also occur in Old Portuguese.[5]

LUNAE DIE	'Monday'	lũes
MARTIS DIE	'Tuesday'	martes
MERCURII DIE	'Wednesday'	mercores
JOVIS DIE	'Thursday'	joves
VENERIS DIE	'Friday'	vernes

9.8.4   Metaphony in nouns

A prominent feature of Portuguese is the assimilating effect of final vowels on stressed mid vowels (§ 9.4). With word-final /a/, stressed high mids /e/ /o/ lower to low mids /ɛ/ /ɔ/:

ĬSTA	'this'	esta	[ɛ]
VĒLA	'sail'	vela	[ɛ]
HŌRA	'hour'	hora	[ɔ]
SŌLA	'alone'	só	[ɔ]
GŬLA	'throat'	gola	[ɔ]

Final [u] (written <o>) has the effect of raising stressed low mids /ɛ ɔ/ to [e o], and /e o/ to [i u].

CŎRVU	'crow'	corvo	[o]
FŎCU	'fire'	fogo	[o]
MĔTU	'fear'	medo	[e]
ĬPSU	'self'	isso	[i]
TŌTU	'all'	tudo	[u]

In nouns and adjectives, alternations in stressed vowels serve to supplement inflection for gender and number. In nouns with Latin stressed ŏ, the masculine singular in Portuguese has stressed /o/ from metaphony, while the other forms have the expected /ɔ/.

ŎVU	m. sg.	ovo	[o]	'egg'
ŎVOS	m. pl.	ovos	[ɔ]	'eggs'
ŎVA	f. sg.	ova	[ɔ]	'roe'

In nouns with Latin stressed ĕ, the masculine singular and plural in Portuguese both have /e/, while the feminine singular and plural nouns have the expected stressed /ɛ/ (examples from Parkinson 1988):

CAPĔLLU	'hood'	capelo	[e]
CAPĔLLOS	'hoods'	capelos	[e]
CAPĔLLA	'chapel'	capela	[ɛ]
CAPĔLLAS	'chapels'	capelas	[ɛ]

These metaphonic alternations have been somewhat blurred. Some nouns that fit these conditions show no metaphony: CAECU 'blind' *cego* [ɛ]. If the stressed vowel is nasal or precedes a nasal consonant, no metaphony occurs. In addition, the patterns of metaphony have extended to nouns which have /o/ from Latin ō or ŭ in the singular but have adopted /ɔ/ in the plural by analogy: FŬRNU 'oven' *forno* [o], FŬRNOS *fornos* [ɔ]. The singular and plural of *olho* 'eye' (< ŎCULU) should both have stressed [o] from the palatalizing of /kl/, but the plural in Modern Portuguese has [ɔ] by analogy with other alternating nouns.

9.8.5   Metaphony in adjectives

As in Spanish or Italian, adjectives fall into the /-o -a/ type from the Latin second and first declensions and the /-e -e/ type from the third declension.

	Masculine		Feminine		Masculine/Feminine	
sg.	BĚLLU	belo	BĚLLA	bela	FŎRTE	forte
pl.	BĚLLOS	belos	BĚLLAS	belas	FŎRTES	fortes

Portuguese adjectives show effects of metaphony, as nouns do (§ 9.8.4). Stressed /ɔ/ raises to /o/ in the masculine singular, while the other three forms have /ɔ/.

NŎVU	'new'	novo	[o]
NŎVOS		novos	[ɔ]
NŎVA		nova	[ɔ]
NŎVAS		novas	[ɔ]

However, stressed high mids /o/ and /e/ remain immune to metaphony in adjectives.

RŬPTU	'broken'	roto	[o]
RŬPTOS		rotos	[o]
RŬPTA		rota	[o]
RŬPTAS		rotas	[o]

Exception: the suffix -ŌSU underwent metaphony by final /a/ in both feminine forms. Its masculine plural adopted [ɔ], analogizing to adjectives like *novos*.

FORMŌSU	'beautiful'	formoso	[o]
FORMŌSOS		formosos	[ɔ]
FORMŌSA		formosa	[ɔ]
FORMŌSAS		formosas	[ɔ]

Adjectives with stressed /ɛ/ have leveled their paradigms in one direction or the other and thus show no metaphony:

GRAECU	grego	[e]	BĔLLU	belo	[ɛ]
GRAECOS	gregos	[e]	BĔLLOS	belos	[ɛ]
GRAECA	grega	[e]	BĔLLA	bela	[ɛ]
GRAECAS	gregas	[e]	BĔLLAS	belas	[ɛ]

9.8.6   Allomorphy in nouns and adjectives

Loss of intervocalic /l/ had the effect of creating singular and plural allomorphs in nouns and adjectives, e.g. SOLE, SOLES *sol, sóis* 'sun(s)' and CRUDELE, CRUDELES *cruel, cruéis* 'cruel' (§ 9.6.4). In the plural, stem-final /l/ is intervocalic and deletes. In the singular, /l/ becomes final and remains intact.

Loss of intervocalic /n/ also created stem alternations in nouns and adjectives. In this pair, the masculine maintains the nasalized stressed vowel, but in the feminine the nasalized vowel in hiatus is denasalized (§ 9.3.2):

BONU	'good, m.'	bõo	>	bom	[bõ]
BONA	'good, f.'	bõa	>	boa	

The spread of final /ão/ in singulars produced unusual stem alternations in words that had undergone nasalization of stressed vowels (§ 9.3.1).

CANE	'dog'	can	>	cão
CANES	'dogs'	cães		
RATIONE	'reason'	razon	>	razão
RATIONES	'reasons'	razões		

9.8.7   Pronouns

Romance pronouns develop a major contrast between tonic (noun-like) and atonic (clitic) forms (§ 8.8). This contrast exists in Portuguese too.

Chart 9.1 Tonic pronouns in Portuguese

1st sg.	Subject	ĔGO	eu
	Non-subj.	MIHI	mim
2nd sg.	Subject	TŪ	tu
	Non-subj.	TIBI	ti
3rd sg. m.	Caseless	ĬLLE	ele
f.		ĬLLA	ela
1st pl.	Caseless	NŌS	nós
2nd pl.	Caseless	VŌS	vós
3rd pl. m.	Caseless	ĬLLĪ	eles
f.		ĬLLĀS	elas

Chart 9.2 Atonic pronouns in Portuguese

	Acc		Dat	
1st sg.	MĒ	me	MIHI	me
2nd sg.	TĒ	te	TIBI	te
3rd sg. m.	ĬLLU	lo > o	ĬLLĪ	li > lhe
f.	ĬLLA	la > a	ĬLLĪ	li > lhe
				(OPo)
1st pl.	NŌS	nos	NOBIS	nos
2nd pl.	VŌS	vos	VOBIS	vos
3rd pl. m.	ĬLLŌS	los > os	ĬLLĪS	lis lhes
f.	ĬLLĀS	las > as	ĬLLĪS	lis lhes
				(OPo)

Tonic pronouns are full-fledged words, used as emphatic subjects and in other stressable positions, notably with prepositions: Portuguese *para mim* 'for me', *para nós* 'for us'. As in Italian and Spanish (Chart 8.7), case contrasts in tonic pronouns are confined to the first and second singular (*eu/mim* and *tu/ti* above, Chart 9.1).

Eu, tu, and *ele* are unmistakably from Latin nominatives, and *ele* 'he' even retains the *-e* of the pronominal declension (Chart 8.8), as do Spanish demonstratives *este, ese* 'this, that'. Portuguese created *eles* 'they, m.' based on *ele* (unlike Spanish *ellos*, § 8.3.3). For *elas* 'they, f.' we can invoke analogy based on *ela* 'she'. Or just as easily, *elas* can derive from the nominative ĬLLĀS of Popular Latin (§ 8.3.2, Chart 8.10).

Atonic subject pronouns are zero (*falo* 'I speak') unless needed to distinguish between *ele/ela* 'he/she' and *você* 'you' (see note 8). Among atonic (light, clitic) pronouns, the distinct third person datives are a pan-Romance feature.[6]

The older accusatives *lo la los las* regularly lost /l/ when it was intervocalic (§ 9.6.4), which was often, given that clitics in Portuguese were mainly post-verbal: *frigo-las > frigo-as* 'I fry them'. The allomorphs *o a os as* later spread to other environments.[7] Old Portuguese dative *li* palatalized in prevocalic positions such as the clitic combination ĬLLĪ–ĬLLA (dative + accusative) > /*li–ella/ > /ʎela/ *lhela*, from which *lhe* was extracted and generalized (Anderson and Rochet 1979:102).

9.9   Verb morphology: infinitives

The Portuguese verb system shares in the trends outlined in § 6.1. Pre-Romance in general, and pre-Portuguese with it, totally effaces the category of deponent verbs (§ 6.1.3), and relocates some of them in different conjugation classes.

Latin	Popular Latin		Portuguese
FABULARĪ	FABULĀRE	'speak'	falar
PISCARĪ	PISCĀRE	'fish'	pescar
MORĪ	MORĪRE	'die'	morrer
SEQUĪ	SEQUĪRE	'follow'	seguir
NASCĪ	NASCĔRE	'be born'	nascer

Like Spanish, Portuguese eliminates all rhizotonic (class III) infinitives, relocating most to class II or IV.

BIBĔRE	'drink'	beber
CAPĔRE	'seize'	caber
DICĔRE	'say'	dizer
FERVĔRE	'boil'	ferver
RECIPĔRE	'receive'	receber
SAPĔRE	'understand'	saber
VINCĔRE	'conquer'	vencer
VIVĔRE	'live'	viver
CADĔRE	'fall'	cair
CINGĔRE	'surround'	cingir
FUGĔRE	'flee'	fugir

A few infinitives become monosyllabic via regular sound change (§§ 9.6.4, 9.5.4, 9.2.4).

TENĒRE	'hold'	tẽer	>	teer	>	ter
VENĪRE	'come'	vẽir	>	viir	>	vir
PONĔRE	'put'	põer	>	poer	>	pôr
LEGĔRE	'read'	leer	>	ler		

9.10   Verb morphology: present indicative

With the class III verbs folded into the other classes, Portuguese has a true three-conjugation system (compare Spanish, § 6.4). The present indicative paradigms are:[8]

I		II		IV	
LAVĀRE	lavar	TĬMĒRE	temer	PARTĪRE	partir
'WASH'		'fear'		'depart'	
LAVŌ	lavo	TĬM(Ē)Ō	temo	PART(Ī)Ō	parto
LAVĀS	lavas	TĬMĒS	temes	PARTĪS	partes
LAVĂT	lava	TĬMĒT	teme	PARTĬT	parte
LAVĀMUS	lavamos	TĬMĒMUS	tememos	PARTĪMUS	partimos
LAVĀTIS	laváis	TĬMĒTIS	teméis	PARTĪTIS	partís
LAVĂNT	lavam	TĬMENT	temem	PART(Ī)ŬNT	partem

9.10.1   Singular endings

The singular forms seen here derive straight from Latin with loss of final /t/ in third singulars. Final /e/ of the third singular deletes after /l n r s z/: FACIT 'does' *faz*, QUAERIT 'wants' *quer*. The yod from vowel hiatus in classes II and IV generally deletes, but may have consequences: VIDĔŌ 'I see' *vejo*, FACĬŌ 'I do' *faço*, TĔNĔŌ 'I have' *tenho* (§§ 9.7.2, 9.7.5–6), CAPĬŌ 'I fit' *caibo* (§ 9.2.1). See also § 9.10.4 on metaphony in the first singular.

9.10.2   Plural endings

The first plural endings are regular. The second plural endings, via lenition, become Old Portuguese *-ades*, *-edes*, *-ides* and later lose the /d/, except in a few irregular verbs where it serves to prevent homonymy with the second singular (Williams 1962:§ 155.4).

TENĒTIS	tendes	'you have'	*VADĒTIS	vades	'you go'
*PONĒTIS	pondes	'you place'	VENĪTIS	vindes	'you come'
VIDĒTIS	vêdes	'you see'	*LEGĒTIS	ledes	'you read'

In third plurals, -ENT > *-em* spreads from class II to class IV, as in Spanish. With so many losses of intervocalic consonants in Portuguese, *-em* was often left in hiatus with a stem vowel. In Brazilian Portuguese, the like vowels contract in *TENENT *tem* 'they have', *VENENT 'they come' *vem*, but hiatus remains in VIDENT 'they see' *vêem*, *LEGENT 'they read' *lêem*, RIDENT 'they laugh' *riem*.

9.10.3   Stress-based allomorphy in class I

Inheriting the pre-Romance system of seven stressed vowels, Portuguese maintained the contrast between high mids [e o] and low mids [ɛ ɔ] under stress. This resulted in paradigm alternations with low mids in the stressed stems (where Spanish would have [je], [we]):

LĔVĀRE	levar	[e]	RŎGĀRE	rogar	[o]
'lift, lighten'	'take away'		'ask'	'implore'	
LĔVŌ	levo	[ɛ]	RŎGŌ	rogo	[ɔ]

LĔVĀS	levas	[ɛ]	RŎGĀS	rogas	[ɔ]
LĔVĂT	leva	[ɛ]	RŎGĂT	roga	[ɔ]
LĔVĀMUS	levamos	[e]	RŎGĀMUS	rogamos	[o]
LĔVĀTIS	levais	[e]	RŎGĀTIS	rogais	[o]
LĔVĂNT	levam	[ɛ]	RŎGĂNT	rogam	[ɔ]

This pattern spreads to other class I verbs even where the stem vowel was a high mid:

SPĒRĀRE	esperar	[e]	CŬRTĀRE	cortar	[o]
'hope'	'wait'		'shorten'	'cut'	
SPĒRŌ	espero	[ɛ]	CŬRTŌ	corto	[ɔ]
SPĒRĀS	esperas	[ɛ]	CŬRTĀS	cortas	[ɔ]
SPĒRĂT	espera	[ɛ]	CŬRTĂT	corta	[ɔ]
SPĒRĀMUS	esperamos	[e]	CŬRTĀMUS	cortamos	[o]
SPĒRĀTIS	esperais	[e]	CŬRTĀTIS	cortais	[o]
SPĒRĂNT	esperam	[ɛ]	CŬRTĂNT	cortam	[ɔ]

Verbs like *esperar* and *cortar* show once again how analogical pressure can induce paradigm disleveling (§ 6.8). Instead of a constant high mid [e] or [o], they adopted analogical forms in the boot template to match verbs like *levar* and *rogar*, which had stem-vowel allomorphy by regular sound change. This process, rather pervasive in Portuguese, recurs in all the verbs we study next (§§ 9.10.4, 9.10.5), except that a further change occurs in first singulars.

9.10.4   Metaphony in the first singular

The stress-based vowel alternations just seen can occur in all conjugations. However, in *-er* and *-ir* verbs, the usual boot template is altered by metaphony in the first singular. The ending /-o/ [u] raises the stressed stem vowels [ɛ] [ɔ] to [e] [o]. For *-er* verbs the resulting alternation is:

VĔRTĔRE	verter	[e]	VŎLVĔRE	volver	[o]
'turn'	'pour'		'roll'	'turn'	
VĔRTŌ	verto	[e]	VŎLVŌ	volvo	[o]
VĔRTĬS	vertes	[ɛ]	VŎLVĬS	volves	[ɔ]
VĔRTĬT	verte	[ɛ]	VŎLVĬT	volve	[ɔ]
VĔRTĬMUS	vertemos	[e]	VŎLVĬMUS	volvemos	[o]
VĔRTĬTIS	verteis	[e]	VŎLVĬTIS	volveis	[o]
*VĔRTĔNT	vertem	[ɛ]	*VŎLVĔNT	volvem	[ɔ]

By regular sound change, only the pre-Romance low mids [ɛ] [ɔ] should participate in this pattern. By analogy, however, *-er* verbs with a high mid stem vowel join the group.

DĒBĒRE 'owe'	dever	[e]	CŬRRĔRE 'run'	correr	[o]
DĒB(Ĕ)Ō	devo	[e]	CŬRRŌ	corro	[o]
DĒBĒS	deves	[ɛ]	CŬRRĪS	corres	[ɔ]
DĒBĒT	deve	[ɛ]	CŬRRĬT	corre	[ɔ]
DĒBĒMUS	devemos	[e]	CŬRRĬMUS	corremos	[o]
DĒBĒTIS	deveis	[e]	CŬRRĬTIS	correis	[o]
DĒBĔNT	devem	[ɛ]	*CŬRRĔNT	correm	[ɔ]

For -*ir* verbs, the picture is similar, except that the stem vowel of the first singu-lar has double raising, [ɛ] > [e] > [i], and [ɔ] > [o] > [u]. A first raising, from low mids to high mids – as in Old Portuguese *servo* [e], *dormo* [o] – is attributable to the old yod. Later, final /-o/ triggers a further raising to *sirvo*, *durmo*. The remaining forms adhere to the stress-based boot template.

SĔRVĪRE 'serve'	servir	[e]	DŎRMĪRE 'sleep'	dormir	[o]
SĔRVĬŌ	sirvo	[i]	DŎRMĬŌ	durmo	[u]
SĔRVĪS	serves	[ɛ]	DŎRMĪS	dormes	[ɔ]
SĔRVĬT	serve	[ɛ]	DŎRMĬT	dorme	[ɔ]
SĔRVĪMUS	servimos	[e]	DŎRMĪMUS	dormimos	[o]
SĔRVĪTIS	servis	[e]	DŎRMĪTIS	dormis	[o]
*SĔRVĔNT	servem	[ɛ]	*DŎRMĔNT	dormem	[ɔ]

This pattern, with its high vowel and three low mids in the boot template, spreads to other -*ir* verbs where the stem vowel had earlier been a high mid. The old yod accounts for the raising [o] > [u] in *subo*, *tusso*, but in the rest of the paradigm the stressed stem vowels become low mid [ɔ], copying verbs like *dormir*.

SŬBĪRE 'go up'	subir	[u]	TŬSSĪRE 'cough'	tossir	[o]
SŬBĔŌ	subo	[u]	TŬSSĬŌ	tusso	[u]
SŬBĪS	sobes	[ɔ]	TŬSSĪS	tosses	[ɔ]
SŬBĬT	sobe	[ɔ]	TŬSSĬT	tosse	[ɔ]
SŬBĪMUS	subimos	[u]	TŬSSĪMUS	tossimos	[o]
SŬBĪTIS	subis	[u]	TŬSSĪTIS	tossis	[o]
*SŬBĔNT	sobem	[ɔ]	*TŬSSĔNT	tossem	[ɔ]

Unstressed stem vowels are leveled to [u] in some verbs (*subir*) and not others (*tossir*).

The leveled template of verbs like *subir* extends even to a few -*ir* verbs where the stem vowel was high. A contrast like *frigo, freges*, where [i] is original and [ɛ] analogical, echoes the pairs like *sirvo, serves* (above), where [i] is raised (by regular sound change), and [ɛ] is original.

FRĪGĔRE	frigir	[i]	SŪMĔRE	sumir	[u]
'fry'			'take up'	'disappear'	
FRĪGŌ	frigo	[i]	SŪMŌ	sumo	[u]
FRĪGĬS	freges	[ɛ]	SŪMĬS	somes	[o]
FRĪGĬT	frege	[ɛ]	SŪMĬT	some	[o]
FRĪGĬMUS	frigimos	[i]	SŪMĬMUS	sumimos	[u]
FRĪGĬTIS	frigis	[i]	SŪMĬTIS	sumis	[u]
*FRĪGĔNT	fregem	[ɛ]	*SŪMĔNT	somem	[o]

The lowered vowels in *somes, some, somem* become [o] rather than remaining [ɔ] because a nasal consonant follows (§ 9.4.1). This rule, raising [ɛ ɔ] to [e o] before a nasal, applies in all three conjugations, creating predictable variants on the patterns displayed in §§ 9.10.3–4.

9.10.5   Stem allomorphy induced by consonant changes

A stem-final consonant may change regularly according to what follows it. In a verb like *dizer*, Latin /k/ remains velar before the back vowel in *digo* but palatalizes elsewhere. *Fazer* has a similar paradigm, except that in FACĬŌ, [kj] yields [ʦ] > [s] (§ 9.7.5).

DĪCĔRE	dizer	FACĔRE	fazer
'say'		'make'	
DĪCŌ	digo	FACĬŌ	faço
DĪCĬS	dizes	FACĬS	fazes
DĪCĬT	diz	FACĬT	faz
DĪCĬMUS	dizemos	FACĬMUS	fazemos
DĪCĬTIS	dizeis	FACĬTIS	fazeis
*DĪCĔNT	dizem	*FACĔNT	fazem

Another source of allomorphic stems in the first singular is [tj] > [ʦ] > [s]: *MĒTĬŌ *meço* (§ 9.7.5). A similar change affects [dj] after a diphthong: AUDĬŌ *ouço* (Williams 1962:§ 89.6):[9]

*MĒTĪRE	medir	AUDĪRE	ouvir
'measure'		'hear'	
*MĒTĬŌ	meço	AUDĬŌ	ouço
*MĒTĪS	medes	AUDĪS	ouves
*MĒTĬT	mede	AUDĬT	ouve
*MĒTĪMUS	medimos	AUDĪMUS	ouvimos
*MĒTĪTIS	medis	AUDĪTIS	ouvis
*MĒTĔNT	medem	*AUDĔNT	ouvem

The group with a consonant change in the first singular attracts at least one recruit. In *perder* 'lose', the first singular analogizes first to the *meço, ouço* type and later to the velar *digo* type: PERDŌ > Old Portuguese *perço* > *perco* 'I lose'.

9.10.6   Patterns of allomorphy: summary

Verb stem allomorphy typically results from vowel alternations, but stem consonant changes can leave their mark too. The present indicative has four principal patterns of allomorphy.

First, the familiar stress-based boot template is seen in verbs like *levar* and *rogar*. Verbs like *esperar* and *cortar* gravitate into this pattern analogically (§ 9.10.3).

1st sg.	1st pl.
2nd sg.	2nd pl.
3rd sg.	3rd pl.

Second, all the remaining patterns of allomorphy surveyed above (§ 9.10.4) involve a metaphonic effect in the first singular. This raising effect is superimposed on what would otherwise be a boot, either an ordinary etymological one (*verter*, *volver*) or one resulting from analogical attraction to the boot template (*dever*, *correr*).

1st sg.	1st pl.
2nd sg.	2nd pl.
3rd sg.	3rd pl.

Third, in *-ir* verbs the raising in the first singular is double, bringing [ɛ ɔ] to [i u], as in SĔRVĬŌ *sirvo* and DŎRMĬŌ *durmo*. These paradigms have three allomorphs:

1st sg.	1st pl.
2nd sg.	2nd pl.
3rd sg.	3rd pl.

Some *-ir* verbs joining this group (such as *subir*) level the vowel in the arhizotonic forms to match the doubly raised vowel of the first singular.

Lastly, stem consonant changes can produce allomorphy in the first singular alone, as in *dizer*, *fazer*, *medir*, *ouvir*. This template can also introduce an anomalous first singular by analogy (as in *perder*):

1st sg.	1st pl.
2nd sg.	2nd pl.
3rd sg.	3rd pl.

9.11   **Paradigm leveling and disleveling**

Analogical forces can be capricious, either reducing allomorphy or increasing it, depending on the model. Allomorphy in the first singular has been eliminated in these paradigms:

VĬNCĔRE	vencer	*CŎCĔRE	cozer
'conquer'		'cook'	
VĬNCŌ	vinco (OPo) > venço	*CŎCŌ	*cogo > cozo
VĬNCĬS	vences	*CŎCĬS	cozes
VĬNCĬT	vence	*CŎCĬT	coze
VĬNCĬMUS	vencemos	*CŎCĬMUS	cozemos
VĬNCĬTIS	venceis	*CŎCĬTIS	cozeis
*VĬNCĔNT	vencem	*CŎCĔNT	cozem

The expected stem-final velar has been changed to match the rest of the paradigm (and in *venço* the stem vowel too is analogical, overriding metaphony). But analogical change doesn't always favor majority rule:

	Expected	Portuguese
*CŎMPLĪRE	*comprir	cumprir
'carry out'		
*CŎMPLĬŌ	cumpro	cumpro
*CŎMPLĪS	*compres	cumpres
*CŎMPLĬT	*compre	cumpre
*CŎMPLĪMUS	*comprimos	cumprimos
*CŎMPLĪTIS	*compris	cumpris
*CŎMPLĔNT	*comprem	cumprem

Latin CŎMPLĒRE, relocated into class IV, developed first like *dormir*, with double raising in the first singular (§ 9.10.4). Modern Portuguese has generalized the stem vowel [u] to the whole paradigm.

   Disleveling was endemic in the Portuguese present indicative, as we saw in § 9.10. Each of the typical patterns of allomorphy – whether from stress or first singular metaphony or consonant changes – gains new adherents as individual verbs analogize to these patterns.

9.12   **A stem extender: -*sc*-**

The formerly inchoative affix -*sc*- survives in certain Portuguese verbs, but today it is neither inchoative nor an affix, but simply part of the verb stem, as in Spanish (§ 6.9). In *parecer* 'seem', in fact, its origin is totally obscured by leveling first singular [sk] to [s]:

*PARĒSCĔRE	parecer		[e]
'seem'			
*PARĒSCŌ	paresco (OPo) >	pareço	[e]
*PARĒSCĬS	pareces		[ɛ]
*PARĒSCĬT	parece		[ɛ]
*PARĒSCĬMUS	parecemos		[e]
*PARĒSCĬTIS	pareceis		[e]
*PARĒSCĔNT	parecem		[ɛ]

Question: Why do the stem vowels alternate between [e] and [ɛ]?

Answer: *Parecer* is one of many verbs that analogize to the *verter* type. Again, we see both leveling (consonant) and disleveling (vowel) in the same paradigm.

9.13   Some truly irregular verbs: be, have, go

As we saw in Italian, Spanish, and French (§ 6.10), some high-frequency verbs maintain irregularities inherited or created in prior stages of development.

9.13.1   Outcome of ESSE 'be'

As in Spanish, the infinitive *ser* 'be' comes from SĔDĒRE 'sit'. The present is:

SŬM	sou
ĔS	es
ĔST	é
SŬMŬS	somos
ĔSTĬS	sois
SŬNT	são

Non-etymological forms are *sou, é, sois*. First singular SŬM yields Old Portuguese *som* / *sõ* and later *são* (after the 1400s, when *-om, -am* and *-ão* merged), but then *são* is replaced by *sou*, allied with *estou, vou, dou* (Williams 1962: § 198.3).[10] The third singular final *-s* fell by analogy with other third singular present forms and to avoid homonymy of ĔS *es* with ĔST **es*.[11] Second plural *sois* developed from **sŭtĭs*, created on the model of SŬM, SŬMŬS, SŬNT. Third plural *som* became *são* with the merger of *-om, -am* and *-ão* (§ 9.3.1).

9.13.2   Outcome of HABĒRE 'have'

Being a high-frequency verb and formerly an auxiliary, *haver* shows greater than normal phonetic attrition (§ 6.10.2). In Old Portuguese, *haver* competed with *ter* 'have' < TENĒRE 'hold' as auxiliary of the perfect periphrastic (§ 9.15.2). Today *ter* has prevailed, and *haver* survives only in high formal register and as a dialectal variant.

Latin	Popular Latin	
HABĒŌ	*[ajo]	hei
HABĒS	*[as]	has
HABĔT	*[at]	ha
HABĒMUS	*[aβemos]	havemos
HABĒTIS	*[aβetis]	haveis
HABĔNT	*[ant]	hão

The first singular shows raising by the yod (§ 9.2.1). In the third plural, Old Portuguese *ham* became *hão* via the same merger seen in *som* > *são* (§ 9.3.1).

9.13.3   Outcome of ĪRE 'go'

As in Italian, Spanish, and French, the Portuguese verb 'go' has a suppletive paradigm (§ 6.10.3), drawing its present forms from ĪRE and VADĔRE.

Latin	Popular Latin	ir
VADŌ	*[vaw]	vou
VADĬS	*[vajs]	vais
VADĬT	*[vajt]	vai
VADĬMŬS		vamos
ĪTĬS		ides
VADŬNT	*[va(w)nt]	vão

Unlike most second plural endings in Portuguese, *ides* preserves the intervocalic /d/. The imperfect retains forms from ĪRE (ĪBAM *ia*). The preterite uses the verb 'be' (*foi, foste*, etc.), as happens in Spanish.

9.14   Verbs: old categories with inherited morphology

Here we take up the present subjunctive, imperfect, preterite, and pluperfect. Portuguese preserves these Latin categories with their original morphology, by and large.

9.14.1   Present subjunctive

Alongside the present indicative (§§ 9.10–13), the present subjunctive also derives more or less directly from Latin, with analogical adjustments to keep each verb in sync with its indicative.

I	LAVĀRE	lavar	II	TIMĒRE	temer
	LAVEM	lave		TĬMEAM	tema
	LAVĒS	laves		TĬMEĀS	temas
	LAVET	lave		TĬMEAT	tema
	LAVĒMUS	lavemos		TĬMEĀMUS	temamos

	LAVĒTIS	laveis		TĬMEĀTIS	temais
	LAVENT	lavem		TĬMEANT	temam
IIIa	VĒNDĔRE	vender	IV	PARTĪRE	partir
	VĒNDAM	venda		PARTĬAM	parta
	VĒNDĀS	vendas		PARTĬĀS	partas
	VĒNDAT	venda		PARTĬAT	parta
	VĒNDĀMUS	vendamos		PARTĬĀMUS	partamos
	VĒNDĀTIS	vendais		PARTĬĀTIS	partais
	VĒNDANT	vendam		PARTĬANT	partam

Subjunctive endings develop a [j] in classes II and IV (above), and in class IIIb, which is like IV. Usually this [j] deletes, but a few verbs of class IIIb metathesize it: CAPĬAT 'fits' *caiba*, SAPĬAT 'knows' *saiba* (Spanish *quepa*, *sepa*). In class IV this [j] could raise an unstressed stem vowel, as in: SERVĬĀMUS, SERVĬĀTIS *sirvamos*, *sirvais*. This forges a bond between raised subjunctive stem vowels and the raised vowels of the first singular indicative. So *sirvo* 'I serve' (§ 9.10.4) gives rise to a matching subjunctive *sirva* that spreads to the other rhizotonic forms. This pattern may extend to other verb classes. For example, VĔRTO 'I pour' *verto* has metaphonic [e] instead of [ɛ], and the subjunctive stem follows suit: VĔRTA *verta* with analogical [e] instead of [ɛ].

9.14.2   Imperfect

This development is straightforward, almost the same as in Spanish (§ 7.4.2). In the first and second plural, stress retracts to the thematic vowel:

I	LAVĀRE	lavar	II	TIMĒRE	temer
	LAVĀBAM	lavava		TIMĒBAM	temia
	LAVĀBĀS	lavavas		TIMĒBĀS	temias
	LAVĀBAT	lavava		TIMĒBAT	temia
	LAVĀBĀMUS	lavávamos		TIMĒBĀMUS	temíamos
	LAVĀBĀTIS	laváveis		TIMĒBĀTIS	temíeis
	LAVĀBANT	lavavam		TIMĒBANT	temiam
IIIa	VĒNDĔRE	vender	IV	PARTĪRE	partir
	VĒNDĒBAM	vendia		PARTIĒBAM	partia
	VĒNDĒBĀS	vendias		PARTIĒBĀS	partias
	VĒNDĒBAT	vendia		PARTIĒBAT	partia
	VĒNDĒBĀMUS	vendíamos		PARTIĒBĀMUS	partíamos
	VĒNDĒBĀTIS	vendíeis		PARTIĒBĀTIS	partíeis
	VĒNDĒBANT	vendiam		PARTIĒBANT	partiam

In the second plural endings, /t/ lenites to zero as in Spanish, but then the resulting hiatus /ai/ raises to /ej/, a regular change in post-tonic position

(Williams 1962:§ 155.2). The intervocalic /b/ > /v/ in class I is regular (§ 9.5.3). Loss of intervocalic /b/ in the other classes, another property shared with Spanish, is variously explained (§ 7.4.2 and Williams 1962:§ 164.2).

Like Italian and Spanish, Portuguese preserves the imperfect of Latin ESSE 'be' (§ 7.4.1). The first and second plural retract their stress to the root: *era, eras, era, éramos, éreis, eram*.

Imperfects of three verbs – *ter* 'have', *vir* 'come', *pôr* 'put' – became irregular via regular sound changes applying to intervocalic /n/ (§§ 9.3.3, 9.6.4).

TENĒBAM	tinha	PONĒBAM	punha
TENĒBĀS	tinhas	PONĒBĀS	punhas
TENĒBAT	tinha	PONĒBAT	punha
TENĒBĀMUS	tínhamos	PONĒBĀMUS	púnhamos
TENĒBĀTIS	tínheis	PONĒBĀTIS	púnheis
TENĒBANT	tinham	PONĒBANT	punham

For *ter* we can posit these stages: */tenia/ > */tẽia/ > */tĩia/ > */tĩĩa/ > */tĩa/. The hiatus of stressed nasal /ĩ/ plus /o/ or /a/ is then broken by the epenthesis of a palatal /ɲ/ (§ 9.3.3), giving *tinha*. For *vir* the process is the same. The imperfect of *pôr* went one step further: PONĒBAT > */poni̯a/ > */poĩa/ > */poi̯ɲa/ > */pui̯ɲa/ > /pui̯ɲa/ > /puɲa/ *punha*.

9.14.3   Preterite

To review § 7.5: the Romance synthetic (one-word) past, known as *pretérito* in Portuguese and Spanish, gets its regular forms from the Latin weak perfect, or more exactly from the popular and well-attested short forms of the weak perfect. The set of verbs having a weak perfect is roughly coextensive with classes I and IV:

CANTAI	cantei		PARTII	parti	
CANTA(I)STI	cantaste		PARTISTI	partiste	
CANTAUT	cantou	[ow]	PARTIUT	partiu	[iw]
CANTA(I)MUS	cantamos		PARTIIMUS	partimos	
CANTASTIS	cantastes		PARTISTIS	partistes	
CANTARUNT	cantaram	[ãw]	PARTIRUNT	partiram	[ãw]

The third plural endings [-arãw -irãw] replaced expected [-arõ -irõ] with the merger of final *-om, -am* and *-ão* (§ 9.3.1).

Portuguese also preserves some preterites from Latin strong perfects. Two points about this group, cited for Spanish (§ 7.5.6), apply equally to Portuguese: (1) their numbers have been greatly depleted by an enduring trend in favor of the weak perfect, and (2) their paradigm retains only two rhizotonic forms, the first and third singular. Here *dizer* 'say' stands for Latin sigmatic perfects and *fazer* 'do' for Latin long-vowel perfects:

DĪXĪ	disse	FĒCĪ	fiz
DĪXISTĪ	disseste	FĒCĬSTĪ	fizeste
DĪXĬT	disse	FĒCĬT	fez
*DĪXĬMUS	dissemos	*FĒCĬMUS	fizemos
DĪXISTIS	dissestes	FĒCĬSTĬS	fizestes
DĪXĔRUNT	disseram	FĒCĔRŬNT	fizeram

Complications include: (1) FĒCĪ > *fiz*, a raising attributed to metaphony, (2) regular loss of final unstressed /e/ or /i/ after /s/ or /k/. The non-homonymy of *fiz, fez* is seemingly echoed in *poder* 'be able' (*pude, pôde*) and *pôr* 'put' (*pus, pôs*), but there are major differences of detail between these facts and the parallel ones in Spanish (§ 7.5.6, end).

Two strong waw perfects, SAPUĬT 'knew' and HABUĬT 'had', undergo metathesis, giving [sawpe] > [soube] *soube* and [awve] > [owve] *houve*. Another verb joins them: from TRAHĔRE 'draw, drag', the sigmatic perfect TRAXIT became (perhaps by way of *TRAXUIT) *trouxe*.

The Latin strong perfect of DARE 'give', by a combination of lenition, vowel coalescence, and analogy, became a weak preterite in Portuguese:

Popular Latin	Expected	Portuguese	
DĔDĪ	dei	dei	
DĔDISTĪ	*deeste	deste	
DĔDIT	*dee	deu	
*DĔDĬMUS	*deemos	demos	
DĔDISTIS	*deestes	destes	
*DĔDĔRUNT	*deeron	deram	[ãw]

This outcome obliterated the last of the Latin reduplicated perfect stems and also helped to legitimize a new class of weak perfects with thematic vowel /e/, where *-er* verbs could go to be regularized. Typical among many examples: TIMĒRE 'fear' with waw perfect TIMŬĪ, TIMŬISTĪ, TIMŬIT becomes Portuguese *temer* with weak perfect *temi, temeste, temeu*.

9.14.4   Pluperfect

Spoken Portuguese expresses the pluperfect with a periphrastic (*tinha cantado* 'had sung'), as do Italian, Spanish, and French. But written Portuguese also has a pluperfect that continues the original Latin pluperfect.

Just as Latin weak perfects had short forms that live on in Romance (Chart 7.7), so do the corresponding pluperfects:

CANTĀRAM	cantara	PARTĪRAM	partira
CANTĀRĀS	cantaras	PARTĪRĀS	partiras
CANTĀRAT	cantara	PARTĪRAT	partira

CANTĀRĀMUS	cantáramos	PARTĪRĀMUS	partíramos
CANTĀRĀTIS	cantáreis	PARTĪRĀTIS	partíreis
CANTĀRANT	cantaram [ãw]	PARTĪRANT	partiram [ãw]

The stress is retracted to the thematic vowel, as also happens in the imperfect in both Portuguese and Spanish (§§ 9.14.2, 7.4.2).

Since the pluperfect belongs to the perfectum system (Chart 7.1), it was destined to have an affinity with the preterite. Verbs that maintain the strong perfect stem in the preterite also do so in the pluperfect, for example *saber* 'know'.

SAPUERAM	soubera
SAPUERĀS	souberas
SAPUERAT	soubera
SAPUERĀMUS	soubéramos
SAPUERĀTIS	soubéreis
SAPUERANT	souberam [ãw]

But as we saw (§ 9.14.3), there was analogical pressure for a thematic vowel /e/ corresponding to -*er* verbs, and DARE 'give' added a push by acquiring that format through sound change. With these endings, -*er* verbs could abandon their predominantly strong perfect stems (TIMUERAT) and create weak ones (*TIMERAT > *temera* 'had feared').

Latin		*Portuguese*	*Portuguese*
DEDERAM	*d<u>ee</u>ra	d<u>e</u>ra	t<u>e</u>mera
DEDERĀS	*d<u>ee</u>ras	d<u>e</u>ras	t<u>e</u>meras
DEDERAT	*d<u>ee</u>rat	d<u>e</u>ra	t<u>e</u>mera
DEDERĀMUS	*d<u>ee</u>ramos	d<u>ê</u>ramos	t<u>e</u>mêramos
DEDERĀTIS	*d<u>ee</u>ratis	d<u>ê</u>reis	t<u>e</u>mêreis
DEDERANT	*d<u>ee</u>ran	d<u>e</u>ram [ãw]	t<u>e</u>meram [ãw]

9.15   Verbs: new periphrastics

Portuguese has widespread periphrastics whose origins in Popular Latin are treated in Chapter 7: the future and conditional (§ 7.8) and the periphrastic perfect (§ 7.9).

9.15.1   Future and conditional

Portuguese shares the main Romance future composed of the infinitive plus reduced forms of HABĒRE:

SCRIBER *[ajo]	escreverei
SCRIBER *[as]	escreverás
SCRIBER *[at]	escreverá

SCRIBER *[emos]   escreveremos
SCRIBER *[etis]   escrevereis
SCRIBER *[a(w)nt]   escreverão

Today this future is rare in spoken or informal registers. Future meaning is conveyed by the present tense or the *ir* + infinitive periphrastic (§ 7.8.3).

The conditional, a spin-off from the future, originally consisted of the infinitive plus a reduced imperfect of HABĒRE (§ 7.8.4). Again, stress is retracted to what was originally the thematic vowel of the auxiliary.

SCRIBER *[ea]   escreveria
SCRIBER *[eas]   escreverias
SCRIBER *[eat]   escreveria
SCRIBER *[eamos]   escreveríamos
SCRIBER *[eatis]   escreveríeis
SCRIBER *[ean]   escreveríam   [ãw]

Like the future, the conditional is now limited to high registers. The imperfect (*disse que escrevia* 'he said he would write') or the imperfect of the *ir* + infinitive periphrastic (*disse que ia escrever*) can replace it.

The future and conditional also share further properties. First, and uniquely in Portuguese among our five languages, object pronouns are either enclitic or interposed between the stem and endings: *escreverá-me* or *escrever-me-á* 'will write to me', *escreveria-me* or *escrever-me-ia* 'would write to me'. Second, only three stems are irregular: *dir-* (*dizer* 'say'), *far-* (*fazer* 'do'), and *trar-* (*trazer* 'bring').[12]

9.15.2   Periphrastic perfects

Periphrastics are powerful (§ 7.9.2) in that they have the potential to yield multiple tenses and moods for the price of one, through inflection of the auxiliary. The Romance periphrastic perfect, formed with an auxiliary plus past participle, did make available a new perfectum system, but Portuguese, rather than discarding the old paradigms, found a niche for each one:

- Latin perfect continues as Portuguese preterite (§ 9.14.3).
- Latin pluperfect indicative is preserved in the written language (§ 9.14.4).
- Latin future perfect and perfect subjunctive fuse to form a future subjunctive (§ 9.16.2).
- Latin pluperfect subjunctive becomes imperfect subjunctive, as happens elsewhere in the West (§ 7.6).

The Romance periphrastic perfect is nonetheless central to Portuguese grammar. In Old Portuguese its auxiliaries were both *haver* (*hei escrito*) and *ter* (*tenho escrito*) < TENĒRE, bleached from the meaning 'hold, keep'. The pluperfect was formed with the imperfect of the auxiliary (*havia escrito* / *tinha escrito*), while the present perfect subjunctive was formed with the present subjunctive of the auxiliary (*haja escrito* / *tenha escrito*). Today *ter* is the preferred auxiliary, but *haver* appears sometimes in formal registers.

9.15.3   Past participles, old and new

With the advent of the Romance periphrastic past, every verb needed a past participle. Class I and IV verbs normally have thematic vowels /a/ and /i/, weak perfects like CANTĀVĪ PARTĪVĪ, and weak participles like CANTĀTU PARTĪTU, Portuguese *cantado partido*. Of the Latin class II and III verbs, a few had participles in -ĒTU, -ĪTU, and -ĬTU. The productive favorite by far was -ŪTU, permanently in Italian and French (§ 7.11.2), temporarily in Old Spanish and Old Portuguese (*avudo, venudo, sabudo*, etc.). By the 1500s Portuguese had replaced -*udo* with -*ido*.

Although strong participles were often replaced by weak ones (Latin SENSU 'felt' but Portuguese *sentido*), some did survive, including:

APERTU	aberto	'opened'	POSĬTU	posto	'put'
COPERTU	coberto	'covered'	SCRIPTU	escrito	'written'
DICTU	dito	'said'	ACCEPTU	aceito	'accepted'
FACTU	feito	'done'	VĪSU	visto	'seen'

Portuguese has also created new rhizotonic participles by "truncation": *cortado* >> *corto* 'cut', *ganhado* >> *ganho* 'won', *gastado* >> *gasto* 'spent', *pagado* >> *pago* 'paid'. This pattern is reportedly productive in Brazilian Portuguese, as in *pego* for *pegado* 'caught', *falo* for *falado* 'spoken' (Mattos e Silva 1994:59).

9.16   Verbs: other new categories

9.16.1   Inflected infinitive

Portuguese is the only major Romance language that has an inflected infinitive – a verb form used in infinitival contexts and resembling an infinitive with personal endings that register subject agreement.[13] Although there are several accounts of its origin, most agree that it derived from the Latin imperfect subjunctive,[14] which died out in most of the West, being replaced by the Latin pluperfect subjunctive (§ 7.6). The forms of the Latin imperfect subjunctive and the Portuguese inflected infinitive are below.

CANTĀREM	cantar	TĬMĒREM	temer	PARTĪREM	partir
CANTĀRĒS	cantares	TĬMĒRĒS	temeres	PARTĪRĒS	partires
CANTĀRET	cantar	TĬMĒRET	temer	PARTĪRET	partir
CANTĀRĒMUS	cantarmos	TĬMĒRĒMUS	temermos	PARTĪRĒMUS	partirmos
CANTĀRĒTIS	cantardes	TĬMĒRĒTIS	temerdes	PARTĪRĒTIS	partirdes
CANTĀRENT	cantarem	TĬMĒRENT	temerem	PARTĪRENT	partirem

The sound changes are regular. Given the usual retraction of stress to the thematic vowel in the first and second plural, syncope of /e/ is regular, as is the loss of final /e/ in the first and third singular. With these changes, then, the imperfect subjunctive began to look like an infinitive with verb endings. Certain syntactic environments fostered the reanalysis. For example, with loss of /-m/ and optional omission of a complementizer such as UT, speakers could take the subordinate verb to be an infinitive.

> MANDAVIT (UT) SCRIBERE(M)   'he commanded that I write'
> MANDAVIT SCRIBERE   'he commanded to write'

With non-zero endings, the subordinate verb looks like an infinitive with inflection.

> MANDAVIT (UT) SCRIBERES   'he commanded that you write'
> MANDAVIT SCRIBERES   'he commanded (you) to write'

Once reanalysed as an inflected infinitive, the paradigm spread to other infinitival contexts, notably after prepositions:

*Não te espantes de Baco nos teus reinos **receberes***
Don't be afraid of receiving Bacchus into your kingdoms

(Camões, *Lusíadas* 6, 15)

9.16.2   Future subjunctive

Recall from § 7.7 that the future subjunctive, a Popular Latin innovation, derives from the conflation of the two similar paradigms below. Both are built on perfectum stems. The short forms shown here, however, coincide with infectum stems (§ 7.7, end). Net result: the future subjunctive paradigm coincides with the inflected infinitive, which is built on infectum stems:

	Latin short forms	*Portuguese*
Future perfect indicative	*Perfect subjunctive*	*future subjunctive*
CANTĀRO	CANTĀRIM	cantar
CANTĀRIS	CANTĀRĪS	cantares
CANTĀRIT	CANTĀRIT	cantar
CANTĀRIMUS	CANTĀRĪMUS	cantarmos
CANTĀRITIS	CANTĀRĪTIS	cantardes
CANTĀRINT	CANTĀRINT	cantarem

However, if the perfectum stem is distinctive (think strong preterite), the future subjunctive uses it, thus diverging from the inflected infinitive. For example, *saber* 'know' has preterite *soube*, so *sabermos* is an inflected infinitive and *soubermos* a future subjunctive.

Exercises

1. Identify at least seven anomalous forms and state how they differ from the expected outcome, without speculating on why the irregularity occurred.

CŎRPU	'body'	corpo	[o]
AMŌRE	'love'	amor	
SŬRDA	'deaf'	surda	[u]
LŬPU	'wolf'	lobo	
SAPŌNE	'soap'	sabão	
SPĒRAT	'hopes'	espera	[ɛ]
DĔCEM	'ten'	dez	
CONDŪCŌ	'I lead'	conduzo	
AUDIŌ	'I hear'	ouço	
HODIE	'today'	hoje	
CŎRDA	'rope'	corda	[ɔ]
PIRA	'pear'	pêra	[e]
COLŌRE	'color'	cor	
TAURU	'bull'	touro	[o]
IŎCU	'game'	jogo	
CABALLU	'horse'	cavalo	
MAIU	'May'	maio	
CAPUĪ	'took'	coube	
TĔNEO	'I have'	tenho	

2. Doublets – a popular word and a *cultismo* deriving from the same Latin etymon – are common in Portuguese. In these pairs (from Azevedo 2005:175) how do you recognize the *cultismo*?

INFLATU	inchado	'bloated'	inflado	'inflated'
CATHEDRA	cadeira	'chair'	cátedra	'bishop's throne'
AURICULA	aurícula	'atrium'	orelha	'ear'
DELICATU	delgado	'slender'	delicado	'delicate'
PLENU	cheio	'full'	pleno	'full'
LACUNA	lacuna	'gap'	lagoa	'pond'
ARTICULU	artigo	'article'	artelho	'toe'
FABULARE	fabular	'invent'	falar	'talk'
STRICTU	estreito	'narrow'	estrito	'strict'

3   Irregularities in the present tense
The verbs *sair* 'go out' and *valer* 'be worth', both from Latin stems ending in /l/, have different outcomes in Portuguese. Below, which forms are regular and which are anomalous? What would be their expected outcomes if they had developed regularly? Review §§ 9.6.4 and 9.7.6.

*SALĪRE	sair	VALĒRE	valer
SAL(Ī)Ō	saio	VAL(Ē)Ō	valho
*SALĪS	sais	VALĒS	vales
SALĬT	sai	VALĔT	vale

*SALĪMUS	saímos	VALĒMUS	valemos
*SALĪTIS	saís	VALĒTIS	valeis
*SAL(Ĭ)ĔNT	saem	VALĔNT	valem

4. Metaphonic allomorphy

Review verb metaphony (§§ 9.10.4, 9.10.6). Which of the paradigms below conform to the pattern of metaphonic allomorphy typical of many class II and III verbs in Portuguese? What surprises do we see below in the tonic stem vowels?

| VĔRTĔRE | verter | | VŎLVĔRE | volver | |
'turn'	'pour'		'roll'	'turn'	
VĔRTŌ	verto	[e]	VŎLVŌ	volvo	[o]
VĔRTĬS	vertes	[ɛ]	VŎLVĬS	volves	[ɔ]
VĔRTĬT	verte	[ɛ]	VŎLVĬT	volve	[ɔ]
VĔRTĪMUS	vertemos	[e]	VŎLVĪMUS	volvemus	[o]
VĔRTĪTIS	verteis	[e]	VŎLVĪTIS	volveis	[o]
*VĔRTĔNT	vertem	[ɛ]	*VŎLVĔNT	volvem	[ɔ]

| QUAERĔRE | querer | | *PŎTĔRE | poder | |
'ask'	'want'		'be able'		
QUAERŌ	quero	[ɛ]	PŎSSUM	posso	[ɔ]
QUAERĬS	queres	[ɛ]	PŎTĒS	podes	[ɔ]
QUAERĬT	quer	[ɛ]	*PŎTĔT	pode	[ɔ]
QUAERĪMUS	queremos	[e]	*PŎTĒMUS	podemus	[o]
QUAERĬTIS	quereis	[e]	*PŎTĒTIS	podeis	[o]
*QUAERĔNT	querem	[ɛ]	*PŎTĔNT	podem	[ɔ]

5. We saw how the OPo dative clitic *li* becomes modern *lhe* (§ 9.8.8). What about the plural? Can you get from OPo *lis* to modern *lhes* by the same path?

6. Pronoun allomorphy

Direct object pronouns *o a os as* (§ 9.8.8) have allomorphs *lo la los las* which appear after /r/ /s/ /z/ and trigger deletion of those consonants: **amar-o > ama-lo* 'to love him', **faz-o > fa-lo* 'do it', **vemos-o > vemo-lo* 'we see it'. Allomorphs *no na nos nas* occur after /m/ /ão/ /õe/ and trigger deletion of /m/: **dão-o > dão-no* 'they give it', **dizem-o > dize-no* 'they say it', **põe-o > põe-no* 's/he puts it'. How did these allomorphs originate?

10 History and structure of Romanian: an overview

Romanian is spoken by about 20,000,000 people in Romania, plus about 3,000,000 in the adjacent nation of Moldavia. Romanian speakers in the rest of Europe as of 2008 numbered 1,000,000 and in the United States and Canada about 500,000.

10.1 Romanian vowels: diachrony and synchrony

Romanian vowel phonology has some salient features unlike anything in the Western languages. Historically, its treatment of the Latin vowel triangle is asymmetrical. Synchronically, the morphology is full of vowel alternations that look complex, although in fact they are satisfyingly regular.

10.1.1 Stressed vowels from Latin to Romanian

Starting from the Latin nine-vowel triangle (§ 1.2.1), the stressed vowels that emerge in Romanian are shown in the array below. What to look for: half of the vowel triangle undergoes the Great Merger characteristic of the Western languages, while the other half neutralizes quantity.

The front half of the vowel triangle undergoes the Great Merger: Latin ĭ and ē merge to high mid /e/. Among the back vowels, both ŏ and ō give /o/, and both ŭ and ū give /u/. Otherwise stated: Latin stressed ŭ merges down in Italian to /o/ and up in Romanian to /u/.

Latin		Romanian	Italian
CRŬCE	'cross'	cruce	croce
CŬRSU	'course'	curs	corso
FŬRCA	'fork'	furcă	forca
MŬLTU	'much'	mult	molto

With the simple loss of quantity, Romanian gets just one /u/ and one /o/. So among the back vowels it doesn't have any contrast between high and low mids.

Latin stressed vowels and their outcomes in Romanian

DĪCIT	'says'
VĪNU	'wine'
FORMĪCA	'ant'
FĪLU	'thread'

zice	
vin	
furnică	
fir	

PISCE	'fish'
VIDET	'sees'
SICCU	'dry'
VIRIDE	'green'
CRĒDIT	'believes'
PARIĒTE	'wall'
RĒGE	'king'
SECRĒTU	'secret'

peşte	crede		
vede	perete		
sec	rege		
verde	secret		

HERI	'yesterday'
*MELE	'honey'
VERME	'worm'
PECTU	'chest'

ieri	
miere	
vierme	
piept	

SALE	'salt'
MARE	'sea'
CASA	'house'
PARTE	'part'

sare	
mare	
casă	
parte	

NŌDU	'knot'
RŌGŌ	'I ask'
FORMŌSU	'shapely'
COGNŌSCŌ	'I know'
FOCU	'fire'
PORCU	'pig'
CORVU	'crow'
NOSTRU	'our'

foc	nod		
porc	rog		
corb	frumos		
nostru	cunosc		

CRŪDU	'raw'
IŪRAT	'swears'
SCŪTU	'shield'
LŪNA	'moon'
GULA	'throat'
IUGU	'yoke'
MUSCA	'fly'
VULPE	'fox'

gură	crud		
jug	jură		
muscă	scut		
vulpe	lună		

There is no diphthong comparable to the /wɔ/ or /we/ from stressed low mid /ɔ/ in Italian, Spanish, and Old French. Compare *fuoco, fuego, feu* with FOCU *foc* 'fire'.

The front half, however, is shaped like the other Romance vowel systems we have seen. Its low mid /ɛ/ does diphthongize to /je/ as in Italian, Spanish, and French.

> Question: In the treatment of /ɛ/ does Romanian more resemble Spanish or Italian?
>
> Answer: Spanish, because /ɛ/ diphthongizes to /jɛ/ (later /je/) in blocked as well as free syllables.

Latin		Romanian	Italian	Spanish
FĔRRU	'iron'	fier	ferro	hierro
PĔLLE	'skin'	piele	pelle	piel
PĔRDIT	'loses'	pierde	perde	pierde

10.1.2   The Latin diphthongs

Of the three inherited diphthongs surviving in Latin, OE and AE probably never reached Dacia. But AU survived longer, and Romanian retains it, not as /aw/ but as /au/ – in fact, some linguists hear these as [ta<u>wur</u>], etc.

Latin		Romanian	Italian
TAURU	'bull'	taur	toro
AURU	'gold'	aur	oro
LAUDAT	'praises'	laudă	loda

10.1.3   Diphthongs induced by metaphony

About fourteen centuries elapse between the six-vowel system that emerged directly from Latin and our earliest documents of Romanian. Since the medieval developments are forever a closed book, we turn abruptly to the vowel system existing today. As in Spanish, low mid /ɛ/ and high mid /e/ collapse at this stage to a single front mid /e/. The high central unrounded vowel /ɨ/ occurs nowhere else in Romance.

	Spellings			Phonemic values		
i	î/â[1]	u	/i/	/ɨ/	/u/
e	ă	o	/e/	/ə/	/o/
	a			/a/	

Important: two diphthongs [ea] [oa] alternate with [e] [o] respectively, depending on the modern word-final vowel.

Latin		Romanian	Latin		Romanian
PLĬCAT	'folds'	pleacă	PLĬCŌ	'I fold'	plec
*IN-CĬRCAT	'seeks'	încearcă	*IN-CĬRCŌ	'I seek'	încerc
ATQUE ĬSTA	'this'	această	ATQUE ĬSTU	'this'	acest
SĒRA	'evening'	seară	SĒRAE	'evenings'	seri
FENESTRA	'window'	fereastră	FENĒSTRAE	'windows'	ferestre
*HELĒNA	'Helen'	Ileana			

> Question: Under what condition does [ea̯] occur instead of [e]?
>
> Answer: When the modern word-final vowel is /ə/ or /a/.

Latin		Romanian	Latin		Romanian
IŎCAT	'plays'	joacă	IŎCŌ	'I play'	joc
TŎRQUET	'twists'	toarce	TŎRQUŌ	'I twist'	torc
TŌTA	'all'	toată	TŌTU	'all'	tot
MŌLA	'mill'	moară	MŌLAE	'mills'	mori
SŌLE	'sun'	soare	SŌLES	'suns'	sori
IOHANNA	'Joanna'	Ioana	IOHANNES	'John'	Ion

> Question: Under what condition do we find [o̯a] instead of [o]?
>
> Answer: When the modern word-final vowel is /ə/, /a/, or /e/.[2]

Oddly, the condition for [ea̯] is more restricted. To remember the difference, think of *foarte rece* 'very cold': word-final /e/ triggers the diphthong [o̯a] but not [ea̯].

PRACTICE

Compute the syllable nucleus. Is there a diphthong?

MŎLLE	'soft'	m___le
VĬDET	'sees'	v___de
CĒRA	'wax'	c___ră
NŎSTRI	'our'	n___ștri
RŎTA	'wheel'	r___tă

10.1.4 Interaction of old and new diphthongs

What happens when the old rule /ɛ/ > [jɛ] > [je] meets the newer metaphonic diphthongization /e/ > [ea̯]? We might expect a triphthong *[jea̯]. Wherever the hypothetical *[jea̯] would arise, it contracts to [ja], written <ia>.

Latin		Romanian	Italian	Spanish
PĚTRA	'stone'	piatră	pietra	piedra
HĚRBA	'grass'	iarbă	herba	hierba
FĚRA	'wild beast'	fiară	fiera	fiera
ĚSCA	'bait'	iască	esca	yesca

PRACTICE

Compare the indicative and subjunctive of these verbs. Compute the syllable nucleus for each.

FĚRVIT	'boils'	f___rbe	FĚRVAT	'boils'	f___rbă
PĚRDIT	'loses'	p___rde	PĚRDAT	'loses'	p___rdă

10.1.5   History of / e̯a/

The diphthongs [e̯a] and [o̯a] already existed in pre-literary Romanian, but the odd asymmetry in their conditioning is more recent. At an earlier stage, final [e] triggered not only [o̯a] but also [e̯a]:

Latin		Old Romanian	Romanian
LĒGE	'law'	leage	lege
MENSAE	'tables'	mease	mese
SĬTI	'thirst'	seate	sete
VĬDĒRE	'see'	vedeare	vedere

The reversion [e̯a] to [e] before final [e] is pervasive, but some words remain as relics of the earlier situation: class II infinitives like *a vedea* 'see', when shortened, no longer had the requisite final [e].[3]

Question: How does *şapte* 'seven' reveal that it used to contain [e̯a]?

Answer: No one sound change could take SĚPTE to *şapte*. But the primary diphthong [je] combined with a metaphonic [e̯a] does the job: SĚPTE > [sjepte] > [sje̯apte] > [sjapte] (§ 10.1.4) > [ʃapte] *şapte*.

The later reversion [e̯a] > [e] did not apply to words like *şapte* (or SĚRPE > *şarpe* 'snake') because they no longer had the requisite [e̯a] on the surface.

10.1.6   Raising before nasals

Stressed vowels raise before a nasal consonant. This change obscures the diphthongization /ɛ/ > [jɛ].

$$\boxed{/e/\ /\varepsilon/ > /i/}$$

Latin		*Romanian*	*Italian*
BĔNE	'well'	bine	bene
DĔNTE	'tooth'	dinte	dente
VĔNIT	'comes'	vine	viene
PRĒ(H)ĔNDIT	'takes'	prinde	prende
ĬNTRAT	'enters'	intră	entra

$$\boxed{/o/ > /u/}$$

BONU	'good'	bun	buono
NOMEN	'name'	nume	nome
FRONTE	'forehead'	frunte	fronte
QUO M(ODO)	'how'	cum	come
RESPONDET	'responds'	răspunde	risponde

Pre-nasal /a/ can raise to /ɨ/, but /ɨ/ also comes from other sources, as we see next.

10.1.7   Sources of central vowels /ɨ/ and /ə/

High central /ɨ/, written <â>/<î>, is unique to Romanian among our languages. Latin stressed /a/ yields /ɨ/ before /n/, or before /m/ plus consonant:

LANA	'wool'	lână
ROMANU	'Roman'	român
ANGELU	'angel'	înger
CANTAT	'sings'	cântă
PLANGIT	'cries'	plânge
QUANDO	'when'	când
CAMPU	'field'	câmp

A dialect variant of this raising produces an extra yod. Several such words entered the standard language:

CANE	'dog'	câine	[kɨjne]
PANE	'bread'	pâine	[pɨjne]
(DE-)MANE	'tomorrow'	mâine	[mɨjne]

Pre-nasal /ɛ/ or /e/, instead of just raising to /i/ as in *bine* 'well' (§ 10.1.6), moves back to /ɨ/, but not if the final vowel is front: TĔMPLA 'temple' *tâmplă*, but LĬMPĬDE 'clear' *limpede*. Before /n/ this backing to /ɨ/ is more narrowly conditioned: it occurs only after a labial, /s/, or /C+r/.[4] These pairs contrast because of the final vowel:

	(final vowel is non-front)			(final vowel is front)	
VĒNA	'vein'	vână	BĔNE	'well'	bine
VĒNDŌ	'I sell'	vând	VĒNDĬT	'sells'	vinde
CONVĔNTU	'word'	cuvânt	*CONVĔNTE	'words'	cuvinte

In the pairs below, the contrast involves the segment preceding the stressed vowel:

(preceding segment is labial, /s/, or /C+r/)			(preceding segment is not labial, /s/, or /C+r/)		
FAENU	'hay'	fân	*GĔNTA	'tribe'	gintă
SĬNU	'breast'	sân	CĒNAT	'dines'	cină
FRĒNU	'brake'	frână	PLĒNU	'full'	plin

Lastly, /i/ backs to /ɨ/ after word-initial /r/. After non-initial /r/ the change is sporadic.

RĪDĬT	'laughs'	râde	
RĪMA	'rhyme'	râmă	
RĪVU	'shore'	râu	
AMARĪRE	'embitter'	a amărî	
FERĪRE	'wound'	a feri	
SALĪRE	'jump'	a sări	'cavort'

The high central /ɨ/ and mid central /ə/ (written <ă>) were at first in free variation, which they still are in some varieties today. In the standard language, they are considered separate phonemes with at least one oft-cited minimal pair: *văr* 'cousin', *vîr* 'I thrust'. Stressed /a/ becomes /ə/ before word-final /C+i/, as in these singular and plural pairs: *mare* 'sea' but *mări* 'seas', *cetate* 'fortress' but *cetăţi* 'fortresses'. Stressed /ɛ/ gives /ə/ after /r/, as in RĔUS > *rău* 'bad' and AMARĒSCO > *amărăsc* 'I become bitter'. Finally, /e/ after a labial becomes /ə/, but not if the final vowel is front. These pairs differ because of the final vowel:

FOETU	'boy'	făt	FOETI	'boys'	feţi
*MĒLU	'apple'	măr	*MĒLE	'apples'	mere
VĬDĔŌ	'I see'	văd	VĬDĔT	'sees'	vede

Mostly, however, /ə/ arises from unstressed /a/ (except word-initial) or /e/:

AMĀRA	'bitter'	amară
*CUMPĂRAT	'buys'	cumpără
REMĀNĔT	'remains'	rămâne
SĔPTĬMĀNA	'week'	săptămână

10.1.8   Word-final vowels

Word-finally, /a/ becomes /ə/ (CASA 'house' *casă*) and /e/ remains /e/ (MOLLE 'soft' *moale*). As for word-final /o/ and /u/, they first merge to /u/, which later deletes,[5] except: (1) /u/ remains intact and syllabic if needed for cluster support, (2) /u/ becomes [w] after a vowel.

LUPU	'wolf'	lup	
QUAERO	'I ask'	cer	
NŎSTRU	'our'	nostru	[nostru]
ĬNTRO	'I enter'	intru	[intru]
SCIO	'I know'	ştiu	[ʃtiw]
MĔU	'my'	meu	[mew]
NŎVU	'new'	nou	[now]

The rules for /i/ parallel the rules for /u/. Like /u/, the /i/ remains syllabic and intact if needed for cluster support and desyllabifies if immediately preceded by a vowel.

NŎSTRI	'our'	noştri	[noʃtri]
ĬNTRAS	'you enter'	intri	[intri]
SCRĪBIS	'you write'	scrii	[skrij]
NŎVI	'new'	noi	[noj]

But unlike /u/, /i/ never just vanishes without effect – it always modifies the preceding consonant (§ 10.3.3).

Another sound change – we call it the Family Rule – affects a specific word-final sequence. Whenever <iă> would arise, it converts to <ie>, whether or not the /i/ is stressed. The rule is living and exceptionless (see Exercise 10.4).

Latin		*Romanian*	*Italian*
FAMILĬA	'family'	familie	famiglia
PATRĬA	'homeland'	patrie	patria
CAMPANĬA	'campaign'	campanie	campagna
MANĪA	'mania'	manie	mania
VĪVA	'alive'	vie	viva

Lastly, Romanian disallows word-final stressed /e/. Wherever it would arise, it breaks to [ea]. We call this the Coffee Rule.

Turkish kahve >		*Romanian*	*Italian*
Romance /kafe/	'coffee'	cafea	caffè
Latin BĬBĬT	'drinks'	bea	beve
Latin NĪVE	'snow'	nea	neve
French canapé	'sofa'	canapea	canapè

10.2   Syllable structure: conservatism and innovation

Romanian shares with Italian two conservative characteristics, but shows them with more consistency: resistance to syncope and absence of lenition.

10.2.1   Resistance to syncope

Words like these keep all their syllables in Romanian, although they syncopate elsewhere:

Latin		Romanian	Italian
PULĬCE	'flea'	purice	pulce
PERSĬCA	'peach'	piersică	pesca
AD-COPĔRĬT	'covers'	acoperă	copre
CUM-PĂRĂT	'buys'	cumpără	compra

Exceptions are the words where syncope occurred early, even before Latin arrived in Dacia. Syncopated CALDU and VIRDE appear in the *Appendix Probi* (§ 2.5.3).

Latin		Romanian	Italian
CALĬDU	'hot'	cald	caldo
VIRĬDE	'green'	verde	verde
OCŬLU	'eye'	ochi	occhio
UNGŬLA	'nail'	unghie	unghia
AMBULAT	'walks'	umblă	....

10.2.2   Absence of lenition

Unlike Italian, where lenition is variable, Romanian keeps intervocalic stops intact. Romanian *stradă* is borrowed from Italian.

Latin		Romanian	Italian
CAPU	'head'	cap	capo
*POTĒTIS	'you can'	puteţi	potete
ACU	'needle'	ac	ago
CAEP(ULL)A	'onion'	ceapă	cipolla
LACTUCA	'lettuce'	lăptucă	lattuga
SPATHA	'sword'	spată	spada
STRATA	'road'	stradă	strada

Romanian is also conservative with respect to [g] deletion, a process related to lenition (same environment), but earlier and more widespread in Romance:

Latin		Romanian	Italian
DIGITU	'finger'	deget	dito
SAGITTA	'arrow'	săgeată	saetta
FRIG(IDU)	'cold'	frig	freddo

NIGRU	'black'	negru	nero
INTEGRU	'entire'	întreg	intero
EGO	'I'	eu	io
MAGIS	'more'	mai	mai

Again, the best explanation for exceptions like *eu* and *mai* is early [g] loss. The Dacians probably never heard these words with [g].

10.2.3   Degemination

Romanian disallows geminates. In this respect it differs from Italian and patterns with the languages farther west.

Latin		*Romanian*	*Italian*
SŬMMA	'sum'	sumă	somma
CŬPPA	'cup'	cupă	coppa
PECCATU	'sin'	păcat	peccato
SICCA	'dry'	seacă	secca
PASSERU	'bird'	pasăre	passero 'sparrow'
PELLE	'skin'	piele	pelle

This fact, in Pan-Romance perspective, shows that degemination is a process independent of lenition. In the West both occur, but the idea that lenition causes degemination runs aground in Romanian.

10.3   Palatal influences on consonants

The segments /e/, /i/, and /j/ exert on preceding consonants an influence that can loosely be interpreted as assimilation. The changes are of three types: those affecting /t/ /d/ /s/, those affecting /k/ /g/, and those occurring word-finally.

10.3.1   Before /i/ or /j/ only

The consonants /t/ /d/ /s/ become /ts/ /z/ /ʃ/ before /i/ or /j/. Since the tongue position for /i/ /j/ is close to the palate, the point of articulation for these consonants is drawn back.

Latin		*Romanian*	*Italian*
SĔNTĪRE	'feel'	a simţi	sentire
AUDĪRE	'hear'	a auzi	udire
TŬSSĪRE	'cough'	a tuşi	tossire
TĔXĔRE	'weave'	a ţese	tessere
DĔCE	'ten'	zece	dieci

In words with Latin stressed Ĕ, the primary diphthong /jɛ/ supplies the yod, which then fuses into the modified consonant.

10.3.2   Before /i/, /j/, and /e/

As in Italian, velars /k/ /g/ palatalize to /ʧ/ /ʤ/ before a front vowel or glide. In this case the point of articulation is drawn forward. The yod of the primary diphthong /jɛ/ fuses into /ʧ/ /ʤ/, as in *cerb* /ʧerb / 'deer', *ger* /ʤer/ 'frost'.

Latin		Romanian	Italian
CĪVITĀTE	'city'	cetate	città
CĔRVU	'deer'	cerb	cervo
PACE	'peace'	pace	pace
CRŬCE	'cross'	cruce	croce
DŬLCE	'sweet'	dulce	dolce
GINGĪVA	'gum'	gingie	gingiva
GĔLU	'frost'	ger	gelo
GÉNĔRU	'son-in-law'	ginere	genero
LĒGE	'law'	lege	legge
ARGĔNTU	'silver'	argint	argento

10.3.3   Consonant + /i/ word-finally

We saw that word-final /i/ remains syllabic if needed for cluster support and becomes /j/ after a vowel. In all other cases, something happens to the preceding consonant (§ 10.1.8). After /t/, /s/, /k/, or /g/, a word-final /i/ has the same effects we just saw. The <i> remains in spelling, and as a **coarticulated** (simultaneous) /j/ in pronunciation.[6]

frate	[frate]	'brother'	frați	[fratsʲ]	'brothers'
cireașă	[ʧireasə]	'cherry'	cireși	[ʧireʃʲ]	'cherries'
joc	[ʒok]	'I play'	joci	[ʒoʧʲ]	'you play'
lege	[ledʒe]	'law'	legi	[ledʒʲ]	'laws'

All other consonants are pronounced with a coarticulated /j/.

lup	[lup]	'wolf'	lupi	[lupʲ]	'wolves'
an	[an]	'year'	ani	[anʲ]	'years'
bolnav	[bolnav]	'sick' (sg.)	bolnavi	[bolnavʲ]	'sick' (pl.)
cer	[ʧer]	'I ask'	ceri	[ʧerʲ]	'you ask'
ied	[jed]	'baby goat'	iezi	[jezʲ]	'baby goats'

Exception: [lʲ] loses the [l] and leaves a plain yod.

gol	'empty' (sg.)	goi	'empty' (pl.)	[goj]
copil	'child'	copii	'children'	[copij]
cal	'horse'	cai	'horses'	[caj]

10.3.4   Velar + /l/: a palatalizing cluster

As in Italian, /kl/ /gl/ become /kj/ /gj/ (§ 4.3.8). But in Romanian, this happens only after velar stops.

Latin		Romanian		Italian	
CLARU	'bright'	chiar	[kjar]	chiaro	[kjaro]
OCŬLU	'eye'	ochi	[okʲ]	occhio	[ɔk:jo]
UNGŬLA	'fingernail'	unghie	[uŋgje]	unghia	[uŋgja]
PLENU	'full'	plin	[plin]	pieno	[pjɛno]
FLORE	'flower'	floare	[flo̯are]	fiore	[fjore]

10.3.5   Effect on /s/ from a distance

When the palatalization of /k/ to /ʧ/ (§ 10.3.2) would create a sequence /sʧ/, this cluster resolves to /ʃt/ – we call it the Fish Rule.[7]

			PĬSCE 'fish'	peşte	[peʃte]
			SCIENTĬA 'knowledge'	ştiinţă	[ʃtiintsə]
			SCĪO 'I know'	ştiu	[ʃtiw]
COGNOSCO 'I know'	cunosc	[kunosk]	COGNOSCĬT 'knows'	cunoaşte	[kuno̯aʃte]
CRESCO 'I grow'	cresc	[kresk]	CRESCIT 'grows'	creşte	[kreʃte]
*NASCO 'I am born'	nasc	[nask]	*NASCIT 'is born'	naşte	[naʃte]

This change applies to native vocabulary and regularly in inflectional endings. In certain *cultismos*, /sʧ/ remains intact: SCENA 'scene' *scena* /sʧena/.

Word-final /i/ palatalizes /s/ to /ʃ/ across the cluster /str/:

nostru	[nostru]	'our' (sg.)	noştri	[noʃtri]	'our' (pl.)
astru	[astru]	'star'	aştri	[aʃtri]	'stars'

When the /kl/ > /kj/ rule takes /skl/ to /skj/, the yod palatalizes the /s/ to produce /ʃkj/: *EX-CLOPPU 'lame' *şchiop* [ʃkjop].[8]

10.4   Other consonant changes

Several other consonant changes shaped the Romanian lexicon. Apart from fortition of initial glides (§ 10.4.4), these changes have no close counterparts in our other four languages.

10.4.1   Consonant losses

Three consonant losses are conspicuous. The first deletes the segment resulting from the /b/ /w/ merger between vowels.

Latin		*Romanian*		*Italian*
ŏVU	'egg'	ou	[ow]	uovo
VĪVU	'alive'	viu	[viw]	vivo
NŎVU	'new'	nou	[now]	nuovo
NĬVE	'snow'	nea	[nẹa]	neve
SCRIBIT	'writes'	scrie	[skrije]	scrive
HIBĔRNA/-U	'wintry'	iarnă	[jarnə]	inverno
CABALLU	'horse'	cal	[kal]	cavallo
BĬBIT	'drinks'	bea	[bẹa]	beve

If this deletion leaves a vowel hiatus that cannot be otherwise resolved, an anti-hiatic glide is inserted:

OVE	'sheep'	oaie	[ọaje]
NOVA	'new' (f.)	nouă	[nowə]

In internal protected position (same as the non-lenition environment in the Western languages) Romanian has [b]. In this position the /b/ /w/ merger is *not* Pan-Romance. Italian keeps the two distinct.

Latin		*Romanian*	*Italian*
PŬLVĔRE	'dust'	pulbere	polvere
FĔRVIT	'boils'	fierbe	ferve
CŎRVU	'crow'	corb	corvo
*EX-VOLAT(-IAT)	'flies'	zboară	svolazza
BULBU	'bulb'	bulb	bulbo
HĔRBA	'grass'	iarbă	erba
BARBA	'beard'	barbă	barba

In word-initial position, /b/ and /w/ remain distinct and intact:

Latin		*Romanian*	*Italian*
BENE	'well'	bine	bene
BONU	'good'	bun	buono
BACCA	'berry'	bacă	bacca
VINU	'wine'	vin	vino
VĬDET	'sees'	vede	vede
VACCA	'cow'	vacă	vacca

Another sound that deletes is /l/ before /j/.

FOLĬA	'leaf'	foaie	[fo̯aje]
PALĔA	'straw'	paie	[paje]
(DE-)SPOLIAT	'plunders'	despoaie	[despo̯aje]
FILĬU	'son'	fiu	[fiw]
LĔPŎRE	'hare'	iepure	[jepure]
LĔVAT	'lifts'	ia	[ja]

In LĔPŎRE, LĔVAT the /j/ comes from the primary diphthong of stressed ĕ (for /ja/ see § 10.1.4).

The third consonant loss is the deletion of geminate /l:/ before Latin word-final /a/. Here, plurals in -AS behave as if already in -E.

Latin		Romanian	Italian
STELLA	'star'	stea	stella
STELLAS	'stars'	stele	stelle
ILLA	'she'	ea	ella (OIt)
ILLAS	'they' (f.)	ele	elle (OIt)

10.4.2   The labial conspiracy

Several rules conspire to change clusters of the form velar + dental to labial + dental. One is /kt/ > /pt/. Original /pt/ remains.

Latin		Romanian	Italian
OCTO	'eight'	opt	otto
NOCTE	'night'	noapte	notte
LACTE	'milk'	lapte	latte
FACTU	'fact'	fapt	fatto
PĔCTU	'chest'	piept	petto
COCTU	'cooked'	copt	cotto
LŬCTAT	'struggles'	luptă	lotta

Another rule of this type is: /gn/ > /mn/. Original /mn/ remains.

Latin		Romanian	Italian
DIGNU	'worthy'	demn	degno
LIGNU	'wood'	lemn	legno
SIGNU	'sign'	semn	segno
PUGNU	'fist'	pumn	pugno
COGNATU	'brother-in-law'	cumnat	cognato
SOMNU	'sleep'	somn	sonno

The cluster /ks/ can give /ps/, but often there is early assimilation, giving /s:/, then regular degemination: /ks/ > /s:/ > /s/.

Latin		Romanian	Italian
COXA	'thigh'	coapsă	coscia
LAXAT	'leaves'	lasă	lascia
EXIT	'goes out'	iese	esce
TEXIT	'weaves'	țese	tesse
DIXIT	'said'	zise	disse

Labiovelars /kw/ /gw/ before front vowels evolve like /k/ /g/. That is, /kw/ > /k/ > /tʃ/ and /gw/ > /g/ > /dʒ/:

QUID	'what'	ce
QUAERIT	'asks'	cere
CINQUE	'five'	cinci
*IN-TORQUET	'turns'	întoarce
SANGUEN	'blood'	sânge

Before non-front vowels, there is a mysterious double development. In one type, /kw/ becomes /k/:

QUANDO	'when'	când
QUAM	'as'	ca
QUANTU	'how much'	cât
QUO M(ODO)	'how'	cum

In the other type, the labial element prevails: /kw/ /gw/ become /p/ /b/, in keeping with the velar-to-labial conspiracy.

QUATTUOR	'four'	patru
AQUA	'water'	apă
EQUA	'mare'	iapă
LINGUA	'tongue'	limbă

10.4.3   Rhotacism of intervocalic [l]

Original intervocalic [l] undergoes rhotacism, i.e. becomes [r]. This rule perceives the syllable structures of Latin, not Romanian: FILU *fir* 'thread'.

Latin		Romanian		Italian	
QUALE	'which'	care		quale	
FILU	'thread'	fir		filo	
SOLE	'sun'	soare		sole	
CAELU	'sky'	cer		cielo	
SCALA	'ladder'	scară		scala	
VIOLA	'violet'	vioară	'violin'	viola	'violet', 'viola'
SALUTAT	'greets'	sărută	'kisses'	saluta	

Original /l:/, when degeminated, does not feed into rhotacism:

	Latin		Romanian	Italian
	CALLE	'path'	cale	calle
	PELLE	'skin'	piele	pelle
	CABALLU	'horse'	cal	cavallo
	MOLLE	'soft'	moale	molle

10.4.4   Fortition

Latin word-initial yod became /ʒ/ in Romanian, probably via the /dʒ/ stage attested in Italian and Old French.

	Latin		Romanian	Italian
	IOCAT	'plays'	joacă	gioca
	IURAT	'swears'	jură	giura
	IOVI (DIE)	'Thursday'	joi	giovedì

Latin /w/ word-initially became /v/, as in Italian. Word-initial /b/ remains intact (§ 10.4.1).

	Latin		Romanian	Italian
	VĪNU	'wine'	vin	vino
	VACCA	'cow'	vacă	vacca
	VĬR(I)DE	'green'	verde	verde

10.5   Present indicative and subjunctive

Romanian infinitives lose the final /re/ of the Latin form.[9] Their citation form includes a particle *a*: *a cânta* 'sing'.

Romanian keeps all four Latin conjugation classes distinct. Like Italian and French, it has distinct infinitives for all.

			Romanian	Italian	French
I	CANTĀRE	'sing'	a cân<u>ta</u>	can<u>ta</u>re	chan<u>ter</u>
II	DOLĒRE	'grieve'	a du<u>rea</u>	do<u>le</u>re	do<u>loir</u> (OFr)
III	PERDĔRE	'lose'	a <u>pier</u>de	<u>per</u>dere	perdre
IV	DORMĪRE	'sleep'	a dor<u>mi</u>	dor<u>mi</u>re	dor<u>mir</u>

But further, unlike the Western languages, Romanian maintains the unique stress pattern of class III throughout the paradigm. Faithful to their Latin source, class III verbs remain rhizotonic in all six forms and do not shift to the boot template (§ 6.2).

	I		II	
	CANTŌ	cânt	DOL(Ĕ)Ō	dor
	CANTĀS	cânţi	DOLĒS	dori

CANTĂT	cântă	DOLĔT	doare
CANTĂMUS	cântăm	DOLĒMUS	du<u>rem</u>
CANTĀTIS	cânta<u>ţi</u>	DOLĒTIS	dure<u>ţi</u>
CANTĂNT	cântă	*DOLŬNT	dor

III		IV	
PERDŌ	pierd	DORM(Ĭ)Ō	dorm
PERDĬS	pierzi	DORMĪS	dormi
PERDĬT	pierde	DORMĬT	doarme
<u>PERDĬMUS</u>	pie<u>r</u>dem	DORMĪMUS	dor<u>mim</u>
<u>PERDĬTIS</u>	pie<u>r</u>deţi	DORMĪTIS	dor<u>miţi</u>
PERDŬNT	pierd	DORM(Ĭ)ŬNT	dorm

In a small subset of class IV verbs (about sixty), the stressed thematic /i/ backs to central /ɨ/, as in *HORRĪRE > *ur<u>i</u>re > /urɨ/ urî 'hate' (and urâm [ur<u>ɨ</u>m], urâţi [ur<u>ɨts</u>ʲ]). Clearly, this change is not random. These verbs are mostly of non-Latin origin and all end in ărî, ârî, orî, or urî (non-front vowel plus stem-final /r/). Of all the class IV verbs having a stem of this shape, nearly one-third show backing to /rɨ/, and if the stem ends in /or/, two-thirds.[10]

10.5.1   Personal endings

In the first singular, word-final /o/ becomes /u/ and deletes (but see below). The second singular gets its underlying /i/ via the same path as Italian (§ 6.3.2). Third singular endings are regular, with loss of word-final /t/.

Crucially, however, word-final /u/ and /i/ conform to the same rules in verb paradigms as anywhere else. They remain intact and syllabic *only* if needed for cluster support: umblu 'I walk', umbli 'you walk'. They lose their syllabicity after a vowel: scriu [skriw] 'I write', scrii [skrij] 'you write'. After anything else, final /u/ deletes, and final /i/ becomes /j/ but makes every possible preceding consonant harmonize with it in some audible way, as outlined in § 10.3.3.

First and second plural endings -AMUS, -ATIS become -ăm [əm], -aţi [atsʲ].[11] Stressed and unstressed -em, -eţi are regular, as are -im, -iţi. In the third plural, Romanian prefers -UNT over -ENT (like Italian and unlike Spanish). Deletion of final /nt/ is regular. In class I, -ANT > -ă leaves third plurals identical to third singulars, and in all other classes -UNT > -u > zero leaves third plurals identical to first singulars.

The subjunctive, always introduced by să, is conspicuous in Romanian because it has largely supplanted the infinitive. The first and second person forms are simply să plus the indicative. In the third person, the subjunctive is distinctive, but its singular and plural are identical. Thus, the subjunctive has only one distinctive form per verb. The subjunctive personal ending is the "opposite" vowel, as in Spanish, Portuguese, and Italian: class I verbs take -e /e/ and the rest take -ă /ə/.

Indicative		*Subjunctive*	
cântă	'sings'	CANTET	să cânte

doare	'grieves'	DOL(Ĕ)AT	să doară
pierde	'loses'	PERDAT	să piardă
doarme	'sleeps'	DORM(Ĭ)AT	să doarmă

10.5.2 Patterns of allomorphy, paradigm leveling and disleveling

By now the paradox of "regularity" is a familiar one: irregular verbs, those that exhibit allomorphy, can result from the regular application of phonological rules. In Romanian, so many phonological rules are at work that a truly regular (non-alternating) verb stem is a rare type. Its stressed vowel must be one that does not undergo metaphony or unleveled pretonic raising, and it must end in a cluster that keeps the second singular /i/ syllabic (but not /str/, which gives /ʃtr/ before /i/).

a umbla 'walk'		a sufla 'blow'	
umblu	umblăm	suflu	suflăm
umbli	umblați	sufli	suflați
umblă	umblă	suflă	suflă
să umble		să sufle	

All other verb stems will have allomorphs, totally computable,[12] created by one or more of the following: (1) the consonant changes that affect /t d s k g l sk str/, which apply exceptionlessly within the realm of inflection (§ 10.3), (2) the metaphonic stressed vowel alternations /e/ ~ /ẹa/ and /o/ ~ /ọa/, which do apply reliably in native words (§ 10.1.3), although they can fail in *cultismos*, borrowings, and neologisms, and (3) pretonic raising, a pattern to be shown below.

First, we examine stem-vowel allomorphy separately from stem-consonant allomorphy. A stress-sensitive rule, if it acts alone, yields the familiar boot template. One such is pre-nasal raising, as in the rhizotonic forms of *a veni* 'come'. Another is pretonic raising in verb stems, which affects /a/ and /o/.

a veni 'come'		a tăcea 'be silent'	
vin	venim	tac	tăcem
vii	veniți	taci	tăceți
vine	vin	tace	tac

Only /a/ gives the boot template. For stem vowel /o/, metaphony in the third person alters the boot template:

a purta 'carry'		a putea 'be able'	
port	purtăm	pot	putem
porți	purtați	poți	puteți
poartă	poartă	poate	pot

In class I verbs like *a purta*, the stem has three allomorphs, /o/ /o̯a/ /u/, arranged in a unique template:

1st sg.	1st pl.
2nd sg.	2nd pl.
3rd sg.	3rd pl.

This pattern has sometimes attracted new verbs, increasing their stem-vowel allomorphy and disleveling their paradigms:

Popular Latin	Expected	Romanian
*EXCUBULĀRE 'wake'	a scula	a scula
*EXCUBULŌ	*scul	scol
*EXCUBULĀS	*sculi	scoli
*EXCUBULAT	*sculă	scoală
*EXCUBULĀMUS	sculăm	sculăm
*EXCUBULĀTIS	sculaţi	sculaţi
*EXCUBULANT	*sculă	scoală

Vice versa, paradigms with these /o ~ u/ alternations are sometimes leveled, either to /o/ (reducing allomorphy) or to /u/ (eliminating allomorphy).

Latin	Expected	Romanian	Latin	Expected	Romanian
DORMĪRE 'sleep'	a durmi[13]	a dormi	MO(N)STRĀRE 'show'	a mustra	a mustra 'scold'
DORM(I)Ō	dorm	dorm	MO(N)STRŌ	*mostru	mustru
DORMĪS	dormi	dormi	MO(N)STRĀS	*moştri	muştri
DORMIT	doarme	doarme	MO(N)STRAT	*moastră	mustră
DORMĪMŬS	durmim	dormim	MO(N)STRĀMŬS	mustrăm	mustrăm
DORMĪTĬS	durmiţi	dormiţi	MO(N)STRĀTIS	mustraţi	mustraţi
DORM(I)UNT	dorm	dorm	MO(N)STRANT	*moastră	mustră

What of the primary diphthong from stressed low mid /ɛ/? Shouldn't it produce a boot template as in Italian *siedo sediamo* and Spanish *pierdo perdemos*? Romanian did have that alternation, but four independent factors dimmed its salience and so depleted the group that it finally dissolved:

- Class III verbs never alternate /je/ ~ /e/, since they have an unchanging stress position (§ 10.5, top).
- Pre-nasal raising eliminates /je/: Italian *viene*, Spanish *viene*, French *vient*, but Romanian *vine* 'comes'.

- Any boot pattern is disrupted when metaphony intervenes in the third person (see *a purta* above).
- Certain consonants assimilate to a following /j/ and absorb it (§ 10.3.1–2). When this happens stem-initially (or stem-internally), the resulting /ts z ʃ tʃ dʒ/ spreads to the whole paradigm, as in SĔD(Ĕ)O 'I sit' > *sjed > [ʃed] *şed*. Here the arhizotonic forms get an initial [ʃ] analogically (*şedem* 'we sit'), effacing the old alternation.

As the pattern fades away, verbs with expected /e/ ~ /je/ alternations tend to level to /e/ or /je/:

Latin	Expected	Romanian	Latin	Expected	Romanian
SĔRVĪRE 'serve'	a servi	a servi	ĔXĪRE 'go out'	*a eşi	a ieşi
SĔRV(I)Ō	*şerv	serv	ĔX(Ĕ)Ō	ies	ies
SĔRVĪS	*şervi	servi	ĔXĪS	ieşi	ieşi
SĔRVIT	*şerve	serve	ĔXIT	iese	iese
SĔRVĪMŬS	servim	servim	ĔXĪMŬS	*eşim	ieşim
SĔRVĪTĬS	serviţi	serviţi	ĔXĪTĬS	*eşiţi	ieşiţi
SĔRV(I)UNT	*şerv	serv	ĔX(Ĕ)UNT	ies	ies

Now for consonants: as we saw, in all verb classes the second singular /i/ alters a stem consonant unless the stem ends in a cluster other than /sk/ or /str/. Thus, most verbs will have at least one allomorph, located in the second singular. Below and in § 10.5.3, shading is used not to signal analogy but rather to help indicate the distribution of allomorphs.

a cânta 'sing'

cânt	cântăm
cânţi	cântaţi
cântă	cântă

In classes II, III, and IV, if the stem consonant is a velar or /sk/, three allomorphs emerge:

a duce 'lead'

duc	ducem
duci	duceţi
duce	duc

a naşte 'be born'

nasc	naştem
naşti	naşteţi
naşte	nasc

Further, since the stem vowel and stem consonant alternations often co-occur, many Romanian verbs have four stem allomorphs. A theorem: in all cases of quadruple allomorphy, three of the forms appear in the first, second, and third singular respectively, and the fourth appears in the arhizotonic forms.

However, due to the different conditions for metaphonic diphthongs, the overall distribution of the allomorphs will differ in third plurals, as shown:

a purta 'carry'   a putea 'be able'

port	purtăm	pot	putem
porţi	purtaţi	poţi	puteţi
poartă	poartă	poate	pot

10.5.3   Two stem extenders

The element -*sc*- has the same status in Romanian as in Italian (§ 6.9). It lost its original inchoative meaning, but is still a segmentable affix, as in Italian and French (not Spanish). In a subset comprising over 80 percent of class IV verbs[14] it occurs in the boot pattern, i.e. in the forms that would otherwise be rhizotonic, as in Italian (but not French).

a vorbi 'talk'   a pârî 'accuse'

vorbesc	vorbim	pârăsc	pârâm
vorbeşti	vorbiţi	pârăşti	pârâţi
vorbeşte	vorbesc	pârăşte	pârăsc

să vorbească   să pârască

The Fish Rule (§ 10.3.5) accounts for the palatalizations of /sk/. The expected backing of /rɛsk/ to /rəsk/ in the -*î* verbs (§ 10.1.7) is sporadic.

Whatever the mysteries surrounding the /sk/ affix (why it was deemed useful despite its bleaching, why it occurs only with some verbs, and why it is confined to class IV in Romanian, Italian, and French), Romanian has another stem extender /ez/ that raises similar questions. Extracted from Latin verbs in -IZARE (§ 11.2.1), it occurs as a semantically empty affix in 60 percent of class I verbs.[15] Like /sk/, it occurs in the boot template and makes those four forms arhizotonic. In verbs like *a studia*, with stem-final /j/, note the regular triphthong reduction (§ 10.1.4).

a lucra 'work'   a studia 'study'

lucrez	lucrăm	studiez	studiăm
lucrezi	lucraţi	studiezi	studiaţi
lucrează	lucrează	studiază	studiază

să lucreze   să studieze

10.5.4   The verbs be, have, want

Latin FIĔRI 'become', remade as *FĪRE, supplies the infinitive *a fi* 'be'. Its indicative reflects the irregular paradigm of ESSE 'be' (§ 6.10.1), drastically rebuilt based on EST and SUNT.

a fi 'be'

sunt	[sunt]	suntem	[suntem]
(sînt	[sɨnt])	(sîntem	[sɨntem])
eşti	[jeʃtʲ]	sunteţi	[suntetsʲ]
		(sînteţi	[sɨntetsʲ])
este	[jeste]	sunt	[sunt]
		(sînt	[sɨnt])

Once *est-* is reanalysed as a stem, the corresponding second singular is *eşti*. Likewise *sunt* (with a vowel of uncertain origin in the older *sînt sîntem sînteţi*) is reanalysed as a stem with the zero ending typical of all but class I verbs. The other two forms take on class II endings, with *suntem, sunteţi* ultimately winning out over variants from SŬMUS, ESTIS.

The subjunctive of *a fi* has six forms. A newly created present indicative of **FĪRE* supplies the first and second persons, and the true subjunctive of FIĔRI supplies the third person. For FĪAT, FĪANT > *să fie*, recall the Family Rule (§ 10.1.8).

*FĪO	să fiu	[fiw]
*FĪS	să fii	[fij]
FĪAT	să fie	[fie]
*FĪMUS	să fim	[fim]
*FĪTIS	să fiţi	[fitsʲ]
FĪANT	să fie	[fie]

The infinitive *a avea* continues HABĒRE with an irregularity: the intervocalic /b/, instead of deleting (§ 10.4.1), gives /v/. As an auxiliary, the verb has a special conjugation (§ 10.6.3), and as a main verb its forms are:

Latin	Popular Latin	Romanian
HABĒRE	**[aβere]*	avea
'have'		
HABĔŌ	**[ajo]*	am
HABĒS	**[as]*	ai
HABĔT	**[at]*	are
HABĒMUS	**[aβemus]*	avem
HABĒTIS	**[aβetis]*	aveţi
*HABŬNT	**[awnt]*	au
HABĔAT	**[abjat]*	să aiba

The origin of first singular *am* is obscure and disputed.[16] One thing is clear: first singular **[ajo]* was discarded, perhaps to avoid homonymy with the second singular. As for *are* 'has', which is /a/ in the Western Romance languages and in the Romanian auxiliary, a plausible explanation is that it was lengthened at a time when long and short infinitives coexisted. Analogically, then: cânta ~ cântare → a ~ are. Another form that boded ill was HABĔAT > *avea, because [ĕa] must be stressed. That outcome would have created an anomaly – a polysyllabic subjunctive with word-final stress – which was forestalled by yod metathesis, a phenomenon common in Romance, though not regular in Romanian.

Popular Latin *VOLĒRE 'want' produced two distinct paradigms. The set that derived more directly from spoken Latin was gradually bleached as it became a future auxiliary (§ 10.6.2). A new set, mostly analogical, was created in the 1600s to supply an unbleached verb meaning 'want':

Latin			Original paradigm	As rebuilt in 1600s
*VOLĒRE			a vrea	a vrea
'want'				
*VOLĔŌ	voiu	>	voi	vreau
VELIS (subjunc.)			vei	vrei
*VOLĔT	*voare	>	va	vrea
*VOLĒMUS	vrem	>	vom	vrem
*VOLĒTIS	vreţi	>	veţi	vreţi
VOLŬNT			vor	vreau
*VOLĔAT			să voaie	să vrea

The main quirk here is syncope in the arhizotonic forms: VOLĒRE > */vorere/ > */vrere/ > */vreare/ > /vrea/ vrea. Syncope also leads to vrem, vreţi with regular class II endings. These later lose their /r/ through leveling.[17] From *VOLĔŌ comes voi by /lj/ > /j/ (§ 10.4.1) and final /u/ deletion (§ 10.1.8). The Latin subjunctive VELIS becomes vei (Lombard 1955:956) by regular sound change (§ 10.3.3).[18] From *VOLĔT, VOLŬNT we expect *voare, vor (§ 10.4.3).[19] Third singular *voare simplifies to vare and then loses /re/ in the same way as are 'has' gains it (see above). Subjunctive *VOLĔAT regularly yields voaie by /lj/ > /j/, the Family Rule, and metaphony.

Based on the infinitive, the finite forms must have acquired initial /vr/. Once the rebuilt verb has vrei instead of vei, its stem can be reanalysed as vre-, consistent with vrem, vreţi.[20] In the third singular, */vree/ > /vre/ > /vrea/ by the Coffee Rule (§ 10.1.8). In the subjunctive, /vre + ə/ coalesces to /vrea/. The -u of vreau is typical of all other verbs with a stem-final stressed vowel (beau 'I/they drink', scriu 'I/they write').

10.6   Verb morphology: systemic reorganization

For the overall structure of the Romanian verb system, Chart 7.2 is a good starting-point: old categories with original morphology. Romanian continues these Latin forms in its present indicative and subjunctive (§ 10.5), imperfect, and preterite (known as perfect simplu). The imperfect subjunctive and pluperfect subjunctive no longer exist as categories. The remaining categories do survive, but are realized with morphology notably different from what we have seen elsewhere.

10.6.1   Imperfect indicative

Deletion of intervocalic /b/ looms large in this derivation: -ABA-, -EBA- reduced to -a-, -ea- respectively.

Latin	Expected	Romanian	Latin	Expected	Romanian
CANTĀRE 'sing'	a cânta	a cânta	VIDĒRE 'see'	a vedea	a vedea
CANTĀBAM	cânta	cântam	VIDĒBAM	vedea	vedeam
CANTĀBĀS	cântai	cântai	VIDĒBĀS	vedeai	vedeai
CANTĀBAT	cânta	cânta	VIDĒBAT	vedea	vedea
CANTĀBĀMUS	cântam	cântam	VIDĒBĀMUS	vedeam	vedeam
CANTĀBĀTIS	cântaţi	cântaţi	VIDĒBĀTIS	vedeaţi	vedeaţi
CANTĀBANT	cânta	cântau	VIDĒBANT	vedea	vedeau

In class II the hiatus /ea/ resolves automatically to /ęa/. Classes IIIb and IV lose the /j/ of -IĒBA- /jeba/ and merge with class II. The expected quadruple homonymy, unparalleled elsewhere in Romanian, has been remedied. The first singular -m spreads from the first plural (1600s) on the model of auxiliary am 'I have', am 'we have'. Likewise the -u of the third plural (1800s) is modeled on au 'they have' (Lombard 1955:248).

10.6.2   Future and conditional

Although infinitive + HABĒRE was the most widespread periphrastic future in Popular Latin (§ 7.8.1), another format also gained favor: *VOLĒRE + infinitive, source of the Romanian literary future. The forms of *VOLĒRE that became future auxiliaries are covered above (§ 10.5.4): voi cânta 'I will sing', vor plânge 'they will weep', veţi vedea 'you will see'. Already in the second century CE, classical VELLE 'want' has a bleached use with future meaning, as in: CUM VELLET DESCENDERE 'as he was about to descend' (Juvenal, Satires 10, 282). Cyprian writes (circa 250 CE): FIDERE UT LIBERARI … VELLENT 'confident that they were going to be freed' (Epistolae 6, 3). And in 550 CE, Corippus says of captive women: MISERAE MODO MATRIBUS AFRIS IAM SERVIRE VOLUNT 'now these miserable women will be serving the matrons of Africa' (De bellis Libycis 6, 89).

Putting the auxiliary from *VOLĒRE into the imperfect, we should get a conditional. Old Romanian did have vrea cânta 'I would sing', vreai cânta 'you would sing', etc. But the Modern Romanian conditional has a different auxiliary:

aş cânta	am cânta
ai cânta	aţi cânta
ar cânta	ar cânta

This auxiliary probably comes from a hybrid paradigm consisting of the imperfect of HABĒRE (both /b/'s delete) with three substitute forms, here bracketed:

[HABESSIM]	>	aş
HABĒBĀS	>	ai
[HABĒRET]	*are >	ar
HABĒBĀMUS	>	am
HABĒBĀTIS	>	aţi
[HABĒRENT]	*are >	ar

The third persons are relics of the Latin imperfect subjunctive (Chart 7.1), which had a conditional value on its own. A periphrastic of exactly this form appears already in Lactantius (d. 325 CE): PRAEDIXISSE QUOD PLURIMAE SECTAE HABERENT EXISTERE 'predicted that many sects would exist' (*Institutiones divinae* 4, 30, 2).[21] The reduction *are* > *ar* obeys the principle that all auxiliaries are monosyllabic. The problematic first singular *aş* is cognate to Italian *avessi*, both being reflexes of the pre-Classical HABESSIM paradigm that ended up infiltrating the pluperfect subjunctive, the Romance imperfect subjunctive (§ 7.6.1).

The Romanian future and conditional remain periphrastic and still admit some interposed adverbs (*vor mai scrie* 'they will write again'), unlike the Western types, which have fused (§§ 7.8.1, 7.8.4).[22] In the conditional, the order of infinitive and auxiliary still vacillates, but *aş cânta* is unmarked, while *cântare-aş* is highly literary.[23]

Periphrastics in general (especially the future) have proliferated in Romanian. Fully three additional future paradigms are attested: (1) *oi cânta* 'I will sing', *om cânta* 'we will sing', which is the literary future discussed above minus the initial /v/, (2) *o să cânt, o să cântăm*, where the auxiliary is neutralized to a uniform *o* (on the model of *oi, om*, and *or*), and, as happens elsewhere in Romanian, the infinitive is replaced by the subjunctive, (3) *am să cânt, avem să cântăm*, the full (non-auxiliary) *a avea* 'have' plus the subjunctive.

10.6.3   Periphrastic perfects

Like all other Romance languages, Romanian has a periphrastic past, the *perfect compus*, consisting of auxiliary 'have' plus past participle. It has both meanings, true perfect ('I have written') and preterite ('I wrote'). Three forms of the auxiliary are shorter than in the main verb 'have' (§ 10.5.4):

am scris	am scris
ai scris	aţi scris
a scris	au scris

Romanian does not use finite auxiliary 'be', as Italian and French do: Italian *è venuto*, French *il est venu*, Romanian *a venit*. But if you change the auxiliary to future or conditional, it switches to 'be': *am scris* 'I wrote/have written' but *voi fi scris* 'I will have written', *aş fi scris* 'I would have written'. Alongside the literary pluperfect (§ 10.6.5), Romanian has a periphrastic pluperfect of popular origin formed by putting the 'be' auxiliary into the *perfect compus*: *am fost scris* 'I had written'. In short, infinitive *avea* and participle *avut* never appear in auxiliaries. They are always replaced by *fi* and *fost*.

10.6.4   Past participles and preterites

Every Romance language creates its own new grammatical regularities. A salient pattern in Romanian is the formal bond that developed between the synthetic preterite (*perfect simplu*) and the past participle. The other languages too tend to place these forms into derivationally linked pairs (§ 7.11.3), but nowhere is the one-to-one matching so pervasive as in Romanian. We examine the weak (arhizotonic) pairs first, then the strong (rhizotonic) type.

Like the other languages, Romanian continues Latin class I and IV weak participles in -ATU and -ITU. Many verbs in classes II and III acquired new weak participles in -UTU (§ 7.11.2).

	Latin		*Popular Latin*	*Romanian*
I	CANTĀRE	CANTĀTU		cântat
	FORMĀRE	FORMĀTU		format
IV	DORMĪRE	DORMĪTU		dormit
	MENTĪRI	MENTĪTU		minţit
II	DOLĒRE	DOLĬTU	*DOLŪTU	durut
	TACĒRE	TACĬTU	*TACŪTU	tăcut
III	CRESCĚRE	CRĒTU	*CRESCŪTU	crescut
	FACĚRE	FACTU	*FACŪTU	făcut

Main fact: the weak perfect stem always echoes the participle stem. The only exception is the stressed /ə/ instead of /a/ in class I third singular, which avoids homonymy with the imperfect.

Short forms of perfectum[24]	*Perfect simplu*		
CANTAI	cântai	făcui	dormii
CANTASTI	cântaşi	făcuşi	dormişi
CANTAT	cântă	făcu	dormi
CANTAMUS	cântarăm	făcurăm	dormirăm
CANTASTIS	cântarăţi	făcurăţi	dormirăţi
CANTARUNT	cântară	făcură	dormiră
	'sang'	'made'	'slept'

Throughout Latin and Romance, perfectum endings are uniform across all classes. In the second singular the loss of /t/ is unexpected: /sti/ > /ʃtʲ/ becomes /ʃ/. The /r/ of the third plural spreads to first and second plurals in the 1600s.

Without it, the first plural would remain identical to the present indicative (a homonymy tolerated in Spanish). For the personal endings after the /r/, the likely source is the hypothetical old paradigm of the pluperfect (§ 10.6.5 below).

We now turn from weak to strong preterites and participles. The strong preterites all have stem-final /s/. How did this pattern arise? First, Romanian kept many Latin sigmatic perfects. For example, UNGĔRE 'anoint':

Latin	Old Romanian	Modern Romanian
UNXĪ	unşu	unsei
UNXISTĪ	unseşi	unseşi
UNXIT	unse	unse
UNXĬMUS	unsemu	unserăm
UNXISTIS	unseţi	unserăţi
UNXĔRUNT	unseră	unseră

The leveled modern paradigm has a stem *unse*-, stressed throughout. This /e/ was regular from ĭ in five forms, and the <ş> from /si/, unique to the first singular, was leveled out. Then the participles, if not already sigmatic, were rebuilt to match the new stem of the *perfect simplu*:

Latin perfectum	Perfect simplu	Latin participle	Romanian participle
UNXĬT	unse	UNCTU	uns
DIXĬT	zise	DICTU	zis
SCRIPSĬT	scrise	SCRIPTU	scris
TRAXĬT	trase	TRACTU	tras

A handful of strong participles have remained non-sigmatic, but the great majority of verbs imposed the principle that the strong *perfect simplu* must always have stem-final /s/. In this case, the strong participles provided the model for a new (non-etymological) *perfect simplu* by changing /t/ to /s/:

Latin participle	Romanian participle	Perfect simplu
COCTU	copt	coapse
FRICTU	fript	fripse
RUPTU	rupt	rupse

The *perfect simplu* is today confined to the written language, as in French. Also shared with French is the rise of a new weak perfect with thematic /u/, e.g. *făcu*.

10.6.5   Pluperfect

The Latin pluperfect subjunctive, converted in the West to the imperfect subjunctive, survives in Romanian as a pluperfect indicative.

Latin short forms	Expected Romanian	a cânta 'sing'	a face 'make'	a durmi 'sleep'
CANTASSEM	cântase	cântasem	făcusem	dormisem
CANTASSES	cântaşi	cântaseşi	făcuseşi	dormiseşi

CANTASSET	cântase	cântase	făcuse	dormise
*CANTASSEMUS	cântasem	cântaserăm	făcuserăm	dormiserăm
*CANTASSETIS	cântaseţi	cântaserăţi	făcuserăţi	dormiserăţi
CANTASSENT	cântase	cântaseră	făcuseră	dormiseră

Just as the *perfect simplu* has a zero ending in the third singular, so also the pluperfect *cântase* was interpreted as a stem with a zero ending. Therefore, the second singular becomes *cântaseşi*, copying the *perfect simplu*. The first singular /m/ cannot be a survivor from antiquity (§ 2.4.4). It has several models within Romanian, such as the imperfect (§ 10.6.1) and *am* 'I have'.

The *perfect simplu* and pluperfect both had a part in creating the innovative plural endings which they now share. The *perfect simplu* (third plural) supplied the /r/, but an older pluperfect, forerunner of the modern one, supplied personal endings *-em -eţi -e* which after /r/ became *-ăm -ăţi -ă*. Then *-răm -răţi -ră* migrated back into the pluperfect.

A regularity then emerges: *perfect simplu* stem + /se/ = pluperfect stem. The formula applies equally to strong stems:

zise	zisese	ziseră	ziseseră
's/he said'	's/he had said'	'they said'	'they had said'
rupse	rupsese	rupseră	rupseseră
's/he tore'	's/he had torn'	'they tore'	'they had torn'

This synthetic pluperfect belongs mainly to the written language. See § 10.6.3 for the popular periphrastic pluperfect.

10.7   Noun and adjective morphology

The most exotic properties of Romanian, from the Western viewpoint, are its two-case system and its postposed definite article. Both are displayed in what follows.

10.7.1   The Romanian case system

The two-case system is organized differently from the system in Old French (Chart 8.5). In Romanian, one case serves as nominative and accusative, the other as genitive and dative. We reconstruct for the Popular Latin of Dacia a three-case system with nominative and accusative – as in the Popular Latin of other regions (Chart 8.2) – plus a dative that has taken over the functions of the genitive.[25]

Reconstructed Popular Latin three-case system

	1 (f.)	2 (m.)	(f.)	3 (m.)
	CAPRA	LUPUS	VULPIS	CANIS
sg.	CAPRA	LUPU	VULPE	CANE
	CAPRE (<AE)	LUPO	VULPI	CANI

	CAPRE (<AE)	LUPI	VULPES	CANES
pl.	CAPRAS	LUPOS	VULPES	CANES
	CAPRIS	LUPIS	VULPIBUS	CANIBUS
	'goat'	'wolf'	'fox'	'dog'

We suggest that final /s/ evolves as in Italian (§§ 6.3.2, 8.4.1 and § 10.5.1), giving the following outcomes for pre-Romanian. The boxed forms represent the modern system in which nominative and accusative are no longer distinct. Analogical forms are shaded.

Reconstructed pre-Romanian noun morphology

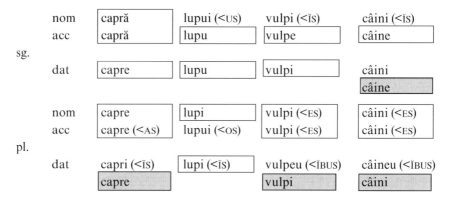

The generalizations that shaped the system are: (1) feminine nouns have a distinct dative singular which is identical to the plurals, (2) case is neutralized in masculine nouns, giving rise to dative *câine*, (3) case is neutralized in the plural. In this analysis, the *lupu* type led the way in the neutralization of case. The best choices were *lupu lupu* and *lupi lupi* because the abandoned plural *lupui* looked too much like a genitive/dative (see below).

Case marking on the isolated noun shows up only in feminine singulars. Most case information resides in function words like articles, as we see below. The definite article is postposed, as promised.

un lup (m.)	'a wolf'	o capră (f.)	'a goat'
unui lup	'of/to a wolf'	unei capre	'of/to a goat'
lupul	'the wolf'	capra	'the goat'
lupului	'of/to the wolf'	caprei	'of/to the goat'
lupii	'the wolves'	caprele	'the goats'
lupilor	'of/to the wolves'	caprelor	'of/to the goats'
un câine (m.)	'a dog'	o vulpe (f.)	'a fox'
unui câine	'of/to a dog'	unei vulpi	'of/to a fox'

câinele	'the dog'	vulpea	'the fox'
câinelui	'of/to the dog'	vulpii	'of/to the fox'
câinii	'the dogs'	vulpile	'the foxes'
câinilor	'of/to the dogs	vulpilor	'of/to the foxes'

Nominative/accusative masculine singular nouns in -*e* have a special definite article -*le*, as in *câinele*.

Question: How is the definite article shown on nominative/accusative singular nouns from the first declension?

Answer: The definite article is -*a*: *CAPRA+A > *capra* (cf. CAPRA *capră*).

Among our five languages, definite articles (and third person pronouns) all derive from the Latin demonstrative ILLE, but only in Romanian do the articles inflect for case. The relevant paradigms appear in Charts 8.8, 8.9, and 8.10.

sg.	nom/acc	lupul	LUPU	+	(I)LLU
	gen/dat	lupului	LUPU	+	(I)LLUI
pl.	nom/acc	lupii	LUPI	+	(I)LLI[26]
	gen/dat	lupilor	LUPI	+	(I)LLORU
sg.	nom/acc	capra	CAPRA	+	(I)LLA[27]
	gen/dat	caprei	CAPRE	+	(I)LLEI[28]
pl.	nom/acc	caprele	CAPRE	+	(I)LLE
	gen/dat	caprelor	CAPRE	+	(I)LLORU

The definite articles on third declension masculine and feminine nouns have the etymologies shown above, except for *câinele* and *vulpii*.[29]

One difficulty for learners: some feminine nouns in -*ă* pluralize with -*i*. By the modern exceptionless rule, their genitive/dative is identical to their plural:

o limbă	'a language'	limba	'the language'
unei limbi	'of/to a language'	limbii	'of/to the language'
		limbile	'the languages'
		limbilor	'of/to the languages'

Further complexities, but predictable ones, arise because the change of word-final vowels may induce metaphony and/or consonant changes.

	Feminine singular		*Plural or gen/dat singular*
fereastră	'window'	ferestre	'windows'
țeastă	'skull'	țeste	'skulls'

neagră	'black' (f. sg.)	negre	'black' (f. pl.)
seară	'evening'	seri	'evenings'
noapte	'night'	nopți	'nights'

> **PRACTICE**
>
> Based on the etymon and plural marker, calculate the regular outcomes in each of these singular/plural noun pairs:
>
> | | | singular | plural |
> |---|---|---|---|
> | CODA | 'tail' | c_____dă | c_____i |
> | *BROSCA | 'frog' | br_____scă | br_____e |
> | PĔTRA | 'stone' | p_____tră | p_____e |
> | FLORE | 'flower' | fl_____re | fl_____i |
> | COXA | 'hip' | c_____psă | c_____e |
> | CEPA | 'onion' | c_____pă | c_____e |

10.7.2   Ambigenerics

Another conspicuous feature of Romanian noun morphology is the class of ambigeneric nouns, masculine when singular and feminine when plural. Italian has about thirty (§ 8.5.3), while in Romanian they form about one-third of nouns. Consistent with the origin of the category in the Latin neuter gender, all but two ambigenerics denote inanimates. Moreover, inanimates fall outside the ambigeneric class with far less than chance frequency.

Only Italian, not Romanian, preserves the Latin neuter plural -A. Romanian replaced it early on with either the feminine plural marker -*e*, or with an ending -*ură*, extracted from third declension neuter plurals (e.g. CORPUS, CORPORA). But -*ură*, apparently as unacceptable as -*ă* (< -A), was replaced by a more plural-looking -*ure*, -*uri*, today only -*uri* [urʲ].

	sg.	pl.	sg.	pl.
'wood'	LIGNUM	LIGNA	lemn	lemne
'bone'	OSSUM	OSSA	os	oase
'people'	POPULUS	POPULI	popor	popoare
'telephone'	Fr *téléphone*	*téléphones*	telefon	telefoane
'chest'	PECTUS	PECTORA	piept	piepturi
'time'	TEMPUS	TEMPORA	timp	timpuri
'wine'	VINUM	VINA	vin	vinuri
'sky'	CAELUM	CAELA	cer	ceruri
'fax'	Eng *fax*	*faxes*	fax	faxuri

Although it originated in the Latin neuter, the ambigeneric class has expanded vastly to include inanimates from other sources: Latin masculines and foreign words.

Chart 10.1 Romanian personal pronouns

	Tonic			Atonic	
	Nom	Acc	Dat	Acc	Dat
1st sg.	eu	mine	mie	mă	(î)mi
2nd sg.	tu	tine	ţie	te	(î)ţi
3rd sg. m.	el	el	lui	îl	(î)i
3rd sg. f.	ea	ea	ei	o	(î)i
1st pl.	noi	noi	nouă	ne	ni
2nd pl.	voi	voi	vouă	vă	vi
3rd pl. m.	ei	ei	lor	îi	le
3rd pl. f.	ele	ele	lor	le	le

10.7.3 Adjective morphology

Romanian adjectives deriving from the Latin third declension are recognizable, as in Italian, Spanish, and Portuguese, because they inflect only for number, not gender, while adjectives from the second and first declension have the familiar four forms. As with nouns, their formal complexity is predictable, in accord with the changing word-final vowels.

Examples of nom/acc adjective forms

m. sg.	bun	'good'	sec	'dry'	mare	'big'	moale	'soft'
f. sg.	bună		seacă		mare		moale	
m. pl.	buni		seci		mari		moi	
f. pl.	bune		sece		mari		moi	

Adjectives inflect for case only in the feminine singular and their genitive/dative forms are predictably identical to the feminine plural.

10.7.4 Pronoun morphology

Romanian pronouns maintain a robust three-case system. In our other languages, distinct dative pronouns do exist, but only in the third person and only in the atonic class. In Romanian, datives distinct from accusatives exist in all persons[30] and among tonic as well as atonic forms, as Chart 10.1 shows:[31]

In the tonic class, Romanian does resemble our other languages in having a single pronoun for both nominative and accusative everywhere except *eu/mine*, *tu/tine*. The loss of gender distinction in third person datives finds parallels in our other languages, but Romanian neutralizes the most, leaving only tonic third person singulars distinct for gender. Easy etymologies include (for tonic forms) NŌS VŌS *noi voi* as in Italian (§§ 6.3.2, 8.8.1), ILLA ILLAE *ea ele* by the Star Rule (§ 10.4.1), ILLUI ILLAEI *lui (l)ei* with an unexpected /l/ loss in the standard language, ILLŌRU *lor*, and (for atonic forms) MĒ > *me > *mă*, TĒ *te* and their analogical followers *ne*, *ve > *vă*.[32] Atonic datives *mi ţi* also attract analogical followers *ni vi*.

First and second person tonic datives display regular sound change combined with analogy. *Nouă* and *vouă* are regular,[33] and from them *mie* and *ţie* acquire their final <e> at a pre-literary stage.

$$\begin{array}{ccccccc}
\text{*NOBI} & \text{*VOBI} & > & \text{/*nowe} & \text{*vowe/} & > & \text{nouă vouă} \\
 & & & \downarrow & \downarrow & & \\
\text{MIHI} & \text{TIBI} & > & \text{/mie} & \text{ţie/} & = & \text{mie ţie}
\end{array}$$

Accusatives *mine tine* come from older *mene tene* by raising before a nasal (§ 10.1.6). But why *-ne*? Some ascribe it to Albanian and/or Greek influence (Rosetti 1986, Du Nay 1996), others trace it to an interrogative particle -NE (Densuşianu 1934, Elcock 1960, Bourciez 1967, Anderson and Rochet 1979, *et al.*). But *paragogy* (addition of an arbitrary final syllable) is a known phenomenon. Central and Southern Italian varieties also add *-ne* to certain words. Rohlfs (1966–69:I, § 336) reviews the data, conceding that the origin of this syllable is obscure.

There are two words *o*, both feminine singular: the indefinite article *o* 'a' and the accusative pronoun *o* 'her'. Neither is well explained in the literature. Nearly all agree that they must derive from UNA and ILLA, but how? An important clue is the unique position of this accusative clitic: in the *perfect compus* it is postposed to the participle. This may reflect a time when ILLA *ea*, with apheresis in unstressed position, had become *a* – inaudible before the auxiliary, as in **a-am văzutu* 'I saw her'. The solution was to place this pronoun after the participle: **am văzutu-a*. Meanwhile, participles without the final <u> (standard today) were alternating with ones that kept it. This allowed a resegmentation of **am văzutu-a* as **am văzut-ua*. The two vowels in hiatus coalesce to /o/, which replaces **a* 'her' in all other contexts. The indefinite article, which by regular change gives *ună*, may have developed the modern variant *o* by analogy. Another possibility: UNA > **ua* by a sporadic or regional change and then **ua* > *o* as described above.

Exercises

1. Compare Lat SPEC- (as in *inspect, spectator, conspicuous*) with its Greek cognate *skep-, skop-* (as in *skeptic, microscope*). Apparently this root was prone to metathesis. Explain why *a aştepta* 'wait' cannot be from **AD-SPECTARE (> It *aspettare*). Posit the correct etymon.

2. Describe the sound changes, shown here in approximate chronological order, leading from Lat *LIBĔRTAT 'frees' to Ro *iartă* 'forgives', and from Lat HIBĔRNA 'wintry' to Ro *iarnă* 'winter'.

LIBĔRTAT		HIBĔRNA	
[libɛrtə]	....	[ibɛrnə]	....
[liertə]	....	[jernə]	....
[jertə]	....	[jɟarnə]	....

[jĕartə]   ....   [jarnə]   ....
                                      iarnă

[jartə]   ....
iartă

For *iartă*, compute the infinitive and second singular. For *iarnă*, compute the plural (two guesses).

3.   Recall that LL deletes adjacent to word-final -A (§ 10.4.1). Pairs like these three underwent reanalysis.

STELLA	'star'	stea	STELLAS	'stars'	stele
MAXILLA	'molar'	măsea	MAXILLAS	'molars'	măsele
ĪLLA	'she'	ea	ILLAS	'they' (f.)	ele

Explain how the following words acquired their plural marker *-le*.

MEA	'my' (f. sg.)	mea	mele	'my' (f. pl.)
*GREVE	'difficult'	grea	grele	'difficult'
Fr *café*	'coffee'	cafea	cafele	'coffees'
Tu *lâle*	'tulip'	lalea	lalele	'tulips'

4.   The frustrated subjunctive
Review the formation of subjunctives (§ 10.5.1, end). Given the forms *scriu* 'I write' and *scrie* 'writes', what should the subjunctive be? How does the Family Rule change it?

5.   Adventures in pseudo-metaphony
Reminiscent of Italian, but more restricted, the Romanian change /kl gl/ > /kj gj/ produces yods that make new diphthongs (§ 10.3.4). If these secondary diphthongs become entangled in metaphonic alternations, strange things happen. It is not clear at first how to explain the /e/ of CLAMĀRE *a chema* 'call' or *IN-COAGULĀRE *a închega* 'curdle'. But try deriving the third person, naming each change shown below:

CLAMAT
[klamə]   ....
[kjamə]   ....   > *cheamă*
IN-COAGULAT
[iŋkwagulə]   ....
[iŋkwaglə]   ....
[iŋkaglə]   ....   (cf. QUALE *care* 'which')
[iɨŋklagə]   ....
[iɨŋkjagə]   ....   > *încheagă*

Now explain the /e/ of the infinitives *a chema* and *a închega*.

6.   Really vulgar Latin
Given the source, derive the unrefined word for 'backside' in these four languages. The reflexes are all regular.

Latin			Italian	Spanish	French	Portuguese	Romanian
CŪLU	'ass'	>	....	....	....	....	....

So why did Romanian need a new word for 'run'? Mention specific sound changes.

Latin		Italian	Spanish	French	Portuguese	Romanian
CŬRRŌ	'I run'	corro	corro	cours	corro	alerg

7. Each of these words departs in some way from the regular sound changes we studied. Identify the irregularity without speculating on why it occurred.

Latin		Romanian	
AUTŬMNU	'fall'	toamnă	
FARĪNA	'flour'	făină	
MŌRU	'mulberry'	mur	
PALŪDE	'swamp'	pădure	'forest'
STRĬCTU	'tight'	strâmt	'narrow'
VĒLA	'sail'	velă	
VETERĀNU	'old'	bătrân	
VŌCE	'voice'	voce	

8. Contemplating death

Given the expected infinitive of the Romanian verb 'perish', reconstruct its present indicative forms. Which of your reconstructed forms differ from the modern ones? What motivates the change in these forms? Another verb meaning 'die' displays extensive allomorphy – all predictable given (1) pretonic raising, (2) effects of final /i/, and (3) conditions for metaphonic diphthongs. Calculate the outcomes for the modern paradigm. Count the stem allomorphs.

Popular Latin	Expected	Romanian	Popular Latin	Romanian
PĚRĪRE 'perish'	a peri	a pieri	*MORĪRE 'die'	....
*PĚRŌ	....	pier	*MORŌ	....
PĚRĪS	....	pieri	*MORĪS	....
PĚRĬT	....	piere	*MORĬT	....
PĚRĪMUS	....	pierim	*MORĪMUS	....
PĚRĪTIS	....	pieriți	*MORĪTIS	....
*PĚRUNT	....	pier	*MORUNT	....

11　Formation of the Romance lexicon

To form a true-to-life image of how the pre-Romance lexicon took shape, the key idea again is the extralinguistic fact that Latin spread over a vast territory. Wherever and whenever Latin was adopted, the non-native speakers acquiring it would at first learn a rudimentary version of the lexicon. Then, new native speakers, using the resources at hand, would build a fully elaborated lexicon, overlapping w-ith the original but reconstituting it.

Even in stable speech communities where Latin had deep roots, its vocabulary evolved. At any given time, Latin was a mix of words destined to vanish, others that remained vigorous, and others newly introduced. The native languages of the conquered or neighboring peoples made their contribution. As the Empire dissolved, an influx of words came from the languages newly arriving in Latin-speaking areas.

11.1　Lexical competition and replacement

Words adopted in popular speech tend to survive in Romance while others recede into disuse. Sometimes the motives are clear: the irregular verb FERRE 'carry' is eclipsed by regular PORTARE, allomorphic PULCHER 'beautiful' by BELLU or FORMOSU.[1] Sometimes colorful or slang words supplanted bland ones.

	Latin	Italian	Spanish	French	Portuguese	Romanian
CAPUT 'head'	TESTA 'clay pot'	capo, testa	cabeza	chef, tête	cabeça	cap, țeastă
DOMUS 'house'	CASA 'hut'	casa	casa	chez	casa	casă
*CUM-EDERE 'eat'	MANDUCARE 'chew'	mangiare	comer	manger	comer	a mânca
EQUU 'horse'	CABALLU 'pack horse'	cavallo	caballo	cheval	cavalo	cal

287

		Italian	Spanish	French	Portuguese	Romanian
FLERE 'weep'	PLANGERE 'wail'	piangere	plañir	....	....	a plânge
	PLORARE 'cry aloud'	....	llorar	pleurer	chorar	....
IGNE 'fire'	FOCU 'hearth'	fuoco	fuego	feu	fogo	foc
ORE 'mouth'	BUCCA 'cheek'	bocca	boca	bouche	boca	....
SCIRE 'know'	SAPERE 'be sensible'	sapere	saber	savoir	saber	a şti

The *Satyricon* of Petronius abounds in examples of lexical choice meant to portray popular speech. In the episode known as *Trimalchio's Dinner*, the characters give us a wine-fueled display of colloquial usage (§ 2.5.1). Among the words listed above we find: BELLUS (25, 42, 57), BUCCA (43, 44, 70), CABALLUS (117, 134), MANDUCARE (46, 55), and PLORARE (54, 71). In one passage the narrator vacillates between formal FLERE and casual PLORARE, evidently near-synonyms:

Haec ut dixit Trimalchio, **flere** coepit ubertim. **Flebat** et Fortunata, **flebat** et Habinnas, tota denique familia, tanquam in funus rogata, lamentatione triclinium implevit. Immo iam coeperam etiam ego **plorare**.

When Trimalchio said this, he began to cry profusely. Fortunata too was crying, Habinnas too was crying, and finally the whole household, as if invited to a funeral, filled the dining-room with sobs. Indeed, even I had begun to cry.

(Satyricon 72)

Sometimes the popular preferences have multiple motives: FARI 'talk' is archaic, deponent (§ 6.1.3), and too short. Romance prefers two other verbs derived from nouns meaning 'tale', FABULA (akin to FARI) and PARABOLA (from Greek):

Latin	Italian	Spanish	French	Portuguese	Romanian
FABULARE	...	hablar	...	falar	...
PARABOLARE	parlare	...	parler	...	...

Impending homonymy may have favored BĬBĔRE 'drink' over PŌTĀRE 'drink' (cf. PŬTĀRE 'deem, consider') and QUASI 'almost' over PAENE 'almost' (cf. PĒNE 'penis'). Some apparently random choices include:

Latin			Italian	Spanish	French	Portuguese	Romanian
AGRU	'field'	CAMPU	campo	campo	champ	campo	câmp
ALIU	'other'	ALTERU	altro	otro	autre	outro	alt
LŬDĔRE	'play'	IOCĀRE	giocare	jugar	jouer	jogar	a juca

Neither the military class nor the people they conquered had any contact with the Roman cultural elite. Words belonging to a high register (e.g. INQUIT 'says', NUPER 'recently', OLIM 'long ago, some day') may even have been unknown to those whose Latin was less than urbane.

11.2   Exploiting the derivational resources of Latin

Derivation is the readiest source of vocabulary. One simple step is to make a noun directly from a verb stem. Examples of these **deverbal nouns** include:

Latin			Italian	Spanish	French	Portuguese	Romanian
DUBĬTAT	(v.)		dubita	duda	doute	duvida	....
'doubts'	(n.)		....	duda	doute	dúvida	....
PERDŌNAT	(v.)		perdona	perdona	pardonne	perdoa	....
'forgives'	(n.)		perdono	perdón	pardon	perdão	....
(EX)-QUIRĪTAT	(v.)		grida	grita	crie	grita	strigă
'shouts'	(n.)		grido	grito	cri	grito	....
(EX)-VOLAT	(v.)		vola	vuela	vole	voa	zboară
'flies'	(n.)		volo	vuelo	vol	voo	zbor
*AD-BRACCHĬAT	(v.)		abbraccia	abraza	....	abraça	....
'embraces'	(n.)		abbraccio	abrazo	....	abraço	....
*(EX)-CAMBĬAT	(v.)		cambia	cambia	change	cambia	....
'(ex)changes'			scambia	....	échange	....	schimbă
	(n.)		cambio	cambio	change	cambio	....
			scambio	....	échange	....	schimb
*(IN)-CARRĬCAT	(v.)		carica	carga	charge	carrega	....
'load'			incarica	encarga	....	....	încarcă
	(n.)		carico	cargo	charge	cargo	....
			incarico	encargo	....	....	....

Vice versa, there are numerous **denominal verbs** created from nouns: SIGNU 'sign' > SIGNARE 'mark', PECTINE 'comb' > PECTINARE 'comb'. Already common in Latin, they continue to spring up in pre-Romance (PARABOLA 'speech' > PARABOLARE 'speak', PAUSA 'rest' > PAUSARE 'cease') and even today (Spanish *fusil* 'rifle' > *fusilar* 'shoot', French *zup* 'urban project' > *zupper* 'urbanize').

11.2.1   Verb-forming suffixes

Nearly all the favorite verb-forming suffixes feed into the favored first conjugation. The suffix -ICARE can make denominal verbs or simply lengthen existing verbs.

Latin		Italian	Spanish	French	Portuguese	Romanian
CABALLU 'horse'	CABALLICARE 'ride horseback'	cavalcare	cabalgar	chevaucher	cavalgar	....
(IN) CARRU '(in) cart'	(IN) CARRICARE 'load'	carricare	cargar	charger	carregar	a încărca
FOLLE 'bellows'	FOLLICARE 'breathe, rest'	....	holgar	....	folgar	....

PEDE 'foot'	IMPEDICARE 'impede'	....	....	empêcher	....	a împiedica
LINGERE 'lick'	LIGICARE 'lick'	leccare	....	lécher	....	....

From Greek *-izein* came the -IZ- of -IZARE, at a time when the borrowing of a derivational affix was unusual (§ 11.5.2). The variant spelling -IDIARE suggests that the letter <z>, freshly borrowed from Greek in Classical times, represented at that time a sound like [ʤ] (§ 4.3.3). Popular reflexes also point to [idʒare]:

Latin		Italian	Spanish	French	Portuguese	Romanian
UNDA 'wave'	*UNDIZARE	ondeggiare	ondear	ondoyer	ondear	....
VIRIDE 'green'	*VIRIDIZARE	verdeggiare	verdear	verdoyer	verdejar verdear	....
FLAMMA 'flame'	*FLAMMIZARE	fiammeggiare	flamear	flamboyer	chamejar chamear	....
LACRIMA 'tear'	*LACRIMIZARE	lacrimeggiare	lagrimear	larmoyer	lacrimejar	....
FESTA 'feast'	*FESTIZARE	festeggiare	festear (OSp)	festoyer	festejar	....

Spanish made *-ear* the default suffix for deriving denominal verbs: Italian *telefonare*, French *téléphoner*, Portuguese *telefonar*, Romanian *a telefona*, but Spanish *telefonear*, plus *flirtear* 'flirt', *jonronear* 'hit a home run', and many others. Reborrowed from Latin (§ 11.5.6), -IZARE supplies numerous *cultismos* all over Europe (e.g. Italian *organizzare*, Spanish *organizar*, French *organiser*, Portuguese *organizar*, Romanian *a organiza*) and is still fully productive.

11.2.2   Frequentatives

Latin has a mechanism for deriving **frequentative** or **iterative** verbs, meaning 'do something repeatedly'.

Infinitive		Perfect	Past participle	Frequentative
ADIŬVĀRE	'help'	ADIŪVIT	ADIŪTU	ADIŪTĀRE
NĀRE	'swim'	NĀVIT	*NATU	NATĀRE
ASPICĔRE	'look at'	ASPEXIT	ASPECTU	ASPECTĀRE
CANĔRE	'sing'	CECĬNIT	CANTU	CANTĀRE
IACĔRE	'throw'	IACŬIT	IACTU	IACTĀRE
PELLĔRE	'push'	PEPŬLIT	PULSU	PULSĀRE
SALĔRE	'jump'	SALŬIT	SALTU	SALTĀRE
STERNUĔRE	'sneeze'	STERNŬIT	*STERNUTU	STERNUTĀRE
VERTĔRE	'turn'	VERTIT	VERSU	VERSĀRE

AUDĒRE	'dare'	AUSU EST	AUSU	*AUSĀRE
OBLIVISCĪ	'forget'	OBLĪTU EST	OBLĪTU	*OBLĪTĀRE

Question: What is the formula for making a frequentative verb?

Answer: Take the past participle stem of the base verb and add -ĀRE.

Although frequentative forms existed in Latin, most had already lost their frequentative meaning. Being learner-friendly class I verbs whose paradigms are fully predictable, frequentatives often supplant the base verb.

Latin	Italian	Spanish	French	Portuguese	Romanian
ADIŪTĀRE	aiutare	ayudar	aider	ajudar	a ajuta
*AUSĀRE	osare	osar	oser	ousar	....
CANTĀRE	cantare	cantar	chanter	cantar	a cânta
IACTĀRE	gettare	echar	jeter	....	....
NATĀRE	....	nadar	....	nadar	....
*OBLĪTĀRE	....	olvidar	oublier	....	a uita
PULSĀRE	....	pujar	pousser	puxar	....
SALTĀRE	saltare	saltar	sauter	saltar	....
STERNUTĀRE	starnutire	estornudar	éternuer	esternudar (OPo)	a strănuta
VERSĀRE	versare	versar	verser	versar	a vărsa

Examples of such frequentatives occur in the *Satyricon* of Petronius: CANTARE (28, 31, 34, 36, 53, 64, 70, 74), NATARE (36, 72), STERNUTARE (98, 102).

A given base may have several derivatives. From FIGĔRE 'fasten' we have FIGICARE > Portuguese *ficar,* while the past participle FIXU gives a frequentative FIXARE > Italian *fissare,* Spanish *fijar.* From QUASSU, past participle of QUATĔRE 'shake,' come QUASSARE > French *casser* and QUASSICARE > Spanish *cascar* 'break'.[2]

11.2.3   Derivation with verb prefixes

Verbs derived with prefixes were already prominent in Latin word formation and continued to proliferate in Romance.

Latin	Popular Latin	Italian	Spanish	French	Portuguese	Romanian
CALĬDU 'hot'	*EX-CALD-ARE	scaldare	escaldar	échauder	escaldar	a scălda
LŎCU 'place'	*CON-LOC-ARE[3]	coricare	colgar	coucher	colgar	a culca
ODĬU 'hate'	*IN-ODI-ARE	....	enojar	ennuyer	anojar	....
RĪPA 'shore'	*AD-RIP-ARE	arrivare	arribar	arriver	arribar	....
SĬGNU 'mark'	*IN-SIGN-ARE	insegnare	enseñar	enseigner	ensinar	a însemna

COLLIGĔRE 'collect'	*AD-COLLIGĔRE	accogliere	acoger	accueillir	acolher	....
EDĔRE 'eat'	COM-EDĔRE[4]	....	comer	....	comer	....
INITIĀRE 'begin'	*COM-INITIĀRE	cominciare	comenzar	commencer	começar	....
TORNĀRE 'turn'	*RE-TORNĀRE	ritornare	retornar	retourner	retornar	....

Multiple prefixes can combine: from PLICARE 'fold' with the prefixes DE- and EX- comes Spanish *desplegar* 'unfold'.

11.2.4   Noun-forming suffixes: old and new

Many noun-forming suffixes enrich the Romance lexicon. Here we mention a few.[5] Nouns in -MĔNTU, already numerous in Latin, may be either abstract or concrete:

Latin		Italian	Spanish	French	Portuguese	Romanian
IACĒRE	'lie'	giacimento	yacimiento	gisement	jazimento	zăcămînt
SENTĪRE	'feel'	sentimento	sentimiento	sentiment	sentimento	simţămînt
VESTĪRE	'wear'	vestimento	vestimiento	vêtement	vestimento	veşmînt

Nouns in -(I)TĀTE, always feminine, denote the abstract quality corresponding to the base word. French -*té* loses the final syllable by regular sound change, while Italian -*tà* is shortened from older Italian -*tade*, an apocope peculiar to this suffix. In a stark change of meaning, CIVĬTĀTE 'citizenship' (CIVE 'citizen') yields words for 'city' and even more concretely Romanian *cetate* 'castle'.

Latin	Italian	Spanish	French	Portuguese	Romanian
BON-(I)TĀTE[6]	bontà	bondad	bonté	bondade	bunătate
CIV-(I)TĀTE	città	ciudad	cité	cidade	cetate
FACIL-ITĀTE	facilità	facilidad	facilité	facilidade	facilitate
VAN-ITĀTE	vanità	vanidad	vanité	vaidade	vanitate

Nouns made of a past participle plus -IŌNE are a staple of the Romance (and modern European) lexicon. Originally abstract names of actions, they often became concrete in popular usage, as in these French examples:

BĬBĬTU	*BĬBĬTIŌNE	'drink'	boisson	'drink'
LĬGĀTU	LĬGĀTIŌNE	'binding'	liaison	'liaison'
MANSU	MANSIŌNE	'staying, abode'	maison	'house'
MESSU	MESSIŌNE	'reaping'	moisson	'harvest'
PĬSCĀTU	PĬSCĀTIŌNE	'fishing'	poisson	'fish'
PŌTU	PŌTIŌNE	'drink'	poison	'poison'
PRE(HE)NSU	PRE(HE)NSIŌNE	'seizing'	prison	'prison'
VENĀTU	VENĀTIŌNE	'hunting, game'	venaison	'venison'

Besides its old popular reflexes, -IŌNE has modern Latinate forms still highly productive in the Western Romance languages. These cognate sets show a mix of the two layers:

Latin		Italian	Spanish	French	Portuguese	Romanian
ORĀTU	ORĀTIŌNE 'praying'	orazione	oración	oraison	oração	oraţiune
PRAEDĀTU	PRAEDĀTIŌNE 'plundering'	predazione	predación	prédation	predação	prădăciune
RATU	RATIŌNE 'reckoning'	ragione	razón	raison	razão	raţiune

Nouns in -ŌRE, already plentiful in Latin, are built on verb stems. In one central group, the meaning relates to the extent or effect:

Latin		Italian	Spanish	French	Portuguese	Romanian
DŎLĔT	'aches'	dolore	dolor	douleur	dor	.....
FAVĔT	'supports'	favore	favor	faveur	favor	favoare
OLĔT	'smells'	odore	olor	odeur	odor	odoare
SŪDAT	'sweats'	sudore	sudor	sueur	suor	sudoare
VALĔT	'is well'	valore	valor	valeur	valor	valoare
VĪGĔT	'is strong'	vigore	vigor	vigueur	vigor	vigoare

Another -ŌRE attaches originally to past participles, and later to other bases, to make agentive nouns. These are highly productive today.

	Italian	Spanish	French	Portuguese	Romanian
'elevator'	ascensore	ascensor	ascenseur	ascensor	ascensor
'creator'	creatore	creador	créateur	criador	creator
'shepherd'	pastore	pastor	pasteur	pastor	păstor

The suffix -ĬTĬA has multiple outcomes in all five languages. The most regular are Italian -ezza, Spanish -eza, French -esse, Portuguese -eza, and Romanian -eaţă. In cultismos, its stressed [i] is a reminiscence of the Latin form: Italian -izia, Spanish -icia, French -ice, Portuguese -ícia, Romanian -iţie.

Italian	Spanish	French	Portuguese	Romanian
finezza	fineza	finesse	fineza	fineţe
franchezza	franqueza	franchise	franqueza	francheţe
tenerezza	terneza	tendresse	tenreza	tinereţe
verdezza	....	....	....	verdeaţă
avarizia	avaricia	avarice	avareza	avariţie
giustizia	justicia	justice	justiça	justiţie
malizia	malicia	malice	malícia	....

Popular Latin also created some new noun-forming suffixes, extracting them from word-final sequences comprising more than one morpheme. Romance -ALIA originates in words like ANIM-AL inflected for neuter plural: ANIM-AL-IA. Reinterpreted as a feminine singular (§ 8.5.2), it forms collective nouns often suggesting a disorderly medley (e.g. Italian *gentaglia* 'riffraff', Italian *ferraglia*, French *ferraille* 'scrap iron').

Popular Latin	Italian	Spanish[7]	French	Portuguese	Romanian
*CANALIA	canaglia	canalla	canaille	canalha	canalie
*FERRALIA	ferraglia	....	ferraille	....	....
*GENTALIA	gentaglia	gentualla	....	gentalha	....
*MURALIA	muraglia	muralla	muraille	muralha	....

The twin suffixes -ANTIA -ENTIA derive abstract nouns. Like -ALIA, they contain a congealed sequence of morphemes: -ANT- and -ENT- are markers of the present participle of verbs, while -IA marks their neuter plural, recast as a feminine singular in Romance:

Popular Latin	Italian	Spanish	French	Portuguese	Romanian
*DISTANTIA	distanza	distancia	distance	distância	distanţă
*SPERANTIA	speranza	esperanza	espérance	esperança	speranţă
*CREDENTIA	credenza	creencia	croyance	crença	credinţă
*PREFERENTIA	preferenza	preferencia	préférence	preferência	preferinţă

Another derivational formula for feminine nouns takes its shape from the Latin future participle, an adjective made of a past participle stem plus -ŪRU, as in TEXĔRE 'weave', TEXTU 'woven', TEXTŪRU 'going to weave' which determines a noun TEXTŪRA.

Popular Latin	Italian	Spanish	French	Portuguese	Romanian
ARMATURA	armatura	armadura	armure	armadura	armătură
CINCTURA	cintura	cintura	ceinture	cintura	centură
TORTURA	tortura	tortura	torture	tortura	tortură
VECTURA	vettura	....	voiture	....	....
*ADVENTURA	avventura	aventura	aventure	aventura	aventură
*FRICTURA	frittura	fritura	friture	fritura	friptură
*MESURA	misura	mesura	mesure	mesura	măsură

These nouns number in the hundreds in Italian and French. Some preserve dead participles, such as VECTURA above (VECTU from VEHĔRE 'convey'). Extracted from these nouns, -ŪRA became productive, spreading to other bases, primarily in Italian: *bravura* 'skill', *frescura* 'coolness', *pianura* 'plane', *premura* 'care', *verdura* 'vegetable'.

Be warned that the foregoing cognate sets are much tidier than is normal for this domain of data. The Romance languages are far from uniform in the way they make selections among the available bases and suffixes. For example, in Romance words for 'beverage', all derived, both the base (a form of BĬBĔRE 'drink') and the suffix vary:

Italian	bevanda	*BĬB-ANDA	(gerundive[8] 'something to drink')
Spanish	bebida	*BĬB-ĪTA	(feminine of Sp participle)
French	boisson	*BĬBIT-IŌNE	(Lat participle plus -IŌNE)
Portuguese	bebida	*BĬB-ĪTA	(feminine of Po participle)
Romanian	băutură	*BĬBUT-URA	(Ro participle plus -URA)

> Question: Which suffixes occur in these words for 'sweetness' (from DŬLCE 'sweet')? Give their Latin etymons: Italian *dolcezza*, Spanish *dulzura*, French *douceur*, Portuguese *douçura*, Romanian *dulceaţă*.
>
> Answer: -ITIA, -URA, -ORE, -URA, -ITIA.

11.2.5   Faded diminutive suffixes

Diminutive suffixes on nouns and adjectives convey the idea that the referent is small, cute, or loveable. Thriving in Popular Latin usage, these suffixes sometimes lose their meaning through overuse. For instance, AURE 'ear' is gradually supplanted by AURICULA 'ear', a faded diminutive. We find in Petronius SI FILIAM HABEREM, AURICULAS ILLI PRAECIDEREM 'if I had a daughter I'd cut her ears off' (*Satyricon* 67), in Cicero AURICULA INFIMA … MOLLIOREM 'limper than a lower ear [= earlobe]' (*Epistolae ad Quintum fratrem* 2, 13, 4), and in Catullus (67) UTPOTE QUAE MI SPERARET NEC LINGUAM ESSE NEC AURICULAM 'as if she imagined I had neither tongue nor ear'. Varro's description of the ideal herding dog confirms that AURICULA no longer means 'little ear': AURICULIS MAGNIS AC FLACCIS 'big, floppy ears' (*De agri cultura* 2, 9).

Latin			*Italian*	Spanish (OSp)	French (OFr)	*Portuguese*	*Romanian*
ACU	ACUCULA	'needle'	….	aguja	aiguille	agulha	….
APE	APICULA	'bee'	pecchia	abeja	abeille	abelha	….
AURE	AURICULA/U	'ear'	orecchio	oreja	oreille	orelha	ureche
GENU	GENUCULU	'knee'	ginocchio	(hinojo)	(genoil)	joelho	genunchi
OVE	OVICULA	'sheep'	….	oveja	ouaille	ovelha	….
PAR	PARICULU/A	'pair'	parecchio	pareja	pareil	parelha	….
PEDE	PEDUCULU	'louse'	pidocchio	piojo	pou	piolho	păduche
VERME	VERMICULU	'worm'	vermiglio	bermejo	vermeil	vermelho	….
VETU	VETULU	'old'	vecchio	viejo	vieil	velho	vechi

These pre-Romance words are just longer versions of the base word, not diminutives. So what accounts for their success? Three factors may be at work. First, short words can be too short. For APE 'bee', surviving only in Italian *ape* and Old French *ef*, lack of substance may have been a handicap. Second, suffixes can avert homonymic collision. For example, AVE 'bird' is replaced by AVICELLU in Italian *uccello* and French *oiseau*. Had AVE and APE both survived, both would have given Old French *ef.* Latin PEDE 'louse' and PEDE 'foot' are nearly exact homonyms, but PEDUCULU means only 'louse'. Likewise, SOLICULU yields French *soleil*, heading off a homonymic clash between SŌLE 'sun', SŌLU 'alone', and SŎLU 'ground'. The sun was no smaller in Gaul than elsewhere. Third, the diminutive suffixes have the welcome property of relocating the derived noun into the favored first and second declensions.

Many other diminutives existed in Latin and did fade in certain words (CEREBER, diminutive CEREBELLU > Italian *cervello*, French *cerveau* 'brain'), but also survive as suffixes with diminutive meaning (-ELLU, -ITTU, etc.) and have reflexes productive in modern Romance languages (Italian *-ello -etto*, French *-eau -ette*, etc.).

11.2.6   From adjectives to nouns

The Romance lexicon replaced many old nouns with derived adjectives recycled as nouns.[9]

Latin		*Italian*	*Spanish*	*French*	*Portuguese*	*Romanian*	
HIBERNU	'wintry'	inverno	invierno	hiver	inverno	iarnă	'winter'
DIURNU	'of the day'	giorno	....	jour	....	....	'day'
HOSPITĀLE	'hospitable'	ostello	hostal	hôtel	hotel	hotel	'ho(s)tel'
*VER-ĀNU	'summery'[10]	....	verano	....	verão	....	'summer'
LIXĪV(I)A	'made into lye'	lisciv(i)a	lejía	lessive	lixívia	leşie	'lye'

A successful new suffix, born from the fusion of two old ones, is -ATĬCU, which followed several paths in Romance. Originally it formed adjectives from nouns and meant 'pertaining to noun'. But many of these adjectives went on to become nouns. In French the suffix produces numerous new nouns in *-age* [aʒ],[11] later borrowed so widely that the other Romance languages ended up adopting noun-forming *-age* equivalents of their own. Italian *-aggio*, Romanian *-aj* come from French *-age* and cannot be directly from Latin -ATĬCU. Spanish *-aje* and Portuguese *-agem* come from Provençal or Catalan *-atge*.

Latin		*Italian*	*Spanish*	*French*	*Portuguese*	*Romanian*
COR	'heart'	coraggio	coraje	courage	coragem	curaj
FORMA	'mold'	formaggio	....	fromage	....	....
LINGŪA	'tongue'	linguaggio	lenguaje	langage	linguagem	limbaj
MISSU	'thing sent'	messaggio	mensaje	message	messagem	mesaj
VIA	'way'	viaggio	viaje	voyage	viagem	voiaj
VILLA	'village'	villaggio	villaje	village	....	....

The modern inventory of French nouns in *-age* (over a thousand and growing) falls into several main patterns. In the one exemplified below, the base is a verb and the output a noun denoting the activity or its result. Like -*age* nouns in general, these often spread to the other languages.

Latin		Italian	Spanish	French	Portuguese	Romanian
LAVĀRE	'wash'	lavaggio	lavaje	lavage	lavagem	....
*MASSĀRE	'knead'	massaggio	masaje	massage	massagem	masaj
*MONTĀRE	'assemble'	montaggio	montaje	montage	montagem	montaj

There are also direct (non-borrowed) reflexes of -ATĬCU in Spanish (-*ádego* in Portuguese). They often have technical meanings, such as the name of a social or legal status, office, or territory: *albaceazgo* 'executorship', *primazgo* 'cousinhood', *papazgo* 'papacy', *bailazgo* 'bailiwick'.[12]

11.2.7   From past participles to nouns

Many nouns derive directly from strong participles:

Latin						
Infinitive	Participle	Italian	Spanish	French	Portuguese	Romanian
COPERĪRE	COPERTU/A	coperto/a	cubierto/a	couvert/e	coberta	copertă
DICĔRE	DICTU	detto	dicho/a	....	dito	....
FACĔRE	FACTU/A	fatto	hecho/fecha	fait	feito	fapt/ă

Some nouns made from participles outlive the base verbs, which themselves died out.

Latin		Italian	Spanish	French	Portuguese	Romanian
DESĔRĔRE	DESĔRTU	deserto	desierto	désert	deserto	....
FLUĔRE	FLUXU	flusso	flujo	flux	fluxo	flux
SPONDĒRE	SPONSU	sposo	esposo	époux	esposo	....

Still other nouns from strong participles end up coexisting with a newly minted weak participle (§ 7.11):

Latin		Italian	Spanish	French	Portuguese	Romanian
SENTĪRE	SENSU	senso	senso	sens	senso	sens
		sentito	sentido	senti	sentido	simţit
HABĒRE	HABĬTU	abito	hábito	habit	hábito	....
		avuto	habido	eu	havido	avut
DEBĒRE	DEBĬTU/A	debito	deuda	dette	dívida/débito	....
		dovuto	debido	dû	devido	....
PERDĔRE	PERDĬTU/A	perdita	pérdida	perte	perda	....
		perduto	perdido	perdu	perdido	pierdut

VENDĔRE	VENDĬTU/A	vendita	venta	vente	venda	....
		venduto	vendido	vendu	vendido	vinzut

Weak participles too, whether old or new, can be redeployed as nouns, often meaning 'instance of action *x*':[13]

	Italian	*Spanish*	*French*	*Portuguese*
(Infinitive)	entrare	entrar	entrer	entrar
(Past participle)	entrato	entrado	entré	entrado
(Noun)	entrata	entrada	entrée	entrada
	andare	ir	aller	ir
	andato	ido	allé	ido
	andata	ida	allée	ida
	uscire	salir	sortir	sair
	uscito	salido	sorti	saído
	uscita	salida	sortie	saída
	mangiare	comer	manger	comer
	mangiato	comido	mangé	comido
	mangiata	comida	....	comida
	gelare	helar	geler	gear
	gelato	helado	gelé	geado
	gelata	helada	gelée	geada
	cadere	caer	choir	cair
	caduto	caído	chu	caído
	caduta	caída	chute	caída

As nouns like these proliferated, the reflexes of -ATA were reinterpreted as noun-forming suffixes sometimes meaning 'contents of x':

	Italian	*Spanish*	*French*	*Portuguese*	*Romanian*
'mouth'	bocca	boca	bouche	boca	gură
	boccata	bocada	bouchée	....	....
'spoon'	cucchiaio	cuchara	cuillère	colher	lingură
	cucchiaiata	cucharada	cuillèrée	colherada	....
'oven'	forno	horno	four	forno	cuptor
	fornata	hornada	fournée	fornada	....

In Italian, -*ata* thrives with further meanings: 'action typical of x' (e.g. *asino* 'ass', *asinata*, *cafone* 'boor', *cafonata*), 'blow inflicted with x' (e.g. *coltello* 'knife', *coltellata*, *gomito* 'elbow', *gomitata*), unit of action or duration (*mangiata* 'feast', *dormita* 'nap', *giornata* 'day'), and main component of (*grigliata* 'barbecue', *spaghettata* 'pasta party').

11.2.8   Adjective-forming suffixes: old and new

Noted here are a few of the more prominent Romance suffixes that derive adjectives from nouns. Already in Latin, -ANU was common. The variant -IANU comes from false segmentation of words where the yod belonged to the stem.

Latin		Italian	Spanish	French	Portuguese	Romanian
ROMANU	'Roman'	romano	romano	romain	romano	roman
HUMANU	'human'	umano	humano	humain	humano	uman
MEDIANU	'median'	mediano	mediano	moyen	mediano	median
CHRISTIANU	'Christian'	cristiano	cristiano	chrétien	cristiano	cristian

Similarly, -OSU acquired a variant -IOSU. The yod in GRATIOSU was in the base GRATIA, but in CURIOSU (from CURA) it reflects the newer suffix:

Latin		Italian	Spanish	French	Portuguese	Romanian
*CORATICOSU	'brave'	coraggioso	corajoso	courageux	corajoso	curajos
SPINOSU	'thorny'	spinoso	espinoso	épineux	espinhoso	spinos
GRATIOSU	'graceful'	grazioso	gracioso	gracieux	gracioso	graţios
CURIOSU	'curious'	curioso	curioso	curieux	curioso	curios

Popular Latin *-ĒSE (< -ENSE) derives ethnonyms and some other demographic terms:

	Italian	Spanish	French	Portuguese	Romanian
'of town'	borghese	burgués	bourgeois	burguês	burghez
'of court'	cortese	cortés	courtois	cortês	....
'Danish'	danese	danés	danois	danimarquês	danez
'Irish'	irlandese	irlandés	irlandais	irlandês	irlandez
'Polish'	polonese	polonés (OSp)	polonais	polonês (OPo)	polonez
'French'	francese	francés	français	francês	francez

This suffix is one of the contexts where French exhibits two outcomes from high mid /e/ in a free syllable. We saw its long development from /e/ to /we/ and finally /wa/ (§ 1.2.4). At the /we/ stage in the 1200s, a social variant /ɛ/ became available. In the 1500s, the court usage /ɛ/ acquired favor and was assigned prescriptively to imperfect and conditional endings (§ 7.4.3, and note 12) and also, randomly, to certain other words.[14] Among the reflexes of *-ĒSE, some were put in the /ɛ/ set and others went on to /wa/.

The suffix -ĬSCU, of disputed and possibly multiple origins,[15] seems to have spread from Italian during the Renaissance. The <s> in French -*esque* marks it as a relatively late arrival. Compare *évêque* < EPĬSCŎPUS 'bishop', with the usual loss of preconsonantal <s> (§ 2.1.1). Romanian gets -*esc* later from French, but the more conservative -*escu* was already frequent in family names.

Italian	Spanish	French	Portuguese	Romanian
burlesco	burlesco	burlesque	burlesco	burlesc
carnevalesco	carnavalesco	carnavalesque	carnavalesco	carnavalesc
grottesco	grotesco	grotesque	grotesco	grotesc
romanesco	romanesco	romanesque	romanesco	romanesc

Of course, we have mentioned only a few of the derivational affixes, easily over a hundred, which continue to thrive in the Romance lexicon.

11.2.9   Adverbs from adjectives

Adverbs in Latin were formed from adjective stems with suffixes -Ē for second and first declension and -ĬTER for third declension: MAGNĒ 'greatly', VELOCĬTER 'rapidly'. This system leaves scarcely a trace today.[16] Instead, Western Romance makes its adverbs with a suffix from the noun MENTE 'mind'. Latin has an **ablative absolute** – a verbless phrase in the ablative case – which expresses attendant circumstance: PRIMA LUCE 'at dawn'. From phrases like SERENA MENTE 'with a serene mind', the noun MENTE was reanalysed as a suffix for forming adverbs from adjectives – a good example of **grammaticalization**. The phrases from which the new adverbs originated had the adjectives in their feminine form because MENTE was a feminine noun. This feature has persisted.[17]

	'slow'	'slowly'	'strong'	'strongly'
Italian	lento	lentamente	forte	fortemente
Spanish	lento	lentamente	fuerte	fuertemente
French	lent	lentement	fort	fortement
Portuguese	lento	lentamente	forte	fortemente

In Romanian, uninflected adjectives serve as adverbs: *copiii joacă tare* 'the children play loud(ly)'. Adjectives in -*esc* form adverbs in -*eşte*: *prostesc* 'foolish', *prosteşte* 'foolishly' (by the Fish Rule, § 10.3.5).

11.3   Cycles of added and lost meaning

Words and morphemes can wear out the same way shoes do. The more AURICULA is used instead of AURE to mean 'ear', the more its diminutive value wears away (recall the dog with AURICULIS MAGNIS AC FLACCIS 'big, floppy ears'). Pre-Romance speech adopted many other nouns in -ICŬLU and -UCŬLU (§ 4.3.8), and in time the suffix lost not only its diminutive meaning, but even the status of a morpheme. Yet new diminutives can still be created: Italian *orecchie* 'ears' < AURICULAE produces, with a fresh diminutive suffix, *orecchiette* 'little ears' (a type of pasta).

In the same way, Latin SUĚRE 'sew, sew together' had a compound CONSUĚRE which overtly adds the meaning 'together'. With regular sound changes CONSUĚRE becomes Popular Latin *COSERE in which the morpheme boundary blurs and the verb means simply 'sew', e.g. Spanish *coser*. So a second-century Roman soldier can write: INVOLUCRUM CONCOSUTUM 'a package sewn together' (Pighi 1964). He feels the need for a copy of the prefix to restore the meaning of the faded original. Again, older Latin MECUM 'with me', TECUM 'with you', vestiges of archaic word order, survive in Spanish as *conmigo*, *contigo*. A new copy of CUM 'with' was added as a preposition: *CUM-MECUM *conmigo*.

11.3.1   Demonstrative adjectives

Emphasis is such a common trait of colloquial style that what was emphatic becomes normal, a typical form of semantic bleaching. Instead of FLĒRE 'weep', the stronger words PLANGĚRE and PLORĀRE gained favor, but their success cost them their emphatic quality as they became the normal words for 'weep'. Demonstratives in Latin and Romance tell a story of semantic bleaching, and a tendency to restore the attenuated meaning by a reinforcing word.

Latin had a four-way system of demonstratives – IS, HIC, ISTE, ILLE – but by Classical times IS EA ID, which lacked any **proximal** versus **distal** value, were being used mainly as third person pronouns. This left a three-way system: HIC HUNC 'this (one)', ISTE ISTU 'that (by you)', ILLE ILLU 'that (over there)'. But already in pre-Romance, HIC lost its place in the demonstrative system, surviving vestigially in scattered lexical items[18] but leaving a gap in the system (middle column below).

Deictic value				Latin	Loss of HIC	Pre-Romance
proximal	(1st p.)	'this'		HIC		ISTE/U
distal	(2nd p.)	'that'		ISTE/U	ISTE/U	
distal	(3rd p.)	'that'		ILLE/U	ILLE/U	ILLE/U

All five languages replace the lost HIC by broadening ISTE/U 'that (2nd p.)' to cover 'this' (1st p.), which in turn leaves no explicitly 2nd person form.

To fill this gap (last column) Italian creates a hybrid form of ISTU, *TIBI ISTU 'that to you'. Ibero-Romance recruits another demonstrative, IPSE, originally meaning 'the very (one)'. Finally, French and Romanian neutralize the contrast between the second and third person distal demonstratives, making ILLE/U cover both senses of 'that' (second chart below).

In the colloquial style of the Latin dramatists, forms of ISTE and ILLE often combine with the prefixed emphatic words ECCE 'look, behold' or AC, ATQUE 'and even, and especially' (Grandgent 1907:35). Meanwhile, forms of ILLE were becoming third person pronouns (§ 8.8) and definite articles (§ 8.9). This same reinforcing prefix ECCE was available to ILLE as it became a personal pronoun:[19]

	Demonstrative	Personal pronoun
simple form	ILLE	ILLE
reinforced form	ECCILLE	ECCILLE

Ultimately, the reinforced forms are specialized as demonstratives while the simple forms yield personal pronouns (and definite articles, § 8.9). The basic demonstrative adjectives are:

		Italian	Spanish	Old French	Portuguese	Romanian
proximal	'this'	questo	este	cist	este	acest/ăst
distal 2nd	'that'	codesto	ese	cil	esse	acel
distal 3rd	'that'	quello	aquel	cil	aquele	acel

Of these forms, only Spanish *este, ese* and Portuguese *este, esse* come directly from Latin demonstratives without reinforcement. Another conservative trait of Ibero-Romance: it keeps the original masculine singular ending of the Latin pronominal declension (§ 8.8.2): ISTE *este, este* and IPSE *ese, esse*. Spanish *esto, eso, aquello* and Portuguese *isto, isso, aquilo* (as pronouns) are only for inanimates.

Among the reinforced Romance forms, the reinforcing word could be ECCU(M),[20] ECCE, AC or ATQUE:

ECCU ISTU	>	It	questo	[kwesto]
ECCU *TIBI ISTU	>	It	codesto	[kodesto]
ECCU ILLU	>	It	quello	[kwel:o]
ECCE ISTU > ECCISTU	>	OFr	cest	[tsɛst]
ECCE ILLU > ECCILLU	>	OFr	cel	[tsɛl]
ATQUE ISTU	>	Ro	acest/ăst	[atʃɛst] / [əst]
ATQUE ILLU	>	Sp	aquel	[akɛl]
	>	Po	aquele	[akeli]
	>	Ro	acel	[atʃɛl]

The bipartite demonstrative system of Old French, contrasting proximal 'this' with a single distal 'that', collapses on the way to Modern French. Today *ce livre, cette maison* mean 'this/that book', 'this/that house'. The older distal forms survive as demonstrative pronouns (*celui, celle*, etc.). Continuing the cycle of reinforcement, these have acquired suffixes, *ci* 'here' and *là* 'there', that restore the proximal/distal contrast – *ce livre-ci* 'this book', *ce livre-là* 'that book', *celui-ci* 'this one', *celui-là* 'that one' – although *là* as a free morpheme has no distal feature (*viens là* 'come here', Smith 1995). Modern colloquial Italian tends to reinforce the proximal/distal contrast – *questo qui* 'this (here)', *quello lì* 'that (there)' – even though the base demonstratives still convey the contrast. Again, emphasis is tending to become the norm.

11.3.2 Negatives

Two trends in the history of negation reflect the colloquial urge to make the message more forceful. One is the *not … never* type, the so-called double negative. The other is the *not … a bit* type, where a word denoting a small unit serves to underscore the negation.

Prescriptive Latin grammar shares with English the unusual property of using one, and only one, negative word to negate a clause:

NUMQUAM OTIUM HABEMUS   NON OTIUM UMQUAM HABEMUS

'We **never** have free time'   'We do **not** ever have free time'

Teachers warn us that two negatives make an affirmative, or, as the Classical grammarians would say: *duplex negatio, affirmatio*. However that may be in English, it is true in Latin:

NON NUMQUAM OTIUM HABEMUS

'We sometimes have free time'

Meanwhile a different principle, more common in the world's languages, prevailed in Popular Latin: multiple negative words, the *not…never* type, add up to one negation:

NON OTIUM **NUMQUAM** HABEMUS

'We **never** have free time'

This pattern is attested amply in our popular sources (Plautus, Petronius, inscriptions)[21] and occasionally throughout Classical times, even in Cicero:

DEBEBAT…NUMMUM NULLUM NEMINI
he owed…a cent [acc.] none [acc.] nobody [dat.]
'He didn't owe a cent to anybody'

(*Actio in Verrem* 3, 60)

Apart from French, which lost nearly all the Latin negative words, the other languages have reflexes of Latin *not…never* type expressions: Italian *non vedo nulla* 'I see nothing', Spanish *no tenemos nunca tiempo* 'we never have time', Portuguese *não come nunca presunto verde* 'he never eats green ham', Romanian *nu văd pe nimeni* 'I see nobody'. Popular Latin also added some words to the *not…never* type by prefixing the negative NE/NEC to an otherwise positive term:[22]

NE-IPSU UNU	It	nessuno	'not any / nobody'
NE-ENTE	It	niente	'nothing'
NEC-UNU	Sp	ningún	'not any'
NE-QUEM	Po	nenhum	'not any / nobody'
	Po	ninguém	'nobody'
NE-MICA	Ro	nimic	'nothing'

But many Romance negative words arise from the *not…a bit* type, already known to Latin and thriving in popular speech:

NULLAQUE **MICA** SALIS NEC AMARI FELLIS…**GUTTA**
'and not a crumb of salt nor a drop of bitter bile'

(Martial 7, 25, 3)

The word meaning something of negligible size or value was at first restricted to contexts where it made sense in its literal meaning. But in time a few such words became fixed collocations and started down the path to grammaticalization:

GUTTA	'drop'	NON…GUTTA	Fr ne…goutte	'not'
MICA	'crumb'	NON…MICA	It non…mica	'not'
			Fr ne…mie	'not'
PASSU	'step'	NON…PASSU	Fr ne…pas	'not'
PUNCTU	'point'	NON…PUNCTU	Fr ne…point	'not'
REM	'thing'	NON…REM	Fr ne…rien	'nothing'
(REM) NATA	'born thing'	NON…NATA	Sp no…nada	'nothing'[23]
			Po não…nada	'nothing'
PERSONA	'person'	NON…PERSONA	Fr ne…personne	'nobody'

In the modern languages except French, 'not' is typically rendered by a single preverbal negator from Latin NON: Italian *non*, Spanish *no*, Portuguese *não*, Romanian *nu*. In Old French too, preverbal *non*, *nen*, *ne* can suffice to mean 'not', but by late Middle French the two-piece expressions have become almost mandatory, and today they are the prescriptive norm.

Once these two-piece negations become fully grammaticalized, the second element becomes a negative in its own right, a **negative polarity item**, and can even form short answers, e.g. French *pas moi* 'not me'. In current French the original negator, now redundant, is increasingly deleted as the negative polarity item assumes the role of negator:[24] *ne bouge pas!* 'don't move!' → *bouge pas!* 'don't move!' By eliminating its redundant *ne*, French is reverting to the original Latin pattern where a single negative word suffices, albeit with a drastically renewed inventory of negative words.

11.4   Reanalysis: how the mind remakes words

Our minds are forever busy identifying morphemes and manipulating them in rule-governed ways. Occasionally our analysis is wrong – unwittingly novel – and this can lead to lexical innovations. Here we survey five types of reanalysis that affected the Romance lexicon.

11.4.1   Resegmentation with articles

Given French *oiseau* [wazo] 'bird' and *les oiseaux* [lezwazo] 'the birds' with a [z] from liaison, why do French toddlers say *un zoiseau* [ẽzwazo]? They think the [z] is part of the noun. The same process, with **hypocoristic** reduplication of the first syllable, creates French *nounours* 'teddy bear' << *nours* << *un ours* [ẽnuʀs].

Question: How did Modern French *lierre* 'ivy' acquire its initial /l/?

Latin	Italian	Spanish	Old French	French	Portuguese	Romanian
ĔDĔRA 'ivy'	edera	hiedra	iere	lierre	hera	iederă

Answer: Old French *l'iere* 'the ivy' was reanalysed as one word, 'ivy'.

Resegmentation can also shorten a noun, as in LATERALES 'lateral' > Spanish *adrales* 'hurdles' and ABBATESSA > Italian *badessa* 'abbess', where segments are reassigned to the definite article.

Resegmentation can result in nouns having initial [l] in some languages and initial [n] in others, as happens with *LIBELLU 'carpenter's level':

Latin		Italian	Spanish	French	Portuguese	Romanian
*LIBELLU	'level'	livello	nivel	niveau	nivel	nivel[25]

In Spanish, French, and Portuguese this [l]-initial form was reanalysed as vowel-initial and then acquired [n] from the indefinite article. By a reverse process, UNICORNE 'unicorn', resegmented as *(UN) ICORNE, gave Old French *icorne* 'unicorn' >> *l'icorne* 'the unicorn' >> *licorne* 'unicorn'.

PRACTICE

Which of these words have undergone resegmentation? In what context?

Latin		Italian	Spanish	French	Portuguese	Romanian
VĔSPA	'wasp'	vespa	avispa	guêpe	vespa	viespe
APOTHĒCA	'store(room)'	bottega	bodega	boutique	bodega	....

11.4.2 Resegmentation with affixes

When a word looks as if it could contain a prefix or suffix, speakers may decide that it does. In *CAULU 'cabbage', the diphthong reduces in French *chou*, but an analysis *CA-ULU, with a diminutive, fosters the treatment Italian *cavolo*, which keeps the pseudo-suffix intact. Again, the metathesis MEDULLA 'marrow' > *MUDELLA helps the word look suffixed, hence French *moelle*.

11.4.3 Back formation

Typically, derivation works in one direction: from a base or simplex form comes a more complex derived form. Backwards derivation or back formation occurs when speakers take a certain form to be derived and create a corresponding simplex form, as when French extracts new singulars like *cheveu* 'hair' and *genou* 'knee' from plurals (§ 4.3.8). Old Spanish *tiempos* < TĔMPUS 'time' became modern *tiempo* via the same process (Lloyd 1987:65). Romanian, among its many borrowings from French (§ 11.5.6), adopts *chauffeur* 'driver', as *şofer*, and creates a corresponding base verb, *a şofa* 'drive'.

11.4.4   Blends

The practice of deliberately blending words to stand for a blended meaning – *brunch* (1898), *smog* (1905), *guesstimate* (1936) – is recent, quite alien to pre-modern European cultures. But Romance speakers did create inadvertent blends (**hybrids** or **contaminations**) where one word analogizes to another with no apparent intent to alter the meaning. Spanish *estrella*, Portuguese *estrela* 'star' probably blended ASTRU 'star' with STELLA (Italian *stella*, French *étoile*, Romanian *stea*). The paired antonyms GRAVE, LĔVE 'heavy, light' motivate *GRĔVE > French *grief* 'grievance' and Romanian *greu* 'difficult'. In Old Spanish, *algun* 'someone' < ALIQUIS UNUS and *nado* 'nobody' < (HOMINE) NATU gave way to newer *alguien* and *nadien* to match *quien* < QUEM (Penny 2002:147). Groups of verbs may cluster into a club (§ 6.10.2): already in pre-Romance, REDDERE 'give back' becomes *RENDERE to join the set *PRENDERE, TENDERE, etc. A more colorful example: Italian *zampogna* [ʦampoɲːa] 'bagpipe' blends Greco-Latin SYMPHŌNĬA 'harmony' (a kind of instrument in Late Latin) with *zampa* 'paw, leg of an animal' because the bag of the bagpipe is traditionally made of leather with the hair still on. This example skirts the boundary of our next topic, folk etymology.

11.4.5   Folk etymology

French *girouette* is the product of **folk etymology**, a type of reanalysis that imposes on the words a more transparent structure with recognizable parts. From Norse *veðr-viti* 'wind indicator', Anglo-Norman has *wirewite* 'weathervane' (eleventh century), which, being opaque, was reanalysed in French as *gyrouette* since it spins (*girer*) like a little wheel (*rouette*).[26] Italian *Campidoglio*, the name of a hill in Rome, derives from its ancient name CAPITŌLĬUM. Why the /m/? Faced with a long word with no discernible parts, speakers made it into *Campi d'oglio* 'fields of *oglio*', where the last element remains opaque but could be a proper name. Visualize the site overgrown with grass, as it was in the Middle Ages, and *campi* makes sense. From VĔRŬCŬLU 'little rod', Old Spanish and Old Portuguese have respectively *berrojo*, *verrolho* 'bolt'. Later both were folk etymologized in different ways: Spanish *cerrojo*, because a bolt serves to *cerrar* 'close', and Portuguese *ferrolho*, because it is made of *ferro* 'iron'. And why does German *Sauerkraut* end up in French not as *surcrute*, as it was in Swiss French (1699), but as *choucroute*? Because the French word for 'cabbage' is *chou*.

11.5   Loan words

The Romance lexicon undergoes renewal not only from within, but also from contact with other languages – those which the Romans encountered during their expansion (**substratum** languages), and those which entered the Latin-speaking territories later (**superstratum** languages).

In the lands where Latin took root, the pre-existing languages have generally left scanty remains. Some are known only by their names. Oscan[27] and Umbrian, closely related to Latin in the Italic family, are known from inscriptions, but their contribution to Latin is small, despite centuries of contact. More consequential as a source of borrowing is the Celtic speech of Gaul, Spain, and Northern Italy.

11.5.1   Celtic

The words from Celtic that enjoy the widest diffusion are those that entered Latin early and rode the waves of expansion. These words typically have a concrete meaning belonging to the sphere of everyday life:

Celtic > Latin		Italian	Spanish	French	Portuguese	Romanian
ALAUDA	'lark'	allodola	aloa (OSp)	alouette	....	....
BRACAE	'trousers'	brache	bragas	braies	bragas	brace
CAMISIA	'shirt'	camicia	camisa	chemise	camisa	cămaşă
CARRU	'cart'	carro	carro	char	carro	car
CAMMINU	'road'	cammino	camino	chemin	caminho	....
CAMBIARE	'change'	cambiare	cambiar	changer	cambiar	....
CEREVISIA	'beer'	cervogia (OIt)	cerveza	cervoise (OFr)	cerveja	....

Trousers and shirts were markedly Celtic and quite foreign to Roman culture.

11.5.2   Greek

The Latin lexicon teems with loan words from Greek attesting to the enduring and evolving bond between the Greek and Roman cultures. Many of these words were ephemeral, such as the comical Greek-tinged locutions in the early Latin dramatists. The Greek loans introduced in imperial times by medical and other technical writers belonged to the jargons of specialized minorities and were mostly destined to an early demise. Yet many Greek loans do survive in Romance:

Greek > Latin		Italian	Spanish	French	Portuguese	Romanian
CHORDA	'string'	corda	cuerda	corde	corda	coardă
CRYPTA	'hidden place'	grotta	gruta	grotte	gruta	criptă
PETRA	'stone'	pietra	piedra	pierre	pedra	piatră
SACCU	'sack'	sacco	saco	sac	saco	sac
SCHOLA	'school'	scuola	escuela	école	escola	şcoală
THESAURU	'stash'	tesoro	tesoro	trésor	tesouro	tezaur
THRONU	'throne'	trono	trono	trône	trono	tron
TYMBA	'tomb'	tomba	tumba	tombe	tumba	....

In Classical times, the Roman alphabet even added the Greek letters *upsilon* (ʏ) and *zeta* (z). These might either stand for the authentic Greek sound in loan words, or at least show off a writer's awareness of the Greek origin of those words.[28] The letter <ʏ> represented a high front round vowel [y] as in French *lune* 'moon'. Popular Latin speech Romanized it in two ways, either front ĭ as in *GĬPSU or round ŭ as in *BŬRSA.

Latin		Italian	Spanish	French	Portuguese	Romanian
GYPSU	'plaster'	gesso	yeso	gypse	giz	ghips
BYRSA	'purse'	borsa	bolsa	bourse	bolsa	bursă

Greek *zeta* entering the Latin alphabet was at first Romanized as <ss>: μάζα > MASSA 'dough, mass' > Italian *massa*, Spanish *masa*, French *masse*, Portuguese *massa*, Romanian *masă*. Once <z> is in use, it affords no graphic clue to how Popular Latin speech was really dealing with *zeta* words. But in a later period the phonetic reality is again uncloaked: from as early as 200 CE, we find <z> standing for a new sound, the palatalizing [dj] on its way to [dʒ]. We find such spellings as OZE for HODIE 'today' (> Italian *oggi*) and ZABULUS for DIABOLUS 'devil', among many other examples (Sturtevant 1940:176).

The new terminology of Christianity brought a wave of Greek borrowings. Christian writers, and crucially Bible translators, tended to leave the Greek terms untranslated. They were reluctant, it seems, to distort the scriptural term by seeking a Latin equivalent that might be inexact or might have mundane connotations.

Greek > Latin		(O)Italian	Spanish	French	Portuguese	Romanian
ANGĔLU	'messenger'	angelo	angel	ange	anjo	înger
DIABŎLU	'slanderer'	diavolo	diablo	diable	diabo	....
ECCLĒSĬA	'assembly'	chiesa	iglesia	église	igreja	....[29]
ELEEMOSYNA	'alms'	(limosina)	limosna	aumône	esmola	....
EPĬSCŎPU	'overseer'	vescovo	obispo	évêque	bispo	episcop
EVANGĔLĬU	'good news'	vangelo	evangelio	évangile	evangelho	evanghelie
PRESBYTER	'elder'	prete	....	prêtre	....	....

The verb-forming affix -IZ-, notable for its perennial productivity, comes from Greek (§ 11.2.1). The verbs that brought it abound in Christian writings: SI OCULUS TUUS DEXTER SCANDALIZAT TE 'if thy right eye offend thee' (Matthew 5:29). Spellings like BAPTIDIARE for BAPTIZARE reflect a popular pronunciation [dʒ] rather than [z].

11.5.3   Germanic

Roman contact with Germanic peoples began along the northern frontier of the Empire long before they entered Roman lands in any significant numbers. Some were recruited into the Roman legions, bringing their military terms. The first true Germanic migration into the Empire came in 376 CE, when the Goths, seeking protection from the Huns advancing from the east, asked and received permission to cross the Danube and settle inside the Empire. Soon, alleging maltreatment at the hands of Roman officials, the Visigoths (western Goths) began a period of wandering westward and southward, culminating in their famous sack of Rome itself in 410 CE. Thereafter, they gradually made their way into Gaul and finally Spain, where they established a kingdom supplanting Roman rule. The traditional date when the Roman Empire ended, 476 CE, did not mark any cataclysmic event. It was then that Odovacar, head of the Roman military and himself of Germanic descent, deposed the emperor and took over. He in turn was defeated and replaced by the Ostrogoths (eastern Goths) under King Theodoric, who founded a kingdom comprising all of Italy. Meanwhile, other Germanic tribes too had streamed into the moribund Empire. Those that crossed the Rhine frontier included the Swabians, Alans, and Vandals, who ended up establishing kingdoms in Spain and Africa, and later the Burgundians, Alamans, and Bavarians.

Of all the Germanic invaders, the most successful in the long run were the Franks. Under the Merovingian kings they spread southward through Gaul, drove the Visigoths into Spain and later effaced the Burgundians. The Frankish king Clovis converted to Christianity about 496, which led to a lasting alliance between the Franks and the Pope. Their religious affiliation fostered their integration with the Roman population of Gaul and worked to their advantage during the ensuing Carolingian dynasty (§ 12.1.1). The Langobards, or Lombards, latecomers to Italy in 568, settled mainly in the Po valley, and they too fell victim to Frankish expansion.

Borrowings from Gothic include:

		Italian	Spanish	French	Portuguese	Romanian	
werra	'war'	guerra	guerra	guerre	guerra	....	
lofa	'palm'	....	luva (OSp)	....	luva	....	'glove'
gans	'goose'	....	ganso	....	ganso	....	
sakan	'claim'	....	sacar	....	sacar	....	'obtain'

Gothic *hleba* 'bread' (cf. English *loaf*) figures in a derivative *gah-hleba* 'one who shares bread', source of the Latin loan translation COMPANIO, COMPANIONE 'comrade' > Italian *compagno*, Spanish *compañero*, French *compagnon*, Portuguese *companheiro*.

Frankish words in Western Romance attest to several centuries of contact with incipient Romance languages, especially French:

		Italian	Spanish	French	Portuguese	Romanian
balla	'ball'	balla	bala	balle	bala	....
blank	'white'	bianco	blanco	blanc	branco	....
busk	'woods'	bosco	bosque	bois	bosque	....
gardo	'yard'	giardino	jardín	jart (OFr), jardin	jardim	....
hanka	'hip'	anca	....	hanche	anca	....

want	'glove'	guanto	guante	gant	....	....
thwahlja	'towel'	tovaglia	toalla	touaille (OFr)	toalha	....

Italian also has a number of loan words from Langobardic:

palla[30]	'ball'	palla
wankja	'cheek'	guancia
skinko	'shin'	stinco
skerzan	'joke'	scherzare
straufinon	'polish'	strofinare
bauzzan	'knock'	bussare

11.5.4   Arabic

Less than a century after the death of the prophet Mohammed (632 CE), the Arabs appear on the European scene, crossing the Straits of Gibraltar from Africa into Spain (711) and dispatching the Visigothic kingdom. They gradually advanced north and crossed the Pyrenees into southern France, where they were turned back by the Franks (732) under Charles Martel, founder of the Carolingian dynasty. Arab rule in the Iberian Peninsula lasted over 500 years and left hundreds of loan words, mainly in Spanish:

Arabic		*Spanish*		*Portuguese*	
al kaadii	'the judge'	alcalde	'mayor'	....	
al kasr	'the fortress'	alcázar	'fortress'	alcácer	
al beitar	'the veterinarian'	albéitar	'farrier'	alveitar	
al humra	'the rug'	alhombra (OSp)	'rug'	....	
al banni	'the builder'	albañil	'mason'	alvanel	
ar ruzz	'the rice'	arroz	'rice'	arroz	
az zayt	'the olive'	aceite	'oil'	azeite	

During these centuries of cultural and material prosperity, Arabic words spread far afield, especially names of commodities and other terms figuring in medieval commerce:[31]

		Italian	*Spanish*	*French*	*Portuguese*
as sukkar	'the sugar'	zucchero	azúcar	sucre	açúcar
al birquq	'the apricot'	albicocca	albaricoque	abricot	albricoque
al qutn	'the cotton'	cotone	algodón	coton	algodão
al karshuuf	'the artichoke'	carciofo	alcachofa	artichaut	alcachofra
an naranj	'the orange'	arancia	naranja	orange	laranja

11.5.5   Slavic

The emperor Trajan's conquest of Dacia was a bold undertaking because Dacia, located north of the Danube, lay outside the natural frontiers of the Empire. This distant eastern province, where today Romanian is spoken, was the last conquered (104–106 CE) and the first abandoned (271 CE). By the mid-600s, Dacia and the rest of the Balkan Peninsula had been colonized by Slavs, and the surviving Romans were assimilated. Their language lived on but remains unattested until 1521 (§ 12.2.5). In medieval times the language of religion and culture was Old Church Slavonic, a source of many loan words:

OCS			Romanian	
popŭ	'priest'		pop	
svętŭ	'holy'		sfînt	
bogatŭ	'rich'		bogat	
sluga	'servant'		slug	
ljubiti	'love'		a iubi	
dragŭ	'dear'		drag	
slabŭ	'weak'		slab	
razboi	'violence'		război	'war'

In addition, Romanian has borrowings from such neighboring Slavic languages as Bulgarian and Serbo-Croatian:

Bulgarian	gradina	'garden'	grădină	
	bolnav	'sick'	bolnav	
Serbo-Croatian	briti	'shave'	briciu	'razor'

The Slavic negative prefix ne- 'un-', as in Old Church Slavonic sŭdravŭ 'healthy', nesŭdravŭ 'unhealthy', became hugely productive in Romanian: neclar 'unclear', nebun 'insane', nevăzut 'unseen', neîntors 'unturned', nebătut 'undefeated', etc.

Also taken from Slavic is the Romanian pattern for forming numbers over ten:

			Italian	Spanish	French	Portuguese	Romanian
Latin	UNDECIM	'eleven'	undici	once	onze	onze	….
OCS	jedin na desęte	'one on ten'	….	….	….	….	unsprezece
Latin	VIGINTI	'twenty'	venti	veinte	vingt	vinte	….
OCS	dŭva desęti	'two tens'	….	….	….	….	douăzeci

Old Church Slavonic supplies the model for Romanian unsprezece (< UNU SUPRA DECEM) and Romanian douăzeci where zece (< DECEM) is pluralized as a noun.

11.5.6 Romance cross-borrowing and reborrowing from Latin

For all their divergence, the Romance languages have nonetheless developed over the centuries an increasingly shared lexicon via the diffusion of loan words among them.

In the Middle Ages, French and Provençal enjoyed immense prestige as vehicles for the spread of courtly poetry and the newly formed tradition of epic poetry (chansons de geste), carried to Italy by the troubadours. Some early loans into Italian are: (Old Italian) *clero* 'light' (< French *clair* [klɛʀ], native Italian *chiaro* < CLARU), *forgia* 'forge' (< French *forge* 'smithy', native Italian *fabbrica* < FABRICA), *roccia* 'boulder' (< French *roche*, native Italian *rocca* < *rukka*). Loans into Spanish include *flecha* 'arrow' (< French *flèche*), *frambuesa* 'raspberry' (< French *framboise*), *español* 'Spanish' (< French *espagnol*, Old Spanish *español*).

The Italian Renaissance of the 1400s and 1500s launched a flow of Italian loan words into much of Western Europe – words referring to the visual arts, music, literature, food, and commerce. Among the hundreds of examples are: *chiaroscuro* (Spanish *claroscuro*, French *clair-obscur*, Portuguese *claro-escuro*), *balcone* 'balcony' (Spanish *balcón*, French *balcon*, Portuguese *balcão*), *concerto* 'concert' (Spanish *concierto*, French *concert*, Portuguese *concerto*), *sonetto* 'sonnet' (Spanish, Portuguese *soneto*, French *sonnet*), *festino* 'banquet' (French *festin* > Spanish *festín*, Portuguese *festim*), *banca* 'bank' (Spanish, Portuguese *banca*, French *banque*). As the Renaissance unfolded in France, French words were exported, especially to Italy: *marcher* 'march' (Italian *marciare*, Spanish *marchar*, Portuguese *marchar*), *chaperon* 'hooded cape' (Italian *ciapperone*, Spanish *chaperón*, Portuguese *chapeirão*), *tranchée* 'trench' (Italian *trincea*, Spanish *trinchea*). The Spanish military victories in Italy in the mid-1500s increased contacts between the two languages. Examples of borrowings include: *camarada* 'comrade' (Italian *camerata*, French *camarade*), *apartamiento* 'living quarters' (Italian *appartamento*, French *appartement*), and *hablar* 'talk' (French *hâbler*).

The heady intellectual and artistic fervor of the Renaissance fed on the rediscovery of ancient science, philosophy, and literature. Great prestige accrued to the kind of scholarly activity that was reviving and reinterpreting the Classical tradition. Vernacular literature and a flowering Neo-Latin literature coexisted in a kind of tension that sometimes drew comment and debate about their relative merits. Greek was added to the mix, increasingly after 1453, when the fall of Constantinople to the Turks drove many Greek scholars to seek refuge in the West. As the ancient languages became ever more central to European intellectual life, writers drew upon them freely, injecting into the Romance languages a relentless stream of loan words we have called *cultismos*. Today's Romance lexicon owes its texture in large part to this ongoing practice of creating words from Latin and Greek material, which proved to be indispensable in keeping pace with the needs of industry, science, and technology.

Romanian meanwhile belonged to distant cultural spheres: Byzantine, Slavic, and Turkish. Written in the Cyrillic alphabet and little known in the West, the language we now call Romanian went by various names (*Vallachian* and cognates), and its Romance affiliation was not recognized. Only after its territory became part of the Austrian Hapsburg lands in the 1700s was there an opening towards the West. The late 1700s saw a movement called the Transylvanian School that embraced the Latin heritage and sought to modernize and westernize the Romanian lexicon, taking French and, to some extent, Italian as its sources for wholesale borrowing. Consequently, while Romanian has words from all its superstrata – Slavic, Turkish, Hungarian, and Modern Greek – its lexicon has become far more Romance with this huge influx of French and Italian words. An 1825 dictionary of Romanian adds such neologisms as *transport* 'transport', *politic* 'political', *militari* 'military', *complement* 'complement', *familie* 'family', *modă* 'fashion', *examen* 'test', *planetă* 'planet', *chirurgie* 'surgery', *poetă* 'poet', *teatru* 'theater', and *coragie* 'courage' (Rosetti 1973:140–141). Correspondingly, the proportion of its unique Eastern vocabulary waned, leaving behind some doublets: for 'century' *secol* from Latin and *veac* from Slavic, and for 'shepherd' *pastor* from Latin and *cioban* from Turkish, among others.

11.5.7   Other sources

The Romanian lexicon, despite its nineteenth-century renovation, remains the most mixed of any in the family. Romanian adopted numerous loan words from the Magyars (Hungarians) in the West, from the Turks in the East, and from Modern Greek.

Hungarian	Romanian		Turkish	Romanian		Greek	Romanian	
szállás	sălaş	'abode'	*oda*	odaie	'room'	*ftinos*	ieftin	'cheap'
határ	hotar	'border'	*çorba*	ciorbă	'soup'	*kounoupida*	conopidă	'cauliflower'
gyengéd	gingaş	'tender'	*kel*	chel	'bald'	*anapoda*	anapodă	'inside-out'
képe	chip	'face'	*tütün*	tutun	'tobacco'	*nostimos*	nostim	'pleasing'

The Western Romance languages acquire words of non-Latin origin not just from their ancient and medieval neighbors – Celtic, Greek, Germanic, Arabic – but also from a widening range of languages that Europeans encountered in the course of their colonial expansion and its aftermath, from 1492 all the way to the present day. Commodities, plants, and animals native to other continents – tea (Portugese *cha* < Chinese *chá*), coffee (< Turkish *kahve*), tobacco, potatoes (Spanish *tabaco*, *patata* < Arawak-Taíno), pineapples (Spanish *ananás* < Guarani), chocolate (< Nahuatl), bamboo (< Malay) and many more – arrived in Europe, bringing their names with them.[32]

The industrial revolution has a lexical impact far outweighing any other event in the history of the Romance languages. From its beginnings in England in the late 1700s, this profound social transformation moves first to France and thereafter tends to form a package with the ideals of the French Revolution as these continue to spread through Europe. The modern world takes shape, and with it the habitat of modern languages: urbanization, growth of the middle classes, improved means of communication and travel, mass literacy, the birth of journalism, and an accelerating stream of innovations in social institutions and technology. Today the vocabulary of every major Romance language is in a state of unrelenting ferment, flooding the language with neologisms at every level, from scientific terms to product names to short-lived slang expressions. Examples? See for yourself:

> **PRACTICE**
>
> Open a Romance language periodical to any page. Find at least eleven words that include obvious *cultismos*, borrowings, and words of a distinctly contemporary stamp (acronyms, concepts of recent vintage, and the like).

Exercises

1. Another verb-forming suffix favored in popular Latin is -ŪLĀRE. Sometimes the base survives alongside the -ŪLĀRE derivative.

Italian	*Spanish*	*French*	*Portuguese*	*Romanian*
tremare	temblar	trembler	tremular	a tremura
tremolare				
miscere	mezclar	mêler	mesclar	....
mescolare				
rotolare	rodar	rouler	rolar	a rula
turbare	....	troubler	....	a tulbura

For each Latin verb below, identify all its Romance outcomes in the list above. What sporadic sound change accounts for Fr *troubler* and Ro *a tulbura*? Identify the three sound changes, regular or sporadic, leading to Sp *temblar*.

*TREMULARE		
TREMARE	'tremble'	

*MISCULARE		
MISCERE	'mix'	

*ROTULARE		
ROTARE	'roll'	

*TURBULARE		
TURBARE	'disturb'	

2. From Latin FŎLLE 'bellows', which derivational process gives FŎLLĬCĀRE 'pant'? From Sp *holgar* 'go on strike', which derivational process gives *huelga* 'strike'? How could FŎLLĬCĀRE 'pant' come to mean *holgar* 'go on strike'? (Hint: What does 'take a breather' mean?)

3. This happens frequently
   Below, what do the Italian, French, and Romanian reflexes have in common that sets them apart from most of the Ibero-Romance outcomes? The Portuguese reflexes are -ar verbs – what other property do they share? In what two ways do Sp *freír* and *tundear* stand out from the other Spanish outcomes? What Popular Latin verbs can we reconstruct to account for It *fallire* and Fr *falloir*?

	Infinitive			*Past participle*	
	FALLĔRE	'fail'		FALLĪTU	'failed'
	FRĪGĔRE	'fry'		FRĪCTU	'fried'
(AD)-	IŪNGĔRE	'join'		IŪNCTU	'joined'
(DE)-	PĬNGĔRE	'paint'		PĪCTU	'painted'
	TŬNDĔRE	'shear'		TŬNSU	'shorn'
	ŬNGĔRE	'anoint'		ŬNCTU	'anointed'

Italian	*Spanish*	*French*	*Portuguese*	*Romanian*
fallire	faltar	falloir	faltar	....
friggere	freír	frire	fritar	a frige
giungere	juntar	joindre	juntar	a ajunge
dipingere	pintar	peindre	pintar	....
tondere	tundear	tondre	tosar	a tunde
ungere	untar	oindre	untar	a unge

4. Prepositional building blocks

Some Romance prepositions come straight from Latin (AD 'to' *a*, DE 'of' *di*, *de*), but others have been built from two or more prepositions.[33] Which of these Latin prepositions have combined to form the Romance prepositions listed below?

DE	INTRO	CUM	ANTE
'of'	'inside'	'with'	'before'
INFRA	AB	AD	TRA(NS)
'under'	'from'	'to'	'through'
VERSU	SUPER	EX	CONTRA
'toward'	'above'	'out of'	'against'
POST	SINE	PER	IN
'after'	'without'	'through'	'in'

.... It *dentro* 'within'   .... Fr *envers* 'towards'
.... It *attraverso* 'across'   .... Po *após* 'after'
.... Sp *después* 'after'   .... Po *perante* 'before'
.... Sp *detrás* 'behind'   .... Ro *despre* 'about'
.... Fr *avant* 'before'   .... Ro *pentru* 'for'

5. De toutes les couleurs

Italian	*Spanish*	*French*	*Portuguese*	*Romanian*	
annerire	ennegrecer	noircir	enegrecer	a înnegri	'turn black'
imbianchire	blanquear	blanchir	branquear	a albi	'turn white'
arrossire	enrojar	rougir	avermelhar	a roşi	'turn red'
ingiallire	amarillar	jaunir	amarelar	a îngălbeni	'turn yellow'
inverdire	enverdecer	verdir	enverdecer	a înverzi	'turn green'
....	azular	bleuir	azular	....	'turn blue'

In forming verbs from adjectives of color, what do Italian, French, and Romanian have in common? What generalization distinguishes Italian? What generalization distinguishes French? What extra affix occurs in *e(n)negrecer* and *enverdecer* (§ 6.9)?

6. Related to the old demonstrative HIC HAEC HOC (accusative HUNC HANC HOC) 'this' are two adverbs of location HĪC, HAC both meaning 'here, in this place'. Pieces of this paradigm survive in various Romance words. Choose from the box the Romance word(s) deriving from each reconstructed Popular Latin combination.

Sp *acá* 'here'	Sp *aquí* 'here'	Po *agora* 'now'	It *ancora* 'still'
Fr *avec* 'with'	Fr *ce* 'that'	It *ciò* 'that'	OSp *ogaño* 'this year'
It *però* 'but'	It *qui* 'here'	Fr *encore* 'still'	OFr *oïl* > Fr *oui* 'yes'
OFr *ouan* 'this year'	Sp *aún* 'even'	It *qua* 'here'	Prov *oc* 'yes'

*HAC HORA

....

*HANC HORA

....

*HOC

....

*HOC ANNU

....

*HOC ILLU

....

*APUD HOC

....

*ECCE HOC

....

*PER HOC

....

*AD HUNC

....

.*ECCU HIC

....

.*ECCU HAC

....

*ATQUE HIC

....

*ATQUE HAC

....

7. Don't be lazinessful
    What suffixes do you see in the Spanish, French, and Portuguese words for 'lazy'? What outcome would we expect for It 'lazy' if it adopted the model of Spanish, French, and Portuguese?

Latin		Italian	Spanish	French	Portuguese	Romanian
PIGER, PIGRU	'lazy'	pigro	perezoso	paresseux	preguïçoso	....
PIGRITIA	'laziness'	pigrizia	pereza	paresse	preguïça	....

8. "Blorrowing"
    In the ninth-century Glosses of Kassel (§ 12.1.4) Celtic *ordigas* is defined as Germanic *zaehun* 'toes'. How might French arrive at *orteil* 'big toe' from Latin ARTĬCŬLU?

9. Folk etymologies in French
    Using your imagination, suggest a plausible motive for the changes made in these words.

*INTER TANTU	>	OFr *entretant*	'meanwhile'	(*tant* 'so much')	[tã]
'during so much'		Fr *entretemps*	'meanwhile'	(*temps* 'time')	[tã]
FINGENTE	>	Fr *feignant* (1306)	'do-nothing'		
'feigning'		Fr *fainéant* (1321)	'do-nothing'	(*néant* 'nothingness')	

12 Emergence of the Romance vernaculars

12.1 Language in the Carolingian world

When do the Romance languages stop being Latin and become Romance? Here are two crude and unsatisfying answers. One is to posit some specific date. But whatever date you choose, there was obviously no sudden change in people's language behavior on that day or in that year or decade. Another answer, equally off target, is to dismiss the question as meaningless, claiming that since languages change continuously, no such break ever occurred. This is true but evasive. Let's restate the question: today there is something called French (Italian, Spanish, etc.), and once there wasn't. What changed, and when?

The question is better framed when we realize that what we are seeking is not the birth of any specific property internal to the phonology, grammar, or lexicon, but rather the birth of a cultural concept. The dawn of the Romance languages is not so much a linguistic change as a discovery, an innovation in people's thinking about their linguistic circumstances.

The key changes in these perceptions occurred in a period of several decades centered around the year 800. Our aim here is to see how the written record reveals people's experience of linguistic change.

12.1.1 The social setting

By the mid 700s, Western Europe was starting to materialize as a cultural zone. For the Romans, the Mediterranean Sea had been MARE NOSTRUM, the center of their world. But Mediterranean unity, both political and commercial, was broken not only with the dissolution of the Western Roman Empire, but especially with the Arab conquest of North Africa and, starting in 711, most of Spain. The historian Henri Pirenne famously argued that these events drew the cultural center of gravity northward and marked the beginning of European history.

In the former Gaul, the descendants of Romanized populations, now ruled by Germanic kings, lived in the country and in the few towns. The livelihood of the rural majority rested on subsistence agriculture, and feudalism was taking root. Government was decentralized, with most functions delegated to local nobles. Illiteracy was the norm except among clergy, public officials, notaries, and a privileged few. While the 700s saw no dramatic changes in these conditions, the rise of a new Frankish dynasty, the Carolingians, did have consequences in the cultural sphere.

The first famous Carolingian, Charles Martel, a high official in the Merovingian dynasty, had halted in 732 the Moorish advance at Poitiers and reasserted Frankish control over southern France. His grandson, Carolus Magnus or Charlemagne (742–814), ranks among the towering figures of the early Middle Ages. During his long reign (768–814) he expanded Frankish territory in all directions and forged a fruitful alliance with the papacy, culminating in his coronation by the Pope on Christmas day in 800, an event meant to mark the restoration of the Western Roman Empire. But alongside his military and political achievements, Charlemagne made a sustained effort to foster the revival of learning by convening in his court a team of distinguished scholars from all over Western Europe. Clerics one and all, they strove mainly to recover and restore Christian writings, but also to preserve the classics of antiquity for their value as models of elegance and correctness. Charlemagne's father, Pépin the Short, had already sponsored an effort to eliminate from the Latin spelling of his time the vernacular influences that had crept in. Charlemagne's court scholars too deplored the low standards of accuracy in Latin and worried that important writings, repeatedly copied, might be so corrupted as to become unintelligible. Alcuin of York (735–804), an accomplished Latinist and head of the palace school, continued to reform the writing and pronunciation of Latin, and trained scribes in a new, more legible script, known today as Carolingian minuscule, which became the model for later Renaissance scripts and ultimately for today's book fonts. Alcuin also systematized the use of upper and lower case letters, punctuation, and spaces between words.

12.1.2   Medieval diglossia and scribal behavior

In the mid 700s, Western European scholars wanting to write had one option: Latin. Literary Latin persists as an ideal, a target, to which the literate must aspire within the limits of their competence and in accordance with their aims, which could range from the artistic to the humble. These educated folk would also use Latin as a spoken language among themselves, in schools, law courts, and the church. The illiterate majority had no contact with this conservative ideal, and their speech was evolving unconstrained by the written norm. Somewhere within the proficiency hierarchy of those who produced Latin documents were many who introduced properties of the vernacular. Their Latin diverges from the standard inadvertently. The coexistence and interaction of the two systems among the literate exemplify a sociolinguistic situation known as **diglossia,** in which two language varieties specialize to different zones of activity. In cases where the two are related there can readily be some seepage from one zone to another, since the linguistic boundaries between the varieties may be unclear. The educated minority who experienced diglossia undoubtedly regarded both varieties – standard Latin and the local vernacular – as facets of a single linguistic system. Scribes could make errors induced by the vernacular without feeling that they were switching to that variety. Hypercorrections (§ 2.4.1) further confirm that the target is Latin and that mastery of it varies among writers. The "Dog Latin" texts of the 700s are best seen as a sign of imperfect education and of the mutual permeability of Latin and the vernacular.

12.1.3   Glosses of Reichenau

Monasteries, like church schools, were islands of literacy and learning. We owe the scribal tradition mainly to the sixth-century cleric and scholar Cassiodorus, who deemed the copying of manuscripts a proper activity for monks (Elcock 1960:302). No literary text composed in antiquity could ever have reached the present day without being sufficiently valued to be copied and recopied. It was in the monasteries that this work was done.

As a product of monastic activity, texts were often supplied with glosses (marginal or interlinear), that is, words or phrases meant to elucidate obsolete words that were no longer understood. Sometimes glosses were extracted from texts and compiled into lists. Highly prized in monastic culture, these glossaries often traveled great distances, and were collected and recopied into larger compilations which amount to forerunners of modern dictionaries.

Among the largest and most revealing is the Reichenau Glossary, named for the monastery that once owned it. Compiled in the 700s, it was intended primarily as an aid to reading the Vulgate, Saint Jerome's early fifth-century Latin translation of the Bible. From the multitude of words that were deemed difficult for eighth-century readers one can see how much the lexicon had changed in the intervening centuries. The words given as glosses were generally those destined to survive in Romance (§ 11.1).

Original	Gloss	Italian	Spanish	French	
AGER	*campus*	campo	campo	champ	'field'
HIEMS	*ibernus*	inverno	invierno	hiver	'winter'
ICTUS	*colpus*	colpo	golpe	coup	'blow'
GECORE	*ficato*	fegato	hígado	foie	'liver'
(IN) ORE	*(in) bucca*	bocca	boca	bouche	'mouth'
NEMINI	*nulli*	nullo	….	nul	'none'
OPORTET	*convenit*	conviene	conviene	convient	'is fitting'
OPTIMOS	*meliores*	migliori	mejores	meilleurs	'better'
PULCRA	*bella*	bella	bella	belle	'beautiful'
RERUM	*causarum*	cose	cosas	choses	'things'
SANIOR	*plus sano*	più sano	….	plus sain	'healthier'
UMO	*terra*	terra	tierra	terre	'earth'

Some Latin words are glossed with terms of Germanic origin, apparently more current:

Original	Gloss	Italian	Spanish	French	
GALEA	*helmus*	elmo	yelmo	heaume	'helmet'
PIGNUS	*wadius*	....	....	gage	'pledge'
SCABRONES	*wapces*	vespe	avispas	guêpes	'wasps'

Several of the glosses are regionalisms, unmistakably Gallo-Romance:

Original	Gloss	French	Spanish	
CASEUM	*formaticum*	fromage	queso	'cheese'
DA	*dona*	donne	da	'give'
OVES	*berbices*	brebis	ovejas	'sheep'
PUEROS	*infantes*	enfants	niños	'children'
UVAS	*racemos*	raisin	uvas	'grapes'
VESPERTILIONES	*calvas sorices*	chauves-souris	murciélagos	'bats'

A few words invite special comment: GALLIA, no longer understood, is glossed as *Frantia*, not *Francia*, which would sound the same (§ 4.3.6). Standard Latin SI VIS 'if you want' has vanished in favor of Popular Latin *si voles* (cf. Italian *vuoi*, French *veux*, Romanian *vrei*), and IACĔRE 'throw' has ceded to the frequentative *iactare* (Italian *gettare*, Spanish *echar*, French *jeter*, and cf. § 11.2.2).

The Reichenau Glossary is famous for showing how far the vocabulary current in the 700s had journeyed away from the ancient standard. At a close look, however, a few items also show speakers navigating between the two codes that they use in their diglossic situation. For Latin TRANSGREDERE 'go beyond', one contributor gives *ultra alare* (not a Latin verb). Thinking [alɛr], he uses his usual rule to map from the pronunciation back to a presumed Latin version. Another contributor, or the same one in a more lucid moment, glosses ISSET 'had gone' as *ambulasset*, presuming to have hit the etymological target. For TAEDET 'is boring', we are offered a rough approximation *anoget* by a writer who couldn't quite recover Popular Latin *IN-ODIAT but tried to convey its sound in the vernacular (§§ 4.3.3, 4.3.4): [anoiɛt], modern French *ennuie* and English *annoy*.

12.1.4   Glosses of Kassel

This brief text, so named because the civic library of Kassel houses it, is not an aid to reading but "a medieval antecedent of the bilingual phrase book, as used by the present-day tourist" (Elcock 1960:317), hence a guide to speaking. Written between 800 and 825, it consists of Latin words (an approximate Latin) translated into a form of Old High German that exhibits features of Bavarian dialect (Bischoff 1971).

The text is in two parts. The first contains 180 items, arranged by semantic sphere: the human being, domestic animals, the house, clothing, tools and utensils, and miscellany. The second part has sixty-five items, mostly whole sentences, many of them questions.

The German part is a consistent, correct Bavarian, but the Latinate part is a mess, hard to localize on the basis of lexical choice, seemingly random in case marking, and peppered with spellings that suggest a German accent (e.g. *callus* for *gallus* 'rooster', *fidelli* for *vitelli* 'calves', *parba* for *barba* 'beard', *puticla* for *buticla* 'bottle').

Latin	Germanic	
mantun	*chinni*	'chin'
oculos	*augun*	'eyes'
pedes	*foozi*	'feet'
boues	*ohsun*	'oxen'
callus	*hano*	'rooster'
cauallus	*hros*	'horse'
fidelli	*chalpir*	'calves'
scruua	*suu*	'sow'
vaccas	*choi*	'cows'
casu	*hus*	'house'
furnus	*ofan*	'oven'
stabulu	*stal*	'stall'
martel	*hamar*	'hammer'
puticla	*flasca*	'bottle'
tundi meo capilli	*skir min fahs*	'cut my hair'
radi meo parba	*skir minan part*	'shave my beard'

The best guess about the birth of this text is that the author, a Bavarian monk, intended it to assist brother monks preparing to travel in the West and wrote from memory, sorely overestimating his knowledge of the foreign idiom. While the spellings are not entirely trustworthy, one thing is clear: what he seeks to represent is the spoken language ("Shave my beard" is something you would say, not write). We value the text as a window into the lexicon and for at least one decisive etymology. The disputed origin of French *aveugle* 'blind' is clear from the gloss *albioculus* : *staraplinter* 'blind from cataracts'. The form *albioculus* 'white-eyed' is certainly the source of *aveugle*.

12.1.5   Emerging awareness of the new languages

Under Charlemagne's sponsorship, his court scholars attained in their circle a standard of correctness in Latin that moved it even farther from the vernacular. Sharing their zeal, Charlemagne, in a letter of 787 to at least one of his abbots, directed that the clergy should upgrade their Latin: "So that those who strive to please God by a decorous life may not neglect to please Him also by decorous speech ... we exhort you to study letters ... precisely with the aim that you may be able to penetrate more easily and accurately into the mysteries of the Holy Scriptures."[1]

Whatever improvements may have resulted from these reforms, they had unintended consequences. A wrenching fact had become evident: ordinary people could no longer understand spoken Latin. Charlemagne had to reverse his policy. In 813 the Council of Tours directed the clergy to give their sermons in the vernacular (not the whole liturgy, just the sermons). This was momentous, because in order to even say that, the decree had to give a name to the vernacular, distinguishing it from Latin:

et ut easdem homilias quisque aperte transferre studeat in rusticam romanam linguam aut thiotiscam, quo facilius cuncti possint intellegere quae dicuntur.
and [we direct that] everyone endeavor to translate those sermons clearly into the *rustica romana lingua* or into *thiotisca* so that all may more easily understand what is said.

The key words, besides the word *translate*, are the names for the vernacular languages, of which several existed within the broad territory of the Carolingian Empire. *Thiotisca* is an established name for Frankish, a form of Old High German spoken in Charlemagne's eastern lands. *Rustica romana lingua* is the phrase that signals to us the advent of conscious bilingualism, the recognition that sermons were now to be given in a different language. No doubt the term is meant to encompass the vernaculars of the whole western half of Charlemagne's lands, including incipient Old French, Old Spanish, Old Italian, and the rest. Distinguishing these from Latin was the first step, soon to be followed by further terminology distinguishing names for the individual vernaculars.

Texts of the 700s present countless examples of bad Latin, which does, especially in Italy, look much like the vernacular, but only because of incompetence, not because of intent:

de uno latere corre via publica

(Pisa, 730)

de uno latum decorre via publica

(Lucca, 746)

'a public road runs on one side'

These examples yield no evidence that the vernacular language had yet been discovered or invented as a concept. The above-cited decree of 813, however, does embody the idea that the *rustica romana lingua* exists as a language distinct from Latin. The newfound distinction was at first binary: Latin versus local vernacular. The vernaculars, however, were following their own paths and were undoubtedly diverging by region long before they began to be written down.

At the close of the millennium we find a three-way distinction in the epitaph of Pope Gregory V (999):

usus francisca, vulgari et voce latina instituit populos eloquio triplici
Using Frankish, Italian, and Latin, he taught the people with a triple eloquence

Francisca here cannot mean 'French'. Gregory was German and spent his short life mostly in Frankish-speaking lands. In the context of Rome, however, *vulgari voce* refers to Italian.

12.2   The earliest Romance texts

According to our criterion, Romance languages are born when medieval people see them as languages. We can regard a text as unambiguously Romance only when that awareness is evident. The discovery of the vernacular as a separate language plainly comes first in France. Why should that be? The answer is simple: sound change went faster and farther in northern France than in any other Romance area, and the Carolingian reform meanwhile restored a more conservative Latin, further widening the gap. Below, we examine what scholars take to be the earliest extant text in each Romance variety.

12.2.1   The Oaths of Strasbourg (842)

This document is the earliest instance of clear intent to record in writing a discourse in a Romance vernacular, as opposed to Latin. The contrast is unmistakable, since these words appear as a quotation within a historical treatise written in impeccable Carolingian Latin.

The background: Charlemagne was succeeded by his son Louis the Pious, who in turn had three sons. Louis the Pious died in 840, bequeathing to each son a part of the Empire. War ensued. Two of the sons, Charles the Bald (western Romance-speaking lands) and Louis the German (eastern Germanic-speaking lands) found it expedient to gang up on the third brother, Lothar, who held the middle lands (*Lotharingia* > French *Lorraine*). The wars among the three sons of Louis the Pious are recorded in a Latin chronicle by Nithard, their cousin, another grandson of Charlemagne, reared and educated at the royal court (a literate non-clergyman). As Nithard recounts in his chronicle, Charles the Bald and Louis the German met at Strasbourg in 842, each accompanied by his troops, and swore an oath of alliance. Two vernacular languages met on this occasion, as they must have met often in the Frankish Empire: the troops of Charles the Bald spoke Gallo-Romance, while the followers of Louis the German spoke Frankish. In the reported staging of the event, each leader took his oath in the language of the other army: Charles the Bald spoke Frankish so as to be understood by the army of Louis the German, and Louis the German spoke Gallo-Romance so that Charles' army could understand him. Then each army took an oath in its own language. Nithard records both versions, Germanic and Romance, and the two texts elucidate each other. What follows are the Gallo-Romance oaths, abbreviations resolved,[2] each with a line-by-line translation and commentary.

Louis the German's oath:

Pro Deo amur et pro Christian poblo et nostro commun salvament, d'ist di in avant, in quant Deus savir et podir me dunat, si salvarai eo cist meon fradre Karlo et in aiudha et in cadhuna cosa, si cum om per dreit son fradra salvar dift, in o quid il mi altresi fazet; et ab Ludher nul plaid numquam prindrai, qui, meon uol, cist meon fradre Karle in damno sit.

Pro Deo amur et pro	'for the love of God and for
Christian poblo et nostro	the Christian people and our
commun salvament	common salvation'

- *Deo*: non-nominative case, serving as genitive.

d'ist di in avant	'from this day forward'

- DE ISTO DIE IN AB-ANTE cf. Italian *avanti*, Romanian *înainte*.

in quant Deus savir et podir	'insofar as God gives me
me dunat	knowledge and power'

- *savir* < SAPĒRE, *podir* < *POTĒRE.
- DARE 'give' has been replaced in Gallo-Romance by DONARE > French *donner*.

si salvarai eo cist meon	'so will I help this my brother
fradre Karlo	Charles'

- *si* < SĪC 'thus', marking assertion, common in Old French, and seen in the frozen English expression 'so help me God'.
- *salvarai* < SALVARE HABEO, Romance future (§ 7.8.1).
- *cist* [tsist] < ECCE ISTU, Romance demonstrative (§ 11.3.1).

et in aiudha et in cadhuna cosa	'both in aid and in every thing'

- *ajudha* [ajyðə], a deverbal noun from AD-IŪTĀRE akin to Italian *aiuto*. The modern noun *aide* [ɛd] must be re-derived after the verb reduced to *aider*.
- *cadhuna* < *KATA UNA. This *kata* 'down' came into Popular Latin from Greek, cf. English *catalog*, *catastrophe*, etc. It survives in Spanish *cada* 'each', and in French *chacun* < *KATA-QUISQUE-UNU.

si cum om per dreit son fradra	'as one by right must help his
salvar dift	brother'

- *cum* < QUŌ MŌDŌ 'in which way', source of Italian *come*, Spanish *como*, French *comme*, Portuguese *como*, Romanian *cum*.
- *om* < HŎMO 'man, person', here used like Modern French *on* 'one' (cf. German *man*).
- *dreit* < DIRECTU.
- *dift* < DEBET (see Exercise 12.1).

in o quid il mi altresi fazet	'on the condition that he does the same for me'

- *o* < HŌC 'that' (= the condition).
- *quid* = QUID: a Latinizing spelling.
- *mi* < MIHI 'to me' (dative). Compare *me* above.
- *fazet* [fatsət] < FACIAT (subjunctive).

et ab Ludher nul plaid	'and with Lothar I will never make
nunquam prindrai	any pact'

- *plaid* < PLACĬTU 'agreement', a notarial term. Contracts often began with the phrase PLACĬTUM EST 'it pleased [the agreeing parties]', open to reinterpretation as 'it's a deal'.
- *nunquam*: a Latinizing spelling, maybe a pure Latinism, not surviving in modern French (but cf. Old French *onques* < UMQUAM 'ever'). Note the double negative, literally 'will never make no pact' (§ 11.3.2).
- *prindrai* < PR(EH)ENDERE HABEO, Romance future (§ 7.8.1).

qui meon uol cist meon fradre	'which, by my consent, might be
Karle in damno sit.	harmful to this my brother Charles'

- *qui*: visibly nominative. Modern French still marks case in relative pronouns: *qui* versus *que*.
- *cist meon fradre*: non-nominative case, prepositionless.

Oath of Charles the Bald's followers:

Si Lodhuuigs sagrament, que son fradre Karlo iurat, conservat, et Karlus meos sendra de suo part [ñ] lo fraint, si io returnar non l'int pois, ne io ne neuls cui eo returnar int pois, in nulla aiudha contra Lodhuwig nun li iv er.

Si Lodhuuigs sagrament, que son	'if Louis keeps the oath which he swore to
fradre Karlo iurat, conservat	his brother Charles'

- *Lodhuvigs*: note the nominative <s>.
- *que*: non-nominative (cf. *qui*, above).
- *jurat*: the context indicates this must be from the perfectum, *jurat* < IURA(VI)T.

et Karlus meos sendra de suo	'and Charles my lord for his part
part [ñ] lo fraint	breaks it'

- *[ñ] lo fraint*: the diplomatic edition has *ñ loftanit*, a source of debate among Romance linguists. The context, and the corresponding Frankish *forbrichit* 'breaks', make a strong case for the reading given. See Elcock (1960:334–339) for an illuminating discussion.

si io returnar non l'int pois	'if I cannot deter him from it'

- *l'* < ILLU: clitic pronoun that survives in modern French.
- *int* < INDE 'thence, from that' (source of partitive clitic *en*).

- *pois* < *POTEO: source of modern *peux* and its formal variant *puis*.

ne io ne neuls cui eo returnar int pois   'neither I nor anyone whom I can
                                                    deter from it'

- *neuls* 'nobody' < NE...ULLU 'not...any': note again the double negative 'nor
  nobody'.

in nulla aiudha contra Lodhuwig   'will be of any assistance to him
nun li iv er   against Louis in this'

- *li* < ILLI 'to him'. Modern *lui* is from ILLUI (§§ 8.8.2, 8.8.3).
- *iv* ([if], cf. *dift*) < IBI 'there' becomes modern locative clitic *y* 'there, to/in it'.
- *er* : a relic of the original Latin future of 'be' (§ 7.8.2).

12.2.2   The Cassino Depositions (960 and 963)

After the oaths in France, it takes over a century in Italy for the same kind
of evidence to emerge. Being far more conservative in its phonology, Italo-
Romance takes longer to be perceived as a language distinct from Latin. In
963/965, Gonzo of Novara, a monk, distinguishes between the two, but says in
effect that he gets confused:

licet aliquando retarder usu nostrae vulgaris linguae quae latinitati vicina est
at times I can be held back by my use of our everyday language, which is close to
Latin

From about this time come the earliest surviving bits of Italo-Romance written deliberately. Court records preserved in the monastery of Monte Cassino
include some depositions concerning the ownership of certain lands. Elsewhere
the formulas used for this purpose appear in Latin:

Scio quia illae terrae per ipsos fines et mensuras quas tibi, Paldafrit comes, mostravi, per
triginta annos possedit pars sancti Vincencii[3]
I know that those lands within the same boundaries and measures that I showed you,
Count Paldafret, the Monastery of Saint Vincent has owned [them] for thirty years.

In specific documents from 960 and 963, composed primarily in Latin, the
testimony of witnesses is recorded verbatim in their southern variety of Italo-
Romance:

Sao ke kelle terre, per kelle fini que ki contene, trenta anni le possette parte sancti
Benedicti.

(Capua, 960)

Sao cco kelle terre, per kelle fini que tebe mostrai, Pergoaldi foro, que ki contene, et
trenta anni le possette.

(Sessa Aurunca, 963)

Sao 'I know' < SAPĬŌ 'I understand', and allied *vao fao dao stao*, are recessive variants in dialects of the region around Naples (compare Tuscan *vo fo* etc., § 6.10.3). *Possette* 'possessed' is mysteriously shortened from *possedette*. *Foro* 'were' derives from FUERUNT > *FURUNT. The reduction of /kw/ to /k/ in *kelle* 'those' < ECCU ILLAE and *ki* 'here' < ECCU HIC is typical of Neapolitan. Akin to *tebe* 'to you' < TIBI are the *meve teve* found in many Southern Italian varieties (Rohlfs 1966–69:II, § 442). The non-diphthong in *contene* 'contains' < CONTĔNET is also a southern feature (Elcock 1960:451). Latinate features are: spellings *que*, *sancte*, explicit genitives *sancti Benedicti, Pergoaldi*, and perhaps the synthetic preterites *foro, possette* with present perfect meaning 'have been', 'has possessed'. A distinctly Romance feature, however, is the accusative clitic *le* 'them' < ILLAE/ILLAS (§ 8.8.3) of *le possette*, which serves to identify preposed *kelle terre* as direct object.

12.2.3   The Glosses of San Millán (900s)

The earliest surviving samples of Ibero-Romance are two sets of glosses discovered in Latin codices belonging to the monastic libraries of San Millán (*Glosas Emilianenses*) and Santo Domingo de Silos (*Glosas Silenses*). The Latin texts that the glosses are meant to elucidate are a miscellany of writings on religious topics. The two sets of glosses, similar in form and regional character, belong to roughly the same period, the San Millán set dating from the mid 900s and the Silos set from later in the century (Menéndez Pidal 1950). Our examples are selected from the 1,007 glosses of the earlier set. There is also one stretch of prose that ranks as the earliest surviving continuous text in Ibero-Romance.

Original	*Gloss*	
ADTENTIUS	*buena mientre*	'carefully, well'
ALICOTIENS	*alquandas bezes*	'sometimes'
ASPERIUS	*plus aspero mas*	'harsher'
BENEFICIA	*elos serbicios*	'the services'
DIVERSIS	*muitas*	'many'
DONEC	*ata quando*	'until'
[ET] TERTIUS VENIENS	*elo tercero[diabolo] uenot*	'the third [devil] came'
ET TU IBIS	*e tu iras*	'and you will go'
EXTERIORES	*de fueras*	'outside'
FENI	*jerba*	'grass'
INCOLOMES	*sanos et salbos*	'safe and sound'
INDICA	*amuestra*	'show'
INERMIS	*sine arma*	'unarmed'
ADMONEO	*castigo*	'I scold'
INVENIEBIT	*aflaret*	'will find'
MANES	*tu siedes*	'you remain'

PAUPERIBUS	*misquinos*	'wretched'
QUID AGAS	*ke faras*	'what will you do?'
REPENTE	*lueco*	'immediately'
SOLLICITI SIMUS	*ansiosu segamus*	'(that) we be avid'
SUSTINUIT	*sufriot*	'suffered'

The primary diphthongs of Spanish are in evidence: *buena, fueras, amuestra, lueco, jerba, siedes, mientre*. Spellings show hesitation between /b/ and /w/: *bezes, serbicios, salbos*, but *uenot*. Recognizably Ibero-Romance words include: *bezes* (Spanish *veces*), *mas* (Spanish *más*), *ata* (Spanish *hasta* < Arabic *hatta*), *tercero, sine* (Spanish *sin*), *aflar* (Spanish *hallar* < *AD-FLARE 'sniff out'), *misquinos* (Spanish *mezquinos* < Arabic *meskin*), and *lueco* (Spanish *luego*). *Segamus* [sejamus?] < SEDEAMUS corroborates the view that SĒDĒRE supplies certain forms in the Spanish paradigm of 'be' (§ 6.10.1). The Romance future is amply attested: *faras, iras*. Finally, such forms as *uenot* and *sufriot* suggest an early spread of class I -AVIT (> -*aut* > -*ot* > -*o*) to other verb classes (§ 7.5.2).

12.2.4   The Sanchiz Act of Partition (1192)

Not until about 200 years after the *Glosas* do we find the earliest sample of Ibero-Romance with distinctly Portuguese features. This notarial document, now preserved in the national archives in Lisbon, records an agreement among four members of the Sanchiz family about how their property is to be divided. It has a companion document in the will of Elvira Sanchiz, drawn up the following year. After the customary notarial formulas in Latin, the text switches abruptly to the vernacular:

> In Christi nomine amen. Hec est notitia de partiçon e de deuison que fazemus antre nos dos herdamentus e dus cout[us e] das onrras e dous padruadigus das eygreygas que forum de nossu padre e de nossa madre en esta maneira....
>
> In Christ's name, amen. This is to give notice of the partition and division which we make between us of the possessions and hunting-reserves and estates and patronages of the churches which belonged to our father and mother, in this way....
>
> (Elcock 1960:429)

The document, 232 words in all, includes several typically Portuguese features: lack of primary diphthongs, as in *nossa* 'our', *fora* 'outside', *sestas* 'sixths' (cf. Spanish *nuestra, fuera, siestas*), and loss of intervocalic /l/, as seen in definite articles *o a os as*, here compounded with prepositions: *do, dos* 'of the', *no, nas* 'in the', etc. Examples of yod metathesis include OLIVARIA *Ulueira* 'Oliveira', MANARIA *maneira*, and ECCLESIAS *eygreygas*. Also attested are the changes /aw/ > /ow/ in CAUTU *coutu*, ALTERU > *[awtru]* > *outro* 'other', and initial /kl/ > /ʃ/ in CLAMANT *chamam* 'they call'. Loss of intervocalic /n/ with nasalization of the preceding vowel appears in such plurals as DIVISIONES > *diuisoes* and

PARTITIONES > *partiçoens* where the tell-tale misplaced <n> reveals that its only job is to indicate nasalization.

12.2.5   Neacşu's letter (1521)

In the medieval diglossia of Western Europe the teeming vernaculars were paired with a stiffly codified Latin that seemed destined to live forever as the language of religion, law, and learning. In the history of Romanian, however, Latin had no such enduring presence. In the period of intensive Romanization ending with the Roman withdrawal from Dacia in 271 CE, Latin had provided the foundation, but there its influence ended. The nascent Romanian, known as Wallachian, was situated in the Greek-speaking half of the Empire, and its later contacts were with Slavic, Hungarian, and Turkish. The primary language of religion and administration was Old Church Slavonic. Thus the standard was far more distinct from the vernacular in the East than in the West. From the 1200s on, though, documents in Slavonic increasingly contain isolated words in Romanian, mainly personal and place names, e.g. *Singuru*, a surname, *Piatra obla*, a place name, *gura isvorului* 'the source of the spring'. The first mention of written Romanian is an oath of allegiance taken in 1238 by Stephen the Great to Casimir IV, king of Poland. Only its Latin translation survives, but it clearly states: *haec inscripcio ex valachico in latinam versa est* 'this document was translated into Latin from Wallachian'.

The earliest surviving continuous text in Romanian is a letter of about 250 words, written in the Cyrillic alphabet, to the mayor of Braşov from a nobleman, Neacşu Lupu of Câmpulung. Datable precisely to June 1521, it warns of an impending attack by the Turks. The document, now preserved in the Museum of Printing and Old Romanian Books in Târgovişte, opens and closes with formulaic salutations in Old Slavonic, but the rest is mostly intelligible to speakers of Modern Romanian:[4]

I pak dau ştire domnie tale za lucrul turcilor, cum am auzit eu că împăratul au eşit den Sofiia, şi aimintrea nu e, şi se-au dus în sus pre Dunăre.
And likewise I let your honor know of the Turks' deeds, as I heard that the Emperor has left Sofia, and it is not otherwise, and sailed up the Danube.

I pak să ştii domniia ta că au venit un om de la Nicopole de miie me-au spus că au văzut cu ochii lor că au trecut ciale corăbii ce ştii şi domniia ta pre Dunăre în sus.
And likewise you should know that a man from Nicopolis came to me and told me he saw with his own eyes that those ships, which you also know of, have sailed up the Danube.

Salient Romanian traits include: the postposed article as in *lucrul, împăratul, oraşele* 'the cities', and case markers as in *turcilor*, and *domniie tale* 'to your honor' versus *domniia ta* 'your honor'. The metaphonic diphthong [ea] is already in place: *Rumânească* 'Romanian', *să treacă* 'may pass'. It displays its older conditioning (§ 10.1.5): *vor treace* 'they will pass', *ciale* (elsewhere *ceale*). The metaphonic diphthong [ọa] appears inconsistently: *toate oraşele* 'all the cities' but *omin*, *umin* 'men' instead of *oameni*, and both *vostre* and *voastre* 'your'. The Family Rule (§ 10.1.8) is also attested in the subjunctive *să nu ştie mulţi* 'not many should know'. Verb phrases with clitics have their modern format: *i va fi voia*, literally 'to him will be desire' = 'he will want'.

12.3   Conclusion: from dialects to standards

We live in a world of nations. The map, with its tidy borders and solid colors, tends to foster the illusion that Italian, Spanish, French, and other national languages sprang up in exactly those areas. Such a misconception skips over at least half the history of the Romance languages.

In reality, Romance vernaculars began to form at a time when centrifugal forces predominated, with no external constraint to check their divergence. The natural result is a mosaic of local vernaculars. Typically, one of these local varieties, when its site becomes a center for commerce, administration, or culture, gains currency over a wider territory. As it spreads, it may embody compromises among the features of nearby local varieties. Out of this develops a **koiné**: a spontaneous regional standard serving for communication among speakers of non-mutually-intelligible vernaculars throughout the area. Over time, the linguistic landscape morphs into a group of koinés, each differentiated somewhat from the local vernaculars it was born of. This development leads to a new kind of diglossia: local vernacular versus regional koiné.[5] That situation can remain stable for centuries. The next step, the creation of a national language, is no more a foregone conclusion than is the making of a nation.

In Western Europe, however, from Carolingian times on, nations gradually arise, some earlier, some later. The creation of national standard languages is a deliberate endeavor in the service of national interests (prestige or solidarity) and typically with some form of governmental intervention. Just as a local variety may, for external reasons, form the basis for a regional koiné, so also one regional koiné may, by historical circumstance, serve as the basis for the standard language. The other regional koinés are then gradually demoted to dialects.

Volumes have been written about how this process unfolded in Romance languages over the last 800 years. Our remarks make no claim to be even a summary. Instead, we draw only the major outlines for our five languages and mention some of the milestones in the growth of each standard.

12.3.1   French

The later Carolingian period sees a rapid return of authority to local feudal lords. But the Capetian dynasty, beginning with Hugh Capet's accession to the throne (987), initiates a centuries-long movement toward a powerful monarchy centered in Paris. The Albigensian Crusade (1208–1213), ostensibly a war against heretics in the South, extended the power of the Capetian kings all the way to the Mediterranean, severely crippling the distinctive Provençal culture and the status of its language.

While Latin continues to coexist with a flourishing French literature up to the Renaissance, a series of edicts illustrate the royal language policy favoring the vernacular and, increasingly, the northern vernacular known as *françois* (Lodge 1993:125–126). From 1530, with the founding of the Collège de France, spoken French was allowed as the language of instruction. Under the Ordinance of Villers-Cotterêts (1539), all legal affairs, written and spoken, were to be conducted *en langage françois maternel et non aultrement*. Codification begins with the first French grammars: *Deffence et illustration de la langue françoyse* (Joachim DuBellay, 1549) and *Traicté de la grammaire françoise* (Robert Estienne, 1557). Among the learnèd societies that formed in the Renaissance to debate all manner of intellectual issues were some that focused on linguistic matters. In keeping with the authoritarian spirit that pervaded most of the next two centuries, one such group was designated as an official organ of language policy by Cardinal Richelieu. Known as the *Académie Française* (1634), its mission was "to exert absolute power...over literature and language" (Hall 1974:180). To that end it was charged with preparing an official dictionary and grammar. *Remarques sur la langue françoise* (1647), which fixed usage for the classical writers of the seventeenth century, was not the Academy's grammar, but the work of one of its members, Claude Favre de Vaugelas. The French Revolution, for all its rejection of the old régime, did not mitigate the enduring tendency toward prescriptivism and state control of language. The Jacobin principle held sway: *la langue doit être une comme la République*. In public elementary education, mandatory since 1882, it was not until the Deixonne Law (1951) that any language but French was allowed for general instruction.

12.3.2   Italian

Nationhood came much later to Italy than to France, Spain, or Portugal. Throughout the thousand years from the decline of Carolingian rule to the *Risorgimento* ('resurgence') that made Italy a nation (1860–1870), the territory comprised many political entities under different kinds of authority. From about 1000, the city states of the North and of Tuscany, nominally affiliated to the Holy Roman Empire but mostly autonomous, gradually grew wealthy and prominent (especially Florence) through their activity in commerce, the textile industry, and banking. Midway in the peninsula were the lands known as Saint Peter's patrimony, the Papal States. The South had a complex history. Usually divided, it was subject to a succession of foreign rulers: Arab, Norman, Bavarian (the Holy Roman Empire), French, and Spanish. There was no material force uniting the disparate lands of Italy, and the vernaculars survived in their separate spheres. To this day, every facet of Italian tradition has a regional character.

The 1200s saw the growth of various regional literatures that sought to establish an elevated (*illustre*) standard for belletristic use. Ultimately, Florentine usage won out as the basis for a national literary standard, and for two reasons: first, the economic prosperity of Florence beginning in the 1200s (the gold florin was the standard European monetary unit), and second, Dante Alighieri (1265–1321), Francesco Petrarca (1304–1374), and Giovanni Boccaccio (1313–1375), who, writing in their Tuscan vernacular, polished it to a level of prestige that assured its acceptance as a literary standard. Like the nascent standard languages of France, Spain, and Portugal, this standard was available only to an educated few. Uniquely among the others, however, the Florentine-based Tuscan standard was entirely the product of intellectuals and artists without government sponsorship and was long confined to the literary sphere.

Some Renaissance humanists questioned the merits of the vernacular, but most embraced it. A landmark in its codification was Pietro Bembo's *Prose della volgar lingua* (1526). Government intervention comes in 1572, when Cosimo dei Medici decides to convert a private literary discussion group into an official body, the *Accademia della Crusca*, charged with adjudicating matters of language. However, it was never a nationally sanctioned entity, and by the 1800s its authority had faded.

The post-Napoleonic era finds Northern Italy chafing under Austrian rule and nationalist sentiment burgeoning. As Italian unification progressed (1860–1870), language policy gained urgency. The statesman Cavour famously said: "We have made Italy, now we must make the Italians." Estimates put somewhere between 2.5 and 9.5 percent that part of the population able to speak Italian (based on the Tuscan literary standard) at that time. Italian needed to become truly national and to serve not just artistic, but also general purposes. The novelist Alessandro Manzoni, a lifelong advocate of promoting Florentine to a national language, recommended in an 1868 report to the Ministry of Education that it be taught in the public schools. Standard Italian has seen its Florentine quality attenuated, but the language has been successfully diffused through compulsory education, military service, and the media. Today, dialects are somewhat in retreat, but the standard does admit some regional variation.

12.3.3   Spanish and Portuguese

After the Moorish conquest, starting in 711, the mountains in the extreme North of the peninsula were the refuge of the remaining Christian kingdoms: Galicia, León, Asturias, and Aragon. The theme of the next seven centuries was the *Reconquista* ('reconquest'), a southward drive to recover lands lost to the Moors. As the Kingdom of León expanded eastward (910–914), many fortresses (*castillos*) were built in the new domains, hence the name Castile. The ongoing rise of Castile to hegemony – political and linguistic – rests upon its military leadership in the *Reconquista*.

Alfonso VI, King of León and Castile, retook Toledo (1085) and made it his capital. He gave to his sons-in-law Raymond and Henry the counties of Galicia and Portugal (1093), a moment in Iberian linguistic history that drove a wedge between the already diverging Galician-Portuguese and its neighbors to the East. Henry's son Alfonso Henriques, after an important victory over the Moors (1139), proclaimed himself King of Portugal and won recognition both from his cousin King Alfonso VII of Castile (1143) and from the Pope (1179). When he retook Lisbon (1147), the center of Portuguese power moved to the south, increasing the distance, both physical and linguistic, between Portuguese and Galician. King Dinis, the best-loved of medieval Portuguese kings, decreed (1290) that the language be used officially and known as Portuguese rather than as "the common language." He also founded (1290) the *Estudos Gerais*, one of Europe's oldest universities.

Writers in medieval Iberia typically commanded more than one of the languages. From the 1100s through the 1300s Galician-Portuguese was deemed better suited to the lyrical *cantigas*, and Castilian to other genres. By the 1500s, while Portuguese enjoyed less prestige in Castile, Portugal's most celebrated author, Luis de Camões, set an enduring literary standard, the basis for the modern language. The Renaissance brought to Portugal the same kind of lexical enrichment as elsewhere in Romance (§ 11.5.6).

In the Old Spanish period the greatest champion of the Castilian vernacular was Alfonso X el Sabio ('the wise'), who reigned 1250–1284 as King of Castile. He sponsored extensive translation (from Latin) and scholarship (in Castilian), and is the reputed author of substantial works in history and law as well as lyric poetry. As the *Reconquista* pushed southward, the retaken lands became nominally Castilian-speaking. Further centralization came when Castile united with Aragon and Catalonia (1479) under Ferdinand and Isabella – at that point Castilian, not Catalan, became the chancery language. In the *annus mirabilis* 1492, among other landmark events, the *Reconquista* concluded with the capture of Granada, and the first Spanish grammar was presented to Queen Isabella by Antonio de Nebrija. In the ensuing Golden Age (*Siglo de Oro*), such renowned authors as Miguel de Cervantes, Lope de Vega, and Pedro Calderón de la Barca, among others, definitively established Castilian as the basis for a literary and national standard. Royal action confirming its status soon followed. Felipe V officially recognized the *Real Academia Española* (1714), a purist and regulatory body modeled on its Italian and French counterparts, but quieter, less pretentious, and more productive (Hall 1974:181) – its dictionary appeared in 1726–1729. Government intervention continued: early in the century Castilian became the language of legal transactions, then of public primary education throughout Spain (1768), and finally of notarial documents (1862). Today *español* and *castellano* are near-synonyms. The successive constitutions of the 1930s reaffirmed Castilian as the national language, but also guaranteed protected status for the other *lenguas españolas* (Catalan, Galician, and Basque). Minority language rights were revoked under Franco's rule, but reinstated by the constitution of 1978.

In Portugal, twentieth-century events confirm that national sentiment goes hand in hand with promotion of the language. Just after the proclamation of the Portuguese Republic (1910), the government convened a commission for orthography, guided by the linguist Aniceto Gonçalves Viana, which produced the first spelling reform (1911). While Portugal has lagged behind other Western

European nations in its literacy rate, it has kept pace in the number of spelling reforms. In 1991, seven Portuguese-speaking countries agreed upon a unified orthography. Recently, Portugal's parliament voted to adopt certain Brazilian spelling conventions (2008).

12.3.4   Romanian

As of about 1500, there were three traditional regions where most of the population spoke Romance varieties that we would now call Romanian: Walachia, Moldavia, and Transylvania. Each was independent at some points in its history, but in other periods they were vassal states: Transylvania to Hungary, Walachia and Moldavia to the Ottoman Empire. Either way, the Romance speakers were a peasant class under rulers of other ethnicities and languages.

The Reformation, in keeping with its ideal of making Christian scriptures accessible to all, sometimes catalyzed the written use of low-prestige, spoken varieties. The earliest literary works in Romanian are religious texts motivated by the Reformation. Coresi, a deacon and printer, published in 1559 a Protestant catechism and in 1560 his own translation of the gospels into his native Walachian. Religious texts in Romanian, most in Cyrillic script but some in the Roman alphabet, continued to appear through the 1600s.

The foundation (circa 1700) of the Uniat Church (Greek Catholic) marked a turn to the West. The intellectuals of the Transylvanian School (mid 1700s to 1800s) sought to legitimate the bond with Rome by demonstrating, historically and philologically, the Latin origin of the people and their language. They promoted the Roman alphabet and introduced many neologisms from Latin, French, and Italian (§ 11.5.6). Pride in the Latin heritage became an element of Romanian national awakening. At the time, however, Romania was not yet a nation.

Walachia and Moldavia, by electing the same individual as prince, united to form the nation of Romania (1859), which later won recognition from the European powers (1878). The speech of Bucharest, the capital, served as the basis for a Romanian standard. A logical extension of the Transylvanian School's agenda was the foundation of the Romanian Academy (1866) to cultivate Romanian language and literature. Its major projects include: a descriptive dictionary (*Dicţionarul explicativ al limbii române*), an etymological dictionary, a dictionary of literature, a historical grammar, and a dialect atlas.

The two world wars again changed the borders of Romania: Transylvania in the West and Moldavia in the East were reincorporated (1920). Part of Moldavia, ceded to the Soviet Union in 1945, now constitutes the nation of Moldavia, where Romanian is still spoken. Romania itself is today a multilingual nation (chiefly Hungarian, German, and the "Gypsy" language, Rom), but the standard is firmly established in public life, education, and the media.

In this book, we chose to deal only with the five Romance languages that are national languages. We have linked that property with standardization.

However, other Romance languages have developed standards, created flourishing literatures, and even established academies, all in the absence of nationhood. Galician, Catalan, Occitan, and Rheto-Romance, for example, all have their loyal promoters and qualify as languages to the same extent as the five we have studied.

Exercises

1. The Oaths of Strasbourg
    Referring back to the text and commentary in § 12.2.1, do these philological projects.

    a. Case system. Collect all the noun phrases that show evidence for the two-case system in Old French (nominative versus non-nominative), explained in § 8.4.3.
    b. Final vowels. We know that a word-final vowel deletes in French, except it becomes [ə] if it comes from Latin word-final /a/ or is needed as support vowel for a consonant cluster. Question: had this development already occurred by the time of our text? Collect the evidence, keeping in mind that medieval scribes used creative spelling. They had to. There was no standard tradition to adhere to, especially for new sounds.
    c. Spelling of high mids. Our scribe has a consistent but odd way of writing diphthongs [ej] [ow] that derived from high mids (§ 1.2.4). Collect the words that derive from the following, and comment:

    > AMŌRE   SAPĒRE   DĒBET   DŌNAT   Pop Lat POTĒRE

    d. *Dift*. Work out the ordering of the regular changes that must have led from DĒBET to *dift* 'ought'. The stressed vowel is a spelling peculiarity treated in the preceding question.
    e. *Sendra*. Latin SĒNĬOR is an imparisyllabic. Using the Penultimate Rule, show where the stress falls on the nominative SĒNĬOR and accusative SĒNĬŌRE(M). Which of these is the source of *sendra*, and how do you know?
    f. To what extent does the language of the text show lenition? Collect examples. What sound is the scribe trying to represent with *dh* (not a possible sequence in Latin)?

2. Anglo-Norman French in the 1100s: The Wolf and the Crow
    The first known French woman poet is Marie de France. Nothing is known of her life, but at one point she writes: *Marie ai nun, si sui de France* 'my name is Marie and I'm from France'. Scholars speculate that she wrote between 1160 and 1200 and frequented the court of Henry II of England and his wife, Eleanor of Aquitaine. Her main works are twelve *lais*, or rhymed tales of courtly love, and her Aesop-like *fables*, exemplified here.

Del lu e del corbel.	On the wolf and the crow.
D'un lu cunte ke vit jadis	It is said of a wolf that he once saw
U un corbel s'esteit asis	where a crow had perched
Sur le dos de une berbiz.	on the back of a sheep.
Li lus parla od nobles diz :	The wolf spoke with noble words:
« Jeo vei, » fet il, «grant merveille.	« I see, » said he, « an amazing thing.
Le corp sur le dos d'une oweille!	The crow on the back of a sheep!

Siet la u siet, dit ceo que dit,	He sits where he will, says what he will,
Fet ceo que fet – sanz cuntredit!	does what he will – nobody objects!
Mal ne crient de nule rien.	They're making no fuss about anything.
Si jeo i seisse, jeo sai bien	If I sat there, I know for sure
Que tute gent me hüereient,	that everyone would howl at me,
De tutes parz m'escrïerent,	from all sides they'd raise a hue,
Que jeo la vodreie manger.	saying I was going to eat the sheep.
Ne me larreient aprismer. »	They wouldn't let me get anywhere near. »
Issi est del tricheür:	So it is with the trickster:
En esfrei est e en poür,	he's in fright and in fear
(Sa conscience le reprent),	(his conscience chides him)
Que tuz cunuissent sun talent.	that everyone knows his intent.
Forment li peise del leal,	Honest folk make him quite uneasy
Que hum ne tient ses fez a mal.	lest they think his actions bode ill.

a. Find the word that derives from each of these sources:

APPROXIMĀRE	ECCE HOC	DORSU	OVICŬLA	UBI
SEDET	FACTOS	IBI	QUIRĪTANT	

b. Find one imperfect subjunctive and four conditionals. For one of the conditionals, set up a pre-Romance reconstruction.

c. Comment on *grant merveille*, today *grande merveille*. What is the gender? (§ 8.4.3)

3. Galician-Portuguese in the 1200s: the Embittered Poet
    Pero Gómez Barroso, author of this text, is one of about 156 poets whose works survive from the heyday of Galician-Portuguese troubadour lyric, about 1200 to 1330 (Jensen 1978:14). Their school did absorb and value Provençal influences, but it is also imbued with its own local traditions, including its typical genres, the *cantigas de amor, cantigas de amigo*, in which a woman sings of her lover, and the mischievous or satirical *cantigas de escarnho e de maldizer*. This poem belongs to a less typical genre, the *serventês*.

Do que sabia nulha ren non sei,	Of what I once knew, I know nothing now
polo mundo, que vej' assi andar,	in this world, the way I see it going,
e, quand' i cuido, ei log' a cuidar,	and when I think of it, I have cause to think,
per boa fé, o que nunca cuidei:	honestly, things I never before thought:
ca vej' agora o que nunca vi	for I see now what I never saw before
e ouço cousas que nunca oí.	and I hear things I never heard.
Aqueste mundo, par Deus, non é tal	This world, by God, is not the same
qual eu vi outro, non á gran sazon,	as the other I saw, not so long ago,
e por aquesto, no meu coraçon,	and for this reason, in my heart,
aquel desej' e este quero mal,	I long for that one, and this one I despise,
ca vej' agora o que nunca vi	for I see now what I never saw before
e ouço cousas que nunca oí.	and I hear things I never heard.
E non receo mia morte poren,	And yet I do not fear my death,
e, Deus lo sabe, queria morrer,	and God knows I would like to die,
ca non vejo de que aja prazer	for I see nothing in which to take pleasure
nen sei amigo de que diga ben,	nor know any friend of whom to speak well,
ca vej' agora o que nunca vi	for I see now what I never saw before
e ouço cousas que nunca oí.	and I hear things I never heard.

E se me a min Deus quisess' atender,	And if God were willing to heed,
per boa fé, ũa pouca razon,	in all honesty, my humble thought,
eu post'avia no meu coraçon	I had decided in my heart
de nunca já mais neun ben fazer,	Never again to do any good deed,
ca vej' agora o que nunca vi	for I see now what I never saw before
e ouço cousas che nunca oí.	and I hear things I never heard.
E non daria ren por viver i	And I wouldn't give a penny to live here
en este mundo mais do que vivi.	in this world any longer than I already have.

    a. Find the word that derives from each of these sources:

        PLACĒRE   ACCU ISTE   ŪNA   COGITĀRE   REM   RECELO   AUDIO

    b. Identify the verbs and place them in these categories: present indicative, present subjunctive, imperfect indicative, imperfect subjunctive, preterite, conditional. Given that *queria* is a conditional (of *querer* 'want'), what special change has it undergone?

    c. What two words are fused in each of these contractions? *do*   *polo*   *no*

4. Castilian in the early 1200s: The Manticore

    The anonymous *Semeiança del mundo* (circa 1223), the earliest geography in Spanish, is freely translated from a Lat *Imago mundi* 'tableau of the world' (circa 1090–1120?) with added material mostly from Isidore of Seville's famous *Etymologiae* (circa 625–630). Mainly it lists lands, cities, rivers, mountains, and the origins of their names, but the section on *tierra de Yndia* turns into a phantasmagoria of bizarre peoples and beasts, as in this excerpt (edition by Bull and Williams 1959).

    De la bestia que dizen mantigora.

    En esta partida ha otrossi huna bestia que ha nombre mantigora. Esta bestia ha la faz como ome, e ha en la bocha tres ordenes de dientes, e ha cuerpo de leon, e ha la cola como de escorpion, e ha muy mala catadura, que ha los oyos uerdes e enbueltos en sangre, e silua como serpente, e come carne de omne muy de grado. Esta bestia da uozes de muchas maneras, e corre mas que aue puede uolar.

    On the beast which they call manticore.

    In this region there is also a beast which has the name manticore. This beast has a face like a man, and it has in its mouth three rows of teeth, and it has the body of a lion, and it has a tail like a scorpion's, and it has a most vile appearance, for its eyes are green and bloodshot, and it hisses like a serpent, and it likes to eat human flesh. This beast utters sounds of many kinds, and it runs faster than a bird can fly.

    a. Find the old words later replaced by: *pájaro* 'bird', *tiene* 'has', *tambien* 'also'.

    b. Judging from this document, have the following changes occurred? Answer *yes*, *no*, or *can't be sure*, and cite any relevant forms.

        Lenition? (§ 3.2.2)
        Intervocalic [kl] > [ʎ] > [j] > [x]? (§ 4.3.8)
        Initial [f] > [h]? (§ 3.3.2)
        Vowel prosthesis? (§ 2.1.1)
        Primary diphthongization? (§ 1.2.5)

    c. From SIBILAT 'hisses' derive *silua* [silβa], naming the changes.

5.   Mantuan (Northern Italy) in the time of Dante: The Eagle
This excerpt is from *Trattato di scienza universal* (circa 1309), a voluminous work by
one Vivaldo Belcalzer of Mantua. Never published in full, it survives in an **autograph
manuscript** (a manuscript in the author's own hand) and two copies. Cian (1902) recognized it as a translation of the medieval Latin best-seller *De proprietatibus rerum*
('On the nature of things') by Bartholomeus Anglicus (circa 1240), the *Encyclopedia
Britannica* of its time. Such vernacular translations, or *volgarizzamenti*, were common in many regions of Italy at a time when the local vernaculars were competing
on a fairly even footing.

Dei oxey e de le colse chi vola.
Le agoie è de tant setil vedir che le monta tant alt ch'a pena che le possa fi vedude e
siant così ad alt le vedera un pizol pexe in mar e tengnant le ale strette e ferme le ven
zoso a mod de preda e de mar traz el pexe … Liberament guarda entrel sol, nè per tanta
clarità se declina lo so vedir e zo dis Ambros e dis Aristotel che l è generaçion d'agoie
che nodrigant ie fioy che y volz contra 'l sol e costrenzey a guardarge dentr e se ad alcun
lagrema l'ocl e ol s'agreva el vedir, l'agoia lo zeta for a del nin no crezante l esser de soa
generaçion. …

On birds and on things that fly.
Eagles have such keen eyesight that they go up so high that they can barely be seen and
while they are so high up they will see a little fish in the sea and, holding their wings tight
and firm, they drop down like a stone and snatch the fish from the sea … They freely look
into the sun, and for all its brilliance their eyesight is not harmed, and so says Ambrose,
and Aristotle says that there is a race of eagles which, in bringing up their young, turn
them to face the sun, and compel them to look at it, and if there is any whose eye waters
or whose eyesight suffers, the eagle throws it out of the nest, believing it to be not of its
own kind.

a. In the text, point out evidence for these statements:
    i   Mantuan has subject pronouns.
    ii Third plural verbs are identical to third singular.
    iii Palatal /ʎ/ deletes in Mantuan.
b. Find the Mantuan cognates for these Italian words: *ciò* 'that', *picciolo* (variant of
piccolo) 'small', *volge* 'turns', *costringe* 'compels', *getta* 'throws', OIt *giuso* 'down'
< DEORSU. Could we argue that letter <z> has two pronunciations?
c. How should we interpret these spellings? Why does our scribe write <l> in
'things'?

ocl	'eye'
tengnant	'holding'
colse	'things'

Notes

1 The evolution of stressed vowels

1 Spanish has at least ten words where stressed high mid /o/ yields a high /u/ that cannot be attributed to the raising effect of a palatal articulation. See Malkiel (1983) for discussion. Some examples are:

SŬLPHŬRE	'sulfur'	azufre	
CRŬCE	'cross'	cruz	
MŬNDU	'world'	mundo	
SŬLCU	'groove'	surco	
SŬMMA	'highest'	suma	'total'

2 Early changes in syllable structure and consonants

1 For the *Corpus Inscriptionum Latinarum* (CIL), see § 2.5.2.

2 For the *Appendix Probi*, see § 2.5.3.

3 See § 1.3.1 for further examples of non-syncope in Italian.

4 Sp *humilde* 'humble', with stressed /i/, is not an exact cognate to the other two. Most likely it was derived backwards from *humildad* 'humility' (§ 11.4.3).

5 In keeping with this tradition, the English letter <w>, called 'double U', may resemble either <uu> or <vv>.

6 We will encounter this pattern again. These same protected positions also inhibit lenition, the process of consonant weakening (§ 3.2.4).

7 The /v/ of inverno was regular when it was still intervocalic. That is: first HIBERNU became */iverno/, then /n/ was inserted under the influence of the prominent prefix *in-* (§ 11.4.2).

8 See § 2.5.3 for further ancient testimony about fads and fashions involving /h/.

9 Augustus quoque in epistulis ad C. Caesarem scriptis emendat, quod is *calidum* dicere quam *caldum* malit, non quia id non sit Latinum sed quia sit odiosum et, ut ipse Graeco verbo significavit, περίεργον   (Book I, vi, 19–20 in Butler 1920:121).

10 Parcissime ea veteres usi etiam in vocalibus, cum *aedos ircos*que dicebant; diu deinde servatum, ne consonantibus aspirarent, ut in *Graccis* et in *triumpis*; erupit brevi tempore nimius usus, ut *choronae, chenturiones, praechones* ...   (Book I, v, 20 in Butler 1920:87–88).

11   Varro also remarks on this obliquely, stating that the form POS could be ambiguous between POS 'having power' and PONS 'bridge'   (*De lingua latina*, Book V, i, 4 in Kent 1951:7).

12   et consules exempta n littera legimus   (Book I, vii, 19 in Butler 1920:143).

13   Atqui eadem illa littera m, quotiens ultima est…etiamsi scribitur, tamen parum exprimitur… adeo ut paene cuiusdam novae litterae sonum reddat
        (Book IX, iv, 37–41 in Butler 1920:529).

3 Consonant weakening and strengthening

1   Word-initial lenition is rare and affects only velars, e.g. QUIRĪTAT > *CRITAT 'shouts' *grida*, CRYPTA 'grotto' *grotta*, CAVEA 'cage' *gabbia*, CON-FLARE 'stir up, blow up' *gonfiare* (and Fr *gonfler*) 'swell', CATTU 'cat' *gatto* (and Sp *gato*). The *Appendix Probi* (§ 2.5.3) cites CALATUS NON GALATUS.

2   In Portuguese this trend went even further (§ 9.6.3).

3   The *Orthographia Gallica*, the oldest treatise on French spelling and pronunciation, composed about 1300, has most recently been edited by Johnston (1987).

4   See e.g. Clements and Keyser (1983), Murray and Vennemann (1983), Vennemann (1988), Milliken (1988).

5   For word-medial fortition see §§ 4.3.1 and 4.3.4.

6   The [gu] of It *Guglielmo* is an example of sporadic rounding of an unstressed vowel in contact with a labial: [gwi] > [gu] (see Exercise 6.8).

7   The element *guad-* seen in many Spanish **toponyms** is not from either of these sources, but rather from Ar *wadi* 'river (bed)': /wadi-al-kabir/ > *Guadalquivir*, /wadi-al-aʃːaraⱡ/ > *Guadalajara*.

8   In explaining the development of French *esprit*, be sure you have first identified the Latin stressed vowel – the Spanish reflex, where a diacritic indicates stress position, is useful for this. Warning: do not invoke syncope to delete the *stressed* vowel, something that can't happen.

4 New palatal consonants

1   The change /w/ > /v/ is a case of word-medial fortition.

2   The Spanish treatment stands out from the other two. There is no epenthesis, but rather metathesis and then /i/ becomes non-syllabic: VIDUA > [biðua] > [biuða] > [bjuða].

3   The *Appendix Probi* cites twenty errors that may reflect confusion about hiatus, if we assume that <I> stands for [j]. These include: VINEA NON VINIA, CAVEA NON CAVIA, LANCEA NON LANCIA, SOLEA NON SOLIA, CALCEUS NON CALCIUS, and TINEA NON TINIA.

4   These two positions, word-initial and postconsonantal, were also seen to pattern together as the protected positions in lenition (§ 3.2.4). We return to this point in § 4.3.8.

5   For vocalism of *hui*, *appui* see § 5.3.5.

6   In *puits* 'well' the spelling reflects the earliest stage, where /tj/ yields /ts/. The vocalism, which involves a secondary yod, raising, and reversal of syllabicity, is complicated but regular (see § 5.3.5).

7   In Sp *coz* < *CALCEU, the /o/ points to a velarization of preconsonantal /l/, as happens in French (§ 3.3.1): *CALCEU 'kick' > [kawts] > [kots] > [kos] (or [koθ]) *coz*, like ALTERU 'other' > [awtru] > [otro] *otro*.

8   For the apparent discrepancies in French, see § 3.3.1.

9   The Ē of FLĒBILE should give a high mid /e/, but, strikingly, the sequence /je/ adjusts to /jɛ/ to match the far more frequent primary diphthong /jɛ/. Likewise PLĒBE 'parish' > [pjɛve] instead of the expected [pjeve].

10   See § 4.3.11 on /r/ plus yod in Italian.

11   SIFILARE 'whistle, hiss' has a variant SIBILARE which yields Sp *silbar*. See Exercise 12.4.

12   Perhaps It *coscia* 'thigh' < COXA 'hip' belongs to this group, but it could just as well be a back formation from the plural COXAE > *cosce*.

13   EXAMEN 'swarm' is an apicultural (bee-keeping) term. Literally, EX-AG-MEN was 'a driving or leading out', referring to a moment when one faction in a hive suddenly emigrates *en masse* to form a new hive. The same etymon also yielded, oddly enough, EXAMEN 'scrutiny, investigation'.

14   Italian also has words in *-iero, -iere, -iera* borrowed from French (§ 5.3.1), e.g. *guerriero* 'warrior', *parrucchiere* 'hairdresser', *caffettiera* 'coffee maker'.

15   Consonant developments sensitive to protected position (word-initial and postconsonantal) have come up before: see §§ 3.2.4, 4.3.2, and 4.3.8. For MASTICAT we posit an early syncope to *MASCAT, where /ka/ is in protected position.

5 More about vowels: raising, yod effects, and nasalization

1   *MŬCULU < CŬMULU 'heap' by metathesis (Pianigiani 1907).

2   NĔBULA 'fog' > *nebbia* [neb:ja] is an isolated case where an expected low mid is actually a high mid.

3   LŎNGU 'long' > *lungo* is an isolated case where the vowel raises two degrees.

4   IANUARIU > *gennaio* appears to be an isolated case of pretonic raising of /a/.

5   Between the vowel and the distant yod, what intervenes is either a labial or a cluster ([tr], [str]).

6   Also perhaps to be placed in this group is LĪMPIDU 'clear' *limpio* 'clean', where [j] arises only after [d] is lost by lenition.

7   For TĔPIDU 'warm' *tibio*, Menéndez Pidal (1966:130) reconstructs *TĒPIDU to account for what would otherwise be a case of "double" raising. Leonese has the expected *tebio*.

8   Linguists disagree about the "cherry" word. Latin had CERASUS (f.) and CERASIU (n.), borrowed from Greek. To judge from Spanish only, the Romance base could be CER[a]SIA (Penny, Menéndez-Pidal) or CER[e]SIA (Corominas) or CER[ɛ]SIA, given that, as we saw, [aj] [ej] [ɛj] all reduce to the [e] seen in *cereza*. However, It *ciliegia* (with the diphthong [jɛ]) and Fr *cerise* (which had the diphthong [jɛ] at an earlier stage, cf. § 5.3.4) point unambiguously to the low mid CER[ɛ]SIA.

9   An exception is VĔTULU > VĔCLU > *viejo*. See Corominas and Pascual (1980) for a detailed critique of opinions about why *viejo* has a diphthong.

10   *Castiello* and *siella* are first attested in tenth-century documents, *cuchiello* in Gonçalvo de Berceo (Corominas and Pascual 1980, quoting Oelschläger 1940).

11   Seemingly exceptional is BĔLLU 'beautiful' > *bello*, not *billo. However, *bello* is not a native word, but rather a thirteenth-century *cultismo* modelled on Provençal *bel* (Corominas and Pascual 1980).

12   *Vowel harmony* is a more inclusive term than *metaphony*: it can refer to any kind of feature spreading to or from stressed or unstressed vowels.

13   Also in this group is Late Latin COFIA, CUFIA 'helmet, headdress', which fails to pattern with other clusters of labial + yod (§ 4.3.11), and yields *coiffe* [kwaf] rather than *[kuʃ].

14   For MFr *huile* see § 5.3.5.

15   A similar reversal of syllabicity is seen in *juillet* [ʒɥijɛ] 'July', a derivative of IŪLIU. See Exercise 5.6.

16   The last stage, fronting of the glide [wi] > [ɥi], fails in some other words too: *oui* [wi] 'yes', *Louis* [lwi], *fouit* [fwi] 'digs'.

17   Modern Standard French has only three, having merged /œ̃/ into /ɛ̃/.

6 Verb morphology: the present indicative

1   Class III has a subset of verbs that share some properties of the class IV (§ 6.2).

2   From class II (-ĒRE) to class I (-ĀRE).

3   From class II (-ĒRE) to class I (-ĀRE).

4   Not Lat GAUDĒRE, but a suffixed *GAUDIĀRE has to be the source of Sp *gozar*.

5   Quintilian alludes to this in his *Institutio oratoria* (Book I, vi, 7–9), where he censures a usage that converts Cl Lat FERVĒRE to *FERVĔRE.

6   Verbs like *luire* 'shine' (*nuire* 'harm', *cuire* 'cook') belong to class III, not class IV. They acquired their stem vowel /i/ via regular sound changes in Old French (§ 5.3.5).

7   Romanian alone faithfully preserves the stress pattern of class III (§ 10.5, top).

8   See Maiden (1995) for more on this analysis and its sources. Extensive discussion is provided in Tekavčić (1972: 108–109, 114, 200–206).

9   This is the account favored by Rohlfs (1968). For an appealing "slightly modified scenario," see Maiden (1995:131).

10   In Old French [pɔrt] is a legal syllable, but [ēntr] is not, since the sonority curve would rise at the end, yielding a second syllable without a permissible nucleus.

11   This <s>, though attested very early, was slow to take hold. By the time it became standard in the 1400s and 1500s it was no longer pronounced (Fouché 1967:182–183).

12   MŎRĪRE is starred because in Classical Latin it is a deponent.

13   Two non -*ir* verbs, *caber* 'fit' and *saber* 'know', show present-stem metaphony in certain forms (§ 7.3.2).

14   MĒTĪRE is starred because in Classical Latin it is a deponent.

15   For example, the yod arising in PARĒŌ 'I appear' leads regularly to *paio* (§ 4.3.10). *Paiono* is created by analogy to *paio*.

PARĒŌ	paio	PARĒMUS	pariamo
PARĒS	pari	PARĒTIS	parete
PARĒT	pare	PARĒNT	paiono

16   Another example is the analogical first singular *duermo* 'I sleep' replacing the expected DŎRMĬŌ > *dormo*, which would have metaphonic raising of low mid [ɔ] to high mid [o], hence no diphthong.

17   OFr *pui*, later *puis* by analogy, still exists as a high-register variant of *peux*.

18   In *chiedere*, intervocalic [r] > [d] is a sporadic (unpredictable) change, cf. RARU > It *rado* 'rare', ARMARĬU > It *armadio* 'cabinet'.

19   In an alternative treatment, *ERĬGĔRE assimilates to the *pedir pido* type (§ 6.6.2), giving *erguir irgo* etc.

20   Portuguese has no /g/ in these verbs. But alongside *tenho* [teɲu] and *venho* [veɲu], both regular, it makes PŌNŌ into *ponho* [poɲu] on the model of the other two. So these verbs form a club in all three languages.

21   In both Spanish and Italian, parallel to the birth of *tengo, vengo*, a similar process involving [ʎ] instead of [ɲ] creates forms like *salgo* and *valgo*.

22   In French, but not Italian, it also occurs throughout the imperfect paradigm: It *finiva*, Fr *finissait* 'was finishing'.

23   In French too, there are verb stems which contained the -*sc*- historically but are no longer segmentable: PARESCĔRE *paraître* 'seem'.

24   The Popular Latin of Spain used SĔDĒRE in a locative sense, e.g. ...*illa valle... ubi sederant filii Israhel* '...in that valley... where the children of Israel were located', *Peregrinatio Aetheriae* 5, 1 (§ 8.9).

25   Rohlfs (1968: II, 267–268).

26   Portuguese too has an anomalous glide in: *sou, estou, dou, vou* (§ 9.13.1). Regarding /ow/ versus /oj/, see § 9.2.3.

27   Anderson and Rochet (1979:266), citing Bourciez (1967:218, 438).

28   Rohlfs (1968:II, 278). He also cites a sixth-century inscription from Carthage: AD MAGISTRU NON AMNAVIT 's/he did not go to the master'.

29   Also from īRE is French *ir-*, the stem for the future and conditional forms of *aller*.

30   ALARE appears four times in a dictionary-like document, the Glosses of Reichenau (eighth century, Northern France). See § 12.1.3.

31   Strikingly, VADĪMŬS VADĪTĬS underwent this syncope early enough to escape the otherwise pervasive shift to arhizotonic first and second plurals that would have given *VADĪMŬS *VADĪTĬS.

32   One trend in sixteenth-century French pronunciation led certain instances of [wɛ] to become [ɛ] rather than [wa] (§ 7.4.3).

7 Verb morphology: systemic reorganization

1   Portuguese alone retains a synthetic pluperfect derived from the Latin pluperfect (§ 9.14.4). Romanian also has a synthetic pluperfect, less directly derived from the Latin form (§ 10.6.5).

2   Some Sardinian dialects preserve the original imperfect subjunctive. The original forms survive in Portuguese, but with another function (§ 9.16.1).

3   The Latin second plural forms did undergo an adjustment: in their final syllable they match the corresponding indicatives, which came from the imperative (§ 6.3.5).

4   For these yod-induced sound changes see § 4.3. Recall (§ 6.8) that the *venga salga* type involves a complex analogical mechanism. Examples in class IV are scarce because so many -IRE verbs acquired the stem extender -*isc*, which effaced the original yod:

FINĬO   'I finish'   finisco   FINĬAT   'finishes'   finisca

5   Analogical *siemo* (from regular *semo*) is the source of back-formed *sie* and *sieno,* which appear in Old Italian texts as recessive variants.

6   Unstressed vowels in Western Romance form a five-vowel system with no distinction between high and low mids. Hence, when any unstressed mid vowel raises it becomes high: *sintamos, durmamos.*

7   The distribution of metaphonic allomorphy has been shaped both by analogical extension (§ 6.6.2) and by an apparently arbitrary restriction to -*ir* verbs even though other classes contained yod-producing hiatus. The only non -*ir* verbs showing metaphony are *caber* 'fit', *saber* 'know'. The present indicative has the metaphonic stem *quep*- only in the first singular (unlike all the -*ir* verbs of this type, which generalize the metaphonic stem to the boot template), but the subjunctive has the stems *quep- sep-* throughout the paradigm.

8   The yod would arise regularly after a stem-final palatal consonant.

9   *Eramo* and *erate* were short-lived and barely attested in Old Italian.

10   For details and a review of scholarly opinion on -*ié-*, see Malkiel (1959).

11   Normally, an intervocalic Popular Latin [β] gives French [v]: FABA 'bean' > *fève,* CABALLU 'horse' > *cheval.* For the standard explanation see Nyrop (I: 362, 457), Pope (1934:346), Fouché (1967:236).

12   "The modern spelling <ai> which sanctioned this change was finally adopted by the Académie Française in 1835" (Anderson and Rochet 1979:272).

13   Evidence for a suppletive relationship between ESSĒRE and STARE comes from the past participle *été* 'been' < STATU (§ 7.10) and the ambiguity of future forms like OFr *estrai* 'you will be', which may derive from either **esseras* or **esteras.*

14   "Yo, dude," he goes, "your homies just pushed me around" (Caplan 1954: Book IV, x, 20–21, trans. ours).

15   Examples from Nyrop (II:130), Diehl (1910:19), Väänänen (1966:45).

16   Both -VĒRUNT and -VĔRUNT were possible for the third plural. They would of course differ in stress. Still, either is consistent with the short forms CANTĀRUNT PARTĪRUNT, given that stress on -ĒRUNT would retract to the thematic vowel, as it does in the second person short forms. Reasons for positing -ĒRUNT come to light in Spanish (§§ 7.5.2, 7.6.2).

17   Although attested in Latin, third singulars in -AIT survive only in Old Sardinian as -ait, later -ât (Tekavčić 1972: §660.3, Wagner 1993:336, Blasco Ferrer 1984:104).

18   Malkiel (1976:446–471) offers a meticulous critical review of the scholarly literature on the Spanish weak perfect, especially -ió, -ieron.

19   Such weak perfects still exist in Portuguese (§ 9.14.3).

20   These endings in turn would be modeled on the strong perfect of DARE 'give'. See also Lloyd (1987:301–302).

21   Similar to the force at work in colloquial American English today, e.g. *Honey, I Shrunk the Kids* instead of *shrank*.

22   Loss of preconsonantal [s], as we saw, is typically marked in French spelling by a circumflex accent on the preceding vowel. In this case, the "lost" <s> had been purely orthographic.

23   Apparently CECĪDĒRUNT 'they fell' was unintelligible by the time of the eighth-century Glosses of Reichenau (§ 12.1.3), where an updated form *caderunt* serves to gloss it.

24   PERDEDI occurs in the CIL III 8447 (Pope 1934:370).

25   There are several opinions about why *ebbi* and *seppi* have stem vowel /e/. For a critical review of the literature, see Tekavčić (1972:II, 387ff).

26   That is, fewer verbs in Spanish preserve the strong type. In terms of token frequency, on the contrary, the strong type is more prominent in Spanish, since the preterite belongs to the spoken language.

27   The OSp variant *troxe* did join the trend, yielding *truje*, attested in Renaissance texts and in some modern dialects. Had it survived, Modern Spanish would have high stem vowels in all its strong *pretéritos*.

28   The yod in third plural *-ieron* is not very consequential, since its metaphonic effect is confined to *-ir* verbs, which rarely had strong perfects. The main example is VĒN- 'came': Old Spanish at first has variants *venieron ~ vinieron*, but the metaphonic effect of the yod prevails decisively from the 1500s on, just as it does in weak perfects like *sintieron* 'they heard', *durmieron* 'they slept' (§ 7.5.2).

29   Lenition is blocked after [aw]: PAUCU > *poco* 'little', *AV(I)CA > *oca* 'goose' (Menéndez Pidal 1966:140–141). Counterexamples: PLACUĪ > OSp *plugo* 'it pleased', PAUPERE > *pobre* 'poor', among others.

30   Others of this class include: HABUIT > *out* > *eut* 'had', PLACUIT > *plout* > *plut* 'pleased', TACUIT > *tout* > *tut* 'kept silent'.

31   Like that invoked to explain the high vowel of Spanish *hice* < FĒCĪ and *vine* < VĒNĪ (§ 7.5.6).

32   The third person forms of this group regularly developed a diphthong:

perdɛdit > perdjɛdt > perdjɛt > perdjɛθ
perdɛderunt > perdɛdrənt > perdɛrənt > perdjɛrənt

On the model of the first singular *perdi* these forms were regularized to *perdi, perdirent* in Central and Northern French by 1200 (Pope 1934:374).

33   The original Latin imperfect subjunctive, which looks like the present active infinitive with personal endings (Chart 7.1), survives marginally. In Portuguese it becomes the inflected infinitive (§ 9.16.1). In Spanish it serves as a literary variant of the periphrastic pluperfect indicative (§ 7.9.2). Only in one dialect of Sardinian does it survive with its original function.

34   'they pledged themselves ready to do willingly whatever he commanded' (*De bello africano* 33). A pluperfect reading ('whatever he had commanded') hardly makes sense, since *whatever* indicates that the commands have not yet been issued.

35   For Italian and Spanish we reconstruct CANTASSEMUS CANTASSETIS with the usual retraction of stress onto the thematic vowel. French shows evidence for CANTASSEMUS CANTASSETIS (§ 7.6.3).

36   As we saw in the imperfect, infectum stems sometimes reflect older, unabbreviated infinitives, e.g. *dire* 'say' but *dicesse* (§ 7.4.1).

37   This change may have been reinforced by the sigmatic strong perfects in *-assero*, *-essero*, *-issero*, e.g. *trassero* 'they pulled', *lessero* 'they read', *dissero* 'they said' (Tekavčić 1972:II, 371).

38   In Old Spanish this paradigm retained its original pluperfect value throughout the medieval period, and only later drifted toward the value of the *-se* paradigm (Chart 7.8). It remains a pluperfect even today in Portuguese (§9.14.4) and in high formal registers of Spanish.

39   On ne peut le nier: l'imparfait du subjonctif est en train de mourir … On embaumera ces flexions, on les roulera dans les suaires de la grammaire historique, et cela sera très bien.
      It cannot be denied: the imperfect subjunctive is dying … These forms will be embalmed and wrapped in the shroud of historical grammar, and that will be just fine.
                        (Rémy de Gourmont (1902:253–254) in Nyrop (II:150), trans. ours)

40   Some scholars attribute these forms to the sources just mentioned (Nyrop II:151–152, Pope 1934:384), while others posit purely phonetic explanations (Fouché 1967:339–340).

41   The fusion of all three occurs in Portuguese, resulting in the formal identity of the future subjunctive with the inflected infinitive (§§ 9.16.1–2).

42   This idea recurs with perfect consistency in the grammatical treatises collected in Keil (1857), including those of Sacerdos, Donatus, Charisius, Diomedes, Priscian, Cledonius, Pompeius, and the supposed Probus, author of the *Instituta artium*. No examples are offered in the grammars themselves, but elsewhere the use of this paradigm with a future subjunctive value is well attested. Consider the formulas often included in epitaphs to lay a curse on possible intruders (examples from Diehl 1961): SI QUIS HUNC SEPULCHRUM UIOLAUERIT 'if anyone shall violate this tomb' (3850), SI QUIS SEPULCRUM HUNC UIOLARIT 'if anyone shall violate this tomb' (3845), QUI HUNC LOCUM BIOLABERIT 'whoever shall violate this place' (3844). These verbs are ambiguous between (according to our tradition) perfect subjunctive and future perfect indicative, but indicative is unlikely in this context and perfect makes no sense. The (moribund) Spanish future subjunctive, however, would translate these examples perfectly.

43   The old future had properties unlikely to endear it to learners. Classes III and IV had their own distinct paradigm, not shown in Chart 7.1. Add to this the impending homonymy with certain forms from other paradigms (-ABIT -ABIMUS with perfects -AVIT -AVIMUS, among many other pairs), and the demise of the old future was assured. See Penny (2002:205–206).

44   in nulla enim re sic fit soloecismus etiam a doctis. praesens est, dum agitur: ceterum si non agatur, non est praesens: non possum dicere lego, nisi dum lego, dum in ipso actu sum. ergo si mihi dicas "lege mihi Vergilium," et dixero lego, soloecismus est. nam cum adhuc in re non sim, quo modo praesens tempus adsumo? ergo debemus dicere legam.
      From *Explicationes artis Donati*, ascribed to one Sergius, whose dates are unknown, but he is commenting on the grammarian Donatus, who lived in the 300s. In Keil (1857:IV, 507–508).

45   Tekavčić (1972:II, 303–305) and Pinkster (1987) offer abundant examples, including those cited here.

46   Fredegarius in Krusch (1888:85).

47   Exceptions are *giacere* 'lie', *piacere* 'please', *tacere* 'be silent', and *sedere* 'sit'.

48   Modern secondary clusters arising from schwa deletion, such as this [tr], remain stable in French. They do not evolve the way the ancient secondary clusters did, such as the [tr] from *POTER-AT > *pourra*.

49   Sp *será* could be from *ESSER-AT, but more plausibly derives from *SEDER-AT, given the evidence for syncretism (§§ 6.10.1, 7.3.2).

50   A singular paradigm *iere, ieres, iere* also occurs in Old French, perhaps arising from confusion with Old French reflexes of the Latin imperfect ĒRAM ĒRAS ĒRAT.

51   Portuguese uses as auxiliary *ter* 'have' < TENERE 'hold' (§ 9.15.2).

52   The next three examples are cited in Pinkster (1987:197, 201).

53   The *Formulae Salicae Merkelianae* is a collection of eighth- to ninth-century ready-made notarial formulas, with blanks to be filled in by users.

54   Ulpianus, *Digesta* 43, 12, 1, 202, cited in Pinkster (1987:198), trans. ours.

55   One school of thought, Relational Grammar, explains auxiliary selection as the mark of a certain syntactic structure, concurrently accounting for adjective and past participle agreement, among other related phenomena, and uncovering some remarkable secrets of Italian grammar. See, for example, La Fauci (2000).

56   Posner (1996:16) also cites some periphrastic perfects with 'be' in certain Romanian dialects.

57   In Old French the two verbs were also linked by a formal similarity: *ester* 'stand', *estre* 'be'. See also § 7.4.3, note 13.

58   There were a few strong participles from classes I and IV, but they were remade as -ĀTU, -ĪTU types (e.g. DOMĀRE 'tame', DOMĬTU > It *domare, domato* and SENTĪRE 'feel', SENSU > It *sentire, sentito*, Sp *sentir, sentido*, Fr *sentir, senti*).

59   It is regular in Spanish for unstressed <ī> to remain [i] in a word-initial syllable and to become [e] in a final syllable: cf. *VĪVĪRE > vivir, *DĪCĪS > dices*.

8 Noun and adjective morphology

1   Latin also has a **vocative** case used for direct address, but it is distinguished only in the second declension, e.g. MARCE 'yo, Marcus!'

2   Old Italian even retained the reflex of its original nominative plural, MANŪS, and thus had invariable *la mano ~ le mano*.

3   In keeping with their origin in the fifth declension, these nouns, in Italian, remain invariant in the plural.

4   In, respectively, the *Regula monachorum* 39 and *De situ terrae sanctae* 11, both cited by Herman (2000: 160), who also notes the accusative CASTAS (more on this below).

5   A few prepositions take different cases to convey different meanings. In such a situation it is the case ending that disambiguates the preposition: e.g. IN CAMERA 'in the room', IN CAMERAM 'into the room'.

6   The rise of nominative -AS may have multiple causes. The first declension may have analogized to the third, which has no case contrast in the plural. Moreover, it would be functionally odd for the plural (marked category) to maintain a case contrast once the singular (unmarked category) loses it. Finally, the Oscan and Umbrian substrata in Southern Italy may have been a factor (Väänänen 1966:83), since these sister languages of Latin had -AS in the corresponding nominative plurals, inherited from Indo-European.

7   Unstressed word-final [oj] > [o] is regular in Italian. Compare tonic *noi* 'we', *voi* 'you' with OIt atonic *no* 'us', *vo* 'you' < NŌS, VŌS (§ 8.8.1), and tonic *poi* 'then' < POST 'after' with atonic *dopo* 'after' < *DE POST. Further examples: MĬNUS > */menoj/ > *meno* 'less', MĒLĬUS > */meʎoj/ > *meglio* 'better'.

8   Old Spanish experienced a trend known today as *apócope extrema*, loss of final -e. During the reign of Alfonso X el Sabio (1252–1284) the trend was reversed and final <e> was restored

except after dental and alveolar consonants (Lloyd 1987:320–322, Penny 2002:58–59, Franchini 2005:326–330).

9   No case contrast is shown in this chart because by Middle French it was vanishing from the language.

10   In the prehistory of Latin, intervocalic [s] becomes [r], a sound change known as **rhotacism**. In words like these we can recognize the long stem, with its intervocalic [r], in such English *cultismos* as *lateral, corporal, temporary, pectoral*.

11   Idiomatic ĒST ŎPUS 'it is needful' leaves some relics. See Exercise 8.4.

12   Usually masculine, Sp *mar* is feminine in some idioms (*alta mar, mar ancha*). In Spain, some regions distinguish *el mar* 'the Mediterranean' from *la mar* 'the Atlantic' (Diego de Acosta, p.c.).

13   Except neuters, which have the short stem in both the nominative and accusative singular.

14   This was quite normal in Old French. Given its two-case system with a *cas sujet* derived from the Latin nominative, there were understandably many nouns with short and long stems distributed according to case, e.g. *suer seror* < SŎROR SORŌRE 'sister', *nies nevou* < NĒPOS NEPŌTE 'nephew', *cuens conte* < CŎMES CŎMĬTE 'comrade'.

15   Plural *uomini* < HOMĬNES.

16   Another possible motivation: since *vos* was also a second singular in certain dialects, *vosotros* could serve as a distinct plural (Penny 2002:134).

17   Other rivals to *no vo* were *ne ve*, both of debated origin (Elcock 1960:82–83, Rohlfs 1968: 158–161, Tekavčić 1972:II, 241–242, 577).

18   Old French *gié* appears to be from tonic ĒGO: [ɛgo] > [ɛo] > [jɛo] > [je] > [dʒe] *gié*.

19   Cited in Väänänen (1966:128), Anderson and Rochet (1979:94).

20   In Latin, the interrogative was identical to the relative pronoun in all but the nominative singular, where QUIS (interrogative) contrasts with QUI (relative). Popular Latin soon took care of that, replacing QUIS with QUI. The Pompeii inscriptions record SI QUI MURIA BONA VOLET 'if anyone wants good brine', and Petronius has QUI DE NOBIS 'who of us?' repeated three times (*Satyricon* 58), among other examples.

21   These examples are cited in Tekavčić (1972:II, 234).

22   Cited in Nyrop (II:390).

23   Pighi (1964), cited in Tekavčić (1972:II, 234).

24   In fact, *loro* also figures in the possessive adjective paradigm, though it remains invariable (*la loro casa* 'their house'), in keeping with its original status as a non-adjective meaning 'of them'.

25   Some varieties of Spanish also expand the sphere of *le*. Penny writes:

Already in Old Spanish (e.g. PMC 655: *al bueno de mio Cid en Alcoçer le van çercar*), *le* is being used as a direct-object form in the case of masculine personal referents (just as in the modern Peninsular standard). Northern dialects go further and use *le* as a direct-object form for masculine countable referents (whether personal or non-personal; e.g. *esto vaso no hay que romperle*), but not for non-countable (or mass) referents... Such extension of the role of *le* is referred to as **leísmo**, while the retention of *lo* in its traditional, etymological function as a personal (as well as a non-personal) masculine pronoun is labelled **loísmo**.

(Penny 2002:135–136).

26   *Els* and *eus* are the Old French forms, *eux* is modern. For an account of word-final <us> and <ux> in French spelling, see Brunot (1899:252–253).

27   For the reversal of syllabicity [uj] > [ɥi], see § 5.3.5.

28   Another title given to this text is *Itinerarium Egeriae* (Egeria's Journey). The discrepancy in the author's name arose because a certain Valerius, a seventh-century monk who must have had a more complete copy than ours, mentions this work and the author's name – but it appears differently in the manuscripts of Valerius.

29   Conjectures range from Arles (she mentions the Rhône river) to Mont-Saint-Michel to Northern Spain.

30   The first line is the *cas sujet*, the second is the *cas régime*.

31   *Lo* also occurs before [ʃ], [ʦ], [ʣ], [ɲ], and [ps].

9 History and structure of Portuguese: an overview

The material of this chapter was compiled by Emily E. Scida, University of Virginia, Charlottesville.

1   European and Brazilian Portuguese also have low central [ɐ] from Lat Ā/Ă. In Brazilian Portuguese, [ɐ] occurs word-finally, e.g. *casa* [kazɐ] and before nasal consonant plus vowel, e.g. *chama* [ʃɐmɐ], while [a] occurs elsewhere. In European Portuguese, the situation is similar, but there are some minimal pairs, e.g. *dá* [da] 'gives' versus *da* [dɐ] 'of the', and present indicative -*amos* [ɐmuʃ] versus preterite -*ámos* [amuʃ] in all -*ar* verbs.

2   See § 6.10.2. Since HABÉŌ > *[ajo], HABĔAT > *[aja].

3   Spanish also reduced this sibilant inventory, but by neutralizing voice and maintaining the place contrast, ultimately /s/ versus /θ/ (§§ 4.3.5, 4.3.6).

4   Medieval Galician-Portuguese lyric kept (*mia*) *senhor* '(my) lady'.

5   These words were replaced by *segunda feira* 'second weekday = Monday' etc., probably through contact with Arabic, which has the same nomenclature (*yaum al-ithnaya* 'second day = Monday', etc.).

6   Romanian has this contrast in all persons, and in both tonic and atonic pronouns (Chart 10.1).

7   In Brazilian Portuguese, clitics are preverbal with finite verbs, if used at all. See also Exercise 9.6 on third person pronoun allomorphy.

8   Brazilian Portuguese has eliminated the inherited second person endings shown here. Second singulars in /s/ with subject *tu* 'you' are replaced by a formerly polite pronoun *você* 'you' with a third singular verb. In second plurals *vocês* takes a third plural verb.

9   In other forms from the AUDĪRE paradigm, loss of [d] induces the anti-hiatic glide [w], which then becomes [v].

10   Obviously, irregular Po *sou estou vou* present the same problem as do Sp *soy estoy voy doy* (§ 6.10.1). Less obviously. OFr *sui voi* belong to the same picture, having a rogue glide as their only anomaly (§ 6.10.1). Should we insist that explanations be applicable across these languages?

11   Spanish took a different route to avoid this homonymy (§ 6.10.1).

12   Actually, the "irregular" stem *trar-* is the genuine reflex of TRAHĚRE 'draw, drag', while *trazer* is an innovation.

13   Sardinian, Galician, Old Neapolitan, Old Leonese, and Mirandese also have an inflected infinitive.

14   Maurer (1968), Martin (1972), Wireback (1994), Martins (1999), Mensching (2000), Miller (2002), Scida (2004).

10 History and structure of Romanian: an overview

1   In the older orthography [ɨ] was normally written <î> except in a few words, such as *român* 'Romanian'. Current (post-1990) orthography prescribes <â> for all positions except initial and final, and for the prefix IN > *în* in any position (*reîncepe* 'begin again').

2   A morphological constraint intervenes here: in masculine noun plurals, [o̯a] remains intact as in *oaspete* 'guest', *oaspeţi* 'guests'.

3   If *vedere* were shortened, the Coffee Rule would take **vede* to *vedea* (§ 10.1.8, end).

4   Unexpected TĔMPU 'time' *timp* may be the result of back formation from an early variant plural *timpi* (Densuşianu 1934:I, 19).

5   Loss of final /u/ is relatively late, between the 1600s and 1700s.

6   Chițoran (2002) offers some minimal pairs: *coş* [koʃ] 'basket', *coşi* [koʃʲ] 'you sew', and *laş* [laʃ] 'coward', *laşi* [laʃʲ] 'cowards'.

7   Word-finally, /ʃti/ > [ʃtʲ]: *peşti* [peʃtʲ] 'fishes'.

8   Word-finally, [ʃkj] > [ʃkʲ]: **MUSCLU* 'moss' > *muşchi* [muʃkʲ].

9   The longer forms with <RE> survive as feminine nouns: *cântare* 'singing'.

10   For further examples showing backing of /ri/ to /rɨ/ under stress, see § 10.1.7.

11   These unexplained vowels are the opposite of what we expect, cf. AERAMEN > *aramă* 'copper', CĪVĪTATES > *cetăţi* 'fortresses'.

12   This is of course not true of verbs altered by analogical forces, as discussed below. Also exceptional is the loss of /n/ in *vii* 'you come', *ţii* 'you hold'.

13   The unleveled *a durmi, durmim, durmiţi* exist as substandard, dialectal forms (Ştefan Oltean, p.c.).

14   Only ten -*î* verbs lack the stem extender. These verbs, e.g. *a coborî* 'descend, lower', have an unusual mixed conjugation with class I endings in the third person: *cobor, cobori, coboară, coborâm, coborâţi, coboară*.

15   The most productive class today, it is used for neologisms (Lombard 1955:487–488).

16   Lombard (1955:905–906) surveys the literature and deems the problem "almost insoluble."

17   *Vem* > *văm* is a change conditioned by adjacent labials. *Văm* > *vom* may reflect further such conditioning or the influence of *voiu* and *vor* (Lombard 1955:957).

18   Perhaps the subjunctive was invoked to avoid a homonymic clash with first person *voi*. Pop Lat indicative **VOLĒS* would give **VOLI* then *voi*.

19   *Voare* is indirectly attested in a variant *oare*, as in *oarecând* 'whenever', *oarecine* 'whoever' (cf. Sp *quienquiera* 'whoever').

20   Regular *vrem vreţi* had probably remained alive alongside *vom veţi*.

21   Cited in Bourciez (1967:604). Our translation concurs with Pierre Monat's 1992 French version.

22   Except for the formal and written Portuguese conditional (and future). See § 9.15.1, end.

23   In Old Romanian the future too admitted both orders: *voiu cânta* and *cântare-voiu*.

24   For the other short forms see § 7.5.3 and Chart 7.8.

25   In Popular Latin, the dative of possession rivaled the genitive, as in PHILOCOMASIO CUSTOS 'guardian to (=of) Philocomasius' (Plautus, *Miles gloriosus* 271), and gained ground in the later language.

26   See § 10.3.3 on word-final /li/.

27   Latin /l:/ before /a/ is lost by the Star Rule (§ 10.4.1, end).

28   The loss of /l/ here is unexpected. The regular outcome *caprelei* is attested in Megleno-Romanian.

29   The source for *câinele* is CANE + (I)LLE. Expected *vulpilei*, attested in Megleno-Romanian, loses its /le/ in Daco-Romanian *vulpii* (Bourciez 1967:580).

30   Exception: the feminine third plural *le* is accusative and dative.

31   All five tonic pronouns written with initial <e> are pronounced with an initial [j]: *eu* /jew/, etc. In the atonic class, parenthesized /i/ is a support vowel whenever these forms cliticize to a main verb or an auxiliary beginning with a consonant: *îmi aduce câinele* 'she brings the dog to me', *îmi va vorbi* 'she will talk to me', but *mi-a vorbit* 'she talked to me'.

32   The preceding labial triggers /e/ > /ə/ (§ 10.1.7).

33   Word-final /we/ to /wə/ is regular, as in: NOVE 'nine' > /nowe/ > /nowə/ *nouă*, **PLOVĬT* 'rains' > /plowe/ > /plowə/ *plouă*.

11 Formation of the Romance lexicon

1   Classical authors were highly sensitive to register in their diction. Forms of BELLU, for instance, occur in Cicero's writings thirty-seven times, of which fully twenty-four are in his letters, a less formal genre (Stefenelli 1962:70).

2   It *cascare* 'fall' has a different source, CASU (participle of CADĔRE 'fall') plus -ICARE.

3   See § 3.3.4 for further details on the reflexes of *COLLOCARE < *CON-LOC-ARE.

4   This popular form is attested in the *Satyricon* (40, 43, 44, 46, 134, 141).

5   In what follows, we do not usually signal differences in meaning among cognates.

6   In older formations, the pretonic [i] usually deletes if the resulting consonant cluster is acceptable.

7   These words came to Ibero-Romance from Italian, cf. CILIA Sp *ceja* 'eyelash', PALEA Sp *paja* 'straw'.

8   The gerundive is an adjective formed productively from verb bases. Examples: ADDENDUM '(thing) to be added', AGENDA '(things) to be done'.

9   Some non-derived adjectives became nouns too, as in APRĪCU 'sunny' > Sp *abrigo*, Fr *abri*, Po *abrigo*, and TAM MAGNU 'so big' > Sp *tamaño*, Po *tamanho* 'size'.

10   Lat VER 'spring' in Popular Latin became *VERA meaning 'summer'. Also attesting to this change are It *primavera* 'spring' and Ro *vară* 'summer', *primăvară* 'spring'.

11   Via a complex process involving lenition, syncope, palatalization as a compromise articulation, and deaffrication: [atiku] > [adigu] > [adgə] > [adʒə] > [aʒ].

12   All five languages also have Latinate versions of -ATICU (It *-atico*, Sp *-ático*, Fr *-atique*, Po *-ático*, Ro *-atic*) but these continue to act as adjective-forming suffixes.

13   In Romanian, long infinitives fulfill this function: *a intra* 'enter', *intrare* 'entry, entrance'.

14   Some words with stressed /wɛ/ that received /ɛ/ are FLĒBILE 'pathetic' > *FĒBILE faible [fɛbl] 'weak', MONĒTA 'coin' *monnaie* /mɔnɛ/, and CRĒTA 'chalk' *craie* /kRɛ/ (compare PRAEDA 'prey' > *PRĒDA proie /pRwa/).

15   Rohlfs (1969: III, 437–438).

16   One notable relic is the word *Romance* itself: it comes from an adverb ROMANICE 'in the Roman way'.

17   Italian adjectives in -*le* or -*re* drop the <e> in forming adverbs: *facile* > *facilmente* 'easily', *regolare* > *regolarmente* 'regularly'. French adjectives in -*ant* and -*ent* from Latin present participles are contracted in forming adverbs: *courant* > *couramment* 'commonly', *évident* > *évidemment* 'obviously'.

18   See Exercise 11.6: *ciò, però, ancora, qui* (< ECCU HIC), *qua, agora, ogaño, pero, oc, oui, ici* (< ECCE HIC), *encore*, etc.

19   Examples of reinforced demonstratives and third person pronouns abound – there are fifty-seven examples of combinations with ATQUE in Plautus alone. Combinations with ECCE include: TEGILLUM ECCILLUD MIHI UNUM ID ARET 'that hood is the only dry thing I have' (*Rudens* 2, 7, 18), HABEO ECCILLAM MEAM CLIENTAM 'I have that girl of mine' (*Miles gloriosus* 3, 1, 94), UBINAMST IS HOMO…? ECCILLUM VIDEO 'where is this man…? I see him' (*Mercator* 2, 3, 98).

20   ECCUM, itself an early combination of ECCE + HUNC, also appears in the early dramatists, but only by itself, never with ILLU, ISTU, etc. It often means 'look, here…': SED ECCUM AMPHITRUONEM ADVENIT 'but look, here comes Amphitruo' (Plautus, *Amphitruo* 3, 4, 22), ATQUE ECCUM VIDEO IPSUM FORAS EXIRE 'and look, I see him coming outside' (Terence, *Andria* 3, 3, 48). Only later does ECCU combine with ILLU, ISTU, etc., as shown above for Italian (which also still has *ecco* 'here is…').

21   Examples: NEC TE ALEATOR NULLUS EST SAPIENTIOR 'nor is there no gambler wiser than you' (Plautus, *Rudens* 2, 3, 29), NEQUE EGO HOMINES MAGIS ASINOS NUMQUAM VIDI 'nor have I never seen men more asinine' (Plautus, *Pseudolus* 1, 136), NEMINEM NIHIL BONI FACERE OPPORTET

'nobody should do nothing good' (Petronius, *Satyricon* 42, 7), QUI NUMQUAM…NIL DEBUIT 'who never owed nothing' (CIL V 6520).

22   These began as *not…a bit* type negations alongside others already established in the Latin lexicon: NULLUS 'none' < NE ULLUS < NE UNULUS 'not a little one', NIHIL 'nothing' < NE HĪLUM 'not a speck', NEMINE 'nobody' < NE HOMINE 'no man'.

23   Similarly, (HOMINE) NATU 'born man' yields OSp *nado* 'nobody'. OSp *nadien* 'nobody' may be a blend with *quien* 'who' (§ 11.4.4). For today's *nadie* see Menéndez Pidal (1966:265) and Elcock (1960:102).

24   When the negative polarity item precedes the verb, Italian, Spanish, and Portuguese do not use the negator from NON, whereas French (at least prescriptively) and Romanian do.

Compare these versions of 'nobody spoke':

Nessuno ha parlato.   Personne n'a parlé.
Nadie habló.   Nimeni n-a vorbit.
Ninguém falou.

25   Ro *nivel* is a borrowing.
26   In a less precise use (not to be encouraged), the term "folk etymology" is applied to historically incorrect etymologies also.
27   Oscan was a major presence in Italy, spoken in most of the peninsula south of Rome. Well represented in the graffiti of Pompeii, it was still alive as late as the 300s CE.
28   The proper use of <Y> becomes an issue in the *Appendix Probi* (§ 2.5.3): GYRUS NON GIRUS, CRISTA NON CRYSTA.
29   Romanian has *biserică* 'church' < Greco-Latin BASILĪCA 'public building'.
30   Langobardic, unlike Gothic and Frankish, underwent a consonant change known to Germanists as the Second Sound Shift. Compare Frk *balla* to Lgb *palla*.
31   Ro *zahăr* 'sugar' came not via Moorish Spain but by an Eastern route (< M Gr *sákharon*).
32   For more examples of Amerindianisms see Penny (2002:275–277).
33   Still others are formed from verbs (DURANTE 'lasting' > It *durante* 'during'), adjectives (BASSU 'low' > Fr *en bas de* 'below') or nouns (TORNU 'lathe' > It *intorno* 'around').

12   Emergence of the Romance vernaculars

1   ut, qui Deo placere appetunt recte uiuendo, ei etiam placere non negligant recte loquendo…Hortamur uos litterarum studia…ad hoc certatim discere, ut facilius et rectius divinarum scripturarum mysteria valeatis penetrare
(Jean Mabillon, *Annales ordinis S. Benedicti*, Liber xxv, 64, cited in Pulgram 1950:460–461)

2   European medieval writing, in whatever language, typically used many abbreviations – not to conserve time, but rather such expensive writing materials as vellum. Modern scholars who prepare such texts for publication usually resolve the abbreviations for the reader's convenience. If, for any reason, a modern edition reproduces exactly the abbreviations, symbols, and word spacing, it is known as a **diplomatic edition**. In the one surviving manuscript, Louis' oath in diplomatic transcription looks like this:

Pro dõ amur & p xp̃ian poblo & nr̃õ cõmun | falvament. dift di en auant. inquantdf | favir & podir medunat. fifalvaraieo. | cift meon fradre karlo. & in aḍ iudha. | & in cad huna cofa. ficũ om p dreit fon | fradra falvar dift. In o quid il miialtre|fi faz&. Et abludher nul plaid nũquã | prindrai qui meon vol cift meon fradre | karle in damno fit.   (Tabachovitz 1932:1)

Clearly one cannot comment on, say, the <s> of *nostro*, since it does not appear in the original.

3   Monteverdi (1952:134), cited in Elcock (1960:450).
4   Among its few archaic features is the use of third plural as an honorific third singular (Rotaru 1981:62–65).
5   Some among the educated minority probably participated in triglossia: Latin, regional koiné, and local vernacular.

Glossary of linguistic terms

ablative absolute A Latin construction with adverbial value, expressing an attendant circumstance. Its predicate and argument are both in the ablative case: TE AUDIENTE 'with you listening'. Romance relics include: It, Sp *durante la guerra*, Fr *pendant la guerre* 'during the war'.

ablative case Latin noun phrases marked with the ablative case typically express the notion 'from location x' or 'by means of x' or, in the ablative absolute, 'in the presence of circumstance x'.

accusative case The accusative case in Latin serves mainly to mark direct objects and the objects of certain prepositions.

allomorphs Different pronunciations of the same morpheme (unit of meaning): Fr *les* 'the (pl.)' has a preconsonantal allomorph (*les fleurs* [le flœr] 'the flowers') and a prevocalic allomorph (*les arbres* [lez aʀbʀ] 'the trees').

analogy A prominent force in language change, analogy is the tendency of the mind to build on models, starting from an existing pattern and extending its domain. In Ro *octombrie*, the [m] is analogical, based on *septembrie, noiembrie, decembrie*.

antepenult The third syllable from the end of a word.

anticipatory assimilation Changing a sound to make it resemble – totally or more closely – a later sound. Also **progressive assimilation**.

apheresis Omission of a word-initial vowel or syllable: EVANGELIU It *vangelo* 'gospel'. Greek for 'taking away'.

apocope Omission of a word-final vowel or syllable: VERITATE It *verità* 'truth'. Greek for 'cutting off'.

arhizotonic Designates a word not stressed on the root.

assimilation Changing any element to make it resemble another, usually in reference to sound change. The sound exerting the attraction may be adjacent (ABDOMEN It *addome*), or non-adjacent (FĒCĪ Sp *hice*, Fr *fis* 'I made').

athematic perfect Any Latin perfect that lacks a thematic vowel. Also **strong perfect**.

autograph manuscript A manuscript written by the hand of the same person who composed the text, as opposed to one that may have suffered from the intervention of copyists.

back formation Reverse derivation. The speaker, interpreting a certain word as a derivative, creates the base form from which it would derive.

blend A word created by combining parts of two words to symbolize a mixture of their meanings: *twizzard* for 'blizzard of twitters' (Maureen Dowd, *New York Times*) or *schnoodle* 'part schnauzer, part poodle'.

blocked syllable A syllable ending in a consonant.

case The categorization of grammatical roles that nouns and pronouns may play in a clause: subject, direct object, indirect object, and various other less central roles. Pronouns display overt marking of their case (Latin and Romance), as do nouns and adjectives (Latin only).

clitic pronouns In Romance, a specific class of pronouns that behave like verb affixes. They cannot stand alone and cannot be conjoined, modified, or moved to sites other than their allotted position. Typically they cannot be stressed (exception: the French type *aidez-moi* 'help me').

coarticulated Pronounced simultaneously with some other sound. Yod is superimposed on [r] in Ro *flori* [florʲ] 'flowers'.

comparative method Procedures used by historical linguists for reconstructing, based on a set of sister languages, the parent language from which they descend (§ 2.5.4).

compositional meaning A meaning computable in a regular way from the meanings of the parts of an expression.

compromise articulation The pronunciation that results when two adjacent sounds that need distinct tongue positions exert a mutual influence, pulling the articulation to a middle position.

contamination A blend that arises inadvertently, not deliberately, from the influence of some conceptually related word.

cultismo Meaning 1: in the context of Romance (and English), a word taken deliberately from Latin or Greek roots, with minimal changes adapting it to the phonology of the borrowing language. Meaning 2: a word that remains in use from antiquity on, but resists the normal sound changes because of its link with cultural zones where Latin remained alive, such as religion, law, or medieval science. Also **learned word** (bisyllabic **learnèd**).

dative case The dative case in Latin serves mainly to mark indirect objects, or to express the notion 'to x', where x may be recipient, benefactee, or person affected.

declension A pattern or paradigm that determines the case-marked forms of a noun, adjective, or pronoun in Latin. Nouns divide into five declensions, while adjectives belong to the first three.

degemination The process that reduces a geminate (long) consonant to a non-geminate (normal) consonant.

denominal verb A verb derived from a noun.

deverbal noun A noun derived from a verb.

diglossia The condition of a speech community where two varieties of speech, related or not, are in regular use, each being specialized to its own set of social contexts.

diphthong A vowel and adjacent glide, in either order, both belonging to the nucleus of the same syllable.

diplomatic edition A diplomatic edition of a text is one that faithfully reproduces the symbols and abbreviations existing in the original.

distal Indicating that which is remote from the speaker, physically or figuratively, such as *that one* as opposed to *this one*.

doublets A pair of words that derive from the same ultimate source but via different paths: HOSPITALE > Fr *hôtel* and, as a semi-*cultismo*, Fr *hôpital*.

elision Deletion of certain word-final vowels before an adjacent word-initial vowel. Fr *la* + *étoile* = *l'étoile* [letwal] 'the star'.

epenthesis Inserting a sound between two others. Often epenthesis serves to resolve a disfavored consonant cluster: *Thom-son* > *Thompson*.

epigraphic Pertaining to inscriptions. From Grk *epi-* 'on' and root *graph* 'write'.

etymon The older word(s) from which a more modern word is derived.

folk etymology The popular tendency to nativize a long, unfamiliar morpheme by resolving it into meaningful (or at least recognizable) parts. Children reportedly convert *cystic fibrosis* to *sixty-five roses*.

fortition Changing a consonant to a stronger one, for example changing a glide to an obstruent: Gmc *werra* > It *guerra* [gwer:a].

free syllable A syllable ending in a vowel.

frequentative verb A derived verb meaning 'perform the action of the base verb often or repeatedly'. Also **iterative verb**.

geminate A long consonant, formed by holding the closure in place for longer than in a plain consonant.

genitive case Latin noun phrases marked with genitive case usually convey the notion 'of x'. The genitive may express possession or virtually any semantic link with the governing noun.

grammatical gender Each noun in Latin belongs to a gender category: masculine, feminine, neuter. For nouns denoting animate beings, grammatical gender correlates well with natural gender, but not perfectly.

grammaticalization The historical process whereby a word evolves into a morpheme with a purely grammatical value. In Fr *je vais rester ici* 'I'm going to stay here', the verb 'go' loses its literal meaning and becomes an auxiliary for the future tense.

h aspiré |aʃaspiʀe| The formerly audible word-initial [h] which entered Old French via Germanic loan words. Though silent today, it still blocks elision: *le heaume* 'the helmet' (not *l'heaume*).

haplology Deletion of one of two adjacent identical syllables.

heavy syllable In Latin, a syllable that ends in a consonant or contains a long vowel or a diphthong.

hiatus Adjacent vowels belonging to separate syllables: It *caos* 'chaos', *poeta* 'poet'.

homorganic Said of a consonant having the same point of articulation (as an adjacent segment). In *RE-MEMORARE* > OFr *remembrer*, the inserted [b] is homorganic to the preceding [m], both being labial.

hybrid A word that has been altered in some irregular way to resemble another individual word of related meaning: Sp *estrella* 'star' < STELLA with [r] from ASTRU 'heavenly body'. Also **contamination**.

hypercharacterization Imposing on a word an extra marking for a certain grammatical feature when the word already has that feature. Much as in dialectal

English *chilluns* (< *children* + *s*), Rheto-Romance has double plurals: Ladino *peresc* [pereʃ] 'fathers' < **peres* + *i*. In Italian the rare plural type *ala* 'wing': *ali* 'wings' probably reflects a double plural **ale* + *i* > *ali* 'wings'.

hypercorrection Errors or innovations of this type occur when people are exposed to a speech register socially higher than their own, and adopt some form that sounds prestigious, but then overzealously generalize it: *the man **whom** we think is guilty.*

hypocoristic Proper to pet names or terms of endearment.

imparisyllabic Describes Latin nouns or adjectives whose nominative singular is one syllable shorter than the other case forms: ARBOR, ARBORE 'tree', LEX, LEGE 'law'.

inchoative Verb forms expressing the idea of entry into a state.

instrumental case Case forms in any language are called instrumental if their chief use is to mark noun phrases meaning 'with x as means or instrument'. Latin has no distinct instrumental case, since the Indo-European instrumental case merged with the dative case in pre-Latin times.

iterative verb A verb form expressing the idea of repeated action. Also **frequentative verb**.

lenition The common (Western Romance) sound change whereby stops and fricatives are progressively "weakened" if situated in an unprotected (postvocalic) position.

lexicon That component of our mental grammar which registers the shape and meaning of all our words or smaller meaningful units (morphemes), together with everything we know about the otherwise unpredictable or idiosyncratic properties of each item.

liaison Formation of a syllable across a word boundary, where a normally silent final consonant becomes overt before an initial vowel of the next word. Fr *mes livres* [melivʀ] 'my books' does not have liaison, *mes amis* [mezami] 'my friends' does. From Lat LIGATIONE 'bond'.

light syllable In Latin, a syllable whose nucleus consists of a short vowel. See **heavy syllable** above and § 1.1.4.

locative Noun phrases meaning "place where something occurs or is situated" are locative expressions. In Latin, the locative case forms inherited from Indo-European had already merged with other cases in pre-literary times.

metaphony A sound change where a vowel later in the word (word-final or not) exerts a harmonizing attraction on an earlier stressed vowel. A term confined mostly to Romance linguistics.

metathesis Sporadic sound change which reverses the order of two segments, either adjacent (**CATENATU* 'chained' > Sp **cadnado* > *candado* 'padlock') or non-adjacent (PERICULU > Sp **periglo* > *peligro* 'danger').

minimal pair A pair of forms that differ in only one way, typically used to demonstrate phonemic contrasts in the sound system of a given language. The minimal pair *version virgin* displays the contrast between fricative [ʒ] and affricate [dʒ] in English.

monophthong A simple vowel, as opposed to a diphthong. In AURU > It *oro* [ɔro] 'gold', an original diphthong becomes a monophthong.

national standard A sociolinguistic term applied chiefly to modern nations. Denotes that variety of a language which is nationally recognized as suitable and proper for governmental, commercial, educational, and other public uses. This recognition may be *de facto*, or it may be conferred by law.

negative polarity item A word confined (strictly or loosely) to contexts colored with unreality, uncertainty, or negation: *did Tub* **ever** *catch* **any** *mice?* / *if Tub* **ever** *caught* **any** *mice*, versus **Tub* **ever** *catches* **any** *mice*. The negation may be overt or implied: *Tub never* / *rarely* / **often catches any mice.*

nominative case The form assigned to a noun, pronoun, or adjective when it occurs as subject of a finite clause. Also used as the citation form (dictionary entry).

paradigm An array showing the possible inflections of a given word, i.e. how it changes its stem and affixes to reflect such features as case, number, gender, or in verbs, person, number, tense, and mood.

paradigm leveling An analogical force that makes a morpheme (especially a verb root) remain invariant throughout its paradigm, overriding any allomorphy (alternating pronunciations) from sound change. English *sword* loses its [w] before [o], but *swore* keeps it, being part of a paradigm.

parisyllabic Describes Latin nouns or adjectives whose nominative singular has the same syllable count as the other case forms: CANIS CANE 'dog', PIGER PIGRU 'lazy'. Compare **imparisyllabic**, above and § 8.7.

Penultimate Rule The phonological rule that determines the placement of stress in Latin words, with results persisting into Romance. Explained in § 1.1.4.

periphrastic A verb form having two parts (*has drawn*), one being a non-finite form of the verb with lexical meaning (*drawn*), and the other an auxiliary (*has*), carrying the inflection.

phonotactic(s) The constraints imposed by a given language on the possible adjacencies of sounds.

pretonic Occurring in a position before the stressed syllable. Sometimes means *immediately* before the stressed syllable.

primary or spontaneous diphthong A term confined to Romance linguistics. Denotes the diphthongs triggered by stress on low mid vowels in Italian, Spanish, and French, and on high vowels in French, with the further requirement (in Italian and French) that the syllable be free. See § 1.2.6.

progressive assimilation Changing any sound to make it resemble – totally or more closely – another later in the word.

proparoxytone A word stressed on the third syllable from the end.

prosthesis or prothesis Adding a word-initial sound for phonetic reasons. Popular Latin in Western lands added prosthetic /e/ before word-initial /s/ + consonant.

protected position The postconsonantal position, where consonants are sheltered from lenition, e.g. PARTE *parte* 'part' in contrast to PATRE *padre* 'father'. Word-initial position is normally protected, exceptions mostly involving Italian velars: CAVEA *gabbia* 'cage'.

proto-language An ancestral language reconstructed in a hypothetical form by comparing its descendants.

proximal Indicating that which is near the speaker, physically or figuratively, such as *this one* as opposed to *that one.*

reflex The newer word (or similar unit) that results from applying normal sound changes to an older one.

register The speech style associated with any particular social ambience, especially as ranked along a scale of formality.

regressive assimilation Changing any sound to make it resemble – totally or more closely – a preceding one.

rhizotonic Stressed on the root.

rhotacism Any sound change that converts some segment into [r]. In archaic Latin, intervocalic /s/ > /r/.

sandhi Systematic alterations of sound that occur at boundaries, especially across word boundaries. Sanskrit for 'joining'.

secondary diphthong Any diphthong newly created in Romance, excluding the primary diphthongs (see under **primary**).

sigmatic perfect A Latin perfect marked by adding /s/ after the root.

sporadic Describes a sound change that occurs unsystematically, not as a general regularity.

standardize A language is standardized when the community of speakers, or an authoritative subgroup among them, agree upon the approved pronunciation, morphology, and lexicon, to the exclusion of disfavored variants.

strong perfect Any Latin perfect that lacks a thematic vowel. Given this feature, and the Penultimate Rule, Latin strong perfects are always rhizotonic (root-stressed) in at least the first and third singular. They form the nucleus for the class of "irregular" Romance preterites.

substratum, superstratum These terms refer to a language contact scenario in which one language becomes dominant and the other recedes. In lands where Latin effaced a pre-existent language, that language is a substratum with respect to Latin. In lands where Latin arrived but did not become dominant (such as Britain), Latin is a superstratum. In lands where invaders settled among Latin-speaking peoples and were assimilated, their languages are superstrata.

suppletion A case where elements of unrelated origin are fused into a single paradigm: Eng *go, went* and *good, better,* Sp *voy* 'I go', *iba* 'I went'.

syncope Loss of a medial unstressed syllable: Eng *every.* The process normally originates in fast speech.

syncretism Loss of contrast between two formerly distinct morphological categories or inflectional forms. Example: in first and second person clitic pronouns of Western Romance (It *mi ti ci vi,* Sp *me te nos os,* Fr *me te nous vous*), dative and accusative case have been conflated. In Latin, dative case does the work of instrumental, due to pre-Latin syncretism.

synthetic Having multiple units of meaning expressed in one unsegmentable piece of morphology. The Latin inflection -STĪ has no parts, yet it registers four features: second person singular perfect indicative. One-word expressions like Latin MINORE 'smaller' are called synthetic in contrast to analytic It *più piccolo,* Sp *mas pequeño,* Fr *plus petit,* Ro *mai mic* 'smaller', where the units of meaning are separated.

thematic vowel In the great majority of Latin verbs, a long [aː], [eː], or [iː] which ends the infectum stem, and to which [w] is added to make the perfectum stem. Its effect on stress position has major consequences for Romance verb developments (§ 7.5).

toponym Place name.

vocative Nouns in the vocative case serve to call or name the person being addressed. Latin uses nominatives for vocatives, except in the second declension: *vale, Marce* 'goodbye, Marcus'.

vowel harmony Any systematic process where one vowel assimilates to another.

waw perfect A Latin perfect marked by adding [w] at the end of the stem.

weak perfect Any Latin perfect containing a thematic vowel. Weak perfects are marked only by stem-final [w] (which is effaced in the popular shortened forms) and always arhizotonic (stressed off the root) in all forms.

Suggestions for further reading

Latin: historical studies

Adams 2003, 2007.
Ernout 1927.
Ernout and Thomas 1951.
Landgraf 1894–1908.
Marouzeau 1922–1949.
Oniga 2004.
Palmer 1961.
Pinkster 1990.
Tagliavini 1962.

Vulgar Latin: general

Battisti 1949.
Grandgent 1907.
Herman 2000.
Hofmann 1951.
Löfstedt 1959.
Muller 1970.
Schuchardt 1866–1868.
Väänänen 1983.
Vossler 1954.

Vulgar Latin: texts

Corpus Inscriptionum Latinarum (CIL) 1862–1975.
Díaz y Díaz 1975.
Diehl 1910.
Diehl 1913.
Muller and Taylor 1932.
Rohlfs 1968.
Stefenelli 1962.
Väänänen 1966.

Romance: general historical studies

Agard 1984.
Auerbach 1965.
Bourciez 1967.
Cornagliotti, Piccat, and Ramello 2001.
Coseriu 1977.
Diez 1836–1843.
Elcock 1960.
Gess and Arteaga 2006.
Harris and Vincent 1988.
Herman 1990, 2006.
Iordan and Orr 1970.
Lausberg 1969.
Lee 2000.
Maiden, Smith, and Ledgeway 2009.
Meyer-Lübke 1890–1902.
Meyer-Lübke 1920.
Posner 1996.
Posner and Green 1980–1982.
Renzi and Andreose 2003.
Renzi and Salvi 1995.
Rohlfs 1957.
Schlösser 2005.
Tagliavini 1964.
Vidos 1956.
von Wartburg 1950.
Wright 1982, 1996, 2002.

Romance: phonology

Hall 1976.
Jensen 1999.
Leonard 1978.
Pulgram 1975.
Schürr 1970.

Romance: morphology

Coseriu 1976.
Hall 1983.
Mourin 1962.
Pountain 1983.
Schwegler 1990.
Vincent and Harris 1982.

Romance: syntax

Harris and Ramat 1987.

La Fauci 1988, 1997.
Loporcaro 1998.
Wanner 1987.

Romance: lexicon

Malkiel 1989, 1992, 1993.

Romance: external history

Hall 1974.
von Wartburg 1941.

Romance: early texts

Iordan 1962–1975.
Moreno and Peira 1979.
Sampson 1980.

Romance: etymological dictionaries

Diez 1887.
Meyer-Lübke 1935.

Romance: bibliographies

Bach and Price 1977.
Bal and Germain, *et al.* 1991.

Italian

Bruni 1984.
Castellani 2000.
Dionisotti and Grayson 1972.
Maiden 1995.
Migliorini 1960.
Rohlfs 1966.
Tekavčić 1972.
Zamboni 2000.

Spanish

Gifford and Hodcroft 1966.
Lapesa 1980.
Lipski 1994.
Menéndez Pidal 1966.
Penny 2002.
Pharies 2007.
Pountain 2001.
Rohlfs 1957.
Wright 1982.

French

Ayres-Bennett 1996.
Fagyal, Kibbee, and Jenkins 2006.
Lodge 1993.
Posner 1997.
Rickard 1993.

Portuguese

Azevedo 2005.
Mattoso Câmara 1972.
Nunes 1960.
Silva Neto 1970.
Teyssiere 1997.
Williams 1962.

Romanian

Juilland and Edwards 1971.
Lombard 1974.
Mallinson 1986.
Sala 2004.

Works cited

Adams, James (2003). *Bilingualism and the Latin Language*. Cambridge University Press.

(2007). *The Regional Diversification of Latin 200 BC–AD 600*. Cambridge University Press.

Agard, Frederick (1984). *A Course in Romance Linguistics*. 2 vols. Washington: Georgetown University Press.

Anderson, James Maxwell, and Bernard Rochet (1979). *Historical Romance Morphology*. Ann Arbor: University Microfilms International.

Auerbach, Erich (1965). *Introduction aux études de philologie romane*. Frankfurt: Klosterman.

Azevedo, Milton M. (2005). *Portuguese: A Linguistic Introduction*. Cambridge University Press.

Ayres-Bennett, Wendy (1996). *A History of the French Language through Texts*. London and New York: Routledge.

Bach, Kathryn, and Glanville Price (1977). *Romance Linguistics and the Romance Languages: A Bibliography of Bibliographies*. London: Grant and Cutler.

Bal, Willy, Jean Germain, Jean-René Klein, and Peter Swiggers (1997). *Bibliographie sélective de linguistique romane et française*. 2nd edn. Louvain-la-Neuve: Duculot.

Battisti, Carlo (1949). *Avviamento allo studio del latino volgare*. Bari: Leonardo da Vinci.

Bauer, J. (1878). "Franz. *aller.*" *Zeitschrift für Romanische Philologie* 2:592.

Bischoff, B. (1971). "Paläographische Fragen deutscher Denkmäler der Karolingerzeit." *Frühmittelalterliche Studien* 5:101–134.

Blasco Ferrer, Eduardo. (1984). *Storia linguistica della Sardegna*. Tübingen: Niemeyer.

Bourciez, Édouard (1967). *Éléments de linguistique romane*. 5th edn. Paris: Klincksieck.

Bruni, Francesco (1984). *L'italiano: Elementi di storia della lingua e della cultura*. Turin: UTET.

Brunot, Ferdinand (1899). *Précis de grammaire historique de la langue française.* Paris: Masson.

Bull, William E., and Harry F. Williams (1959). *Semeiança del Mundo: A Medieval Description of the World.* University of California Publications in Modern Philology, vol. LI. Berkeley and Los Angeles: University of California Press.

Butler, Harold E. (1920). *The Institutio Oratoria of Quintilian.* Loeb Classical Library. New York: Putnam.

Cano, Rafael, ed. (2005). *Historia de la lengua española.* 2nd edn. Barcelona: Ariel.

Caplan, Harry, ed. (1954). *Rhetorica ad Herennium.* Loeb Classical Library. Cambridge, MA: Harvard University Press.

Castellani, Arrigo (2000). *Grammatica storica della lingua italiana. I. Introduzione.* Bologna: Il Mulino.

Chiţoran, Ioana (2002). *The Phonology of Romanian: A Constraint-Based Approach.* New York: Mouton de Gruyter.

Cian, Vittorio (1902). *Vivaldo Belcalzer e l'enciclopedismo italiano: Giornale storico della letteratura italiana.* Supplemento no. 5. Turin: Ermanno Loescher.

Clements, George N., and Samuel Jay Keyser (1983). *CV Phonology: A Generative Theory of the Syllable.* Cambridge, MA: MIT Press.

Cornagliotti, Anna, Marco Piccat, and Laura Ramello (2001). *Lineamenti di linguistica romanza.* Alessandria: Edizioni dell' Orso.

Corominas, Joan, and J. A. Pascual (1980). *Diccionario crítico etimológico castellano e hispánico.* Madrid: Gredos.

Corpus Inscriptionum Latinarum (CIL) (1863–1975). Berlin: Mouton de Gruyter.

Coseriu, Eugenio (1976). *Das romanische Verbalsystem.* Tübingen: Narr.
  (1977). *Estudios de lingüística románica.* Madrid: Gredos.

de Gourmont, Rémy (1902). *Le problème du style.* Paris: Mercure de France.

Densuşianu, Ovid (1902/1938). *Histoire de la langue roumaine.* Paris: Ernst Leroux.

Díaz y Díaz, Manuel (1975). *Antologia del latín vulgar.* Madrid: Gredos.

Diehl, Ernst (1910). *Vulgärlateinische Inschriften.* Bonn: Marcus and Weber.
  (1913). *Lateinische altchristliche Inschriften.* Bonn: Marcus and Weber.
  (1961). *Inscriptiones latinae christianae veteres.* Berlin: Weidmann.

Diez, Friedrich (1836–1843). *Grammatik der romanischen Sprachen.* 3 vols. Bonn: Weber.
  (1887). *Etymologisches Wörterbuch der romanischen Sprachen.* Bonn: Marcus.

Dionisotti, Carlo, and Cecil Grayson (1972). *Early Italian Texts.* 2nd edn. Oxford: Blackwell.

Du Nay, André (1996). *The Origins of the Romanians: The Early History of the Romanian Language.* Toronto: Matthias Corvinus.

Elcock, William D. (1960). *The Romance Languages.* London: Faber and Faber.

Ernout, Alfred (1927). *Morphologie historique du latin.* Paris: Klincksieck.
  and François Thomas (1951). *Syntaxe latine.* Paris: Klincksieck.

Fagyal, Zsuzsanna, Douglas Kibbee, and Fred Jenkins (2006). *French: A Linguistic Introduction.* Cambridge University Press.

Fleischman, Suzanne (1982). *The Future in Thought and Language: Diachronic Evidence from Romance.* Cambridge University Press.

Fouché, Pierre (1967). *Le verbe francais, étude morphologique.* Paris: Klincksieck.

Franchini, Enzo (2005). "Los primeros textos literarios: Del Auto de los Reyes Magos al Mester de Clerecía." In Rafael Cano (ed.), *Historia de la lengua española.* 2nd edn. Barcelona: Ariel.

Gamurrini, Gian Francesco (1888). *Sanctae Silviae Aquitanae Peregrinatio ad Loca Sancta.* 2nd edn. Rome: Ex Typis Vaticanis.

Gess, Randall, and Deborah Arteaga (2006). *Historical Romance Linguistics: Retrospective and Perspectives.* Amsterdam and Philadelphia: J. Benjamins.

Gifford, Douglas J., and Frederick W. Hodcroft (1966). *Textos lingüísticos del medioevo español.* Oxford: Dolphin.

Grandgent, Charles (1907). *An Introduction to Vulgar Latin.* Boston: D. C. Heath & Co. Republished (2007) by University Press of the Pacific.

Hall, Robert A. Jr. (1974). *External History of the Romance Languages.* New York: Elsevier.

(1976). *Proto-Romance Phonology.* New York: Elsevier.

(1983). *Proto-Romance Morphology.* Amsterdam: J. Benjamins.

Hanssen, Friedrich (1913). *Gramática histórica de la lengua castellana.* Halle: Niemeyer.

Harris, Martin, and Paolo Ramat, eds. (1987). *Historical Development of Auxiliaries.* Berlin: Mouton de Gruyter.

and Nigel Vincent, eds. (1988). *The Romance Languages.* London: Croom Helm.

Herman, Jószef (1990). *Du latin aux langues romanes. I Études de linguistique historique.* Tübingen: Niemeyer.

(2000). *Vulgar Latin.* University Park: Pennsylvania State University Press. Translated by Roger Wright from: Herman (1975), *Le latin vulgaire.* Paris: P. U. F.

(2006). *Du latin aux langues romanes II. Nouvelles études de linguistique historique.* Tübingen: Niemeyer.

Hofmann, Johann B. (1951). *Lateinische Umgangssprache.* 3rd edn. Heidelberg: Winter.

Iordan, Iorgu, ed. (1962–1975). *Crestomaţie romanică.* 5 vols. Bucharest: Ed. Academiei R.S.R.

and John Orr (1970). *An Introduction to Romance Linguistics: Its Schools and Scholars.* 2nd edn. Oxford: Blackwell.

Jensen, Frede (1978). *The Earliest Portuguese Lyrics.* Odense University Press.

(1999). *A Comparative Study of Romance.* New York: Peter Lang.

Johnston, Ronald C. (1987). *Orthographia Gallica.* London: Anglo-Norman Text Society from Birkbeck College.

Juilland, Alphonse, and P. M. H. Edwards (1971). *The Rumanian Verb System.* Janua Linguarum Series Practica 28. The Hague: Mouton de Gruyter.

Keil, Heinrich, ed. (1855–1880). *Grammatici latini.* 8 vols. Leipzig: Teubner.

Kent, Roland G. (1951). *Varro: On the Latin Language.* Loeb Classical Library. Cambridge, MA: Harvard University Press.

Krusch, Bruno (1888). *Monumenta Germaniae Historica, Scriptores Rerum Merovingicarum, II.* Hanover.

La Fauci, Nunzio (1988). *Oggetti e soggetti nella formazione della morfosintassi romanza.* Pisa: Giardini.

(1997). *Per una teoria grammaticale del mutamento morfosintattico. Dal latino verso il romanzo.* Pisa: Edizioni ETS.

(2000). *Forme romanze della funzione predicativa: Teorie, testi, tassonomie.* Pisa: Edizioni ETS.

Landgraf, Gustav, ed. (1894–1908). *Historische Grammatik der lateinischen Sprache.* Leipzig: Teubner.

Lapesa, Rafael (1980). *Historia de la lengua española.* 8th edn. Madrid: Gredos.

Lausberg, Heinrich (1969). *Romanische Sprachwissenschaft.* 3 vols. Berlin: Mouton de Gruyter.

Lee, Charmaine, and Sabrina Galano (2000). *Linguistica romanza.* Rome: Carocci.

Leonard, Clifford (1978). *Umlaut in Romance: An Essay in Linguistic Archaeology.* Grossen-Linden: Hoffmann.

Lewis, M. Paul, ed. (2009). *Ethnologue: Languages of the World.* 16th edn. Dallas, TX: SIL International. Online version at www.ethnologue.com.

Lipski, John (1994). *Latin American Spanish.* London: Longman.

Lloyd, Paul M. (1987). *From Latin to Spanish.* Philadelphia: American Philosophical Society.

Lodge, R. Anthony (1993). *French: From Dialect to Standard.* London and New York: Routledge.

Löfstedt, Einar (1959). *Late Latin.* Oslo: Aschehoug.

Lombard, Alf (1955). *Le verbe roumain: Étude morphologique.* Lund: C. W. K. Gleerup.

(1974). *La langue roumaine: Une présentation.* Paris: Klincksieck.

Loporcaro, Michele (1998). *Sintassi comparata dell'accordo participiale romanzo.* Turin: Rosenberg and Seiler.

(2007). "L' 'Appendix Probi' e la fonologia del latino tardo." In Lo Monaco, Francesco (ed.), *L' 'Appendix Probi': Nuove Ricerche.* Florence: SISMEL. pp. 95–124.

Maiden, Martin (1995). *A Linguistic History of Italian.* New York: Longman.

John Charles Smith, and Adam Ledgeway (2009). *The Cambridge History of the Romance Languages. Volume I: Structures.* Cambridge University Press.

Malkiel, Yakov (1959). "Toward a Reconsideration of the Old Spanish Imperfect in -ia~ -ie." *Hispanic Review* 27.4:435–481.

(1975–1976). "From Falling to Rising Diphthongs: The Case of Old Spanish io < eu (with excursuses on the weak preterite, on possessives, and on judío, sandío, and romero)." *Romance Philology* 29:435–500.

(1983). "Alternatives to the Classic Dichotomy: Family Tree/Wave Theory? The Romance Evidence." In Irmengard Rauch and Gerald Carr (eds.), *Language Change.* Bloomington: Indiana University Press. pp. 192–256.

(1989). *Theory and Practice of Romance Etymology: Studies in Language, Culture and History.* London: Variorum.

(1992). *Diachronic Studies in Lexicology, Affixation, Phonology: Edita and Inedita, 1979–1988.* Amsterdam: J. Benjamins.

(1993). *Etymology.* Cambridge University Press.

Mallinson, Graham (1986). *Rumanian.* London: Routledge.

Marouzeau, Jules (1922–1949). *L'ordre des mots dans la phrase latine*. Paris: Champion.

Martin, John W. (1972). "Remarks on the Origin of the Portuguese Inflected Infinitive." In James M. Anderson and Jo Ann Creore (eds.), *Readings in Romance Linguistics*. The Hague: Mouton de Gruyter.

Martins, Ana Maria (1999). "On the Origin of the Portuguese Inflected Infinitive." In L. J. Brinton (ed.), *Historical Linguistics 1999*. Amsterdam: J. Benjamins.

Mattos e Silva, Rosa Virginia (1994). *O português arcaico: Fonologia, morfologia e sintaxe*. São Paulo: Editora Contexto.

Mattoso Câmara, Joaquim (1972). *The Portuguese Language*. Translated by Anthony J. Naro. University of Chicago Press.

Maurer Jr., Theodoro H. (1968). *O infinito flexionado português*. São Paulo: Companhia Editora Nacional.

Menéndez Pidal, Ramón (1950). *Orígenes del español: Estado lingüístico de la península ibérica hasta el siglo XI*. Madrid: Espasa-Calpe.

(1966). *Manual de gramática histórica española*. 12th edn. Madrid: Espasa-Calpe.

Mensching, Guido (2000). *Infinitive Constructions with Specified Subjects*. Oxford University Press.

Meyer-Lübke, Wilhelm (1890–1902). *Grammatik der romanischen Sprachen*. 4 vols. Leipzig: Reisland.

(1920). *Einführung in das Studium der romanischen Sprachwissenschaft*. Heidelberg: Winter.

(1935). *Romanisches etymologisches Wörterbuch*. 3rd edn. Heidelberg: Winter.

Migliorini, Bruno (1960). *Storia della lingua italiana*. Florence: Sansoni.

Miller, D. Gary (2002). *Nonfinite Structures in Theory and Change*. Oxford University Press.

Milliken, Stuart R. (1988). Protosyllables: A Theory of Underlying Syllable Structure in Nonlinear Phonology. Dissertation, Cornell University.

Moliner, Maria (1998). *Diccionario de uso del español*. Madrid: Gredos.

Monat, Pierre (1992). *Institutions divines / Lactance: Introduction, texte critique, traduction et notes*. Book IV. Paris: Éditions du Cerf.

Monteverdi, Angelo (1952). *Manuale di avviamento agli studi romanzi: Le lingue romanze*. Milan: Fr. Vallardi.

Moreno, Jesús, and Pedro Peira (1979). *Crestomatía románica medieval*. Madrid: Cátedra.

Morin, Yves-Charles (1991). "Old French Stress Patterns and Closed Syllable Adjustment." In Dieter Wanner and Douglas A. Kibbee (eds.), *New Analyses in Romance Linguistics*. Amsterdam/Philadelphia: J. Benjamins.

Mourin, Louis (1962). *Introduction à la morphologie comparée des langues romanes*. Bruges: De Tempel.

Muller, Henri (1970). *A Chronology of Vulgar Latin*. Hilderheim: Gerstenberg.

and Pauline Taylor (1932). *A Chrestomathy of Vulgar Latin*. Boston: D.C. Heath.

Murray, Robert, and Theo Vennemann (1983). "Sound Change and Syllable Structure in Germanic Phonology." *Language* 59.3: 514–528.

Neue, Friedrich, and Carl Wagner (1897). *Formenlehre der lateinischen Sprache*. Vol. III. *Das verbum*. Berlin: Calvary.

Nunes, José Joaquim (1960). *Compêndio de gramática histórica portuguêsa*. 6th edn. Lisbon: LCE.

Nyrop, Kristoffer (1899–1930). *Grammaire historique de la langue française*. Copenhagen: Gyldendalske. (Vol. I, 3rd edn., 1914. Vol. II, 2nd edn., 1924. Vol. III, 1908. Vol. IV, 1913. Vol. V, 1925. Vol. VI, 1930.)

Oelschläger, Victor R. B. (1940). *Medieval Spanish Word-List: A Preliminary Dated Vocabulary of First Appearances up to Berceo*. Madison: University of Wisconsin Press.

Oniga, Renato (2004). *Il latino: Breve introduzione linguistica*. Milan: Franco Angeli.

Palmer, Leonard R. (1961). *The Latin Language*. London: Faber and Faber.

Parker, Eugene (1934). "A Defense of the Etymology Allatus, Allare, Aller." *Publications of the Modern Language Association* 49.4:1025–1031.

Parkinson, Stephen (1988). "Portuguese." In Martin Harris and Nigel Vincent (eds.), *The Romance Languages*. London: Croom Helm.

Penny, Ralph (2002). *A History of the Spanish Language*. 2nd edn. Cambridge University Press.

Pharies, David A. (2007). *A Brief History of the Spanish Language*. University of Chicago Press.

Pianigiani, Ottorino (1907). *Vocabolario etimologico della lingua italiana*. Rome/ Milan: Società Editrice Dante Alighieri di Albrighi.

Pighi, Giovanni Battista (1964). *Lettere latine di un soldato di Traiano*. Bologna: Zanichelli.

Pinkster, Harm (1985). "The Development of Future Tense Auxiliaries in Latin." *Glotta* 63: 186–208.

   (1987). "The Strategy and Chronology of Future and Perfect Tense Auxiliaries in Latin." In Martin Harris and Paolo Ramat (eds.), *Historical Development of Auxiliaries*. Paris: Mouton de Gruyter.

   (1990). *Latin Syntax and Semantics*. London: Routledge.

Pope, Mildred K. (1934). *From Latin to Modern French*. Manchester University Press.

Posner, Rebecca (1996). *The Romance Languages*. Cambridge University Press.

   (1997). *Linguistic Change in French*. Oxford: Clarendon.

   and John Green, eds. (1980–1982). *Trends in Romance Linguistics and Philology*. Berlin: Mouton de Gruyter.

Pountain, Christopher J. (1983). *Structures and Transformations: The Romance Verb*. London: Croom Helm.

   (2001). *A History of the Spanish Language through Texts*. London and New York: Routledge.

Pulgram, Ernst (1950). "Spoken and Written Latin." *Language* 26.4:458–466.

   (1975). *Latin-Romance Phonology: Prosodics and Metrics*. Munich: Fink.

Quirk, Ronald J. (2006). *The Appendix Probi: A Scholar's Guide to Text and Context*. Newark, DE: Juan de la Cuesta.

Renzi, Lorenzo, with Giampaolo Salvi (1995). *Nuova introduzione alla filologia romanza*. Bologna: Il Mulino.

   and Alvise Andreose (2003). *Manuale di linguistica e filogia romanza*. Bologna: Il Mulino.

370 Works cited

Rickard, Peter (1993). *A History of the French Language.* London: Routledge.

Rohlfs, Gerhard (1951–1952). *Romanische Philologie, I. Allgemeine Romanistik. Französische und provenzalische Philologie, II. Italienische Philologie. Die sardische und rätoromanische Sprache.* Heidelberg: Winter.

(1957). *Manual de filología hispánica: Guía bibliográfica, crítica y metódica.* Bogotá: Instituto Caro y Cuervo.

(1966–1969). *Grammatica storica della lingua italiana e dei suoi dialetti.* 3 vols. Turin: Einaudi.

(1968). *Sermo vulgaris latinus: Vulgärlateinisches Lesebuch.* Tübingen: Niemeyer.

Rosetti, Alexandru (1973). *Brève histoire de la langue roumaine des origines à nos jours.* The Hague: Mouton de Gruyter.

(1986). *Istoria limbii române de la origini pînă la începutul secolului al XVII-lea.* Bucharest: Editura Ştiinţifică şi Enciclopedică.

Rotaru, Ion (1981). *Literatura română veche.* Bucharest: Editura Didactică şi Pedagogică.

Sala, Marius (2004). *Dal latino al romeno.* Alessandria: Edizioni dell'Orso.

Sampson, Rodney, ed. (1980). *Early Romance Texts: An Anthology.* Cambridge University Press.

Schlösser, Rainer (2005). *Le lingue romanze.* Bologna: Il Mulino.

Schuchardt, Hugo (1866–1868). *Der Vokalismus des Vulgärlateins.* 3 vols. Leipzig: Teubner.

Schürr, Friedrich (1970). *La diphtongaison romane.* Tübingen: Narr.

Schwegler, Armin (1990). *Analyticity and Syntheticity: A Diachronic Perspective with Special Reference to Romance.* Paris: Mouton de Gruyter.

Scida, Emily E. (2004). *The Inflected Infinitive in Romance Languages.* New York: Routledge.

Silva Neto, Serafim da (1970). *História da língua portuguêsa.* 2nd edn. Rio de Janeiro: Livros de Portugal.

Smith, John Charles (1995). "L' évolution sémantique et pragmatique des adverbes déictiques *ici, là,* et *là-bas*." *Langue française* 107: 43–57.

Stefenelli, Arnulf (1962). *Die Volkssprache im Werk des Petron im Hinblick auf die romanischen Sprachen.* Stuttgart: Wilhelm Braumüller.

Stok, Fabio, ed. (1997). *Appendix probi IV. Università di Studi di Salerno. Quaderni del Dipartimento di Scienze dell'Antichità,* No. 18. Napoli: Arte Tipografica.

Sturtevant, Edgar (1940). *The Pronunciation of Greek and Latin.* Linguistic Society of America, University of Pennsylvania.

Tabachovitz, A. (1932). *Étude sur la langue de la version française des Serments de Strasbourg.* Uppsala: Almqvist and Wiksells Boktryckeri-A.-B.

Tagliavini, Carlo (1962). *Fonetica e morfologia storica del latino.* Bologna: Pàtron.

(1964). *Le origini delle lingue neolatine.* 4th edn. Bologna: Pàtron.

Tekavčić, Pavao (1972). *Grammatica storica dell'italiano.* 3 vols. Bologna: Il Mulino.

Teyssier, Paul (1997). *História da língua portuguêsa.* São Paulo: Martins Fontes.

Väänänen, Veikko (1966). *Le latin vulgaire des inscriptions pompéiennes.* Berlin: Akademie-Verlag.

(1983). *Introduction au latin vulgaire.* 3rd edn. Paris: Klincksieck.

Valesio, Paolo (1968). "The Romance Synthetic Future Pattern and Its First Attestations." *Lingua* 20:114–161 and 297–307.

Vennemann, Theo (1988). *Preference Laws for Syllable Structure and the Explanation of Sound Change: With Special Reference to German, Germanic, Italian, and Latin*. New York: Mouton de Gruyter.

Vidos, Benedek (1956). *Handboek tot der romaanse taalkunde*. 's Hertogenbosch: Malmberg.

Vincent, Nigel, and Martin Harris, eds. (1982). *Studies in the Romance Verb*. London: Croom Helm.

von Wartburg, Walther (1941). *Les origines des peuples romanes*. Paris: P. U. F.

(1950). *Die Ausgliederung der romanischen Sprachräume*. Berne: Francke.

Vossler, Karl (1954). *Einführung in Vulgärlatein*. Munich: Hüber.

Wagner, Max Leopold (1993). *La lingua sarda: Storia, spirito e forma*. Tübingen: Francke.

Wanner, Dieter (1987). *The Development of Romance Clitic Pronouns: From Latin to Old Romance*. Berlin: Mouton de Gruyter.

Williams, Edwin B. (1962). *From Latin to Portuguese*. 2nd edn. Philadelphia: University of Pennsylvania Press.

Wireback, Kenneth J. (1994). "The Origin of the Portuguese Inflected Infinitive." *Hispania* 77:544–554.

Wright, Roger (1982). *Late Latin and Early Romance in Spain and Carolingian France*. Liverpool: Francis Cairns.

ed. (1996). *Latin and the Romance Languages in the Early Middle Ages*. University Park: Pennsylvania State University Press.

(2002). *A Sociophilological Study of Late Latin*. Turnhout: Brepols.

Zamboni, Alberto (2000). *Alle origini dell'italiano: Dinamiche e tipologie della trasizione dal latino*. Rome: Carocci.

Index

9908434R00219

Made in the USA
San Bernardino, CA
30 March 2014